Corporate Communication

Eighth Edition

Paul A. Argenti
*The Tuck School of Business
at Dartmouth*

CORPORATE COMMUNICATION

Published by McGraw Hill LLC, 1325 Avenue of the Americas, New York, NY 10019. Copyright ©2023 by McGraw Hill LLC. All rights reserved. Printed in the United States of America. No part of this publication may be reproduced or distributed in any form or by any means, or stored in a database or retrieval system, without the prior written consent of McGraw Hill LLC, including, but not limited to, in any network or other electronic storage or transmission, or broadcast for distance learning.

Some ancillaries, including electronic and print components, may not be available to customers outside the United States.

This book is printed on acid-free paper.

1 2 3 4 5 6 7 8 9 LCR 26 25 24 23 22 21

ISBN 978-1-265-09225-2
MHID 1-265-09225-7

Cover Image: *Ferbies/Shutterstock*

All credits appearing on page or at the end of the book are considered to be an extension of the copyright page.

The Internet addresses listed in the text were accurate at the time of publication. The inclusion of a website does not indicate an endorsement by the authors or McGraw Hill LLC, and McGraw Hill LLC does not guarantee the accuracy of the information presented at these sites.

mheducation.com/highered

For my grandchildren, Amalia, Helen, and Luca.
Papa loves you more than you will ever know.

Preface to the Eighth Edition

This book grows out of more than 40 years of work developing the field of study referred to in this book as *corporate communication*. Although the term itself is not new, the notion of it as a functional area of management equal in importance to finance, marketing, human resources (HR), and information technology (IT) is more recent. In the past 40 years, senior managers at a growing number of companies have come to realize the importance of an integrated communication function.

In this introduction, I would like to talk a bit more about my expertise, what this book is all about, and why I think everyone involved in organizations today need to know about this important discipline.

Author's Expertise

For the past 40 years, I have been a professor of management and corporate communication at the Tuck School of Business at Dartmouth. Prior to that, I taught at the Columbia and Harvard Business Schools.

The tradition of teaching communication has been a long one at Tuck, but as at most schools, the focus was on skills development, including primarily speaking and writing. The first development in the evolution of this field was an interest among businesspeople in how to deal with the media. Because this requirement mostly involved applying oral presentation skills in another setting, the faculty teaching communication were a logical choice for taking on this new task.

So when I began teaching the first management communication course at Tuck in 1981, I was asked to include a component on dealing with the media and handling crises. I became interested in this topic through my study of marketing at Columbia and had already written a case on the subject, which appeared in earlier editions of this book.

Over the years, my interest in the subject grew beyond how companies deal with the media to include how they deal with *all* communication problems. As I wrote more case studies on the subject and worked with managers inside companies, I saw the need for a more integrated function. That's because most companies were conducting communication activities in a highly decentralized way.

For example, the employee communication function at Hewlett-Packard (HP) in the mid-1980s was in the HR department, where it had always been, when I wrote a case on how HP dealt with voluntary severance and early retirement programs. As I looked at other companies, I found similarities to HP. Yet the people in those various HR departments were doing exactly the same thing internally that a communication specialist in the public relations (PR) department was doing for the external audience–sending a specific company message to a specific audience.

The same was true of the investor relations (IR) functions, which typically resided exclusively in the finance department in most companies until the 1990s. Why? Because the chief financial officer was the one who knew the most about the company's financial performance and historically had been responsible for developing the annual report. Communication was seen as a vehicle for getting that information out rather than as a function in itself.

Again, as I worked with companies to develop new characters and brand, I found marketing people involved because they had traditionally dealt with brand and image in the context of products and services. Yet those marketing experts didn't always know what was being communicated to the press or to securities analysts by their counterparts in other functional areas.

These experiences led me to believe that corporations and other organizations, from universities to churches to law firms, could do a much better job of communicating if they integrated all communication activities under one umbrella. That was the theory at least, but I could find precious little evidence in practice.

Then, in 1990, I was fortunate enough to be given a consulting assignment that allowed me to put into practice what I had been talking about in theory for many years. I received a call from the chairman and chief executive officer of a major corporation after my picture appeared on the front page of *The New York Times* Sunday business section in an article about how professors were teaching business students about dealing with the media.

Ostensibly, the chairman's call was about how his company could get more credit for the great things it was doing. Specifically, he wanted to know if I had a "silver bullet." My silver bullet, as it turned out, was the development of a new corporate communication function for the company.

This company, like most, had let communications decentralize into a variety of other functional areas over the years, with the predictable result: no integration. The media relations people were saying one thing, the investor relations department was saying another; the marketing team was developing communication strategies for the outside, the human resources department for the inside.

No one except the chairman, who sat at the top of this $30 billion organization, could see the big picture, and none of those intimately involved with the various activities had an inside track on the overall strategy for the firm. Over the next year and a half, the chairman and I came up with the first integrated communication function that had all the different subsets I had tried unsuccessfully to bring together at other companies and even at my own university.

We changed everything–from the company's image with customers to its relationship with securities analysts on Wall Street. Today, this company has one totally integrated communication function. This book explains what all the component parts of that function are all about.

What Is This Book About?

Chapter 1, "The Changing Environment for Business," provides a context for the rest of the book. It describes changes in the environment for business that have taken place over the past 100 years, with particular emphasis on this past decade and its implications for corporate communication. Companies must contend with two seemingly at-odds phenomena these days: an all-time low trust in corporations and a seemingly all-time high in the expectation that companies speak out on topics of social justice and the broader impact on the world. The shifting perspective on the purpose of a company has had broad implications not just for the structure of the communications function but also for corporate strategy and mission more generally.

In the Redwood Health System case, we examine how one company had to contend with the challenges of a changing of the guard, ushering in new leadership with a new company mission intended to match the challenges of the day.

Chapter 2, "Communicating Strategically," explains how companies need to use a strategic approach to communications. In the past, most communication activities were dealt with reactively as organizations responded to events in the world around them. With the framework for strategic communication provided in this chapter, companies can proactively craft communications tailored to their constituencies and measure their success based on constituency responses.

In the Carsen Molding case, we find an example of a manager who failed to use a strategic approach to communication in a rapidly changing corporate environment.

In Chapter 3, "An Overview of the Corporate Communication Function," we take a look at the evolution of the corporate communication function and some of the different ways it can be structured within organizations. This chapter also describes each of the subfunctions that should be included in the ideal corporate communication department.

The John Deere case provides an excellent example of how a company evolved its communication function to better match with modern demands.

Chapter 4, "Corporate Brand and Reputation," describes the most fundamental function of a corporate communication department: to reflect the reality of the firm itself through control of its brand and ultimately its reputation. This chapter places particular emphasis on the manner in which the digital world, and in particular social media, has changed the way in which corporations can manage these foundational elements.

The case for this chapter allows students to examine the challenges of maintaining a stronghold on brand and reputation through the United Airlines disaster of 2017 when a passenger was violently dragged off a flight.

In Chapter 5, "Corporate Responsibility," we see how companies try to do well by doing good, manage the so-called triple bottom line, and deal with increasing demands from antagonists and pressure groups.

The Starbucks Coffee Company case reveals how one company balanced its responsibilities to its customers with demands from a nongovernmental organization (NGO) to improve its sourcing.

In Chapter 6, "Media Relations," we look at how today's corporate communications function has evolved from the "press release factory" model to a more sophisticated approach of building relationships with both traditional and new media before having a specific story to sell them and targeting the appropriate distribution channel for different kinds of stories.

The Adolph Coors Company serves as our case in point for this chapter. In this classic case, which I wrote for the first edition, we see how this company dealt with the formidable *60 Minutes* when it approached Coors with a controversial story idea.

One of the most important functions within corporate communication deals with an internal rather than an external constituency: employees. In Chapter 7, "Internal Communication," we look at employee communications' migration away from the HR area toward a function that is more connected with senior management and overall company strategy.

The Go Travel case explores one company's attempt to deal with voluntary severance and outplacement issues related to layoffs.

In Chapter 8, "Investor Relations," we see how companies use communication strategies to deal with analysts, shareholders, and other important constituencies. In the past, this communication subfunction often was handled by managers with excellent financial skills and mediocre communication skills. Today, as IR professionals interact regularly with the media and need to explain nonfinancial information to investors, strong communication skills are equally critical to a solid financial background.

Our case for this chapter, Steelcase, Inc., examines how an IR function was built at that company.

Chapter 9 covers government relations. The business environment historically has fluctuated between periods of relatively less regulation and relatively more, but government relations is always a consideration for companies, whether at the local, state, federal, or international level.

The Disney case provides an example of how a large corporation dealt with challenges from government and local communities in Virginia as it tried to open an historical theme park.

Organizations inevitably will have to deal with some kind of crisis. In Chapter 10, "Crisis Communications," we look at how companies can prepare for the unexpected and provide examples of both good and poor crisis communications, as well as practical steps to creating and implementing crisis communication plans.

Our case at the end of this chapter focuses on the *Costa Concordia* Crisis, in which Carnival Cruises tried to navigate the challenges of dealing with the largest cruise line sinking in modern history.

What Is New to the Eighth Edition?

The eighth edition of *Corporate Communication* reflects valuable feedback received from both users and reviewers of the previous editions. In addition to new research findings and new examples to illustrate the latest economic, social, political, and corporate trends, changes in this edition include the following:

- New case and case questions.
- Expanded coverage of the history of communication theory.

- Additional discussion of the impact and role of social media and digital communications.
- Additional recommendations for crisis communication.
- Timely analysis of the challenges that companies are facing today in this time of increased consumer expectation that companies take a stand of the major challenges society faces today.

Why Is Corporate Communication So Important Today?

Every functional area, at one time or another, was the newest and most important. But in the twenty-first century, the importance of communication is obvious to virtually everyone. Why?

First, we live in a more sophisticated era in terms of communication. Information travels at lightning speed from one side of the world to another as a result of digital communications and social media.

Second, the general public is more sophisticated in its approach to organizations than it has been in the past. People tend to be more educated about issues and more skeptical of corporate intentions. Moreover, consumers and community members affected by corporations are more frequently and more vocally stating their opinions on company actions—opinions that are quickly amplified in the digital world. Companies, it seems, most contend with the opinions of nearly everyone.

Third, information comes to us in more beautiful packages than it did before. Slick social media design and easy user interfaces are table stakes at this point from the perspective of most consumers. The department store experience has been replaced by the direct-to-consumer trend, and a few "flagship stores" are now expected to offer immersive experiences as opposed to serving as purely points of sale. The bar is high for a company's message to stand out in this environment.

Fourth, organizations have become inherently more complex. Companies in earlier times (and the same is true even today for very small organizations) were small enough that they could get by with much less sophisticated communications activities. Often, one person could perform many different functions at one time. But in organizations with thousands of employees throughout the world, it is much more difficult to keep track of all the different pieces that make up a coherent communication strategy.

This book describes not only what is happening in an era of strategic communication, but also what companies can do to stay one step ahead of the competition. By creating an integrated corporate communication system, organizations will be able to face the next decades with the strategies and tools that few companies in the world have at their fingertips.

When working on the introduction for the last edition of this text, I wrote that I had hope that managers would soon come to realize the importance of an integrated, strategic communication function. While much progress has been made in giving communications an official seat at the strategic table, the function still has a long ways to go not only in terms of full appreciation of its importance from all important decision makers at most companies, but also in terms of learning how to grapple with the nuances of a much more integrated world, where nearly everyone can communicate with everyone else. Most likely, the field will continue to need to evolve as new challenges, and new opportunities, arise. Along the way, I hope you enjoy reading about this exciting field as much as I have enjoyed chronicling its development and thinking about its future.

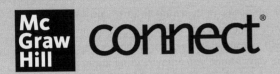

Instructors: Student Success Starts with You

Tools to enhance your unique voice

Want to build your own course? No problem. Prefer to use an OLC-aligned, prebuilt course? Easy. Want to make changes throughout the semester? Sure. And you'll save time with Connect's auto-grading too.

65%
Less Time Grading

Laptop: McGraw Hill; Woman/dog: George Doyle/Getty Images

Study made personal

Incorporate adaptive study resources like SmartBook® 2.0 into your course and help your students be better prepared in less time. Learn more about the powerful personalized learning experience available in SmartBook 2.0 at **www.mheducation.com/highered/connect/smartbook**

Affordable solutions, added value

Make technology work for you with LMS integration for single sign-on access, mobile access to the digital textbook, and reports to quickly show you how each of your students is doing. And with our Inclusive Access program you can provide all these tools at a discount to your students. Ask your McGraw Hill representative for more information.

Padlock: Jobalou/Getty Images

Solutions for your challenges

A product isn't a solution. Real solutions are affordable, reliable, and come with training and ongoing support when you need it and how you want it. Visit **www.supportateverystep.com** for videos and resources both you and your students can use throughout the semester.

Checkmark: Jobalou/Getty Images

Students: Get Learning that Fits You

Effective tools for efficient studying

Connect is designed to help you be more productive with simple, flexible, intuitive tools that maximize your study time and meet your individual learning needs. Get learning that works for you with Connect.

Study anytime, anywhere

Download the free ReadAnywhere app and access your online eBook, SmartBook 2.0, or Adaptive Learning Assignments when it's convenient, even if you're offline. And since the app automatically syncs with your Connect account, all of your work is available every time you open it. Find out more at **www.mheducation.com/readanywhere**

> *"I really liked this app—it made it easy to study when you don't have your textbook in front of you."*
>
> - Jordan Cunningham, Eastern Washington University

Calendar: owattaphotos/Getty Images

Everything you need in one place

Your Connect course has everything you need—whether reading on your digital eBook or completing assignments for class, Connect makes it easy to get your work done.

Learning for everyone

McGraw Hill works directly with Accessibility Services Departments and faculty to meet the learning needs of all students. Please contact your Accessibility Services Office and ask them to email accessibility@mheducation.com, or visit **www.mheducation.com/about/accessibility** for more information.

Top: Jenner Images/Getty Images, Left: Hero Images/Getty Images, Right: Hero Images/Getty Images

A Note on the Case Method

Throughout this book, you will find cases or examples of company situations that typically relate to material covered in each of the chapters.

What Are Cases?

Cases are much like short stories, in that they present a slice of life. Unlike their fictional counterparts, however, cases are usually about real people, organizations, and problems (even though the names may sometimes be disguised for proprietary reasons). Thus, a reader has an opportunity to participate in the real decisions that managers had to make on a variety of real problems.

The technique of using actual business situations as an educational and analytical instrument began at Harvard in the 1920s, but the use of a "case" as a method of educating students began much earlier. Centuries ago, students learned law by studying past legal cases and medicine through the use of clinical work.

Unlike textbooks and lectures, the case method of instruction does not present a structured body of knowledge. This approach often proves frustrating to students who may be used to more traditional teaching methods. For example, cases are frequently ambiguous and imprecise, which can easily confuse a neophyte. This complexity, however, represents what practitioners usually face when making decisions.

In cases, as in life, problems can be solved in a variety of ways. Sometimes one way seems better than others. Even if a perfect solution exists, however, the company may have difficulty implementing it. You also may find that you have come up with a completely different solution to the problem than another student has. Try to forget the notion of finding an "answer" to the problem. The goal in using this method is not to develop a set of correct approaches or right answers, but rather to involve you in the active process of recognizing and solving general management problems.

In class, you will represent the decision maker (usually an executive) in a discussion that is guided by the professor. The professor may suggest ideas from time to time or provide structure to ensure that students cover major issues, but each student's insight and analytical prowess is displayed in this context. Often, a professor will play devil's advocate or pursue an unusual line of reasoning to get students to see the complexities of a particular situation. As a teaching device, the case method relies on participation rather than passive learning.

Although cases come in all shapes and sizes, two categories define the scope of most cases: evaluative and problematic. An evaluative case presents the reader with a description of a company's actions. The purpose of an analysis is thus to evaluate what management has done and then to determine whether the actions were well founded.

Problem cases, which are far more common, describe a specific problem a manager faces, such as whether to launch a new corporate advertising program, choose one method of handling the media over another, or even choose one form of communication rather than another. Such problems call for development of alternative strategies, leading to a specific recommendation.

Case Preparation

No matter what type of case you're dealing with, a common approach will help you prepare cases before you have time to develop what will eventually become your own style. In time, you will no doubt find a method that works well and proves more suitable to you. Regardless of the approach, a thorough analysis requires a great deal of effort.

Begin with a quick reading of the case. This read-through gives you a sense of the whole rather than what often can appear as a dazzling array of parts if you start by analyzing each section in detail. You should extract a *sense* of the organization, some impressions of what *could be* the problem, and a working knowledge of the amount and importance of information presented in the case.

A more careful second reading of the case will allow you to begin the critical process of analyzing business problems and solving them. What you should hope to cull from this analysis follows.

Problem Definition

First, you must establish a specific definition of the problem or problems. Although this definition may be clearly stated in the case, usually problem definition is a crucial first step in the analysis. You need to go beyond simple problem definition and look for symptoms as well. For example, as part of the analysis, you might wonder why or how the defined problem has developed in the company. Avoid, however, a repetition of case facts or a historical perspective. Assume that your reader has all the facts that you do and choose reasoning that will serve to strengthen, rather than bloat, your problem definition.

Company Objectives

Second, once you have defined the problem, place it within the context of management's objectives. How does the problem look in this light? Do the objectives make sense given the problems facing management?

In some cases, objectives are defined explicitly, such as "increase stock price by 10 percent this year." If the problem in the case proves to be that the company's investor relations function is a disaster, this objective is probably overly optimistic. Goals can be more general as well: "Change from a centralized to a decentralized communication organization in five years." In this instance, a centralized department with independent managers at the divisional level has a good chance of meeting its objectives.

Data Analysis

Third, you next need to analyze information presented in the case as a way of establishing its significance. Often, this material appears in exhibits, but you also will find it stated within the case as fact or opinion. Remember to avoid blind acceptance of the data, no matter where they appear. As in the real world, information presented in the case may not be reliable or relevant, but you may find that if you manipulate or combine the data, they ultimately will prove valuable to your analysis. Given the time constraints you will always be under in case analysis and in business, you should avoid a natural tendency to spend more time than you can really afford analyzing data. Try to find a compromise between little or no data analysis and endless number crunching.

Alternative Strategies and Recommendations

Fourth, after you have defined the problem, identified company objectives, and analyzed relevant data, you are ready to present viable alternative strategies. Be sure the alternatives are realistic for the company under discussion, given management's objectives. In addition, you must consider the implications of each alternative for the company and management.

Once you have developed two or three viable alternative solutions, you are ready to make a recommendation for future action. Naturally, you will want to support the recommendation with relevant information from your analysis. This final step completes your case analysis, but you must then take the next step and explore ways to communicate all the information to your reader or listener.

Cases in the Real World

Here are some further thoughts to help you distinguish a case from a real situation: Despite the hours of research time and reams of information amassed by the case writer, he or she must ultimately *choose* which information to present. Thus, you end up with a package of information in writing. Obviously, information does not come to you in one piece in business. A manager may have garnered the information through discussions, documents, reports, websites, and other means. The timing also will be spread out over a longer period than in a case.

Also, given the necessary selectivity of the case writer, you can be sure a specific teaching objective helped focus the selection of information. In reality, the "case" may have implications for several different areas of a business.

Because a case takes place within a particular period of time, it differs in another important way from management problems. These tend to go on and change as new information comes to light. A manager can solve some of the problems now, search for more information, and decide more carefully later on what is best for a given situation. You, on the other hand, must take one stand now and forever.

Finally, case analyses differ from the realities of management in that students do not have responsibility for implementing decisions. Nor do they suffer the consequences if their decision proves untenable. You should not assume that this characteristic removes you from any responsibility. On the contrary, the class (in a discussion) or your professor will be searching for the kind of critical analysis that makes for excellence in corporate communication.

Acknowledgments

Without the help and support of the Tuck School at Dartmouth, I could not have completed this book. Over the past 40 years, I have been given funds to write cases and conduct research as well as time to work on the material in this book. I am particularly grateful to Dick West for initially investing in my career here at Tuck and encouraging me to develop a new area of study, and to Paul Danos and Bob Hansen for their support over a period of two decades. I would also like to thank Matt Slaughter and Brian Tomlin for their support more recently.

I also must thank my other friends and colleagues at Tuck who first made me sit down and finally produce a text after years of collecting materials and thoughts in files and boxes: specifically, the late John Shank. The International University of Japan also deserves credit for providing me with the contemplative setting I needed to write the first edition of this book.

Many clients helped me to test the ideas I have developed over more than 40 years, but I am particularly indebted to Joseph Antonini, former chair and chief executive officer of Kmart, for allowing me to think creatively about the possibilities for a unified corporate communication function. I also would like to thank the late Jim Donahue, former head of learning, and Andy Sigler, formerly chairman and CEO, both of Champion International, for allowing me to test new ideas with top managers at their company; Michael Sneed, Chief Communication Officer at Johnson & Johnson, for his input on Chapter 3; Maura Downing, VP of Global Brand Management and Corporate Communications at John Deere, for serving as the basis of our newest case for Chapter 3; Greg Efthimiou for his permission to use the Disney case in Chapter 9; and Emily Maine, of McKinsey & Company, for her brand management research help. David McCourt, former chairman and CEO of RCN, also allowed me to work on developing a corporate communication function in his company. In addition, I thank my many colleagues at Goldman Sachs, where I was fortunate to work as a consultant for more than eight years, and to Peter Verrengia, my dear friend Suzanne Klotz, and all of my colleagues at Fleishman Hillard for their support over an eight-year period.

I am indebted as well to the students I have taught, especially at Tuck, but also at Erasmus University, Singapore Management University, Hanoi School of Business, the International University of Japan, the Helsinki School of Economics, Columbia Business School, and Harvard Business School. They have tested these ideas in their fertile minds and given me inspiration for coming up with new ways of thinking about communications.

Many research assistants helped me with this project over the years, but I am particularly grateful to Christine Keen, Patricia Gordon, Mary Tatman, Adi Herzberg, Thea Haley Stocker, Kimberley Tait, Abbey Nova, Suzanne Klotz, Courtney Barnes, Alicia Korney, Alina Everett, Genoa Terheggen, Alexandra Angelo, Katie Rosenberg, Lenore Feder, Jordan Fleet, Kelly Sennatt, Joanie Taylor, Andrew Miller, Avanti Maluste, Cassandra Harrington, and Georgia Aarons for their incredible help with previous editions. I would also like to thank my longtime former academic assistant at Tuck, Annette Lyman, and my current assistant Jessica Osgood for their help with previous editions as well as this one. But the person I owe the greatest thanks to for the eighth edition is Anne Bozik, T21. I would not have been able to complete this task without her, and the book is so much better because of the countless hours she spent on this project. I cannot imagine having a better team in place to work on a project like this.

The reviewers who helped with the eighth edition also deserve special thanks for their helpful comments and advice:

Irv Shenkler
NYU Stern School of Business

Donald K. Wright
Boston University

Linda Lopez
Baruch College CUNY

James Scofield O'Rourke, IV
University of Notre Dame

I also wish to thank the reviewers from the previous editions who made this book better through their honesty and input:

Bill McPherson
Indiana University of Pennsylvania

Elizabeth Powell
University of Virginia

Cory Lynn Young
Ithaca College

Frank Jaster
Tulane University

Donna J. Kain
East Carolina University

Gary Kohut
University of North Carolina–Charlotte

Bill Margaritis
FedEx

Irv Schenkler
Stern School of Business, New York University

Carter A. Daniel
Rutgers University

James O'Rourke
University of Notre Dame

Cees van Riel
Erasmus University

Jane Gilligan
Clark University

Charlotte Rosen
Cornell University

Jerry Dibble
Georgia State University

Chris Kelly
New York University

Jon Iwata
IBM

Cynthia Buhay-Simon
Bloomsburg University

JoAnne Yates
Massachusetts Institute of Technology

Don Bates
Columbia University

Joan M. Lally
University of Utah

Don Wright
Boston University

Joel T. Champion
Colorado Christian University

Dr. Sherry Roberts
Middle Tennessee State University

Jonathan Slater
State University of New York at Plattsburgh

Judith Sereno
Medaille College

J. S. O'Rourke
University of Notre Dame

Karen Gersten
Evelyn T. Stone University College

Linda Lopez
Baruch College

Lynn Russell
Columbia University

Otto Lerbinger
Boston University

Margo Northey
Acknowledgments
University of Western Ontario

Mary E. Vielhaber
Eastern Michigan University

Michele Marie Bresso
Bakersfield College

Michael Putnam
University of Texas–Arlington

Paul Ziek
Pace University

Rick Calabrese
Dominican University

Robert Mead
Aetna

Robert Stowers
College of William & Mary

Sherron B. Kenton
Emory University

Sherry Southard
East Carolina University

Stephen Greyser
Harvard Business School

Suzette Heiman
University of Missouri

Valerie Haertel
Alliance Capital Management

Wayne Moore
Indiana University of Pennsylvania

Yunxia Zhu
UNITEC (New Zealand)

My thanks also go to the staff of McGraw Hill: senior project manager, Melissa Leick; associate portfolio manager Laura Spell, editors Sarah Blasco and Diana Murphy, and former executive editor at Irwin, Bevan O'Callaghan, who initially signed the book. Their patience allowed me the freedom to develop this material for eight editions over a much longer period of time than I would have guessed it would take at the outset.

Finally, I would like to thank my parents for giving me the raw material in the beginning and the education later on that allowed me to become an academic.

Paul A. Argenti
Hanover, New Hampshire
2021

The author welcomes any comments or questions as well as corrections to the text. Please write to Professor Paul A. Argenti, The Tuck School of Business, Dartmouth College, Hanover, NH 03755, or e-mail comments to paul.argenti@dartmouth.edu.

Brief Table of Contents

Table of Contents

CHAPTER ONE

The Changing Environment for Business

Most of today's business leaders grew up in a different era from the one they find themselves in now: A typical senior executive grew up during one of the most prosperous and optimistic periods in American history. The difference between the world these people knew in their childhood and the one their grandchildren will face in the mid-twenty-first century is nothing short of staggering.

The public's current expectations of corporations are also different from what they were 50 years ago. To attract customers, employees, and investors, companies need to be progressive leaders about a host of global issues and put their vision in a broader social context. Public scrutiny of business is constant and intense, and in the past decade, disillusionment has grown regarding excesses in executive pay, questionable accounting practices, drug recalls, and moral laxity on the part of corporations.

In this chapter, we put our discussion of corporate communication in context by looking at some of the events that have influenced the operating environment for business. We begin by looking at a history of public attitudes toward American business and their reflection in traditional and social media. Next, we turn to the effects of globalization on business. Finally, we look at how improved corporate communication can help companies compete in this constantly changing environment.

Attitudes toward American Business through the Years

Business has never had a completely positive image in the United States. In the 1860s, the creation of the nation's transcontinental rail systems and the concomitant need for steel created hazardous working conditions for steelworkers and railroad builders alike. Soon thereafter, the Industrial Revolution moved American industry away from a model of small workshops and hand tools to mechanized mass production in factories. This shift had the effect of lowering prices of finished goods, but it also contributed to harsh and dangerous working conditions for laborers, as documented in Upton Sinclair's book, *The Jungle.* The exploitation of young women and children working in factories, highlighted by the deadly Triangle Shirtwaist Factory fire in 1911, only added to negative perceptions of business.

As the patriarchs of big business, the Carnegies, Mellons, and Rockefellers—"robber barons," as they came to be known—were perceived as corrupt businessmen looking out for their own interests rather than the good of all citizens. And yet these negative attitudes toward the first modern corporate businessmen were coupled with envy of their material wealth. Most Americans wanted the lifestyle of these business magnates and came to see the pursuit of wealth and the security it provided as part of the "American Dream." The concept of social mobility, captured in author Horatio Alger's rags-to-riches novels, seemed to many to be a tangible reality in America's cities, and immigrants came to the United States in large numbers.

The 1920s were characterized by a sharply rising stock market following the conclusion of World War I and by increasing disparities in wealth distribution. These disparities—between rich and middle class, between agriculture and industry—made for unstable economic conditions, while speculation in the stock market fueled its growth to unprecedented levels. The stock market "bubble" finally burst in 1929, giving way to the Great Depression, which would last a decade and affect the rest of the industrialized world. It was a dark time for businesses and individuals alike.

By the mid-1940s, however, businesses started rebounding from the Depression as companies geared up for the Second World War. The steel industry, the automotive industry, the military-industrial complex—all of which made the prosperity of the 1950s and 1960s a reality—got their start during World War II.

Perhaps the epitome of this era, considered by many a "golden age," was the "Camelot" years of the Kennedy administration. The economy was booming, and in the aftermath of the Cuban Missile Crisis, the United States felt it had defused the tensions of the Cold War. Even after Kennedy's death, prosperity continued, and public approval of business soared.

Over a period of 30 years, the marketing consultancy firm Yankelovich asked the question of American citizens: "Does business strike a balance between profit and the public interest?". In 1968, 70 percent of the population answered yes to that question. By the time Richard Nixon was on his way to the White House, however, the nation was torn apart by civil unrest, with the continuation of the civil rights struggle and demonstrations against U.S. involvement in the Vietnam War. Disagreement over the role of the United States in Vietnam marked a serious deterioration in public attitudes toward all institutions, including business. For those who were against the war, the executive branch of government came to stand for all that was wrong with America.

Because it helped to make the war possible and profited from the war, American industry was the target of much of the public's hostility. Dow Chemical's manufacture of Napalm and Agent Orange, which would be used to defoliate Vietnamese jungles, led to student protests on American university campuses. Young people in the United States came to distrust the institutions involved in the war, whether government agencies or businesses. This belief represented a dramatic change from the attitudes Americans had during World War II. Those in power failed to see how the Vietnam War was different because Americans were ambivalent about what the country was fighting for.

Toward the end of the 1960s and coinciding with the war in Vietnam, a rise in radicalism in America marked the beginning of a long deterioration of trust in institutions. The events of the early 1970s also contributed to this shift. For example, Watergate only confirmed what most young Americans had believed all along about the Nixon administration.

TABLE 1.1
How Much Confidence Do You Have in These Institutions?*

	1970s	1980s	1990s	2000s	2010s
Big Business	31%	27%	26%	22%	21%
U.S. Congress	39	33	46	22	10
U.S. Supreme Court	46	50	46	42	36
Military	56	58	68	74	74

Sources: Gallup Poll, http://www.gallup.com/poll/1597/Confidence-Institutions.aspx#3.

*Answers reflect proportion of consumers who responded with "great deal" and "quite a lot" of confidence.

The aftermath of the oil embargo, imposed by Arab nations after the 1973 Middle East war, had even more of an effect on attitudes toward business in America. Cheap, abundant petroleum—the lubricant of the American way of life—suddenly became scarce and expensive as Saudi Arabia and other Arab producers punished the United States for supporting Israel in the war. The cutoff lasted less than three months, but its effects on consumer attitudes are still with us today.

As a result of Watergate, Vietnam, and the oil embargo, by the mid-1970s American attitudes toward business reached an all-time low. In answer to the same question "Does business strike a fair balance between profit and the public interest?" those answering yes in a poll conducted by Yankelovich dropped to 15 percent in 1976 when Jimmy Carter took office. This drop of 55 points in just eight years says more about the changing attitudes toward business than a thousand anecdotes.

An opinion research poll conducted by Gallup that asked members of the general public to rate their confidence in a number of institutions showed declines in all areas, except in the military, as shown in Table 1.1.

As you read this, you may be asking yourself whether the 1980s and 1990s, which together constituted the final economic boom of the twentieth century, restored America's faith in business to where it had been in the 1960s. They did not, as a Harris Poll found that by the late 1990s, confidence in American institutions had fallen to its lowest level recorded in the previous thirty years.[1]

In response to a question about whether business strikes a fair balance between profit and the public interest, the percentages climbed back to a high of 30 percent answering yes in 1984. And the percentages dropped slightly to 28 percent in 1999 (the last year Yankelovich asked this question). (See Table 1.2.)

In a Gallup poll conducted over the first two weeks of January 2020, just 8 percent of respondents described themselves as "very satisfied" with the size and influence of major corporations, while another 33 percent considered themselves "somewhat satisfied." Some of the dissatisfaction was attributable to concerns about the regulation (or lack thereof) of big business on the part of the U.S. government. By a slight margin (44 percent to 41 percent) more respondents were dissatisfied than satisfied with government regulations of big business, according to that same Gallup survey. Of those upset with governmental regulation of large firms, half wanted more regulations, while the other half wanted less.[2]

[1] Harris Poll 2017.

[2] Gallup Poll, "Confidence in Big Business," https://news.gallup.com/poll/5248/big-business.aspx.

TABLE 1.2
Does Business Balance Profit and Public Interest?*

Source: *Yankelovich Monitor.*

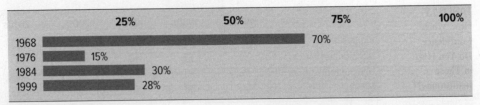

	25%	50%	75%	100%
1968			70%	
1976	15%			
1984	30%			
1999	28%			

*Percent yes responses.

The 1990s saw the phenomenal rise of the NASDAQ index to 4,000 points by the end of the decade. Individual investors were actively participating in the equity markets and reaping enormous gains as stock prices seemed to be on an unstoppable upward trajectory. Then, in the spring of 2000, the markets came crashing down. By December, the NASDAQ had sunk to less than half its peak level of 5,000, reached at the beginning of the year. And unfortunately for the 100 million individual investors who had poured money into the market during the Internet-fueled boom of the 1990s, it did not stop there in its downward spiral. By early 2002, these individuals had lost $5 trillion since the "Internet bubble" burst, representing 30 percent of their stock wealth.[3]

With the bursting of the "dot.com bubble," the exposure of corporate fraud at large companies such as WorldCom, Adelphia, and Tyco, and the collapse of Enron and its auditor, Arthur Andersen, due to fraudulent accounting, Americans perceived business as actively trying to deceive them. This perception was reflected in the media as well, such as in the *NBC Nightly News* segment entitled "The Fleecing of America."

In the midst of this market turmoil, the actions of unscrupulous financial analysts (see Chapter 8 for more on analysts) and companies like Enron angered the American public further. By February 2002, some 81 percent of investors polled "did not have much confidence in those running Big Business."[4] This attitude is not surprising when you consider the many highly publicized stories of top executives who sold millions of dollars' worth of shares in their own failing enterprises, further enhancing their wealth as rank-and-file employees lost much of their retirement savings.

The public also has been embittered by the growing pay gap between senior executives and ordinary workers that reached enormous proportions over recent decades. According to the Economic Policy Institute, since 1978, CEO compensation rose 1,007.5 percent, compared with 11.5 percent for average workers, with CEOs in 2019 making 278 times the average worker.[5] In December 2019, the Congressional Budget Office reported that the middle 60 percent of the American population experienced a growth in household income of 47 percent between 1979 and 2016 (after taxes and adjusted for inflation), while the top 1 percent of earners experienced a growth in household incomes of 218 percent. The study also projected that income for the lowest quintile would grow a mere 1.3 percent by 2021 to $21,900, while income for the top 1 percent would grow 2.3 percent

[3] Marcia Vickers, Mike McNamee, et al., "The Betrayed Investor," *BusinessWeek,* February 25, 2002, p. 105.

[4] Ibid., p. 106.

[5] Jeff Cox, "CEOs See Pay Grow 1,000% in the Last 40 Years," *CNBC,* August 16, 2019, https://www.cnbc.com/2019/08/16/ceos-see-pay-grow-1000percent-and-now-make-278-times-the-average-worker.html.

from \$1.8 million to \$2.0 million.[6] While top earners enjoy lucrative compensation packages, today 40 million Americans rely on food stamps,[7] and 21.3 percent live in households receiving some form of government assistance, according to 2015 data from the Census Bureau.[8] Nobel Prize–winning economist and *The New York Times* contributor Paul Krugman refers to this period of increasing income inequality, which he believes started in the late 1970s, as "The Great Divergence." He writes that it is more a product of conservative politics, tax law that is favorable to the wealthy, and inflated executive compensation than it is a product of less personal forces including globalization and technology.[9,10] Alan Binder for *The Wall Street Journal* similarly argued in 2019 that more recent tax cuts have likewise aggravated income inequality.[11]

Although executive compensation in general is a controversial subject, in the wake of the 2008 subprime credit crisis, public scrutiny has focused on the outsized annual bonuses doled out on Wall Street. Americans were especially outraged that financial firms receiving public TARP (Troubled Asset Relief Program) rescue funds could use the money to pay out executive bonuses. In March 2009, insurance giant A.I.G. earned negative press when it decided to award multimillion-dollar bonuses to its executives despite having just received a \$US 100 billion government bailout. In the summer of 2009, then New York attorney general Andrew Cuomo released a report that detailed compensation at the largest New York–based banks that received public bailout money. The report revealed that Merrill Lynch had paid 149 bonuses greater than \$US 3 million and 696 bonuses greater than \$US 1 million, despite being in such dire financial straits that it had to merge into Bank of America in early 2009.[12] In July 2010, Kenneth R. Feinberg, who was appointed by President Obama to oversee executive compensation during the bailouts, released a report claiming that nearly 80 percent of the \$US 2 billion that banks paid out in 2008 bonuses were unmerited.[13]

Increased tension over growing income inequity combined with relatively high unemployment rates in the United States sparked the Occupy Wall Street movement, a protest against corporate greed and corruption. The largely peaceful Occupy Wall Street movement started in September 2011 in Zuccotti Park in lower Manhattan and quickly spread to other U.S. cities as well as cities around the world, including Paris, London, Berlin, Hong Kong, and Rome.[14] Occupy Wall Street organizers made extensive use of social media and published a daily newspaper to communicate news and marching orders with

[6] "CBO Household Income Report," Congressional Budget Office, December 2019, https://www.cbo.gov/system/files/2019-12/55941-CBO-Household-Income.pdf.

[7] "Snap Data Tables," USDA, https://www.fns.usda.gov/pd/supplemental-nutrition-assistance-program-snap.

[8] "21.3 Percent of U.S. Population Participates in Government Assistance Programs Each Month," U.S. Census Bureau, May 28, 2015, https://www.census.gov/newsroom/press-releases/2015/cb15-97.html.

[9] Paul Krugman, "Introducing This Blog," *The New York Times*, September 18, 2007, http://krugman.blogs.nytimes.com/-2007/09/18/introducing-this-blog.

[10] "Trends in the Distribution of Household Income between 1979 and 2007," Congressional Budget Office, October 2011, http://www.cbo.gov/ftpdocs/124xx/doc12485/10-25-HouseholdIncome.pdf.

[11] Alan S. Blinder, "Tax Cuts for the Wealthy Make Inequality Worse," *The Wall Street Journal*, October 31, 2019, https://www.wsj.com/articles/tax-cuts-for-the-wealthy-make-inequality-worse-11572561280.

[12] Stephen Grocer, "Wall Street Compensation–'No Clear Rhyme or Reason,'" *The Wall Street Journal*, July 30, 2009.

[13] Louise Story, "Topics: Executive Pay," *The New York Times*, December 5, 2011.

[14] Alan Taylor, "In Focus: Occupy Wall Street Spreads Worldwide," *The Atlantic*, October 17, 2011.

participants. Organizers executed a branding campaign for the movement based on the slogan "we are the 99%," meant to highlight the growing income gap between the top 1 percent of earners and the remaining 99 percent. Critics of the Occupy Wall Street movement deride the movement for lacking clear focus and actionable objectives. However, the Occupy Wall Street movement emphatically underscore the growing public discontent with the traditional big business.

In more recent years, two additional movements pertaining to issues of social justice—the #MeToo movement and the Black Lives Matter movement—finally came to the forefront of social consciousness in a way that businesses could not fail to ignore. The phrase "Me Too" was initially used by sexual assault survivor and activist Tarana Burke in 2006 to highlight shared experiences of sexual assault and harassment—especially those experienced by women and girls of color, which Burke had experienced firsthand. The movement took off even further in 2017 following allegations of assault against Hollywood producer Harvey Weinstein.[15] As #MeToo gained traction, the business world has been compelled to confront a wide range of challenges the movement has highlighted, from outright assault and harassment to gender inequity and the gender pay gap, in which women in 2020 still only earned, on average, 81 cents to every dollar made by a male counterpart, and Black women, Native American women, and Latinas earned $0.62, $0.57, and $0.54 for every dollar earned by a white male counterpart.[16,17] In the year following the Harvey Weinstein expose, over 200 men in powerful positions from media to finance to technology stepped down, with over half their positions filled by women.[18] However, while the movement has brought conversations regarding gender inequity and workplace harassment to the forefront, considerable progress remains to be made, as noted by a 2019 Harvard Business Review study, which found that, while in the years following the emergence of the #MeToo movement, reports of unwanted sexual advances declined (in their survey) from 66 to 25 percent, reports of gender harassment increased from 76 percent in 2016 to 92 percent in 2018. Such results highlight that, while progress may be made in the workplace regarding some of the most egregious behaviors, "backlash effects" can unfortunately erode progress.

The Black Lives Matter movement likewise has shone a spotlight on long-standing social ills. The movement was founded in 2013 after the acquittal of George Zimmerman in the shooting death of 17-year-old Trayvon Martin and originally had a primary focus of protesting against police brutality and racism in the United States.[19] The movement

[15] Abby Ohlheiser, "The Woman Behind 'Me Too' Knew the Power of the Phrase When She Created It—10 Years Ago," *The Washington Post*, October 19, 2017, https://www.washingtonpost.com/news/the-intersect/wp/2017/10/19/the-woman-behind-me-too-knew-the-power-of-the-phrase-when-she-created-it-10-years-ago.

[16] Kathleen Elkins, "Here's How Much Men and Women Earn at Every Age," *CNBC*, July 18, 2020, https://www.cnbc.com/2020/07/18/heres-how-much-men-and-women-earn-at-every-age.html.

[17] Courtney Connley, "More than 1 in 3 Black Women Are on the Front Lines of the Pandemic," *CNBC*, August 13, 2020, https://www.cnbc.com/2020/08/13/black-women-are-on-the-front-lines-of-the-pandemic-but-they-arent-even-close-to-equal-pay.html.

[18] Audrey Carlsen, Maya Salam, Claire Cain Miller, Denise Lu, Ash Ngu, Jugal K. Patel, and Zach Wichter, "#MeToo Brought Down 201 Powerful Men. Nearly Half of Their Replacements Are Women," *The New York Times*, October 29, 2018, https://www.nytimes.com/interactive/2018/10/23/us/metoo-replacements.html.

[19] "Black Lives Matter," *Newsweek*, https://www.newsweek.com/topic/black-lives-matter.

returned to national headlines following the 2020 killing of George Floyd by a Minneapolis police officer, with 15 to 26 million Americans participating in demonstrations around the country following his death, making the movement one of the largest, if not the largest, social justices movements in U.S. history.[20] Companies have finally felt compelled to respond in turn, with Twitter declaring Juneteenth a corporate holiday to commemorate the end of slavery, and Reddit founder and husband to Serena Williams, Alexis Ohanian, resigning his position on the company's board to make way for the first Black director in the company's history.[21] Numerous other companies, from Netflix to Nike to WarnerMedia brands, utilized social media channels such as Twitter to declare their support for the movement. An obvious tension exists, though, in companies taking a stand on such deep social injustices in the absence of any real action to combat their underlying causes. Americus Reed, a marketing professor at the Wharton School at the University of Pennsylvania, has described such actions as "values and identity-driven targeted marketing," further noting that, "They're taking a stand, hopefully, because it's moral but also because they understand the long-term economic game."[22] Notably, Black-owned businesses have witnessed an up-tick in business as the movement has gained increasing traction.[23] Skepticism, however, remains as to whether these gains will be short-lived or whether the world of business (and beyond) will continue to commit, in a sustainable and meaningful way, to eradicating the ills of racial inequity, where the average Black family has one-tenth the net worth of the average white family in the United States and where the coronavirus pandemic has disproportionately ravaged communities of color.[24,25]

Television, Social Media, and the Online World

Literature and the arts have both affected and reflected perceptions about institutions throughout human history. Greek attitudes about government and religion manifested themselves in theater; Shakespeare shaped notions about English history for generations; and today, in the United States, television, social media, and the online world have both reflected and helped to create some of the public's negative attitudes about business.

[20] Larry Buchanan, Quoctrung Bui, and Jugal K. Patel, "Black Lives Matter May Be the Largest Movement in U.S. History," *The New York Times*, July 3, 2020, https://www.nytimes.com/interactive/2020/07/03/us/george-floyd-protests-crowd-size.html

[21] Tracy Jan, Jena McGregor, Renae Merle, and Nitasha Tiku, "As Big Corporations Say 'Black Lives Matter,' Their Track Records Raise Skepticism," *The Washington Post*, June 13, 2020, https://www.washingtonpost.com/business/2020/06/13/after-years-marginalizing-black-employees-customers-corporate-america-says-black-lives-matter.

[22] Tiffany Hsu, "Corporate Voices Get Behind 'Black Lives Matter' Cause," *The New York Times*, June 1, 2020, https://www.nytimes.com/2020/05/31/business/media/companies-marketing-black-lives-matter-george-floyd.html

[23] Fredreka Schouten, "The Black Lives Matter Movement Is Driving Customers to Black-Owned Businesses," *CNN*, June 20, 2020, https://www.cnn.com/2020/06/20/politics/black-owned-businesses/index.html.

[24] Tracy Jan, "White Families Have Nearly 10 Times the Net Worth of Black Families," *The Washington Post*, September 28, 2017, https://www.washingtonpost.com/news/wonk/wp/2017/09/28/black-and-hispanic-families-are-making-more-money-but-they-still-lag-far-behind-whites.

[25] "Health Equity Considerations and Racial and Ethnic Minority Groups," CDC 2019 Coronavirus Report, July 24, 2020, https://www.cdc.gov/coronavirus/2019-ncov/community/health-equity/race-ethnicity.html.

For many Americans today, what they see in fictional or "factional" accounts on TV and online helps shape their attitudes more than educational institutions. With three in ten American adults spending time online nearly "constantly" and eight in ten going online daily, it is very clear that the online depiction of a corporation can easily and readily be viewed by many Americans.[26]

The Media Institute, a research organization funded by corporations, has been tracking media coverage of business for more than 40 years. Each time it issues a report, the results are the same: businesspeople are portrayed negatively in almost two-thirds of all television programs. Researchers have concluded that half of the time, businesspeople portrayed on television were involved in criminal activities.

In addition, most Americans (44 percent) get their news from television.[27] As a result, the negative portrayals viewers see in fictional programming blend into the negative news they watch on the nightly news. An individual might, for example, watch an episode of *Law & Order* in which a woman is framed for murder after raising questions about her company's back-dating of stock options one night, then see an in-depth story about United Health doing the same thing on *Dateline NBC* the following evening.

Similarly, though, the share of Americans receiving their news from online is growing, with 34 percent of U.S. adults getting their news in this way. Given that individuals can just as easily (if not more easily) switch from reading the news from reliable sources to watching shows online to stumbling into less thoroughly vetted sources of information on a company, it is clear that there are many avenues to reinforce negative perceptions of business.

It is eerie how Hollywood has mirrored events in business at exactly the right time. The movie *Wall Street* is another such example. Oliver Stone's movie came out just ahead of the great scandals that rocked the real Wall Street in the late 1980s. Even within the film itself, reality and fiction were intertwined. Gordon Gekko, the evil financial genius meant to represent someone like the notorious arbitrageur Ivan Boesky, makes a speech in the film about greed. "Greed is good, greed purifies, greed cuts through and captures the essence of the evolutionary spirit," Gekko says in a passionate speech at an annual meeting. Months earlier, the real Ivan Boesky had made a similar speech to a group of graduates at the University of California's Berkeley campus.

Are these examples instances of "life imitating art"? More likely, it is the other way around. As long as business has a negative public image, movies and television will continue to dramatize real-life tales of corporate wrongdoing. As Hollywood exports a large number of American films to countries around the world, these images become part of a global informational tapestry that we explore in more detail in the next section.

---

[26] Andrew Perrin and Madhu Kumar, "About Three-in-Ten U.S. Adults Say They Are 'Almost Constantly' Online," Pew Research Center, July 25, 2019, https://www.pewresearch.org/fact-tank/2019/07/25/americans-going-online-almost-constantly.

[27] A.W. Geiger, "Key Findings About the Online News Landscape in America," Pew Research Center, September 11, 2019, https://www.pewresearch.org/fact-tank/2019/09/11/key-findings-about-the-online-news-landscape-in-america.

The Global Village

Technology has strengthened communication channels around the globe, disintegrating national borders to produce what Canadian philosopher Marshall McLuhan foresaw decades ago—the creation of a world so interwoven by shared knowledge that it becomes a "Global Village."[28] This trend has had a monumental impact on business, particularly over the past two decades.

In 2002, the U.N. Conference on Trade and Development published an article stating that 29 of the world's top 100 economies were multinational businesses rather than countries.[29] As of 2018, this has reversed, with 29 of the world's top 100 economies being countries and the other 71 being multinational businesses.[30] Thus, it may not be surprising that individuals have begun to turn to large companies to provide the direction that distinct national cultures, communities, and inspirational narratives offered more strongly in the past. Coupled with this shift is a heightened level of interest in social responsibility on the part of organizations. Later in this book, we will discuss the growing importance of corporate social responsibility and its implications for corporate reputation, but generally, the public is looking for companies to demonstrate care for the communities in which they operate from both an environmental and human perspective.

In his book *The Mind of the CEO,* Jeffrey Garten explains, "As the world gets smaller, CEOs will be unable to escape involvement in some of the most difficult political, economic and social problems of our times. There will be no way to avoid operating in countries with fragile economies, weak democratic structures and mega-cities with severely overburdened infrastructures."[31]

Today, companies recognize that the ability to tap into the benefits of globalization is imperative for a company's survival, but at the same time are grappling with the ways to best take advantage of that. The 2019 PwC Global CEO survey underscores the complexities and concerns that come with competing within the global market, with 60 percent of CEOs stating they are "extremely concerned" about protectionism and an increasing number stating they "don't know" where they would like to expand to next.[32]

An anticorporation sentiment was formalized on paper in October 1997, when Earth First! produced a calendar listing important anticorporate protest dates and announcing the first "End Corporate Dominance Month."[33] Since then, organizations such as Vancouver-based Adbusters Media Foundation, which was founded in 1989, have risen to

---

[28] Marshall McLuhan and Bruce R. Powers, *The Global Village: Transformations in World Life and Media in the 21st Century* (New York: Oxford University Press, 1989).

[29] Progressive Policy Institute, "The World Has over 60,000 Multinational Companies," April 27, 2005, http://www.ppionline .org/ppi_ci.cfm?knlgAreaID=108&subsecID=900003&contentID=253303.

[30] "Of the World's Top 100 Economic Revenue Collectors, 29 Are States, 71 Are Corporates," Oxfam, August 3, 2018, https://oxfamblogs.org/fp2p/of-the-worlds-top-100-economic-entities-29-are-states-71-are-corporates.

[31] Jeffrey Garten, *The Mind of the CEO* (New York: Basic Books, 2001), p. 24.

[32] "22nd Annual Global CEO Survey," PwC, https://www.pwc.com/gx/en/ceo-survey/2019/report/pwc-22nd-annual-global-ceo-survey.pdf.

[33] Naomi Klein, *No Logo: Taking Aim at the Brand Bullies* (New York: Picador USA, 1999), p. 327.

a dominant position as nonprofits that devote themselves to deriding corporate giants—a practice now officially referred to as *culture jamming*.[34] Plastering the image of Charles Manson's face over a Levi's jeans billboard, hurling pies at Bill Gates, and dumping garbage bags full of shoes outside of Nike Town to protest Pakistani children manufacturing Nike soccer balls for six cents an hour are some of the routine tactics culture-jamming activists have employed to make anticorporate statements to the public.[35]

This past decade has witnessed an even greater shift in consumer sentiment, from one that distrusted corporate action to one that actually demands companies take a stand on the most challenging societal issues of our time. The Edelman Trust Barometer report from 2020 notes that brand trust—and specifically trust defined as "doing what is right"—is a top five purchase criterion for consumers. In many ways, this is reflective of the newfound belief that brands have the potential to act as positive agents of social change, and consumers are able to participate in this by "voting" with their wallets.[36]

The continual technological advances of the Internet—namely, social media—also have made it difficult for companies to prevent both positive and negative news about them from reaching individuals in virtually all corners of the world. Media outlets have expanded their reach such that events are no longer confined to local communities; rather, they can create reverberations felt worldwide. In 2018, the United Nation's Big Data Working Group estimated that the average mobile subscription rate was 107.0 per 100 inhabitants.[37] As of July 2020, almost 4.6 billion people were active Internet users, encompassing 59 percent of the global population.[38] In the United States, the level of Internet access is far higher, and thus the amount of Internet usage is far higher too, with roughly eight in ten U.S. adults going on online daily and three in ten reporting nearly "constant" Internet usage, according to the Pew Research Center.[39] Data suggest that these numbers will only continue to increase as consumers assume further control of corporate reputations and communicate with one another in real time, 24/7. According to a 2016 Nielsen Social Media study, surprisingly, the heaviest social media user group was not Millennials but Generation X (ages 35–49), who spend almost seven hours per week on social media versus Millennials who spend approximately six hours.[40]

Business leaders today therefore must be prepared not only to handle the international media spotlight but also to proactively counter the advocacy groups looking to use today's media environment to compromise their corporate reputation—and bottom line—globally.

[34] Ibid., p. 280.

[35] Ibid.

[36] United Nations Big Data Report, https://unstats.un.org/bigdata/taskteams/mobilephone.

[37] Ibid.

[38] "Global Digital Population as of October 2020," Statista, https://www.statista.com/statistics/617136/digital-population-worldwide.

[39] Andrew Perrin and Madhu Kumar, "About Three-in-Ten U.S. Adults Say They Are 'Almost Constantly' Online," Pew Research Center, July 25, 2019, https://www.pewresearch.org/fact-tank/2019/07/25/americans-going-online-almost-constantly.

[40] "2016 Nielsen Social Media Report," Nielsen, https://www.nielsen.com/wp-content/uploads/sites/3/2019/04/2016-nielsen-social-media-report.pdf.

How to Compete in a Changing Environment

Even well-respected companies face attacks in this new environment. Gillette (now part of Procter & Gamble), for example, was the target of animal rights groups that successfully used teachers and children to create a stir over the company's research methods. One letter to Gillette's former chairman, Alfred Zeien, said: "Let this be a warning to you. If you hurt another animal, if I find out, one month from [the day] this letter arrives to you, I'll bomb your company. P.S. Watch your back." The letter came from a sixth grader at a school in Philadelphia. As homework, his teacher had assigned letters to companies about animal testing.[41] While the children's campaign had no effect on market share, the company worried about potential long-term effects: "Long term, this could be a very bad trend for the business," said CEO Zeien.[42]

When Walmart faced allegations of unfair treatment of employees, including forcing hourly wage earners to work off the clock, favoring men over women in pay and promotion, and locking employees in stores after closing until managers visited every department, the media pounced on the opportunity to deface the corporate behemoth. In 2000, a female Walmart employee named Betty Dukes filed a sexual discrimination suit against the company that would eventually become a class-action suit representing 1.6 million females. The case finally made its way to the highest court in the United States, the Supreme Court, in 2011, and although the court ruled that the plaintiffs had too much variation in their complaints to merit a class-action suit, Walmart endured negative press for 11 years during the proceedings. A journalist who covered the story turned her research into a book called *Selling Women Short: The Landmark Battle for Workers' Rights at Wal-Mart*, and likened Betty Dukes to civil rights activist Rosa Parks.

Beyond the scrutiny it receives in traditional media outlets, Walmart is also the target of vitriolic social commentary online, with an ever-growing list of anti-Walmart blogs and social groups forming to collectively criticize its controversial business practices. This added dimension of communication, coupled with the reputational risk factors it fosters, raises a key question: how can managers adapt to the challenges of a business environment that is constantly in flux but seems to be moving in the direction of greater scrutiny and less favorable impressions of corporations? In the next section, we look at some of the ways companies can stay on course while navigating these choppy waters.

Recognize the Changing Environment

First, managers need to recognize that the business environment *is* constantly evolving. The short-term orientation of today's managers rarely gives them an opportunity to look at the big picture of how this changing environment affects the company's image with a variety of constituencies. Over the long term, this perspective can have damaging results.

---

[41] Barbara Carton, "Gillette Faces Wrath of Children in Testing of Rats and Rabbits," *The Wall Street Journal*, September 5, 1995, p. A1.

[42] Ibid.

Coca-Cola took note when, in January 2006, the University of Michigan suspended the purchase of its products on campus.[43] This now classic business case had nothing to do with pricing or the products themselves; rather, it was taken based on concerns over environmental concerns in India and labor issues in Colombia. Among the allegations was a contention that products contained unacceptable levels of insecticides (PepsiCo's products were also found to contain unacceptable levels of pesticides).

The business and communication implications of this revelation and the university's subsequent reaction are manifold: first, the University of Michigan's decision was prompted by one man, Amit Srivastava, who ran a small nonprofit out of his home in California. He mobilized students on campus to petition for the ban—an organizational feat that, just a few years before, would have been unthinkable. Second, these visceral reactions on the part of students applied so much pressure that the company agreed to open its overseas facilities to independent, transparent, third-party environmental and labor audits.[44] Third, the event points to a major evolution in business: Sustainable business practices are becoming core brand values that can inspire change. Coca-Cola's sustainability efforts changed dramatically over the course of a year, and the company appeared among the 2007 Global 100 Most Sustainable Corporations in the World. It is still considered a leader in sustainability today, sitting on Barron's 100 Most Sustainable Corporations List as of 2020.[45]

One of the most important challenges facing senior managers is the profoundly unsettling impact of technological change. Andrew Grove, cofounder and senior advisor to the executive management of Intel Corporation, explained, "We make a cult of how wonderful it is that the rate of [technological] change is so fast. But . . . what happens when the rate of change is so fast that before a technological innovation gets deployed, or halfway through the process of being deployed, [an] innovation sweeps in and creates a destructive interference with the first one?"[46] Although many agree that technology has helped business, it also has led to greater uncertainty for business leaders and consumers alike.

Unlike many shifts in the market that companies can anticipate by keeping their fingers on the pulse of change, such as evolving consumer tastes, technological innovations can happen swiftly and have profound effects. Companies need to quickly determine what, if anything, they need to do to respond to such changes.

Adapt to the Environment without Compromising Principles

Second, companies must adapt to the changing environment without changing what they stand for or compromising their principles. In the summer of 2011, Netflix announced that it would "no longer offer a plan that includes both unlimited streaming and DVDs by mail." Subscribers would have to join two separate services—one of them ludicrously dubbed Qwikster—and pay $16 a month instead of $10. The ensuing backlash and exodus stunned investors; more than 800,000 customers fled Netflix in a single quarter, sending

---

[43] http://www.umich.edu/news/?BG/procmemo.

[44] Ibid.

[45] Evie Liu, "The 100 Most Sustainable Companies, Reranked by Social Factors," Barron's, June 28, 2020, https://www.barrons.com/articles/these-companies-rank-best-on-social-criteriaand-could-reward-investors-51593215993.

[46] Garten, *Mind of the CEO*, p. 32.

its stock plunging from $300 a share to around $65 by year's end. Netflix quickly scrapped Qwikster and apologized, but the company only truly recovered from the gaffe with original series such as *Orange is the New Black*, which launched in 2013. Soon profit was skyrocketing, stock hit $400 per share, and Netflix has continued to persist as a streaming giant offering high-quality programming at a low cost.[47]

Arie de Geus of the MIT Sloan School of Management analyzed the strengths of what he defined as "living companies"—a group of 30 companies ranging in age from 100 to 700 years scattered throughout North America, Europe, and Japan.[48] One of the primary reasons these companies—including DuPont, W.R. Grace, Sumitomo, and Siemens—have managed to endure has been their ability to adapt to the rapidly evolving environment in which they live. De Geus explains: "As wars, depressions, technologies, and politics surged and ebbed, they always seemed to excel at keeping their feelers out, staying attuned to whatever was going on. For information, they sometimes relied on packets carried over vast distances by portage and ship, yet they managed to react in a timely fashion to whatever news they received. They were good at learning and adapting."[49]

Don't Assume Problems Will Magically Disappear

Third, assume things will only get worse in today's complex environment, especially with the ever-growing prevalence of consumer-generated media and online communications platforms. For example, Chemical giant Monsanto faced challenges when its foray into genetically engineered crops met with resistance from protesters who labeled its products "Frankenfoods." Protests were not limited to the company's headquarters in St. Louis but spread to some of Monsanto's large, visible customers, forcing McDonald's, for one, to announce that it would no longer use the company's genetically modified (GM) potatoes.[50]

This issue ultimately took its toll on the company's stock price in the late 1990s, even though the company met Wall Street expectations. In response, Monsanto adopted a new approach to handling the "GM backlash" through education and outreach. However, the problems with the Monsanto brand never truly dissipated. Bayer acquired the company in 2018 and entirely nixed the Monsanto name, as it had consistently been ranked as one of the most hated companies in the world. Today, Bayer itself seems to be suffering from its acquisition of Monsanto, as it faces a mountain of legal trouble regarding claims that Roundup causes cancer, leading to the ousting of Bayer's chairman.[51,52]

The Monsanto case clearly underscores the extent to which certain brand challenges, including brand perception and underlying brand integrity, do not just dissipate. Most

[47] "The Biggest Business Comebacks of the Past 20 Years," *Fast Company*, March 17, 2015, https://www.fastcompany.com/3042431/the-biggest-business-comebacks-of-the-past-20-years.

[48] Arie de Geus, "The Living Company," *Harvard Business Review*, March 1, 1997.

[49] Ibid.

[50] Jonathan Low and Pam Cohen Kalafut, *Invisible Advantage: How Intangibles Are Driving Business Performance* (Cambridge: Perseus Books, 2002), p. 114.

[51] Caitlin Dewey, "Why 'Monsanto' Is No More," *The Washington Post*, June 4, 2018, https://www.washingtonpost.com/news/wonk/wp/2018/06/04/why-monsanto-is-no-more.

[52] Ruth Bender, "Bayer Chairman Steps Down in Midst of Roundup Legal Battle," *The Wall Street Journal*, February 26, 2020, https://www.wsj.com/articles/bayer-chairman-steps-down-in-midst-of-roundup-legal-battle-11582714274.

managers assume that the American public has a short memory about the problems companies face. In fact, consumers have longer memories than you might think, as witnessed by boycotts of companies such as Coors, Walmart, Nike, and Shell.

Some companies seem to be getting it right, but most are still getting it wrong. What's more, all constituent groups—from employees to investors to consumers—are taking advantage of changes in the business environment that empower them to increase their personal gains. For example, in autumn 2007, two separate situations took place on opposite coasts, in New York City and Los Angeles, that illustrate unique communication strategies.

On November 5, 2007, screenwriters took to the streets of Hollywood, initiating the first industrywide strike in more than 19 years.[53] Under the representation of the Writers Guild of America, approximately 12,000 movie and television writers formed picket lines in response to failed negotiations with Hollywood producers over their stake in new media revenue, including downloaded movies and online promotional showings of movies and television shows.

The strike crippled the industry, as networks such as CBS and ABC had to shut down production of major primetime shows. Clearly, producers could not just hope the problem would disappear, but their communications and negotiation strategies posed interesting nuances. For example, a *BusinessWeek* article entitled "Behind the Hollywood Strike Talks" highlights an underlying factor driven by conflicting business model challenges from each side:

> The traditional business models of both sides worked well when there were a handful of movie studios and three major TV networks. But now everyone can be a writer or a producer, and every computer is potentially a studio, able to create and publish content. More than 1 billion people on the planet are connected to the Internet, a healthy portion of them via high-speed broadband.[54]

The author of the article, Henry Chesbrough, executive director of the Center for Open Innovation at the Haas School of Business at University of California Berkeley, also highlighted another detail that will continue to play a more prevalent role in management and communication:

> Much of the new online entertainment content is not coming from professional writers or producers at all. Rather, as others have noted, it is coming from users and user communities that stimulate one another to create content.

Unsure of how the negotiations between writers and producers will end, Chesbrough believes that both sides need to make sizable changes and concessions to their business models to take advantage of the shifting industry and the new opportunities provided. He also underscores the massive opportunity that these user communities have to upend Hollywood as we know it. Chesbrough indicates that if Hollywood refuses to meet the challenge that the emergence of these communities creates, they are positioned to lose.

[53] Michael Cieply, David Carr, and Brooks Barnes, "Screenwriters on Strike over Stake in New Media," *The New York Times*, November 6, 2007, https://www.nytimes.com/2007/11/06/business/media/06strike.html.

[54] Henry Chesbrough, "Behind the Hollywood Strike Talks," *BusinessWeek*, November 1, 2007, http://www.businessweek.com/innovate/content/nov2007/id2007111_779706.htm?chan=search.

Coincidentally, as this contention heated up in Hollywood, a similar situation percolated in the Big Apple. On November 10, 2007, stagehands announced a strike of their own, and Broadway went dark. It was the first in the stagehand union's 121-year history, and it darkened 31 theaters.[55] Unlike the writers' strike, which hinged in the proliferation of new media and its role in generating revenue, the stagehand dispute focused on work rules in their contracts that the producers' league claimed to be expensive and inefficient. The league wanted to change these rules, and the consideration was not well received by the stagehands.

The strike lasted 19 days, during which time New York Mayor Michael Bloomberg offered to provide a mediator and a neutral place to negotiate; both offers were declined. What *The New York Times* called "a series of back-channel conversations between league members and union officials" eventually precipitated talks that ended with a resolution.

Again, it is difficult to assume a problem such as one that left Broadway dark would magically disappear, but the communications strategy proved to be much more traditional, and the strike itself was relatively brief compared with the writers' strike. Negotiations focused on work rules and were not clouded by the nebulous laws governing cyberspace. However, with digital communications platforms playing an increasingly integral role in overall management and communications, competition in the changing business environment continues to evolve.

Keep Corporate Communication Connected to Strategy

Fourth, corporate communication must be closely linked to a company's overall vision and strategy. Few managers recognize the importance of the communication function, and they are reluctant to hire the quality staff necessary to succeed in today's environment. As a result, communication people are often kept out of the loop.

Successful companies connect communication with strategy through structure, such as having the head of corporate communication report directly to the CEO. The advantage of this kind of reporting relationship is that the communications professional can get the company's strategy directly from those at the top of the organization. As a result, all of the company's communications will be more strategic and focused (see Chapter 3 for more on structure).

The aforementioned Arthur Page "Authentic Enterprise" report also urged enterprises to define and activate their core values in new ways, which "demands increased delegation and empowerment, while maintaining consistency of brand, customer relationships, public reputation and day-to-day operations. Values are the 'glue' shaping behavior and uniting goals. However, building a management system based on values is a significant challenge. Understanding what the company and its people truly value and turning that into pervasive behavior require new kinds of leadership, tools and skills."[56]

In Chapter 10, we will take a look at how Johnson & Johnson (J&J) handled the Tylenol cyanide crisis of the early 1980s. Part of what helped the company deal so successfully

---

[55] Campbell Robertson, "Stagehands End Walkout on Broadway," *The New York Times*, November 29, 2007, https://www.nytimes.com/2007/11/29/theater/29broadway.html.

[56] "The Authentic Enterprise," Arthur W. Page Society, 2007.

with this dire situation was the existence of the J&J Credo, a companywide code of ethics that spells out J&J's promises to its many constituencies. This credo helped guide the company's actions during an episode that could have irreparably damaged the Tylenol brand and possibly J&J itself. Thirty years later, the company was again under attack for its faulty production practices but still feeling the halo effect from its handling of this situation.

Companies' corporate communications teams play a pivotal role in defining a corporate mission—the cornerstone of a company's overarching strategy—and communicating that mission to internal and external constituents. Given today's rapidly changing environment, a clear-cut corporate mission not only keeps employees aligned with what the company is striving to be but also can act as a source of stability for consumers weary of the constant change surrounding them.

Conclusion

The business environment is constantly changing. Everyone in business today, whether at a large corporation with a national union to deal with or a small business looking to make its mark in the international arena, needs to communicate strategically. The way organizations adapt and modify their behavior, as manifested through their communications, will determine the success of American business in the twenty-first century.

Case 1-1

Redwood Health System

On September 15, 2018, the Board of Directors of Redwood Health System simultaneously announced at its annual physician retreat the retirement of its beloved CEO of eight years, Eric Bell, and the hiring of Elizabeth Wells as his replacement. Founded in Marin County in 1980, Redwood Health System was recognized as a leader in health care delivery in California and across the United States. Rooted in the principles of teaching, research, and patient-centered care, Redwood was an academic medical center that served patients from Marin County and across Northern California.

Originally founded as a single hospital called Valley Clinic, Redwood Health System began to acquire community hospitals throughout the region in the 1980s to gain greater contract leverage over local payers and, due to increased demands for specialty care in the region, it eventually grew to become a ten-hospital system. Redwood served a spectrum of patients throughout the Northern California region, ranging from low-income patients suffering from multiple chronic conditions to higher-income patients looking for concierge health services. Physicians within the system had historically been paid on a traditional fee-for-service (FFS) model. The system also provided care through a number of revenue-generating specialty service lines that produced maximum reimbursement for the hospitals under this FFS system. These profitable centers of the hospital included Cardiology, Orthopedics, Oncology, and Plastic Surgery. As is the case with many hospitals under FFS systems, specialists earned significantly more than primary care physicians, and as such, controlled much of the purse strings during capital budgeting deliberations at Redwood. Despite this pay-and-power discrepancy between specialists and primary care physicians, Redwood still enjoyed relatively high employee morale, with employees frequently citing the pride in their work as being among the top reasons they stayed at the health system.

Unifying all ten hospitals under the Redwood banner was the health system's finance and billing department that brought together service line leaders from each institution for annual capital budget meetings, reimbursement updates from payers, and little else. Though the Redwood system had tried to move to a managed care model in the early 2000s, managed care proved to be too administratively burdensome for the system and Redwood abandoned the model by the late 2000s. Overall, physicians felt the attempt at managed care jeopardized their professional autonomy and the scattered rollout simply increased their existing paperwork burden; subspecialist physician leaders were especially pleased to see a return to the original model and the greater autonomy that came with it.

However, the passage of the Affordable Care Act (ACA) in 2010, and its particularly comprehensive changes that came into effect in 2014, forced Redwood to once again contend with the need to move to a managed care model and similarly to find leadership capable of ushering in such a change.

Dr. Eric Bell had been the long-time CEO of Redwood since 2004, leading the system through the previous attempt at a transition to a managed care model. Bell had completed his fellowship in gastroenterology at Valley Clinic, met his wife (a primary care physician) during his fellowship year, and had been with Valley Clinic for 30 years. He moved to the administrative side of the system in 1990 and eventually was promoted to Chief Medical Officer (CMO) in 1996. Bell was a beloved member of the hospital, well-liked among providers and staff. As CMO, he fostered strong bonds across specialty areas, resulting in high physician satisfaction and low attrition. Primary care physicians also extolled Bell's ability to promote a positive relationship between them and the health system's specialist groups through monthly "listening lunches" he hosted for all physician groups to join and provide feedback on their perspective of Redwood's organizational direction. Believing his effectiveness was dependent on good rapport with those both above and below him, he also forged friendly relationships with members of the Board, especially its current chairman Harry Anders.

Anders had been on the Redwood Board for 10 years and acted as Chairman for the past two. He was well-liked among the physician community and among his colleagues on the Board, and he similarly viewed Bell as a strong leader and good friend. However, he recognized the need to move to leadership better positioned to usher in the changes demanded by the ACA, and thus was in support of the decision to hire Elizabeth Wells. Although Anders had a strong relationship with Bell, Redwood was beginning to lose market share at some of its smaller hospitals where patients were increasingly frustrated by long waiting times to schedule appointments with primary care and specialist physicians alike. While this predicament was a growing concern of the Board, it was subsumed by the belief that the high demand for its medical services was the primary driver behind the long wait times for appointments. Without plans to expand the capacity of workforce or facilities, it was unclear how this market trend would be resolved in the coming years, nor was it of much concern to hospital leaders unaffected by such developments.

Anders announced Wells' appointment at the annual physician leadership retreat at The Lodge at Pebble Beach. A favorite event among physicians, the retreat historically represented an event in which major strategic decisions were discussed across all hospitals within the system. This time, the announcement about the imminent change in leadership was made at the annual banquet in the beautiful Tap Room without discussion. Elizabeth Wells would assume the role of CEO of Redwood, replacing Bell, and usher Redwood through a time of significant policy, reimbursement, and operational change in health care. Her strategy and approach, however, were left to rumor among those in attendance.

Some speculated that Redwood would not be able to successfully align with the policy requirements of the ACA—a path that was met with decidedly mixed results even at larger and more technology-savvy organizations in the state. Others wondered how it might affect their autonomy, with flashbacks to the managed care debacle of decades prior. Even younger physicians worried whether their attending paychecks were in jeopardy with the heavy burden of medical school loans still sitting squarely on their shoulders.

Introducing Wells, Anders pointed out the outstanding record of Redwood's new CEO: "Wells received her MBA from the Tuck School of Business in 2005, spent five years at McKinsey and Company, and then began at Aetna in the early-2010s. Working heavily in finance, Wells was in charge of Aetna's purchase of a number of physician practices and developing integrated delivery networks. Please help me in welcoming Elizabeth to the Redwood family."

"I want to thank Eric and the entire Board of Trustees," Wells said as she took to the podium. "I am thrilled at the opportunity to join the Redwood system. These are exciting times in health care, but there are great challenges ahead of us. As the system embarks on its path over the coming years, we have the opportunity to reshape the way we deliver care to our patients. I have seen in my role at Aetna the value of reducing costs to make care more affordable for the community. This requires a hard look at the way we practice medicine, run our hospitals, and pay our physicians, with a focus on cost containment and value-based physician compensation. It's a bit like running a marathon, which I have done successfully three times, once while I was pregnant."

In a later break-out meeting with the individual hospital CEOs and VPs, Wells spoke about her respect for Redwood and the pressing need to position the system for the upcoming changes in health care delivery. An affable woman but a stickler for details as a self-proclaimed "quant-savant," Wells began making the rounds of the dinner tables that night, discussing her plans to prepare Redwood for a significant transition from "volume to value" and touting the early success of some Accountable Care Organizations in making that change. She vaguely referred to her "new strategy" for reorganizing service lines within Redwood to maximize referral streams through primary care and reworking the systems' physician incentive structure to align with the goals of her future vision for Redwood.

The mood at the end of the retreat was relatively positive, yet a bit inquisitive about Redwood's future direction. Everyone agreed, however, that there would be many upcoming challenges facing Wells and Redwood during this period of significant transition.

CASE QUESTIONS

1. What problems does Redwood face?
2. What problems will Elizabeth Wells have in executing her strategy?
3. How has the business environment changed following the challenges of COVID-19?

CHAPTER TWO

Communicating Strategically

In the first chapter, we examined the changing environment for business over the last half century. In this chapter, we explore how these changes have affected corporate communication and why it has become imperative for modern companies to communicate strategically.

Strategic communication can be defined as "communication aligned with the company's overall strategy, [intended] to enhance its strategic positioning."[1] An effective strategy should encourage a company to send messages that are "clear and understandable, true and, communicated with passion, strategically repetitive and repeated, [and] consistent (across constituencies)."

We begin this chapter with a summary of the basic theory behind all communication, whether individual or organizational in nature. We also briefly discuss influential models in modern communication theory. Although many communication experts have adapted these theories to help leaders communicate in writing and speaking, few have looked at how these same basic theories apply in the corporate communication context; that is, the way organizations communicate with various groups of people (who we will refer to as constituencies).

Communication, more than any other subject in business, has implications for everyone within an organization—from the newest administrative assistant to the CEO. Thanks in part to important strategy work by academics such as Michael Porter, Gary Hamel, and C. K. Prahalad, most managers have learned to think strategically about their business overall, but few think strategically about what they spend most of their time doing—communicating.

This chapter discusses what it means to develop a cohesive and coherent communication strategy within an organization, emphasizing the critical link between corporate communication and the firm's overall corporate strategy.

Communication Theory

Most modern theories associated with communication can be traced back thousands of years to a single common ancestor, the Greek philosopher Aristotle.

---

[1] Paul A. Argenti, Robert A. Howell, and Karen A. Beck, "The Strategic Communication Imperative," *MIT Sloane Management Review*, Spring 2005.

Aristotle, who studied under Plato and taught in Athens from 367–347 BCE, is most often associated with the development of rhetoric, the ancient antecedent to modern persuasive communication. In his book *The Art of Rhetoric*, Aristotle defined the three basic components of every speech, which have been adapted to meet the needs of the modern corporation.

This strategy depends on thinking carefully about the same three parts that Aristotle used to describe the components of speech: (1) a "speaker," or in our case, a corporation, with something to say; (2) a "subject," or message that needs to be conveyed; and (3) a "person" or group to whom the message will be delivered.

Aristotle's observations on message communication laid the foundation for modern communication theory, which developed in the United States along with several other social sciences following World War II. In 1948, law professor and political scientist at Yale University Harold Lasswell proposed a communications model that he believed applied especially well to mass communications.[2] His linear model can be summarized as "who (Aristotle's speaker) says what (Aristotle's subject or message) in which channel (medium) to whom (Aristotle's recipient) with what effect (effect)." Several years later, professor of communication skills Richard Braddock proposed an expansion of Lasswell's model to include more reflection on the intent of the message, as well as more analysis of the circumstances under which the message was being delivered.[3]

Further in 1948, mathematician and engineer Claude Shannon published his *"A Mathematical Theory of Communication"* in the in-house scientific journal at Bell Labs. The following year, Warren Weaver helped Shannon to publish the article as a book, and as a result this communications model is called both the Shannon-Weaver model and the Shannon model. The model, used today in social sciences, mathematics, and engineering, is linear and focuses on the physical transmission of information. It follows the creation of a signal by an information source (using a transmitter) to the reception of the signal by the recipient. The model also includes a "noise source," which can be anything that interferes with the integrity of the signal.[4]

In 1956, professor of communications George Gerbner proposed a communication model that built on both the Lasswell and Shannon-Weaver models and emphasized the important role that perception plays in communication as well as the transactional nature of communications.[5]

The Corporate Communication Strategy Framework presented in Figure 2.1 incorporates these and other communication models to provide a valuable framework for effectively analyzing corporate communications.

---

[2] Harold D. Lasswell, "The Structure and Function of Communication in Society," in Lyman Bryson, ed., *The Communication of Ideas: A Series of Addresses* (New York: Institute for Religious and Social Studies), pp. 203–243.

[3] Richard Braddock, "An Extension of the 'Lasswell Formula,'" *Journal of Communication*, 8, no. 2 (June 1948), pp. 88–93.

[4] Claude Elwood Shannon and Warren Weaver, *The Mathematical Theory of Communication* (University of Illinois Press), 1964.

[5] George Gerbner, "Toward a General Model of Communication," *Audio-Visual Communication Review*, 4 (1956), pp. 171–199.

FIGURE 2.1
Consolidated
Corporate
Communication
Strategy
Framework

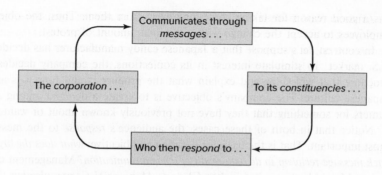

Looking at the framework, one can easily visualize the connections between each component. As communication theorist Annette Shelby[6] states: "The unique interrelationships of these variables determine which messages will be effective and which will not." These interrelationships will also determine the most effective tools for communicating the message. In addition, this framework is circular rather than linear, which reflects the reality that communication of any kind is an ongoing process rather than one with a beginning and an end.

Whether an organization is trying to enhance its reputation through social media, communicate a new health care plan to employees, or convince shareholders that the company is still worth investing in, it is critical to use a coherent communication strategy. An effective strategy should consider the effect that the message will likely have on its audience.

Developing Corporate Communication Strategies

Let's further develop each of these variables and apply them to real situations and see how they operate in practice.

Setting an Effective Organization Strategy

The first part of an effective corporate communication strategy relates to the organization itself. The three subsets of an organization strategy include (1) determining the *objectives* for a particular communication, (2) deciding what *resources* are available for achieving those objectives, and (3) diagnosing the organization's *reputation*.

Determining Objectives

An organization, like an individual, has many different reasons for deciding to communicate. For example, a company might want to announce to employees a change in its benefits package for the upcoming year. Let's suppose the organization has decided to eliminate retiree health benefits as a result of increasing health care costs. In this case, its objective is more than just announcing the change; it also must convince employees it

---

[6] Annette Nevin Shelby, "Organizational Business, Management, and Corporate Communication: An Analysis of Boundaries and Relationships," *Journal of Business Communication* 30, no. 3 (June 1993), pp. 241–267.

has a good reason for taking something away from them. Thus, the objective is to get employees to accept the change with a minimal amount of protest.

In contrast, let's suppose that a Japanese candy manufacturer has decided to enter the U.S. market. To stimulate interest in its confections, the company decides to produce a brochure that will show and explain what the product is and how it is an extension of Japanese culture. The company's objective is to create a demand among American consumers for something that they have not previously known about or wanted.

Notice that in both of these cases, the audience's *response* to the message is what is most important. That is the basis for defining an objective: *what does the organization want each message recipient to do as a result of the communication?* Management communication expert Mary Munter writes in her *Guide to Managerial Communication* that managerial communication is only successful if you get the desired response from your audience.[7] To get that response, you must think strategically about your communication, including setting measurable objectives for it. In general, effective communication can be a differentiator for a business and can drive strategy. It not only allows executives to connect with their constituencies, but also to solicit and act on feedback from those constituencies.

Deciding What Resources Are Available

Determining how to communicate about something like an employee benefits plan or the introduction of a new product depends heavily on what resources are available within the organization, including money, human resources, technology, and time.

Money   In our earlier example involving cutbacks in health benefits for employees, the company must decide whether it is better to simply announce the program as clearly as possible to its employees—for example, through the company newsletter, via e-mail, or on the company's intranet—or to hire a benefits consultant with experience in helping other companies sell employees on benefits reductions. The first option looks less expensive than the second in the short term, but if the employees revolt because they feel they are losing something for no good reason, the company might end up spending far more than it would have if it had hired the more experienced consultant in the first place.

Most companies, unfortunately, often err on the side of short-term, inexpensive solutions to communication problems because they are not looking at the problem from the perspective of the constituency in question. This issue is similar to a problem individuals often have in communicating: they look at their own needs rather than the needs of their audience and end up having difficulty reaching their communication objective.

Human Resources   Human resources are also an important factor in determining the success or failure of a company in achieving its objectives. Typically, too few are assigned to deal with communication tasks, and those involved are often inexperienced or unqualified.

Imagine a company that has just gone public and has decided to create an investor relations function to deal with shareholder relations and communication with financial analysts. It could assign one person to do all of these things, or it could decide that it really needs three. The best approach depends on the size of the company and its shareholder base.

[7] Munter, *Guide to Managerial Communication* (Upper Saddle River: Prentice Hall, 2013).

Let's look at the case of a well-known, multibillion-dollar company that turned this function over to one person with weak communication skills rather than devote two or three experts to deal with the different constituencies involved. In this company's case, it wasn't a question of whether it could afford to pay more people to do the job correctly; it was the lack of understanding about how important corporate communication really is and the limitations put on the human resources needed to accomplish a specific task.

This Fortune 500 company changed its approach after analysts started to downgrade its stock despite healthy prospects for the company's future. The CEO discovered that the analysts felt that the investor relations person at the company was not interested in giving them sufficient information to rate the company's stock. This perception led them to believe that something was wrong at the company. The investor relations person, on the other hand, was actually trying to do two or three tasks at the same time and simply could not keep up with the demands of the job. After this incident, the company hired two more professionals to handle the job properly, creating a more effective and efficient investor relations function, and its stock price shot back to where it should have been all along.

Technology   As we will discuss in Chapter 5, the 4.57 billion people who are online today have fundamentally changed the way organizations connect with their constituents.[8] The organization now has a tertiary audience with whom to communicate—beyond employees, customers, and investors—and those are the millions of Facebook, Twitter, Instagram, and other social media users who have the power to shape a company's reputation. In an increasingly interconnected world, companies are less able to afford lapses in communication.

In 2012, for example, a cruise ship operated by Costa Crociere (owned by Carnival Cruises), sank off the Tuscan coast, claiming 31 lives and injuring 64. The CEO of Carnival Cruises at the time was informed of the disaster via his Twitter newsfeed. This was instead of a phone call, or even an e-mail, from his team on the ground in Italy. The response to the crisis from the home office, both on the ground and on social media, was similarly uncoordinated and was instrumental in compromising the company's public perception and its stock price. The case of Carnival Cruises highlights the importance of leveraging social media to provide a consistent, coordinated message to an audience beyond a company's immediate stakeholders.

Time   Time, like human resources and money, is also a critical factor in determining an organization's corporate communication strategy. Let's look at two approaches for dealing with the same problem involving the allocation of time.

In the case of the Japanese confectioner mentioned earlier, the company decided to produce a brochure (with the help of a communications consulting firm) describing its product more than two years before it was actually necessary. So much time was involved, however, in getting everyone in the company to buy into both the proposed text and the design for the brochure that it took almost the full two years to produce an eight-page pamphlet. Cultural differences between Japanese and American business styles contributed to the tremendous amount of time needed to develop the brochure.

---

[8] "Global Digital Population as of October 2020," Statista, https://www.statista.com/statistics/617136/digital-population-worldwide.

For an American firm, it is unheard of to devote so much time to what would be viewed as such a simple project. American firms produce brochures like this from start to finish in a matter of weeks. But is this really a better approach?

The allocation of time, like the allocation of all resources, should be determined by what it will really take to achieve the company's objective rather than to seek a short-term solution (often to save money). In some cases, this might mean allocating more resources than the organization would like to achieve the desired result, but almost always, the organization is better off allocating the resources up front. Correcting mistakes in corporate communication after the fact can be a costly proposition. Too often, qualified communicators are brought in only after a crisis has erupted or to combat rumors that have materialized to fill a "communications void." This scenario is often the case when a company is in the midst of a merger or acquisition and employees hear details about the company's merger plans through media outlets before they hear it from the company itself. When rampant rumor mills and third-party information inspire fear and uncertainty among employees, productivity and customer service typically suffer, in some cases enough to reduce shareholder value.[9] The company then suddenly has a much larger—and potentially more costly—problem to solve.

Diagnosing the Organization's Reputation

In addition to setting objectives for communication and deciding what resources are available to accomplish that objective, organizations must determine what kind of image credibility they have with the constituencies in question. An organization's overall reputation with constituencies is based on several factors. We will get into this in greater detail in Chapter 4 when we talk about image, identity, and reputation, but it is also a critical factor in the development of all communication strategies, whether specifically related to image or not.

Image credibility is based on the constituency's perception of the organization rather than the reality of the organization itself. As an example, think about a university that is trying to generate positive publicity in the national media. If the university is not well known outside its region, this effort might prove very difficult. Its image credibility in this situation would be low because the national media would have limited experience with the institution compared with an institution that already has a national reputation. Thus, no matter what kind of resources the university puts behind this effort, it will be an uphill battle.

Worse than limited image credibility is credibility that is lacking or damaged. In the fall of 2010, top toy company Mattel had to recall 7 million of its Fisher-Price brand tricycles when ten young children reportedly injured themselves on the sharp, protruding plastic ignition key. During this same period, 3 million Fisher-Price toys were recalled due to concerns that small parts could cause choking. The 2010 recalls unfortunately followed a series of other reputation-damaging recalls for Mattel, including that of magnetic toys with faulty designs in November 2006, a recall of Fisher-Price-brand toys with high levels of lead paint in August 2007, and a recall of lead paint-laden Barbie accessories in September 2007.

---

[9] Michael Kempner, "When RUMORS Thrive Your Deal's in Trouble: Damage Control Techniques to Seize the Communications High Ground," *Mergers & Acquisitions*, May 1, 2005, pp. 42–47.

Once the most credible of toy makers, Mattel had damaged its credibility with investors and customers. During the height of the high-profile recalls, the stock value fell as much as 25 percent. However, Mattel executives took aggressive action to help upend the credibility crisis, opting for complete transparency and leveraging digital communications channels to deliver messages to constituents. Mattel's communications team also launched an advertising campaign with the headline "Because your children are our children, too," and spokespeople constantly reiterated the company's investigation of the safety breaches and communicated openly with the media. Mattel's response to the recalls of 2006 and 2007 likely reassured investors during the 2010 recalls: the company's stock price actually increased slightly immediately following the September 30, 2010, tricycle recall announcement.

Sometimes, damaged image credibility can result from circumstances beyond an organization's control, rather than from any specific actions or missteps by the company itself. Mattel fits this description to some degree because some of its recalls were caused by issues with overseas manufacturing partners. Although Mattel's executives should have ensured more stringent safety requirements and monitoring standards, there are really two credibility crises at play: the handling of the product recall by Mattel and the reputation crisis at Fisher-Price, which was responsible for regulating the overseas production of its toys.

Also victims of circumstances beyond their control, global energy companies faced a collective image credibility challenge in the wake of the Enron collapse. Many began having problems with bondholders, regulators, and investors following the scandal because they were presumed guilty of engaging in practices similar to those of the former energy giant. One possible strategy to combat this "guilt by association" would have been for a company to craft a communication program that would actively seek to distinguish it from Enron in a highly visible way.[10]

We can see that an organization's reputation is an important factor in setting a coherent communication strategy. For simple tasks, this is not a problem, but in other cases, the image credibility an organization has built with a specific constituency can make a huge difference in determining the success or failure the organization has in achieving its objectives. Companies increasingly are recognizing this fact and, accordingly, are dedicating resources to assessing their corporate reputation. One such company is FedEx. Once a year, the company's senior executives gather at its Memphis headquarters to assess the different risks the company faces. In addition to considering the possible financial impact and implications for the business continuity of each scenario, they examine what would happen to the company's reputation. "We believe that a strong reputation can act as a life preserver in a crisis and as a tailwind when the company is on the offensive," explained Bill Margaritis, FedEx's former vice president for global communications and investor relations. In addition to this hypothetical scenario analysis, FedEx conducts a survey to find out how the company is perceived by external stakeholders and performs a similar exercise with its employees annually.[11]

---

[10] Duncan Wood, "Not Cleaning Up Your Act Can Be Costly," *Treasury & Risk Management*, September 2004.

[11] Ibid.

The three considerations for creating an effective organization strategy—setting objectives, deciding on the proper allocation of resources, and diagnosing the organization's reputation—are the building blocks upon which all other steps in communication strategy depend. A second set of issues the organization can turn to is an assessment of the constituents involved.

Analyzing Constituencies

Analyzing constituencies is similar to analyzing your audience when you want to plan a speech or write a memo. This analysis determines (1) who your organization's constituencies are, (2) what each thinks about the organization, and (3) what each knows about the communication in question. We look at each of these in turn.

Who Are Your Organization's Constituencies?

Sometimes, the answer to this question is obvious, but most of the time, it will take careful consideration to analyze who the relevant constituencies are for a particular corporate message. Do not be fooled into thinking that it is always obvious who the main constituency is. Usually, constituencies come from a group that is primary to the organization, but a secondary group also can be the focus for a particular communication (see Table 2.1).

Companies have different sets of constituencies depending on the nature, size, and reach (i.e., global or domestic, local versus regional or national) of their businesses. Although a company may list its constituencies on a piece of paper, as in Table 2.1, it should resist thinking of them as too fixed or too separate. An organization's primary constituency or constituencies can change over time. In a time of crisis, for example, it may be wise for a company to focus more intently on its relations with the media—which it may normally consider a secondary constituency—to manage its reputation and attempt to minimize negative coverage. Additionally, constituencies should not be thought about in "silos," as the lines between them can blur. When employees are also shareholders in a company, for instance, they belong simultaneously to two constituency groups. For example, Starbucks formally blends employees and investors by offering all employees "bean stock" based on the number of hours they work, a practice that Starbucks began in 1991 and considers to be core to its mission.[12]

Companies should acknowledge and pay special attention to the role of their own employees as "brand ambassadors." From the consumer perspective, employees are viewed as highly credible representatives of a brand, and thus it is imperative that employees fully understand what the corporation aims to be in the mind of its customers and other constituencies to best serve as an ambassador.[13] Hilton has established itself as a leader in this area, ranking #1 in *Fortune* magazine's "100 Best Companies to Work For" list in both 2019 and 2020, becoming the first non-tech company to do so two years in a row. The company offers a wide range of benefits for its employees, from generous parental leave for mothers, fathers, and adoptive parents to a new employee stock purchase

---

[12] Starbucks press release: http://news.starbucks.com/2014annualmeeting/program-that-turned-employees-into-partners.

[13] "Special Report: Brand Trust in 2020," Edelman Trust Barometer, June 25, 2020, https://www.edelman.com/research/brand-trust-2020.

TABLE 2.1
Constituents of
Organizations

Primary	Secondary	Tertiary
• Employees	• Traditional media	• Primary and secondary
• Customers	• Suppliers	constituents' social
• Shareholders	• Creditors	media connections
• Communities	• Government	
	• Local	
	• Regional	
	• National	
	• Influencers	
	and activists	

program for all levels of employees to a travel program that offers its people highly discounted rates. CEO Chris Nassetta has noted that, "We try to care for our people in the right way so they will care for our customers. And as a result of doing good things for our people, we are doing very well." Similarly, software company Salesforce has also consistently ranked high on *Fortune's* list for over a decade. As a testament to the extent to which employees have enjoyed their tenure at Salesforce, and thus served as positive brand ambassadors, 52 percent of new hires come from employee referrals. Moreover, employees get $2,000 for every successful referral, with employees collecting a total of $7 million in 2019.[14]

However, constituencies can have competing interests and different perceptions of a company. For example, cutting employee benefits may be welcomed by shareholders but will likely be highly unpopular with employees. In addition, communications intended for one constituency often reach others.

The individual communication experience of one marketing vice president (VP) brings this last point to life. The executive VP to whom he reported had decided to cut the group's administrative support staff due to the increased use of technology to handle communications while professionals were away from their desks. This vice president detailed his plan for cutting the support staff by almost two-thirds in a memo to the vice president in charge of human resources. The plan involved laying off five assistants in the department over a period of six months. Many of them had been with the firm for several years.

As usual, the marketing VP drafted his thoughts in rough form and e-mailed it to his assistant, asking her to format the letter and place the final draft on his letterhead. Although his assistant was not one of the five affected by the layoffs, she couldn't help but empathize with her colleagues of many years, and within an hour, the marketing VP had a revolt on his hands. Now, with a constant news cycle that is aided and abetted by online communications, a scenario like this one could be prompted by information that gets into the hands of an influencer for example, as we see later in this chapter.

The aforementioned VP didn't intend for his assistant to be a part of his constituency, nor did he stop to think about her reaction to the change when he asked her to print the letter to the human resources VP. Nonetheless, she became a conduit to a more important constituency: the employees who would actually be affected by the plan.

This simple example is instructive to organizations seeking to communicate at a more macro level, as well. Just as we cannot always control the flow of information to one constituency alone on an individual level, on the corporate level, the same set of problems arises.

What Is the Constituency's Attitude toward the Organization?

In addition to analyzing who the constituencies for a particular communication really are, organizations also need to assess what each constituency thinks about the organization itself.

We know from personal experience that it is easier to communicate with people who know and like us than it is with those who do not. The same is true for organizations. If a company has built goodwill with the constituency in question, it will be much easier to reach its objective.

The classic example of good corporate communication is Johnson & Johnson's redemption of the Tylenol brand in 1982, when poisoned capsules killed seven people in Chicago (see Chapter 10 for more on the Tylenol crisis). That the company was able to succeed against all odds—when people like advertising executive Jerry Della Femina and several other experts in communication declared Tylenol impossible to save at the time—was a tribute to the hard work the organization had done before the tragedy actually happened. The company was known in the industry, by doctors, by consumers, and by the media as rock solid—willing to stand by its products and do the right thing, no matter what the cost. In this case, the cost ran into the hundreds of millions of dollars when the company decided to recall more than 31 million bottles of Tylenol capsules.

Convincing people to buy a product that had been laced with cyanide was not an easy proposition, but because the company had the trust of many different constituencies, it was able to achieve its objective, which was to revive the brand. If people hadn't trusted the company, or if they had questioned its behavior in any way, this revival would not have been possible.

When goodwill or trust is lacking, communication can be a struggle. And companies cannot expect to be trusted until they prove themselves trustworthy through concerted actions that demonstrate care, concern, and understanding for their constituencies. As stated in "Authentic Enterprise," mentioned in Chapter 1 as a document produced by the Arthur W. Page Society:

> In addition to the familiar intermediaries and constituencies with whom corporations have interacted in the past, there is now a diverse array of communities, interests, non-governmental organizations and individuals. Many of these new players represent important interests, while others are not legitimate stakeholders, but rather simply adversarial or malicious. Regardless of motive, all are far more able to collaborate among themselves around shared interests and to reach large audiences. At the same time, companies and institutions themselves are seeking similar kinds of engagement with multiple constituencies . . . Constituent relationships have always been important for businesses and institutions, but the proliferation and empowerment of new kinds of stakeholders have profoundly altered the landscape. First, in a radically more transparent world, organizations can no longer be different things to different constituencies; an enterprise must be one thing across its entire ecosystem.
>
> Source: Reprinted with permission from the Arthur W. Page Society.

Building trust often must start from within the organization—by communicating up and down with employees, hearing them out on the topics that concern them, and making constructive changes based on their input. Companies with high levels of trust with employees are also those that take the time to clearly communicate the company's business goals to employees and help them understand the vital roles they play in achieving those goals.[15]

What Does the Constituency Know about the Topic?

In addition to the constituents' attitudes toward the company, we also must consider their attitudes toward the communication itself. If they are predisposed to do what the organization wants, then they are more likely to help the organization reach its objective. If they are not, however, the organization will have difficulty in trying to achieve its goals.

Consumers are often wary of new or unknown products. The Japanese confectioner mentioned earlier was a victim of such bias as it tried to convince Americans to buy a product that was well known and liked in Japan but completely foreign to Americans. In Japan, the company is seen as the highest-quality manufacturer of *wagashi*, or candy. The company, Toraya, is one of the oldest companies on earth. It can trace its roots back to the ninth century, and the same family has been in control of the firm for 17 generations. It has been serving the imperial family since its inception.

Given its long history and aristocratic roots, the president of the company assumed that the product would speak for itself in the U.S. market. Because no one else was around to compete with the firm, middle managers in charge of the U.S. operation assumed that its introduction of *wagashi* would be a huge success.

Unfortunately, they didn't think about how American palates would react to the taste of a candy made out of red beans and seaweed. Most of the people who heard about the product couldn't even pronounce its name, and when they tasted the gelatinous form of the product, known as *yokan*, they didn't like it.

To get consumers in the United States interested in the product, Toraya had to educate people about the role of *wagashi* in Japanese history and its exclusivity, as demonstrated by its aristocratic roots. Those who tasted the product in focus groups early in the process of its introduction to the United States likened the experience to the first time they had tasted caviar or espresso.

Though Toraya retreated from its initial foray into the U.S. market, closing its New York store in 2003, the company is now cautiously, but optimistically, looking to make a re-entry into the market, this time seizing upon American consumers' increasing interest in vegan-friendly desserts and the naturally vegan-friendly composition of their product. This second go-round has garnered attention from the likes of Bill Yosses, the former Obama White House Executive Pastry Chef, and Vogue, but only time will tell if the company will be able to address consumer sentiment more effectively.[16]

Japanese candy isn't the only example of misjudged consumer feelings. Take Walmart, for example. The retail behemoth tried to break into the German market for nine years before retreating with its proverbial tail between its legs in 2006. Walmart had 85 stores

[15] Shari Caudron, "Rebuilding Employee Trust," *Workforce Management*, October 2002, pp. 28–34.

[16] Zoe Ruffner, "This Vegan Japanese Dessert Is the Feel-Good Treat to Turn to This Holiday Season," *Vogue*, November 8, 2019.

in the country but eventually lost the battle to local rivals such as Aldi and Lidl because it failed to adapt to the German consumer and business culture. Among the many missteps: German Walmarts imported the U.S. practices of bagging groceries for customers at check-out counters and requiring employees to smile and greet every customer. The service-with-a-smile approach was seen as distasteful and unnecessary by shoppers. Executives also imparted the company's American policy of forbidding romances between employees. This restriction was seen as inappropriately intrusive by German standards. In misjudging its target consumer and subsequently abandoning its German business, Walmart took a $1 billion hit. Ironically, Lidl made the same mistakes with its own attempt at a U.S. expansion. Lidl kicked off its American expansion in 2017 but ultimately had to pull back on its efforts after failing to account for American shopping preferences, with CEO Klaus Gehrig describing the company's foray as a "catastrophe."[17]

Companies that try to sell an idea to the public are always in danger of failing as a result of the lack of information or the negative feelings consumers may have about it. The U.S. automaker General Motors (GM) realized, after several failed attempts to penetrate the U.K. market with Cadillacs, that rather than spending money on a U.K. advertising campaign, it was better served to hire an automotive public relations specialist to help the company educate people about Cadillac's new approach to the market, including an increased range of right-hand-drive models.[18]

When companies are communicating to their employees about something like a change in benefits—from a defined benefit pension plan to a cash balance plan, for instance—understanding what employees know about the topic, as well as how they feel about it, is critical. Without this insight, valuable time and resources can be spent on a communications campaign that ends up completely missing the mark. For example, a company may assume that employees' greatest concern is the competitiveness of their new benefit plan relative to other companies, when, in fact, they are most concerned about understanding how the new plan differs from the existing one. Absent this knowledge, the company's communication strategy may focus too heavily on the benchmarking issue and fail to address the issue of most concern to this constituency.[19]

Clearly, then, after a firm has set objectives for its corporate communication, it must thoroughly analyze all the constituencies involved. This requirement means understanding who each constituency is, finding out what each thinks about the organization, and determining what each already knows and feels about the communication in question. Companies should consider allocating a portion of their marketing budget to this kind of research. Armed with this intelligence, the organization is ready to move to the final phase in setting a communication strategy: determining how to deliver the message.

Delivering Messages Effectively

Delivering messages effectively involves a three-step analysis for companies. A company must first identify its (primary) target constituency, then select a communication channel, and third, choose what approach to take in structuring the message itself.

[17] Bryan Pearson, "German Lessons: What Walmart Could Have Learned from Lidl, and Vice Versa," *Forbes*, February 5, 2018.
[18] Richard Cann, "Cadillac Media Push Aims to Crack the UK," *PRWeek*, July 9, 2004.
[19] "Communicating Cash Balance Plans," *Watson Wyatt Insider*, April 2000, http://www.watsonwyatt.com.

Identify the Target Constituency

Identifying the target constituency, or target audience, for a piece of communication is the first step a company must take in delivering a message effectively, but the identification of the appropriate target audience is not as straightforward as it once was. As described earlier in this chapter, companies have reason to interact with a wide range of constituencies. Importantly, individuals can be members of multiple constituencies, and constituencies can interact with each other far more easily and frequently as a consequence of today's digital world. Thus, a company must keep in mind not only its primary audience but the many ways in which such an audience can interact with other constituencies.

For example, if a company were to notify employees of a change to its benefit package, the company ought to be aware of the multiple constituencies to which employees can belong (such as the employee-shareholder), as well as the other constituencies that the employee might interact with (such as the media). Therefore, though a company should keep its primary target top of mind when crafting a piece of communication, companies ought also to always keep top of mind the interconnected nature of today's world and structure its messages accordingly.

Choose the Appropriate Communication Channel

Just as identifying a target constituency is no longer as straightforward as in days past, so too has the selection of the appropriate communication channel become more challenging. The number of communication channels available to a corporation has grown exponentially over the past few decades (Table 2.2); similarly, the speed with which information is exchanged, and thus leaps from one channel to another, has markedly increased. Thus, corporations must be mindful of choosing not only the most appropriate channel for communication from a far more robust menu of options but also remain cognizant of the ways in which one channel interacts with another.

TABLE 2.2
Communication
Channels

Old Channels	New Channels
Spoken word	E-mail
Letter	Facebook
Print media	Instagram
Printed documents	Twitter
Video	Slack
	LinkedIn
	YouTube
	Company external website
	Company intranet
	Television
	Podcast
	Text messaging
	Digital newsroom
	Videoconferencing

Companies must also bear in mind both the end-audience as well as the content of the message when selecting a communication channel. Letting employees know of a casual happy hour? Slack will likely do. Announcing layoffs? A more personalized channel like an in-person meeting is a far more appropriate first step.

The unicorn Bird offers an example of poor selection of a communication channel when delivering challenging news. In 2018, Bird, a Silicon Valley-backed startup that rents out electric scooters, became the fastest company in history to reach unicorn status and reached a valuation north of $2 billion less than a year later, expanding to 120 cities in 14 months.[20] Despite its bright start, however, Bird was not immune to the challenges presented in 2020 by COVID-19 and was faced with laying off a significant portion of its employees in the pandemic's early stages. While many companies were faced with the difficult decision of laying off employees in order to keep the lights on, Bird's communication channel and strategy hardly displayed the compassion necessary in such challenging times. Employees (amounting to about 30 percent of the company's workforce) were invited to a last-minute Zoom meeting titled only "COVID-19." Within two minutes, they were told they were being let go and the meeting ended. All video was turned off, the participant list remained hidden, and the deliverer of the news was kept anonymous, aspects that Bird had emphasized were intended to respect employee privacy but ultimately only added to the cold and impersonal nature of the call. Moreover, some employees found that their e-mail and Slack access were turned off during those two minutes. Shortly thereafter, a wide range of media sources, from online news sources to Twitter to YouTube, were reporting on Bird's mishandling of the layoffs.[21] Beyond the very obvious need for dealing with challenging situations with greater compassion, this example further illustrates the preeminent importance of selecting a more appropriate communication channel and remaining aware of the many means by which a communication can spread to a far greater range of channels very quickly.

On the other hand, TaskRabbit offers an important example of how to deal compassionately with challenging news through selecting an appropriate communication channel. Leah Solivan, the founder and former CEO of TaskRabbit, an online marketplace that lets people hire freelancers for odd jobs, was faced with the similarly challenging situation of needing to let go a significant portion of her workforce in 2014. As opposed to selecting an impersonal communication channel like a mass video conference, however, Leah elected to first craft a message to each affected employee and followed up immediately with an in-person meeting, in which generous severance packages were offered as well as support in finding new job opportunities. While it is worth noting that TaskRabbit was tasked with letting go 20 employees and not 400, as was the case with Bird, and that this was not occurring during the very challenging times of a global pandemic when in-person meetings were not an option, the key points of TaskRabbit's approach are worth replicating in other settings: choose more personal communication channels when delivering challenging news and offer means for individual follow-up conversations through additional channels.

---

[20] Will Yakowicz, "14 Months, 120 Cities, $2 Billion: There's Never Been a Company Like Bird. Is the World Ready?" *Inc. Magazine*, Winter 2018/2019.

[21] Bani Sapra, "Bird Employees Say They Were Locked Out of Their Email and Slack Accounts as They Were Told Their Jobs Were Gone," *Business Insider*, April 2, 2020.

Each time a corporate communication strategy is developed, the question of which channels to use and when to use them should be explored carefully. Finally, the company needs to think about the best way to structure the message and what to include in the message itself.

Structure Messages Carefully

According to most experts in communication, the two most effective message structures are commonly referred to as *direct* and *indirect*. Direct structure means revealing your main point first, and then explaining it in more detail; indirect structure means giving context first, and then revealing your main point.

When should a company choose to be direct and when should it decide to be indirect? Normally, organizations should be as direct as possible with as many constituencies as possible, because indirect communication is confusing and harder to understand.

Take the example of Nissan: when the car manufacturer first introduced the Infiniti series in the United States, the company took a more indirect (and typically Japanese) approach by showing impressions of landscapes and creating a mood without actually showing the car, instead of just coming out with photographs of the new cars (as it does now). This effort was a creative success compared with the approach its direct competitor, Toyota, took by showing traditional pictures of its comparable Lexus model. Unfortunately, Nissan's campaign didn't sell many cars. The company wanted to create a strong identity in the American market through this type of advertising, but this mixture of product and image advertising was completely lost on American consumers.

A third option in terms of message structure is to simply have *no* message. Today, this approach simply doesn't work with a public hungry for the next sound bite and the media looking for an "angle" on the story. Usually, saying that the company cannot talk about the situation until "all the facts are in" is better than just saying "no comment" or nothing at all, but managers (especially in the United States) are often influenced by lawyers who are thinking about the legal ramifications of saying anything. Deciding to be direct often means taking the court of public opinion into consideration as well, which, to some companies, is often far more important than a court of law.

Constituency Responses

After communicating with a constituency, you must assess the results of your communication and determine whether the communication had the desired result. In some instances, this feedback can be gathered nearly immediately after the delivery of an important message or set of messages. For example, employees can be provided a short questionnaire to confirm an understanding of the main points of the communication and uncover areas where they would have wanted more information or clarification. In other cases, it may take some time to measure the success of the communication, such as determining whether sales rose in response to an advertising campaign. After the results are in, you must determine how you will react. Has your reputation changed? Do you need to change your communication channel? Hence the circular nature of the corporate communication framework.

Creating a coherent corporate communication strategy, then, involves the three variables we have discussed in detail: defining the *organization's* overall strategy for the

FIGURE 2.2
**Expanded
Corporate
Communication
Strategy
Framework**

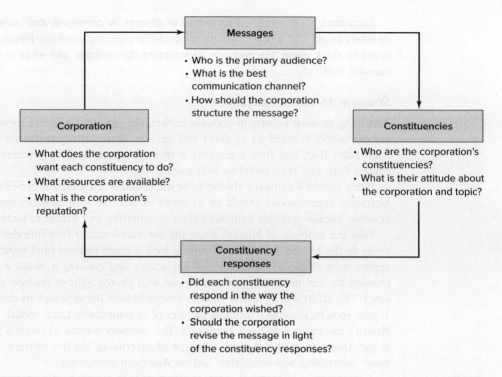

Messages
- Who is the primary audience?
- What is the best communication channel?
- How should the corporation structure the message?

Corporation
- What does the corporation want each constituency to do?
- What resources are available?
- What is the corporation's reputation?

Constituencies
- Who are the corporation's constituencies?
- What is their attitude about the corporation and topic?

Constituency responses
- Did each constituency respond in the way the corporation wished?
- Should the corporation revise the message in light of the constituency responses?

communication, identifying and analyzing the relevant *constituencies*, and delivering *messages* effectively. In addition, the organization needs to analyze constituency *responses* to determine whether the communication was successful. Figure 2.2 summarizes this more complete version of the corporate communication strategy model introduced earlier.

Conclusion

By creating a coherent communication strategy based on the time-tested theories presented in this chapter, an organization is well on its way to reinventing how it handles communications. Just as important for the firm, however, is its ability to link its overall strategy to its communication efforts.

As discussed in Chapter 1, firms are facing increased scrutiny from external groups (e.g., the NGO Environmental Working Group, which launched the Skin Deep Cosmetic Database to "create online safety profiles for cosmetics and personal care products") as well as their key constituencies (such as consumers, who are increasingly turning to companies to take stands on the social justice issues of our day as well as to carry out their core functions). By linking corporate strategy to corporate communication, managers can mitigate the potential loss in reputation (see Chapter 4) that can result from a weak or negative response from an organization to challenges from external groups and its own constituencies.

The extent to which an organization is affected by external forces is also determined by what industry the firm is in, where it does business, and how public its operations are. In addition to staying competitive, the question of how the firm is perceived externally must be considered. Just as the company's awareness about competitive forces protects it from competitors, its awareness of external forces also protects it from attacks.

Despite a recent challenge to its baby powder product in the consumer division, the pharmaceutical firm Johnson & Johnson has benefited from a largely undamaged reputation, simply because the company reinforced its commitment to the J&J Credo, the company's written values system, in its communications with its key stakeholders during moments of crisis (see Chapter 10).

When developing an overall strategy, firms need to consider their corporate communication effort as manifested in the company's vision and mission statement. By doing so at the inception of an overall strategy, the firm avoids repercussions later. Because all organizations operate at the behest of the public will, this egalitarian approach to communications will be appreciated by a society that has come to depend on its organizations more than ever before.

Case 2-1

Carson Molding Company

Carson Molding Company was a large, regional plastic injection-molding manufacturer, supplying medical-grade parts to the medical, pharmaceutical, and dental industries. Carson had 30 plants, located primarily in the Eastern part of the United States. Their procurement procedures were not coordinated. Carson's corporate headquarters had even encouraged plant managers to act as separate entities. In addition, each plant bought many items from local suppliers. Carson's decentralized approach to procurement was indicative of its overall strategy toward dealing with its constituencies including employees, customers, shareholders, and communities.

The need for high-quality, custom-made medical parts took off in the early 2010s, and thus demand for Carson's parts heated up. As it became clear that this trend would continue through the coming years, Carson faced increasing competitive pressures to drive prices down, and company management recognized that dealing with such a fragmented supplier base was hindering "efficiency" at the company. Aileen Wuornos, the company's president, hired an experienced materials manager, Richard Haskell, in January of 2019 as Vice President of Corporate Procurement, a new position in the company. Wuornos gave Haskell lots of flexibility in organizing his work, and placed Rachael Friberg as Haskell's executive assistant. Friberg had worked for 15 years at Carson in several different positions, and thus knew many plant employees. Haskell's appointment was announced on the company's Slack Channel and in a memo to plant managers.

Haskell wanted to centralize the company's procurement procedures and reduce the number of suppliers overall. To begin the process he asked each of the executives who handled materials management in the various plants to clear with headquarters all contracts over $100,000. Haskell thought that if headquarters was going to coordinate in a way that would help each plant and Carson overall, he had to know about bigger contracts being negotiated at

least a week before they were going to be signed. He discussed the idea with Aileen Wuornos, who discussed it with the board of directors, who approved the idea.

Carson's plants made purchases and negotiated deals with suppliers continuously, but the beginning of its busiest buying season was only two weeks away when the new plan was put into place. Haskell drafted a memo to send to the 30 materials managers:

Daer Materials Manager:

Carson's board of directors has approved a new procurement process. Henceforth, all materials managers in each plant will alert the Vice President of Corporate Procurement about contracts above $100,000 which they plan to negotiate at least a week before the day they will be signed.

I know you must understand that this change is critical to coordinate the procurement requirements at Carson and consolidate relationships with national suppliers when we are finding it more difficult to secure good deals at the local level. This step will provide us in the head office the information we need to see that each plant procures the optimal supply of materials at the best prices. As a result the goals of each plant and for Carson as a whole will more likely be achieved.

Sincerely,
Richard Todd Haskell, II
Vice President of Corporate Procurement

Haskell gave Rachael Friberg the memo and asked for her input. She told him she thought the memo was great. She said, however, that, since he had met only three of the materials managers, he might like to meet all of them and discuss procurement with each of them individually. Haskell declined because he had so many things to do at home and in his office that he was unable to travel. He also felt it would cost too much to visit all the plants, and he was keenly aware of the need to limit spending.

Over the next few days, responses came in from all but a few plants. Some managers wrote longer responses, but the following e-mail message was typical:

Dear Dick:

Welcome to Carson! We wish you every success as the new procurement coordinator. We got your recent communication about notifying headquarters a week in advance of our intention to sign contracts with suppliers. This suggestion seems very practical. We would like to let you know that you can be sure of this plant's cooperation in your new job. ☺

Best regards,

Over the next several weeks headquarters heard nothing from the plants about contracts being negotiated with suppliers. Carson executives in other departments who visited the plants frequently reported that they were quite busy, and the usual procedures for that time of year continued.

CASE QUESTIONS

1. What problems does Carson Molding Company have that will affect its communications?
2. What specific problems does Mr. Haskell have as a result of his communication to materials managers?
3. What advice would you give Haskell to help solve his and Carson's problems?

Source: This case was written by Professor Paul A. Argenti of the Tuck School of Business at Dartmouth. This is a fictional case based on real events as well as ideas presented in both the "Dashman Company" case (9-462-001) published by HBS Case Services, Harvard Business School, Boston, 1947 and the "Marathon Plastics" case published by W. H. Newman, E. K. Warren, and J. E. Schnee's *The Process of Management*, 5th ed., Prentice Hall, Englewood Cliffs, 1982.

CHAPTER THREE

An Overview of the Corporate Communication Function

The past two chapters painted a broad picture of the business environment and provided a framework for communicating strategically. Against this backdrop, we now discuss the corporate communication function itself. More and more companies recognize the value of corporate communication and are adapting their budgets and internal structures accordingly. The global communications industry grew by 5 percent in 2018, as measured by growth in the top 250 Public Relations firms, for a total global industry size of $15.5 billion.[1] Additionally, the Global Communications Report, released by the Center for Public Relations at the University of California, projected industry growth would reach $19.3 billion by 2022, requiring a total increase in headcount in the industry of 26 percent.[2]

This chapter traces the evolution of corporate communication and the developments in recent years that have led to heightened recognition for the field. After examining corporate communication's roots, we discuss the most appropriate structure for the function within an organization, including reporting relationships. We also briefly showcase each corporate communication subfunction, all of which are developed in greater detail later in this book.

From "PR" to "CorpComm"

Public relations (PR), the predecessor to the corporate communication (CorpComm) function, grew out of necessity. Although corporations had no specific strategy for communications, they often had to respond to external constituencies whether they wanted to or not. As new laws forced companies to communicate in many situations they hadn't

[1] Arun Sudhaman, "2019 Agency Rankings: Global PR Industry Growth Holds Steady At 5%," PRovoke, April 29, 2019, https://www.provokemedia.com/long-reads/article/2019-agency-rankings-global-pr-industry-growth-holds-steady-at-5.

[2] "Global Communications Report," USC Annenberg, https://annenberg.usc.edu/sites/default/files/USC_REPORT_New.pdf.

previously confronted, the constant need for a response meant that dedicated resources were required to manage the flow of communications.

This function, which was tactical in most companies, was almost always called either *public relations* (PR) or *public affairs*. Typically, the effort was focused on preventing the press from getting too close to management. Like a Patriot missile, designed to stop incoming missiles during war, the first PR professionals were asked to protect the company from bad publicity, often by "spinning" damaging news in a positive light. Thus, the term "flak" came to be used to describe what PR people were actually doing: shielding top managers from "missiles" fired at them from the outside.

The "flak" era of public relations lasted for many decades, and when companies needed other communications activities, public relations personnel were the obvious choice to take them on. In the 1960s, for instance, it was fairly typical to find public relations officials handling speechwriting, annual reports, and the company newsletter. Given that the majority of work in this area involved handling print media (television wasn't truly a factor until the early 1970s), many companies hired former journalists to manage this job. The former-journalist-turned-flak brought the organization the first dedicated expert in the area of communication.

Until recently, the top managers in large companies came from backgrounds such as engineering, accounting, finance, production, or, at best (in terms of understanding the company's communication needs), sales or marketing. Their understanding of how to communicate depended on abilities they might have gained by chance or through under-graduate or secondary school training rather than years of experience. Given their more quantitative rather than verbal orientation, these old-style managers were delighted to have an expert communicator on board who could take the heat for them and offer guidance in times of trouble.

PR professionals often were seen as capable of turning bad situations into good ones, creating excellent relations with their former colleagues in journalism, and helping the chief executive officer become a superb communicator. In some cases, this reputation was true, but for the most part, the journalists were not the answer to all of the company's communications problems. When situations turned from bad to worse, they were the obvious ones to blame—easy scapegoats for irresponsible managers.

The First Spin Doctors

In addition to the internal PR staff, outside agencies often helped companies that either couldn't afford a full-time person or needed an extra pair of hands in a crisis. The legends of the public relations field—such as Ivy Lee and Edward Bernays and, later, Howard Rubenstein and Daniel Edelman—helped the public relations function develop from its journalistic roots into a more refined and respected profession.

For many years, PR agencies dominated the communications field, billing companies hefty fees for services they could not handle in-house. Few large companies were willing to operate without such a firm for fear that they might be missing an opportunity to solve their communications problems painlessly by using these outside "spin doctors."

Some of the top public relations firms today—such as Fleishman-Hillard and Edelman in the United States, Weber Shandwick in the United Kingdom, and BlueFocus in China—still provide some of the best advice available on a number of communications-related issues.[3] But outside agencies cannot handle all the day-to-day activities required for the smooth flow of communications from organization to constituents. Therefore, they often work alongside in-house communication professionals on strategic or project-based communications activities.

A New Function Emerges

By the 1970s, the business environment required more than the simple internal PR function supplemented by the outside consultant. The rise in importance and power of special-interest groups, such as Ralph Nader's Public Interest Research Group, and environmentally oriented nongovernmental organizations (NGOs), such as Greenpeace, forced companies to increase their communications activities. During the Arab oil boycott and embargo in the 1970s, the entire oil industry came under fire as consumers had to wait hours for a tank of gasoline while big oil companies reported what many consumer groups felt were "obscene" profits running into the hundreds of millions of dollars.

This situation led Mobil Oil to develop one of the most sophisticated public relations departments of its time. Mobil's Herb Schmertz revolutionized the field by solving communications problems with strategies that no one had thought of before. His series of advertisements, called "issue ads" (see Chapter 4 for more on this subject), which ran on *The New York Times* and *The Wall Street Journal* op-ed pages once or twice a week, directly attacked the allegations of both "obscene" profits and hoarding of oil to inflate prices. Instead of merely reacting to these allegations, the Mobil issue ads put the blame on the government, explained why the oil companies needed hefty profits for exploration, and refocused discussion on other issues the company's chief executive officer (CEO) thought were important to shareholders.

With a budget in the tens of millions of dollars, Schmertz created a new communications function that changed the nature of Mobil's communications effort from old-style public relations to the first significant corporate communication department. A senior vice president of the corporation, Schmertz was also one of the very few communications executives with a seat on the board of directors—further proof of Mobil's commitment to enhanced communications.

Thus, as individual corporations and entire industries were increasingly scrutinized and had to answer to a much more sophisticated set of journalists, the old-style public relations function was no longer capable of handling the flak. As a result, what at first had been deemed a waste of resources at Mobil in the early 1970s became the norm in corporate America. The focus now shifted to structuring these new corporate communication departments effectively to fit the function into the existing corporate infrastructure.

Corporate Communications Today

In more recent years, the corporate communication function has continued to evolve to meet the demands of the ever-changing business and regulatory environments. At the outset of the millennium, a string of financial scandals at corporations including WorldCom and Enron resulted in the Sarbanes-Oxley Act of 2002, which although only legally affecting public

---

[3] "Global Top 250 PR Agency Ranking 2020," PRovoke, https://www.provokemedia.com/ranking-and-data/global-pr-agency-rankings/2020-pr-agency-rankings/top-250.

companies, increased the public's expectations for transparency, responsiveness, and corporate responsibility for all companies large and small. The need to maintain this level of transparency has elevated the corporate communication function within companies to a new strategic level. Messages, activities, and products—from investor conferences and annual reports to philanthropic activities and corporate advertising—are now analyzed by regulators, investors, and the public at large with unprecedented scrutiny. And the proliferation of online communication vehicles, from Twitter to Instagram to traditional websites, has accelerated the flow of information and the public's access to it to record speeds. (Chapter 6 covers media relations in more detail and Chapter 8 discusses investor relations at length.)

In its report "The New CCO," the Arthur W. Page Society, an association of chief communications officers of large corporations, notes that, "The CCO of today is at an inflection point. The environment in which enterprises operate is fraught with emergent challenges: new competitors reinventing traditional business models; changing demographic, regulatory, and sociopolitical conditions; new modes of work; and an ongoing paradigm shift in how individuals communicate with one another and engage more actively with organizations." Thus, the Page Society suggests that the contemporary CCO must be able to operate effectively across three dimensions: (1) as a "foundational CCO" who advises with all of a company's constituencies in mind; (2) as an "integrator" who encourages cross-functional collaboration; and (3) as a "builder of digital engagement systems," in which they lead the charge in integrating higher levels of data use into their day-to-day decision-making.[4]

Under today's higher-resolution microscope, constituents' perceptions of how companies are addressing issues of social impact and how responsive they are to issues that matter most to them are of increasing importance as well. In fact, 85 percent of consumers feel that responsiveness to issues of social import rank higher in judging company reputation than what the media says (76 percent) and what employees say (68 percent). Clearly, proactive reputation management matters more now than ever.[5]

Specific Responsibilities of Corporate Communications

While organizations may have unique combinations of needs at any given time, the Corporate Executive Board identified in its Resource Allocation Benchmarks report almost 20 distinct responsibilities that a modern communications team is likely to have.

Responsibilities categorized as *external communication activities* include:

- Press and Media Relations
- Investor Relations
- Financial Relations
- Corporate Website
- Corporate Advertising
- Marketing Communications
- Executive Communications

[4] "The New CCO: Transforming Enterprises in a Changing World," Arthur W. Page Society, https://knowledge.page.org/report/the-new-cco-transforming-enterprises-in-a-changing-world.

[5] "The Company Behind the Brand II: In Goodness We Trust," Weber Shandwick, February 15, 2017, https://www.webershandwick.com/news/the-company-behind-the-brand-ii-in-goodness-we-trust.

- Community Relations
- Government Relations

Responsibilities categorized as *internal communication activities* include:

- Employee Communications
- Corporate Intranet
- Leader/Manager Communications Training

Responsibilities categorized as *other communication activities* include:

- Social Media
- Graphics or Creative Services
- Measurement and Monitoring
- Corporate Social Responsibility
- Charitable Activity
- Corporate Sponsorship
- Communications Staff Development
- Operational Costs
- Other Miscellaneous Costs[6]

However, this list misses a key functional area that Chief Communications Officers are responsible for overseeing today: reputation management. In fact, per the Korn Ferry Institute survey of Fortune 500 CCOs, the vast majority of respondents (91 percent) identified "providing leadership on reputation, values and culture across the enterprise" as requiring "more attention and effort today" than ever before. Clearly, the CCO wears many hats these days.[7]

To Centralize or Decentralize Communications?

One of the earliest problems organizations confronted in structuring their communication efforts was whether to keep all communications focused by *centralizing* the activity under one senior officer at headquarters or *decentralizing* the activities and allowing individual business units to handle communications. The more centralized model provided an easier way for companies to achieve consistency in and control over all communication activities. The decentralized model, however, gave individual business units more flexibility in adapting the function to their own needs.

The same structural challenges persist today, and the answer to the centralization/ decentralization debate often depends on a company's size, the geographic dispersion of its offices, and the diversity of its products and services. For organizations as large and diversified as General Electric, for example, the question is moot: there is no way such a sprawling organization involved in activities as diverse as aerospace and health care could remain completely centralized in all of its communication activities.

[6] CEB Resource Allocation Benchmarks Study, 2013.

[7] Korn Ferry F500 "The Influencer" Survey, 2015.

The same is true for Johnson & Johnson (J&J): With more than 132,000 employees in 260 operating companies in 60 different countries, complete centralization of communications would be difficult, if not impossible.[8,9] Instead, Bill Nielsen, the legendary former corporate vice president of corporate communication at J&J, described the function as "a partnership of professionals in communication."[10] J&J even avoids centralizing its external communications counsel with a single public relations firm. Instead, the company uses both small firms on a project basis and large, global agencies with resources around the world, amounting to a total of more than 20 different agencies worldwide to support various elements of its business.

Global events and economic trends also affect decisions about the structure of an organization's communication function. Not only did the shock of the September 11, 2001, attacks teach companies the importance of expecting the unexpected in terms of crises, but it also gave decentralized communication structures a new appeal for many companies. As Jim Wiggins, first vice president of corporate communication for Merrill Lynch (now part of Bank of America), explained at the time, "Companies will have to look at less centralization of key activities if we now live in a world where terrorism is a key possibility."[11]

Increased security threats are not the only catalyst for the decentralization of communications; economic downturns can have a similar effect. Consider a major international airline that imposed significant staff reductions on its corporate communication department due to across-the-board cost cuts. As a result, the director of communications explained that the department became more selective about what they committed to, saying: "We don't do everything for everybody anymore." Instead, other departments throughout the company established communication positions, doing some of the activities formerly handled by the centralized corporate communication department.[12]

In instances of scaled-back budgets, delegating tasks is doubly important because economic uncertainty can also force the communications department to handle activities it would generally outsource to a full-time PR agency. This appears to be happening particularly at government agencies and at NGOs, who anticipate decreased staffing resources within communications, and who increasingly turn to social media as a cost-effective means of mobilizing support and raising funds.

Although decentralization allows for more flexibility in tough economic times, these advantages are not without accompanying risks. Dispersing corporate communications across individual operating units without some central oversight significantly raises the potential for inconsistent messages. In decentralized structures, a company's communication professionals must be diligent about assuring quality, consistency, and integration of messages across the board. In addition, organizations in which communications is not integrated may struggle with internal success factors, such as recommendations being

[8] "Johnson & Johnson Annual Report," U.S. Securities and Exchange Commission, 2019, https://www.annualreports.com/HostedData/AnnualReports/PDF/NYSE_JNJ_2019.pdf.

[9] "Subsidiaries," Johnson & Johnson, https://johnsonandjohnson.gcs-web.com/static-files/f61ae5f3-ff03-46c1-bfc9-174947884db2.

[10] Interview with Bill Nielsen, February 2002.

[11] Shane McLaughlin, "Sept. 11: Four Views of Crisis Management," *Public Relations Strategist*, January 1, 2002, pp. 22–28.

[12] Jack LeMenager, "When Corporate Communication Budgets Are Cut," *Communication World 3* (February 3, 1999), p. 32.

taken seriously.[13] Companies often require formal mechanisms to ensure that this integration takes place.

To this end, the adoption of more agile corporate structures can help businesses walk the fine line between the need to quickly respond to a fast-paced world while maintaining the appropriate levels of structure and process. As noted in McKinsey's "Guide to Agile" 2017 report, "Agile development has largely become synonymous with digitization: senior business leaders have realized that their companies cannot take full advantage of digital tools and technologies without having new, amped up processes for managing them. The value of these processes is immense."[14] The immense challenges presented by the 2020 COVID-19 pandemic underscored the deep-seated benefits of an agile model, particularly as it pertains to the communications function. *PRWeek*'s 2020 Communications Bellwether Survey was conducted at the early stages of the pandemic, as businesses and individuals alike sought ways to adjust to a rapidly changing new normal. Respondents from high-agility organizations and communications functions reported they are doing better across every organizational measure, including preparedness for disruption, effective change management, advances in diversity, application of technology to PR, and commitment to purpose and value creation.[15] While it remains to be seen if this perception of high performance will translate into long-term, concrete gains, it is hard to ignore these early signs that agile businesses, and especially agile communications departments, are better suited for the digital world in which we now live.

The Bellwether study also noted further convergence between communications and marketing departments, with 56 percent of client-side respondents stating that these functions were either somewhat or fully integrated. Notably, respondents who rated their organizations as more highly agile also reported greater integration between communications and marketing.[16] At Xerox, Anne Marie Squeo, Chief Communications and Brand Officer, pushed for heavier integration between these functions when she first joined the company in 2019. "It eliminated a lot of tension that often exists between marketing and comms teams. I am now convinced this is the right model, no matter what kind of company it is," Squeo said. "We have a unified sense of purpose and can act more quickly."[17]

Where Should the Function Report?

Surveys conducted over the last decade have consistently shown that a high percentage of the average CEO's time is spent communicating. Indeed, a 2018 study in the *Harvard Business Review* found that the vast majority of a CEO's time is spent communicating, with 61 percent of their time focused on face-to-face interactions and another 24 percent

---

[13] "Eighth Annual Public Relations Generally Accepted Practices Study," Strategic Public Relations Center, University of Southern California, June 12, 2014, http://ascjweb.org/gapstudy/wp-content/uploads/2014/06/GAP-VIII-Presentation-Final-6.12.2014.pdf.

[14] Santiago Comella-Dorda, Krish Krishnakanthan, Jeff Maurone, and Gayatri Shenai, "A Business Leader's Guide to Agile," *McKinsey Digital*, July 25, 2017, https://www.mckinsey.com/business-functions/mckinsey-digital/our-insights/a-business-leaders-guide-to-agile.

[15] Chris Daniels, "Bellweather Survey 2020," *PRWeek*, September 10, 2020, https://www.prweek.com/article/1693824/bellwether-survey-2020-amid-era-constant-evolution-agility-will-win.

[16] Ibid.

[17] Ibid.

FIGURE 3.1 Ideal Structure for CorpComm Function for Larger Companies

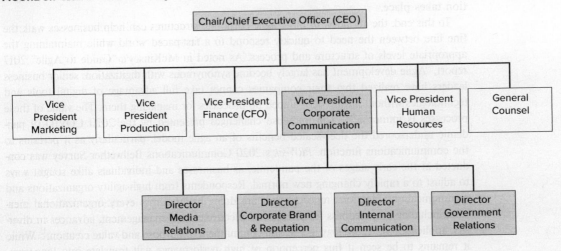

spent on electronic communications.[18] Former Johnson & Johnson CEO James Burke estimated that he spent more than 40 percent of his time as CEO communicating the J&J Credo alone (see Chapter 10 for more on the Credo).[19]

In many respects, CEOs themselves are an embodiment of the corporate brand. As such, their behavior and commentary can easily and markedly affect a company's financial performance. Recall Martha Stewart, founder and CEO of Martha Stewart Living Omnimedia, sentenced to five months in prison in 2004 after being found guilty on four counts of obstructing justice and lying to investigators regarding a stock sale. Expectations of a not-guilty verdict caused the company's stock price to rally prior to the announcement, only to nose-dive 22 percent on the New York Stock Exchange following the guilty verdict.[20]

All of this evidence implies that the CEO should be the person most involved with both developing the overall strategy for communications and delivering consistent messages to constituencies. Ideally, the corporate communication function will have a direct line to the CEO (see Figure 3.1). Even if reporting lines do not, on paper, go directly to the CEO, it is vital that the head of corporate communication have access to the highest levels of senior management and that those executives believe in the value and necessity of corporate communication as a means to achieve corporate goals. Without this connection, the communications function will be less effective and far less powerful.

While direct reporting to the CEO is the ideal structure, not all companies have yet shifted to this approach or are able to accommodate it. To date, only 51 percent

[18] Michael E. Porter and Nitin Nohria, "How CEOs Manage Time," *Harvard Business Review*, July–August 2018, https://hbr.org/2018/07/the-leaders-calendar?#how-ceos-manage-time.

[19] James C. Collins and Jerry I. Porras, *Built to Last* (New York: Harper Business, 1994, 1997), p. 80.

[20] Jim Robinson, "Leader of the Brand—Keeping the Best CEOs in Step," *Management*, June 1, 2005, p. 26.

of CCOs report directly to the CEO, according to the USC Annenberg 2018 Global Communications Report.[21]

To keep the number of direct reports to the CEO down to a handful of senior executives (often the biggest stumbling block to getting the corporate communication function "plugged in" at the top), some companies are now integrating the corporate communication function into the strategic planning function. Given the importance of tying communications to the overall strategy of the firm, this approach may benefit the growing corporate communication function.

In some cases, however, the function still reports to the catch-all executive vice president (EVP) in charge of administration. This person also has responsibility for areas such as HR, security, and buildings and grounds. This structure can present tremendous problems for the communication function—especially if the EVP has little knowledge of or lacks an interest in communications.

In this classic example, when Union Carbide Corporation was dealing with the aftermath of its Bhopal plant accident in India in 1984, the company transferred its communication responsibilities to the vice president of strategic planning. In a letter to executives, the chairman and CEO of the company at the time, Robert Kennedy, said:

> The Corporation's strategic direction is a key element of our communication to shareholders, employees and the public at large. . . . It is therefore more important than ever to be open and consistent in our communications to all of these groups, to keep them informed of our progress as we implement strategy, and to make sure that we address the special concerns and interests of all the groups and constituencies with a stake in Union Carbide's future. . . . To ensure the closest possible alignment of our communications with management directed at strategic planning developments, the management of those functions is being consolidated under . . . [the] Vice President of Strategic Planning and Public Affairs.[22]

Dan Bartlett, U.S. president and CEO of Hill & Knowlton, observed that the increased recognition of communications and public relations by senior management over the last decade has meant that "CEOS are demanding more strategic communications. . . . This calls for a lot more coordination internally."[23] The global financial crisis and the slew of recent corporate scandals have made CEOs more aware of the frailty of their companies' reputations, which has ushered corporate communications' ascendancy: 89 percent of corporate communicators found that they are under pressure to act as the guardian of their company's reputation; more than half say their C-suite has paid more attention to corporate reputation issues in the last year.[24]

Often such studies focus on larger corporations, but many of the lessons that we learn from large companies can be translated and applied to smaller companies. Small and mid-size businesses may not have the luxury of an experienced communications team, but these companies still have important communications needs just as larger companies do. All companies need to communicate with a consistent voice to all of their constituencies.

[21] "The Relevance Report 2019," USC Annenberg, http://assets.uscannenberg.org/docs/relevance-report-2019.pdf.

[22] Letter from Union Carbide's CEO, Robert B. Kennedy, to Executive List, dated March 5, 1992.

[23] Hill & Knowlton/*PR Week* Corporate Survey, 2011.

[24] Ibid.

TABLE 3.1

Why Companies Choose to Work with External PR and Communications Agencies: Top Reasons, Two Tiers

Source: Eighth "Public Relations Generally Accepted Practices Study," Strategic Public Relations Center, University of Southern California, June 2014.

Creative thinking	5.56
Additional arms and legs	5.55
Objective, independent council	5.44
Strategic insight	5.41
Expertise, media relations	4.72
Expertise, digital and social media	4.55
Limit on internal head count	4.25
Expertise, crisis management	4.24
Expertise, specific product markets	4.23
Expertise, specific geographic markets	4.22
Cheaper than adding staff	4.20
Increased geographic reach	4.08
Expertise, measurement and evaluation	3.93
Expertise, research and analysis	3.82
Expertise, socially diverse audiences	3.40

Working Strategically with External PR and Communication Agencies

No matter how they structure their marketing and PR functions, all companies may benefit from the strategic use of external PR and communication agencies. For the best results, external agencies need to be actively managed and provided with clear expectations for deliverables. In some cases, companies and organizations engage external PR and communication agencies due to a lack of internal manpower or expertise. This is particularly common in smaller organizations where the external agency may report to an internal employee who has responsibilities in several functions. Table 3.1 highlights the main reasons that companies choose to work with external PR and communications agencies.

No matter how it staffs and organizes the communications function, when senior management shows commitment to communications by allocating significant resources, all employees will begin to rightfully appreciate communications as a critical management tool. Now let's take a look at what that function should include.

The Subfunctions within the Function

According to recent surveys, more than half of the heads of corporate communication departments oversee communications functions that include corporate communications/reputation, crisis management, executive communications, employee/internal communication, and marketing PR/product. Moreover, CCOs are increasingly being called upon to devote a greater amount of time to significant global issues, including cybersecurity, shifting consumer habits, and financial crises, with four in ten CCOs from the 2016 Rising CCO Report stating they spend at least a lot of their time on these topics.[25]

The best approach to building a corporate communication function is to begin with the most global and strategic issues and then move into the narrower aspects of the

[25] "The Rising CCO VI," Weber Shandwick, October 5, 2016, https://www.webershandwick.com/news/the-rising-cco-vi.

function. We begin this section with a discussion of identity, image, and reputation, and then move on to the various subfunctions of corporate communication.

Identity, Image, and Reputation

Difficult to classify as a separate subfunction, an organization's identity, image, and reputation strategy is the most critical part of any corporate communication function. (In the next chapter, we explore these constructs in greater detail.) What is the difference between image, identity, and reputation, and how do they shape the operations of a corporate communication department?

Image is the corporation as seen through the eyes of its constituencies. An organization can have different images with different constituencies. For example, cigarette companies might be reprehensible to many American consumers looking for a healthier lifestyle but a delight to shareholders reaping the profits from international sales of the same product. On the other hand, customers might have been perfectly happy with what Macy's had to offer in its many stores throughout the United States, but securities analysts were reluctant to recommend the parent company's stock, knowing that inevitably it would enter bankruptcy.

Determining the organization's image with different constituencies is usually less obvious than in these examples—particularly given the increasingly blurred lines separating one constituency from another, as discussed in Chapter 2. For example, many employees today are encouraged to own stock in their own company and can be the most visible ambassadors of their company's brand by also being consumers of its products or services. The corporate communication department should conduct research to understand and monitor each constituency's evolving needs and attitudes. With the accessibility of social media metrics, this is an easy and necessary measurement task. Obviously, the organization cannot please everyone, but by monitoring what constituencies are thinking about, it can make a conscious effort to avoid hostility with a particular group. Similar monitoring and measurement systems can also help to gauge the impact and success of the company's communication activities.

Unlike its image, however, the organization's *identity* should not vary from one constituency to another. Identity consists of a company's defining attributes, such as its vision and values, its people, products, and services. An organization has an identity whether it wants one or not, based in part on the reality it presents to the world. People all over the world know Coca-Cola's red can and white script lettering and McDonald's golden arches in front of a store, whether they are in Singapore, or California.

Because identity building and maintenance require a variety of skills, including developing strategy and the ability to conduct research, to design effective social media platforms, and to enforce identity standards and cohesion, it should be spread around several different functions in the absence of a single, centralized corporate communication function. For example, the research needed to determine a firm's image with various constituencies might be a minor by-product of the overall marketing research effort currently under way at a company, to determine customer attitudes toward particular products and services rather than the firm as a whole.

Determining how a firm wants to be perceived with different constituencies and how it chooses to identify itself is the cornerstone function of corporate communication. If the firm is making serious changes in its identity, this subfunction can easily be a full-time job for a team of corporate communicators for a period of time.

At nearly all companies, outside agencies specializing in identity and image, such as Lippincott, Siegel+Gale, or Landor, would definitely be involved in the makeover as well, if the company alters significant components of its identity. These changes can range from the merely cosmetic—to keep the "look" of the company up to date—to the more momentous—such as a name change or a new logo.

Whereas identity represents the reality of an organization and image its reflection by key constituents, *reputation* is the sum of how all constituents view the organization. As a result, the idea that an organization can manage its reputation is unrealistic. Instead, corporations should focus on developing and implementing strategies in an integrated fashion across constituencies.

Corporate Branding

A company's reputation also can be enhanced or altered through *corporate advertising*. This subfunction of corporate communication is different from its product advertising or marketing communication function in two ways. (See Chapter 4 for more on corporate advertising.)

First, unlike product advertising, corporate advertising does not necessarily try to sell a company's particular product or service. Instead, it tries to sell the company itself—often to a completely different constituency from customers. For example, in 2017, Adobe launched a corporate advertising campaign focused on showing Adobe as a whole functioning as a partner for creatives, whether they were working individual photography projects or full creative campaigns. As opposed to focusing on a single Adobe offering or piece of software, the series of ads highlighted the Adobe ethos as one in line with that of the creative individuals they look to serve, a marked departure from focusing on a single product.[26]

Adding a new layer to traditional television and print campaigns, corporations must also turn to social media to create viral marketing campaigns that can influence consumers' opinions. Whether online or off, employees are important word-of-mouth advertising vehicles for a company's advocacy efforts. GE kept this in mind in its "Ecomagination" launch, conducting a simultaneous internal communications program in 2007 that featured a children's magazine conveying Ecomagination's core messages to employees' children and local communities.[27]

When the upscale discount retailer Target began running an extensive corporate advertising campaign back in the late 1990s featuring products ranging from satin lingerie to earplugs, accompanied only by the product name and Target's bull's-eye logo, the goal was not to sell more of these products but rather to showcase the company's diverse merchandise and potential to be the discount retailer that "looks like Barneys, priced like Kmart."[28] In much the same way, the aerospace and defense firms that advertised extensively in publications such as *The New Republic* in the 1980s were not trying to sell F-15s to liberals but rather to influence public opinion and facilitate approval for increases or allocations in the defense budget.

[26] "20 Top Corporate Advertising Campaign Examples Using Videos," Advids, December 18, 2017, https://blog.advids.co/20-top-corporate-advertising-campaign-examples-using-videos.

[27] Matthew Creamer, "GE Sets Aside Big Bucks to Show off Some Green," *Advertising Age 76*, no. 19 (May 9, 2005), p. 7.

[28] Shelly Branch, "How Target Got Hot," *Fortune*, May 24, 1999, p. 169.

Even though product advertising is the purview of the marketing department in many large companies, corporate advertising is usually run from the CEO's office or through corporate communication departments instead. During the 1980s and 1990s, this area was the fastest-growing segment of the advertising industry, as senior officers tried to present a coherent company identity for opinion leaders in the financial community.

An important subset of corporate advertising is *issue advertising*, in which corporations speak on broader topics that affect both their business dealings and society at large. For example, during the global coronavirus pandemic in 2020, nine pharmaceutical companies issued a rare joint pledge that they would "stand with science" and not seek approval for any COVID-19 vaccine that did not meet the highest standards of safety and efficacy.[29] The companies, which included Pfizer, Moderna, and AstraZeneca, took out large ads in publications from *The New York Times* to *The Wall Street Journal* to make their stance on vaccine safety publicly known in an attempt to assuage fears that the rapidly developed coronavirus vaccines would be rushed in a way that compromised safety. The rare issuance of a joint statement and ad by these otherwise rival firms underscored the importance, and therefore weight, of issue advertising when used appropriately.

While traditionally this type of advertising as referred to advertising meant to influence key constituencies about issues that affect a company, that approach has also broadened in more recent years to businesses taking stands on social justice issues of the day, whether they are obviously connected to a business's core strategy or not. These "movement-oriented marketing campaigns," as described by Brayden King, Professor of Management & Organizations at the Kellogg School of Management, notes that authenticity and commitment are two key ingredients to the successful execution of such campaigns. He notes, "The companies that do this best have a founder story that their current messaging has evolved from. Instead of trying to reinvent themselves through a campaign, they look back to their history, find the fine-line leading the present day, and project those values into the future."[30]

As we will see in Chapter 4, however, issue advertising is risky. By taking a stand on a particular issue, the company is automatically creating a negative image with one or several constituencies. Many companies take this risk nonetheless, facing the consequences of adding their opinions to debates that they consider important.

Corporate Responsibility

Many companies have a separate subfunction in the human resources area to deal with community relations and a foundation close to the chairman that deals with philanthropy, but the two should be tied closely together as companies take on more responsibilities in communities in which they operate.

Taking on these social responsibilities has a number of positive outcomes for corporate leaders. (See Chapter 5 for more on corporate responsibility.) According to the Edelman Trust Barometer, people are increasingly turning to CEOs to act as change agents, with 76 percent of respondents to the 2019 Expectations for CEOs Survey

---

[29] Katie Thomas, "9 Drug Companies Pledge to 'Stand With Science' on Coronavirus Vaccines," *The New York Times*, September 8, 2020, https://www.nytimes.com/2020/09/08/health/9-drug-companies-pledge-coronavirus-vaccine.html.

[30] Laura Montgomery, "When Activism and Advertising Collide," *The Economist*, https://execed.economist.com/blog/industry-trends/when-activism-and-advertising-collide.

reporting that they look to CEOs to take the lead on change rather than waiting for government intervention.[31]

There are also serious internal implications of a strong corporate citizenship record. A growing body of literature indicates that people, particularly in the Millennial generation, are looking to imbue their professional lives with a greater sense of purpose, and consequently, are willing to turn to lower-paying jobs in order to achieve this. A study from the University of Toronto found that participants reported salaries that were 32 percent lower for personally meaningful jobs compared to jobs they considered personally meaningless.[32] This study, among others, has many implications for today's corporations and the sense of purpose with which they imbue their workplace; clearly a commitment to prioritizing corporate social responsibility offers an advantage in terms of attracting and retaining talent.

Corporate philanthropy has also become increasingly important as companies are expected to do more than just give back to the community. Firms now feel a greater obligation to donate funds to organizations that could benefit the firm's employees, customers, or shareholders. Examples include donations to universities that might be conducting research in the industry and organizations representing minority interests.

And with increased globalization and international corporate expansion, constituents' expectations for corporate citizenship also have grown more global in scope. In December 2004, the devastating tsunami that struck 11 countries in Southeast Asia, killing 180,000 people, demonstrated this broadened focus; the U.S. Chamber of Commerce's Center for Corporate Citizenship reported that more than 400 U.S. companies donated $528 million to the tsunami relief efforts, many of these representing a company's first-time disaster relief donation.[33]

In turn, many companies are publishing environmental and social performance information in the same manner as they would traditionally report financials.[34]

Media Relations

Although the old-style public relations function, focused almost exclusively on dealing with *media relations*, may be a thing of the past, the subfunction we now refer to as media relations is still central to the corporate communication effort. Most of the average company's corporate communication staff typically reside within this subfunction, and the person in charge of the communications department as a whole must be capable of dealing with the media as a spokesperson for the firm. Although the media relations subfunction started off as a "flakking" service for managers in response to requests from news organizations, today the best corporate communication departments actively set the discussion agenda of the firm in the media. (See Chapter 6.) There is little debate about whether

[31] "2019 Edelman Trust Barometer," Edelman, April 2019, https://www.edelman.com/sites/g/files/aatuss191/files/2019-04/2019_Edelman_Trust_Barometer_CEO_Trust_Report.pdf.

[32] Jing Hu and Jacob B. Hirsh, "Accepting Lower Salaries for Meaningful Work," *Frontiers in Psychology*, September 29, 2017, https://www.frontiersin.org/articles/10.3389/fpsyg.2017.01649/full.

[33] Michael Casey, "Tsunami Prompts Companies to Play Greater Role in Humanitarian Relief Efforts," Associated Press, June 28, 2005.

[34] "Corporate Sustainability: A Progress Report," KPMG and The Economist Intelligence Unit, 2011, http://www.kpmg.com/Global/en/IssuesAndInsights/ArticlesPublications/Documents/corporate-sustainability-v2.pdf.

media relations, unlike other subfunctions, should come under the purview of corporate communication versus other corporate functions.

Due to the challenges associated with media relations, this function is more frequently outsourced to PR agencies than any other communications function, according to *PRWeek*'s 2019 Bellwether Report.[35] Firms have looked to outsource this function for a number of reasons, a major one of which includes having the perception of a more neutral third party serving as a source for press coverage. Social and digital media have also impacted the business, with firms' earned media work focused on not only generating positive buzz for a company but also generating links back to company websites, translating into end purchases.[36]

Marketing Communications

The marketing communications department coordinates and manages publicity relating to new or existing products and also deals with activities relating to customers. It also may manage corporate advertising. Product publicity almost always includes sponsorship of events for major corporations, such as product introductions, golf tournaments, car races, and marathons. In addition, celebrities are often involved in these activities, which requires coordination within the company. Given how important such events and sponsorship agreements can be in shaping a company's image, corporate communication experts are often involved in setting the events' agendas.

During the 2016 Rio Olympics, for example, corporate sponsorships reached the hundreds of millions, and many required board level approval and were closely watched by senior managers.[37]

One of the biggest recent changes in the customer relations function is the rise of customer-centricity, a trend facilitated by the widespread adoption of digital communications platforms. Pressure groups use digital channels to rally their peers, comment on issues and put the heat on corporate management teams, who are forced to monitor social media sites on a 24/7 basis. Responsiveness is key. Following the *Costa Concordia* disaster in 2012, the worst in its corporate history, cruise line company Carnival was doubly indemnified when a fire broke out on another ship a year later, and CEO Micky Arison was unavailable for comment. Worse, he was at a Miami Heat game, tweeting about basketball. Scores of Carnival customers and investors excoriated his Twitter remarks, damaging the company's reputation and ultimately its stock price, which dropped 5 percent in the week following the fire.[38]

While digitization has created some pressures on companies, like needing to respond immediately to consumer issues, it has also created tremendous opportunities in terms of being able to measure the efficacy of various campaigns. Companies are increasingly

[35] Chris Daniels, "Bellwether Survey: C-Suite Dinosaurs Hold Back Communications," *PRWeek*, October 3, 2019, https://www.prweek.com/article/1660664/bellwether-survey-c-suite-dinosaurs-hold-back-communications.

[36] Ibid.

[37] Charles R. Taylor, "Sponsorship and Advertising Trends in the 2016 Rio Olympic Games: Three Things to Watch For," *Forbes*, August 4, 2016, https://www.forbes.com/sites/onmarketing/2016/08/04/sponsorship-and-advertising-trends-in-the-2016-rio-olympic-games-three-things-to-watch-for/#2bf205a418c7.

[38] Jose Pagliery, "Carnival's CEO Is Loud About His NBA Team, Quiet About His Company," *CNN Money*, February 15, 2013, https://money.cnn.com/2013/02/15/news/carnival-cruise-micky-arison.

turning to big data in order to improve company positioning and to competitively differentiate themselves.[39] Michael Sneed, CCO for Johnson & Johnson, notes that, "We now have the ability to launch a campaign on a Monday and see if it has any impact by Friday. This allows us to make real-time changes to our marketing and communications without having to waste the time and money we used to in the past."[40]

Internal Communications

As companies focus on retaining a contented workforce given changing values and demographics, they have to think strategically about how they communicate with employees through *internal communications*. (See Chapter 7 for more on this subfunction, also referred to as *employee communication*.) Although strong internal communications have always generated a more engaged, productive, and loyal workforce, the bursting of the dot-com bubble, the collapse of several of America's most respected firms, the proliferation of outsourcing jobs to foreign countries in recent years, and cuts in workforces as a result of the financial crisis have further necessitated strong communication channels between management and employees to win back employee trust and loyalty.

Often, internal communications is a collaborative effort between the corporate communication and human resources departments, as it covers topics from employee benefit packages to the company's strategic objectives. More and more, companies are making sure their employees understand the new marketing initiatives they are communicating externally and are uniting the workforce behind common goals and corporate strategies. Employers increasingly have a number of ways to communicate with employees today, from digital options such as Slack and Google Hangouts to more traditional ones such as in-person meetings.

The choice of communication channel ought largely be dependent upon the seriousness of the message being relayed. For example, during difficult economic times, layoffs, and uncertainty require open, honest communication from senior management to all employees, and the decision to communicate via Zoom or an in-person meeting ought to be heavily weighed.[41] The sensitive nature of some of these messages further speaks for the involvement of seasoned communications professionals alongside their human resources counterparts and, most importantly, of the CEO or of senior executives who are the individuals communicating messages to internal and external audiences most frequently.

Finally, as mentioned previously, due to the blurring of constituency lines companies must recognize that employees may also represent investors and members of community advocacy groups—making thoughtful communications even more critical.

Investor Relations

Investor relations (IR) has emerged as the fastest-growing subset of the corporate communication function and an area of intense interest at all companies. (See Chapter 8 for more on investor relations.) Traditionally, investor relations was handled by the finance

[39] Sergio Cortés and Eva Pedrol, "Big Data as a Tool for Corporate Communications Strategies," PRovoke, November 28, 2016, https://www.provokemedia.com/agency-playbook/sponsored/article/big-data-as-a-tool-for-corporate-communications-strategies.

[40] Interview with Michael Sneed, October 2020.

[41] Rebecca Knight, "How to Talk to Your Team When the Future Is Uncertain," *Harvard Business Review*, April 20, 2020, https://hbr.org/2020/04/how-to-talk-to-your-team-when-the-future-is-uncertain.

function, often reporting to the company's chief financial officer (CFO), but the focus in recent years has moved away from "just the numbers" to the way the numbers are actually communicated to various constituencies.

IR professionals deal primarily with shareholders and securities analysts, who are often a direct source for the financial press, which this subfunction cultivates in conjunction with experts from the media relations area. IR professionals interact heavily with both individual and institutional investors. IR professionals also are highly involved with the financial statements and annual reports that every public firm must produce. In recent years, the IR function has increasingly come under pressure to manage activist investors, who mobilize online via digital communications. These shareholders take an active rather than passive role in the companies in which they invest and demand consistent and ongoing communications management.

Given the quantitative messages that are the cornerstone of the IR subfunction, as well as the need for IR professionals to choose their words carefully to avoid any semblance of transferring inside information, this subfunction must be a coordinated effort between communications professionals and the chief financial officer, comptroller, or vice president for finance. The need for this coordination has only increased in recent years with more stringent regulatory demands in the age of Sarbanes-Oxley and Reg. FD. (Regulation Fair Disclosure was an SEC ruling implemented in October 2000. It mandated that all publicly traded companies must disclose material information to all investors at the same time.)

Government Relations

The *government relations* function, also referred to as *public affairs*, is more important in some industries than others, but virtually every company can benefit by having ties to legislators on both a local and a national level. (See Chapter 9 for more on government relations.) Many companies have also established offices in Washington to keep a finger on the pulse of regulations and bills that might affect the company. Because of their critical importance in heavily regulated industries such as public utilities, government relations efforts in such companies are often both staffed internally and supplemented by outside government relations specialists in Washington.

Either firms can "go it alone" in their lobbying and government affairs efforts, or they can join industry associations to deal with important issues as a group. For example, the Edison Institute acts as a lobbying group for electric companies. Either way, staying connected to what is happening in Washington through a well-staffed and savvy government relations team is important to virtually all businesses given the far reach of government regulations within industries from pharmaceuticals to computer software. As companies expand internationally, building or outsourcing government relations efforts in key major foreign hubs—for example in Brussels to concentrate on European Union legislation—will become equally important.

Crisis Management

Although not really a separate function requiring a dedicated department, crisis communications should be coordinated by the corporate communication function, and communications professionals should be involved in crisis planning and crisis management. Ideally, a wider group of managers from throughout the organization—including the senior management spokesperson who will be facing the public—is included in all planning for such eventualities. (See Chapter 10 for more on crises.)

Although company lawyers typically need to be involved in crises, this need presents problems for both the organization and the corporate communication function, because lawyers often operate with a different agenda than that of their communications counterparts and do not always consider how actions might be perceived by specific constituencies or the public at large. A research study on the subject of communication versus legal strategies stated: "legal dominance is shortsighted and potentially costly . . . organizations [must] reconcile the often contradictory counsel of public relations and legal professionals and take a more collaborative approach to crisis communication."[42]

Working collaboratively with in-house counsel and, importantly, senior management, corporate communications professionals can make the difference between good and poor crisis management. We will see examples of both in Chapter 10.

Conclusion

The success of a company's communication strategy is largely contingent on how closely the communication strategy is linked to the strategy of the business as a whole.[43] In addition to thoughtful design and careful planning of firm strategy, a company must have a strong corporate communication function to support its mission and vision.

Although the investor relations function could be in the finance function of a company, the internal communications function within the human resources department, and the customer relations function within the marketing department, all of these activities require communication strategies that are connected to the central mission of the firm.

Corporate communications professionals must be willing to perform a wide variety of subfunctions within the function, and their roles will continue to broaden and diversify as globalization and information from a variety of sources demand that communications be strategic and purposeful. The greater number of global firms and the increasing demand for senior management to travel and speak in international venues place additional pressure on the communication function to communicate successfully with even more diverse, foreign audiences.[44]

Many corporations have made strides in building strong corporate communication functions that are closely aligned with overall strategy; however, there is still much work to be done. A 2020 poll released by Gallup revealed that public confidence in "big business" was the fourth-lowest rated of 16 leading institutions in the United States, just above "news on the Internet" and Congress, though notably "large technology companies" were trusted considerably more than "big business" itself.[45] In this light, managing reputation and building trust are more important than ever, and a strong corporate communication program is a means to achieve those goals.

[42] Kathy R. Fitzpatrick and Mareen Shubaw Rubin, "Public Relations vs. Legal Studies in Organizational Crises Decisions," *Public Relations Review 21* (1995), p. 21.

[43] David Clutterbuck, "Linking Communication to Business Success: A Challenge for Communicators," *Communication World*, April 1, 2001, p. 30.

[44] Norm Leaper, "How Communicators Lead at the Best Global Companies," *Communication World 4* (April 5, 1999), p. 33.

[45] "Confidence in Institutions," Gallup, https://news.gallup.com/poll/1597/confidence-institutions.aspx.

John Deere

The week before Thanksgiving in 2018, Mara Downing was attending a Quad City Mallards hockey game in Moline, Illinois, with other members of the John Deere executive team. Heading down the hallway on the way to her seat, Downing ran into her boss, Marc Howze, Chief Administrative Officer for the company, who asked her if she had a second to chat. After exchanging a few pleasantries, Marc cut right to the chase: "Mara, you did a remarkable job leading our brand re-imagining study, and the CEO staff has decided you're the perfect person to lead both brand and communications as our new Vice President of Global Brand Management and Corporate Communications. I have to run to drop the game puck, but we do hope you'll accept soon."

Mara had sensed that she was going to be tapped for such a position but was surprised to have the news sprung upon her in the hallway, on her way to her seat, right before puck drop. As she hurried to her box to get settled in for the start of the game, though, her mind was already well past whether she should accept (an easy yes) but onto exactly how to structure the new department, create a strategy for the function, and which issues she would need to tackle on her first day in her new role.

A STORIED COMPANY

John Deere traces its roots back to 1837 in Grand Detour, Illinois, where founder John Deere worked as a blacksmith. Hearing farmers' concerns that their plows, designed for the sandy soil of the eastern United States, weren't holding up in the thicker prairie soil of Illinois, Deere fashioned a sturdier plow from steel and a broken sawblade. At first just making a few plows for local farmers, Deere found himself needing to fulfill over 100 orders by 1842. To keep up with ever-increasing demand, Deere moved the nascent company to Moline, Illinois, in 1848, building a water-powered factory

right on the Mississippi and doubling production in that first year. Over 170 years and just eight CEOs later, John Deere was still headquartered in Moline in 2018. By then, the company's operations had expanded well beyond producing a single plow to include equipment for everything from construction and landscaping to forestry and the military and enjoyed a market cap north of $45 billion.

Like many other corporate communication functions at Fortune 100 companies that can trace their roots back nearly 200 years, Deere's communication function faced challenges in adapting to an increasingly fast-paced, digitized world while remaining true to its heritage.

SHARED HISTORY

As a third-generation employee who had joined the company more than 20 years ago, Mara Downing could easily relate to the communication challenges John Deere faced in balancing its desire to respect its family-oriented history and its loyal fan base with its need for modernization. With a background in accounting and finance, Mara had originally joined the company's tax department, later moving to a lobbying position, and then from public affairs to corporate citizenship. Throughout the years, Mara continued to move up the ranks, and by 2015, she was named Director of Global Brand Management and Corporate Citizenship, as the company sought to more directly link its brand with the soul of the company and its understanding of corporate citizenship, identity, and responsibility.

STRONG HEADWINDS

When Mara took over as head of brand and citizenship in 2015, the company was facing brand and communication challenges on a variety of fronts. Deere was no longer ranked on Fortune's World's Most Admired Companies List or recognized on key sustainability rankings; media buzz about the company was at an all-time low; and the communications department was struggling to support the many functions that turned to them to articulate Deere's purpose and vision. At the same time, then-CEO Sam Allen turned to Mara to find opportunities to build on the company's success in past sponsorship events. For example, the company had sponsored the John Deere Classic for the PGA Tour since 1998, and it had done much to grow the business's golf and sports turf segment. Thus, Sam turned to Mara wondering what Deere's next big sponsorship event should be. Something for college football? For Disney? For some other overlooked segment?

GETTING TO THE RIGHT DIAGNOSIS

Mara was hesitant, however, to double down on corporate sponsorship. Aware of the complex dynamics that feed into morale, brand, and reputation, and also not wanting to misdiagnose the problems Deere was facing, Mara sought to comprehensively, and as much as possible quantitatively, get to the heart of what had led to the company's issues.

Mara began by bringing in some external assistance, turning to researchers from the Tuck School of Business to conduct over 30 interviews at Deere to better understand what challenges and opportunities existed for the corporate communications and brand functions. Across the board, a key theme emerged: that while, internally, Deere employees understood and believed in the company's mission, externally, they were failing to effectively communicate that to the outside world. As one interviewee noted, "John Deere has a good message. Shame on us for not getting that out."

Mara knew, however, that she needed to supplement this qualitative assessment with a quantitative one, turning to the RIG tracking system to more concretely measure gaps in the company's performance. Just as had emerged during the qualitative interviews, the areas where Deere was falling short were largely ones where they effectively remained silent.

STARK RESULTS

With the results of the survey in hand, it was abundantly obvious to Mara where the greatest work needed to be done. Clear gaps emerged between what information was viewed as most important to share from the perspective of shareholders, employees, and the general public, and the actual information Deere put forth. The company needed to finally start talking about gender and people of color in its employment base; to more fully articulate its commitment to sustainability; and to make it clear that diversity and inclusion were topics they weren't afraid of discussing. Moreover, Mara quickly realized that resources were not being effectively allocated. The communications department was also facing major issues, in terms of its tone, structure, and process. The department had been dominated by more traditional voices, who often turned to long form editorials and utilized a more formal tone of voice, regardless of which audience that sought to reach, including employees. Additionally, the department operated in a very reactionary matter, almost like a classic news desk waiting for information to come into them. Other than knowing what events the CEO was going to be attending and preparing remarks for him, there was no editorial calendar and no sense of who else needed to be supported from a communications perspective.

Another consequence of this more reactionary approach was that common themes in terms of concerns or challenges brought to the department were being missed. For example, five different members of the Human Resources team might come to the corporate communications department in a day with similar questions around statements on company purpose, but the corporate communications team was not stepping back to analyze trends in issues that were being brought before them.

Thus, Deere faced an issue not only of resource mismanagement but of fundamental misalignment between purpose and practice. Mara knew, then, that keeping the brand and communications functions separate was no longer a viable option for Deere.

PUCK DROP

As Mara rushed down the hallway to make it to her seat on time, her mind turned to her new role, and the challenges she knew she would face in leading the newly combined brand and communications departments. How would she handle the budget constraints she knew Deere was facing? How would she organize this now much larger department that was gluttonous in some areas and starved for support in others? How would she gain credibility with the far larger number of staff for whom she was now responsible? All these questions, and many more, raced through her mind as she made it into her seat just in time for the puck to drop, signaling the start of the game and a far more challenging stage of her career.

CASE QUESTIONS

1. Given the pain points outlined in the case, would you advocate for a centralized or decentralized communications structure at John Deere? Explain.

2. Within an organization like John Deere, who should be responsible for handling external and internal communications? Should the responsibility lie within the communications department, or should the C-suite play a role in execution?

3. Consider the results from employee surveys at John Deere. Based on these insights, how do you think Mara can use both internal and external communications to improve the brand's image externally?

4. If you were in Mara's position, what communications activities would you prioritize first to enhance cohesion between the brand and communications departments? Why?

CHAPTER FOUR

Corporate Brand and Reputation

Chapter 3 covered the various components of the corporate communication function. This chapter examines the first and most critical part of that function: character, which creates its brand and is ultimately filtered into its reputation. While on the surface these are somewhat abstract topics, they each have very tangible impact on a company's long-term success and its bottom line. Take, for example, Coca-Cola. Its Spencerian script logo was developed in 1886, the contoured bottle from 1916, and distinct red color from 1920.[1] Throughout the decades, Coca-Cola has leveraged its history to be an enduring brand in customers' psyches. It has accordingly reaped the benefits in its corporate valuation, which far exceeds its total tangible assets because of its strong brand name.

Looking at an example of image at the personal level might be a good place to start. People choose certain kinds of clothing, drive particular cars, or style their hair a certain way to express their individuality. The cities and towns in which we live, the music we prefer, and the restaurants we frequent all add up to an impression, or identity, that others can easily distinguish.

The same is true for corporations. Walk into a firm's office, and it takes just a few moments to capture those all-important first impressions and learn a great deal about the company. The effort is relatively easy to understand at the personal level but significantly more difficult at the organizational level. One reason for this complexity is that many more potential opportunities to interact with a company's identity exist. Take, for instance, the following example from the hotel industry:

> An executive and her husband decide to treat themselves to one of life's great pleasures: a weekend in a suite at the Oriental Hotel in Bangkok. During their stay, their daily copies of the Asian *Wall Street Journal* and the International *New York Times* are ironed for them to eliminate creases; the hotel staff, omnipresent, run down the hallway to open their door lest they should actually have to use their room keys; laundry arrives beautifully gift-wrapped with an orchid attached to each package; every night, the pillows are adorned with a poem on the theme of sleep; and, outside the lobby, Mercedes limos are lined up, ready to take the couple anywhere at any time of the day or night.

---

[1] The Coca-Cola Company, "125 Years of Sharing Happiness," https://www.coca-colacompany.com/content/dam/journey/us/en/our-company/history/coca-cola-a-short-hisotry-125-years-booklet.pdf.

A few weeks later, they return to the United States, and she is giving a presentation to a group of fellow executives at a midwestern resort. A *USA Today* appears on the outside doorknob squeezed into a plastic bag; the staff, invisible if not for their cleaning carts left unattended in the hallway, are unable to bring room service in under 45 minutes; her pillow is "adorned" with a room-service menu for the following morning and a piece of hard candy; the vehicle waiting to whisk guests to various destinations is a Chrysler minivan; and for flowers, the resort provides silk varietals in a glass-enclosed case that plays the song "Feelings" when the top is lifted.

Both hotels have strong identities, and the choices each has made about its business are at the heart of what brand and reputation are all about. These choices contribute to and shape the identities of these hotels, and ultimately, their reputations.

Just then compromises brand and reputation? How do organizations distinguish themselves in the minds of customers, shareholders, employees, communities, and other relevant constituencies? How do they use their corporate communications function to enhance their image? Above all, how does an organization manage something so seemingly ephemeral?

The Frameworks: Understanding the Building Blocks

In order to best understand how a corporate reputation is created, we first must be clear on *how* to think strategically about communication. As discussed in Chapter 2, the Corporate Communication Strategy framework is iterative and centered around the constituencies the firm hopes will receive the message. In this chapter, we will build upon this framework to structure our approach to building an effective, resonant narrative, and communication strategy (see Figure 4.1). The framework starts with organization character. This is internally created and is perceived by customers, communities, investors, and employees who all communicate among each other. Company reputation is the aggregate of those perceptions.[2]

FIGURE 4.1
Reputation Framework

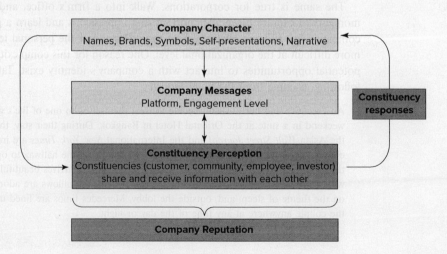

2 Paul Argenti and Bob Druckenmiller, "Reputation and the Corporate Brand," *Corp Reputation Rev* 6, (2004), pp. 368–374.

Similar to the Corporate Communication Strategy Framework itself, this iterative process ensures that there is alignment between what a corporation says or does and how customers understand it.

Company character is firm-created through tangible artifacts from the organization, whether they are brand logos, messages, websites, services, or buildings. An organization's character is best communicated through stories and narratives. They engender emotions from those on the receiving end and stick with the audience. Companies can develop these artifacts with feedback from core constituencies.

Just as a company analyzes how constituencies respond to a message, it can analyze how constituencies respond to artifacts. Are the artifacts that we are releasing resonating in the way we would expect? Are our constituencies responding positively to our character? Does our representation of ourselves match what constituencies perceive to be the truth? Federal Express's change to FedEx in 1994 is a great example of this point, when the company formally changed its name to match the abbreviation already used by thousands of customers (and competitors' customers) as its official name. As a launch advertisement read in 1994: "We're changing our look to FedEx. Isn't that what you call us anyway?"[3]

One of the most effective ways to communicate who you are as a company is through your *narrative*. Stories are sticky. They engender emotions. They develop connections. If you were writing a novel, you develop the character—in this case your company—and weave together a plausible and persuasive story about how it fits into your broader context: your competitors, your customers, and their experience. Moreover, research shows that our brains think of companies as people, with personalities and emotions. Companies must create a narrative for a company that harnesses that power.[4] People have feelings about the character, and they resonate with the character as you would in a movie. The following examples help to illustrate this point:

- Warby Parker, a direct-to-consumer eyewear company, has a textbook narrative:
  - *It frames a problem:* Glasses are too expensive. Warby's narrative goes into as much detail as describing one of the founders losing their glasses on a backpacking trip and forgoing them for a semester of graduate school because of the expense. We can all imagine ourselves there. We immediately have empathy for the character and the situation.
  - *It describes the villain:* The eyewear industry is dominated by one company that "keeps prices artificially high while reaping huge profits from consumers who have no other options."[5]
  - *It presents our heroes:* The founders of Warby Parker come to the rescue.
  - *It delivers a solution:* The company provides an easy, fun way to shop for affordable stylish eyewear.

[3] "Chapter 11: The Image Is the Reality (If You Work at It)," *The World on Time*, July 1, 1996, p. 115.

[4] Mark Bonchek, "How to Build a Strategic Narrative," *Harvard Business Review*, March 25, 2016, https://hbr.org/2016/03/how-to-build-a-strategic-narrative.

[5] Warby Parker, "History," https://www.warbyparker.com/history.

- Innocent Juice, a UK-based drink company, distills their narrative down to 109 words:

> We started innocent in 1999 after selling our smoothies at a music festival. We put up a big sign asking people if they thought we should give up our jobs to make smoothies, and put a bin saying 'Yes' and a bin saying 'No' in front of the stall. Then we got people to vote with their empties. At the end of the weekend, the 'Yes' bin was full, so we resigned from our jobs the next day and got cracking. Since then we've started making coconut water, juice and kids' stuff, in our quest to make natural, delicious, healthy drinks that help people live well and die old.[6]

In those short words, we have a sense for who the heroes are and what they want to achieve through the company.

Corporate brand spans the entire company and conveys expectations of what the company will deliver. A corporate brand can be aspirational. It should answer the question "Who do you say you are and want to be?", and it conveys this through its messaging, logos, tone of voice, marketing esthetic, and so on. In many ways, a corporate brand is a type of shortcut, or mental heuristic. The goal is to activate a set of accurate and positive associations when a constituency thinks of a brand. A company engages in corporate branding when it markets the company itself as a brand; companies create corporate brands.

Perception, on the other hand, is how individual constituencies view a company's artifacts, brand, narrative, and self-presentations. A company has a vast array of constituencies: customers, communities, employees, shareholders, suppliers, etc. Within those constituencies, there are further cleavages. Customers, for example, might be segmented based on their identity and needs. Gen-Zers with pocket change from their parents will react differently to a message than young professionals with disposable income.

Inevitably, the differences between how various constituencies perceive these artifacts can vary. For example, shareholders and the community might perceive a piece of information or message differently based on their context. These perceptions do not exist in isolation. Perceptions between constituencies interact. How employees, for example, perceive an organization's character can affect how customers perceive an organization's character. This is because perception does not just come from artifacts released by an organization. Incorporating constituencies' perspectives in messaging produces a more resonant perception.

Reputation is an aggregate of perceptions across consistencies. While companies create a brand, they earn a reputation. A brand is directly crafted by a company, whether through a logo, message, or set of artifacts. Companies have direct control over their brand. Reputation, while affected by a company's actions, is not a direct reflection of any one message or one artifact that a company has released. It is the collective perceptions of a vast and diverse set of constituencies. While companies can hope that what they release to the universe will lead to a specific reputation, it is ultimately largely out of their hands. A firm thus has control over its actions and representations, but it does not have control over other organizations' actions that affect constituencies' perceptions or how constituencies perceive a firm's actions.

---

[6] Innocent Drinks, "Our Story," https://www.innocentdrinks.co.uk/us/our-story#.

Companies should strive for alignment between a company's self-presentations, constituents' perception, and reality. Simply put, companies should present a truth that aligns with reality as constituents see it. Consistency creates more positive brand awareness and associations. Consistency is critical in cultivating the highest levels of awareness and most favorable associations. Consistency and cohesiveness of brand perception supports consumer recall of brands, and as such, builds brand awareness and positive associations.[7]

In each framework (see again Figure 4.1), arrows are all bi-directional, indicating that not only does information flow both ways, but it also must flow both ways to ensure that companies and brands are responding to what they hear from constituencies. Social media and new online technologies have amplified the importance of these arrows. What was once a more purposeful exchange has become second nature, particularly for digital natives. As a result, companies must ensure that they are harnessing the power of social media and online technologies as they craft their brand and communicate with constituencies. The question for companies today is how do they apply this foundational framework to an increasingly online and connected world. Companies and their constituents are increasingly online; brands must be there too.

Understanding the Elements That Contribute to a Brand

As stated earlier, corporate brand answers the question: "Who do you say you are and what do you want to be?" A wide range of elements help to answer this question; they are comprised of artifacts the company puts into the world through its logos, ads, annual reports to shareholders, and so on, as well as things from the tone of voice it chooses to adopt to the esthetic selected for marketing campaigns.

Brands serve as identification tags that can allow us to gauge everything around us quickly and effortlessly. Given this phenomenon, a company's value can be significantly influenced by the success of its corporate branding strategy. Coca-Cola, for example, has a valuation that far exceeds its total tangible assets because of its strong brand name.

Branding and strategic brand management are critical components of identity management programs. Although it is beyond the scope of this book to fully explore corporate branding, this chapter focuses on a subset of corporate branding—names and logos—to help illustrate the conscious actions that organizations can take to shape their identity and further differentiate themselves in the marketplace.

Companies often institute name changes to signal identity changes, to make their identities better reflect their realities, or to account for organizational changes due to an acquisition or merger. In September 2018, Dunkin' Donuts announced that it would be formally changing its name to Dunkin'.[8] The change was driven by two factors: first, to better reflect the way its customers perceived and talked about the brand; and second, to usher in a new era for the brand with a focus moving beyond just donuts. When the company announced

[7] Keven L. Keller, *Strategic Brand Management: Building, Measuring, and Managing brand Equity.* 2008.

[8] "Welcome to Dunkin': Dunkin' Donuts Reveals New Brand Identity," Dunkin' press release, September 25, 2018, https://news.dunkindonuts.com/news/releases-20180925.

Dunkin' simplified its branding to better reflect the way customers talked about it as well as to signal a new direction for the brand. Source: "Dunkin' Donuts Reveals New Brand Identity." Dunkin' Press Release, September 25, 2018, https://news.dunkindonuts.com/news/releases-20180925.

the name change, it was in some ways reminiscent of FedEx's name change, when customers across social media noted, "Don't we call it Dunkin' anyway?"

Distinct from FedEx's name change, however, was the importance of signaling a new direction for the brand. It had already planted the seeds of change in 2013 when it declared itself a "beverage company," when sales from beverage reached 58 percent of total sales.[9] By dropping the "Donuts" from its name, Dunkin' gave itself room to be known for more than just its pastry offerings. Starbucks had made a similar move in 2011, when it changed its name from Starbucks Coffee to just Starbucks. Then-CEO Howard Schultz noted, "It's possible we'll have other products with our name on it and no coffee in it."[10] Similarly, Chief Marketing Officer Tony Weisman spoke to the future ahead for Dunkin' when he noted, "By simplifying and modernizing our name, while still paying homage to our heritage, we have an opportunity to create an incredible new energy for Dunkin', both in and outside our stores."[11]

[9] Vanessa Romo, "Dunkin' Deletes Donuts from Its Name," NPR, September 26, 2018, https://www.npr.org/2018/09/26/651905960/dunkin-deletes-donuts-from-its-name.

[10] Eliza Brooke, "Companies Are Rebranding with Intentionally Vague Names. Dunkin' Donuts Is the Latest." *Vox*, September 26, 2018, https://www.vox.com/the-goods/2018/9/26/17902620/dunkin-donuts-name-change.

[11] "Welcome to Dunkin': Dunkin' Donuts Reveals New Brand Identity," Dunkin'.

At nearly the exact same time as Dunkin', Weight Watchers announced that it would be changing its over 55-year-old name to "WW," as well as announcing a new tagline, "Wellness that Works." The name change announcement came on the heels of changing cultural norms and values around body image and dieting, where weight loss as an end in and of itself was no longer viewed as important as overall health and self-care. Its simplified name, however, was not met with as much positivity as Dunkin's was. In the first quarter following the change, sales dipped over $60 million and overall membership actually decreased.[12] In many ways, however, this was to be expected, as assistant professor at the University of Nebraska's Yanhui Zhao found in 2017 that 40 percent of rebranding efforts were met with negative reactions from shareholders.[13] While WW has since retained its name-change, it has continued to deal with the tension between its superficial change with little strategic change; perceived inauthenticity in rebranding that comes in the absence of actual strategic change is a considerable stumbling block.

Netflix met with even less success when it quickly reversed a name change it attempted to make in 2011. Having already announced a 60 percent price hike that infuriated customers, Netflix Inc. introduced "Qwikster." The plan, part of Netflix's attempt to separate its streaming video service from its DVD mailing service, was an instant flop. Customers decried not just the higher costs but also the inconvenience of two separate websites and two separate bills. The Qwikster decision lasted just a few weeks. In a 2011 conference call, CEO Reed Hastings said of the Qwikster plan, "In hindsight, it's hard to justify." He also added, "Qwikster became the symbol of Netflix not listening."[14] Netflix's stumble underscores the need to approach rebranding and name changes with caution; they cannot serve as a band-aid for some other issue, like addressing customer concerns.

As these examples illustrate, though organizations can differentiate themselves based on identity through names and logos, they also can risk losing whatever identity they have built up very quickly through changes in the use of names and logos that are not communicated properly.

Logos are another important component of corporate identity—perhaps even more important than names because of their visual nature (which can allow them to communicate even more about a company than its name) and their increasing prevalence across many types of media. When upscale discount retailer Target placed an ad in *The New York Times* in 1999 depicting only its bull's-eye logo and inviting readers to call a toll-free number if they knew what the symbol meant, its phone lines were tied up immediately. The company was soon forced to shut down the toll-free number due to the staggering response.[15]

One of the most recognizable logos in the world today (perhaps second only to Coca-Cola's) is Nike's "swoosh," which was designed for Nike founder Phil Knight by Portland State graduate Carolyn Davidson in 1972 for $35. Some experts believe the swoosh is better.

---

[12] Dearbail Jordan, "What's Gone Wrong at Weight Watchers?" *BBC News*, March 1, 2019, https://www.bbc.com/news/business-47392730.

[13] Ibid.

[14] Michael B. Sauter and Samuel Stebbin, "These 15 Companies Have One Thing in Common: They All Had to Change Their Names," *USA Today*, January 13, 2020, https://www.usatoday.com/story/money/2020/01/12/companies-forced-to-change-their-names/40963349.

[15] Shelly Branch, "How Target Got Hot," *Fortune*, May 24, 1999, pp. 169–74.

A young woman in Hanoi, Vietnam, sports a counterfeit version of the Nike swoosh on her hat.
Source: Paul Argenti

known today than McDonald's golden arches. The world's greatest athletes from LeBron James to Maria Sharipova wear the famous swoosh on their jerseys and shoes. Teams in hockey's Canada Cup and national soccer teams also have worn the swoosh in competition. With Nike as their sponsor, Team USA athletes will wear the swoosh at both Summer and Winter Olympics through at least 2028.[16]

Logos can simply be symbols, like the Nike swoosh, or they can be symbols that represent names, like the Target "bull's eye" or Arm & Hammer's arm and hammer. Logos can be stylized depictions of names or parts of names (like the "golden arches" that form the "M" in "McDonald's"), or stylized names with added mottos or symbols. Accenture's logo, for example, is the company name with a "greater than" symbol above the "t" that is meant to connote the firm's goal of pointing the way forward and exceeding clients' expectations.[17]

Sometimes logos are altered as companies grow and take on more subsidiaries. In 2019, Facebook changed its corporate logo to a minimalist rendering of the Facebook name, a move the company stated was to help bring the broad swath of other companies it owns, from Instagram to WhatsApp, under the Facebook parent umbrella and to also help differentiate the actual social platform of Facebook, which continued to retain its signature blue.[18]

Brand in a Hyperconnected World

Because of the nature of the hyperconnected world we now live in, brand identity creation is no longer confined just to the hands of the company itself, but it also extends to the broad range of constituencies that interact with a brand. We can all conjure up images from the hit American television program *Mad Men*—an executive sitting in a smoky room drinking scotch and attempting to craft a company's brand. In the middle of the twentieth century, crafting a brand was left to experts. Today, successful brands are crafted iteratively and with the help of constituents. Take, for example, makeup company Glossier. Launched in 2014, it is now valued at more than $1.2 billion.[19] This company started as a blog *Into the Gloss* with 1.5 million passionate readers, focused on accessible products with authentic reviews. From there, founder Emily Weiss launched a customer-centric makeup and skincare brand. Products were developed based on what she and her team had heard on their website and tested using their core group of followers. Glossier

---

[16] Tom Bassam, "Report: Nike sign US Olympics deal for LA 2028," Sports Pro, March 7, 2019, https://www.sportspromedia.com/news/nike-us-olympics-sponsor-la-2028.

[17] Sandra Guy, "Consultant to Launch Big Effort to Advertise Its New Identity," *Chicago Sun-Times*, November 16, 2000, p. 66.

[18] Katie Fazzini, "Facebook Has a New All-Caps Logo," *CNBC*, November 4, 2019, https://www.cnbc.com/2019/11/04/facebook-has-a-new-logo.html.

[19] Emily Canal, "Fresh Off Its $1.2 Billion Valuation, Glossier Proves It's More Than Just a Buzzy Beauty Brand," Inc., December 24, 2019, https://www.inc.com/emily-canal/glossier-makeup-skincare-emily-weiss-unicorn-valuation.html.

took customer voice so seriously that early on, it developed a Slack channel where its top 100 customers could interact with each other and company representatives, invited New York-based customers to its offices for pizza and rosé,[20] and crowdsourced ideas for attributes of its new facewash.[21]

It is easier to create a brand *with* stakeholders through online channels. Why? Because a brand lives outside of an organization once it is released online. With the increased connectivity, we not only see our conception of a brand broaden, but also lines around ownership and creation blur.[22] The risk in creating a brand image divorced from constituent perspectives is inconsistency. One small mistake can quickly become magnified on the Internet; there is no putting the genie back in the bottle.

Branding has thus become blurred. Companies cannot fully control a message or narrative because so much branded content lives beside constituent-generated content.[23] It can even be hijacked by consumers and firm partners.[24] Historically, brands provided consumers with expectations around what the company would deliver. Image comes from constituency impressions of a company's behavior, and reputation is the aggregate of those perceptions. Now, brands continue to create expectations, *but so do constituents*. "A brand is no longer what we tell the consumer it is—it is what consumers tell each other it is," according to Scott Cook of Intuit.

Authority has thus shifted. The center of control and influence has changed from institutions to communities of individuals (see Figure 4.2). As a result, communications today is about *creating* rather than *controlling* constituencies. Individuals are no longer primarily getting their information from companies; they are getting it from those around them and online.

As customers access more information on brands, expectations, on average, rise. In a study of American and Indian consumers, researchers found that high-involvement

FIGURE 4.2 **The Role of Communities of Individuals**
Brand narrative control has shifted from fully in the hands of the company to diffuse between the company and its many constituencies, thanks in large part to the rise of social media, mobile, and the Internet more broadly.

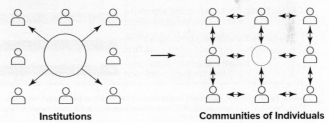

Institutions   Communities of Individuals

[20] Jill Avery, "Glossier: Co-Creating a Cult Brand with a Digital Community," *Harvard Business School*, October 22, 2019.

[21] Glossier Instagram, January 29, 2020, https://www.instagram.com/p/B76PgymBV34.

[22] Swaminathan 2020.

[23] Ibid.

[24] Susan Fournier and Jill J. Avery, "The Uninvited Brand," October 1, 2010, Boston University School of Management Research Paper No. 2010-32, Available at SSRN: https://ssrn.com/abstract=1963056.

customers—customers who accessed more electronic word-of-mouth about two categories of products, hotel services, and cell phones—had higher expectations about the brands. In other words, the more electronic word-of-mouth a customer accesses, the higher the expectations around a brand. This indicates that what stakeholders hear from each other, and not just from the brands themselves, affects how stakeholders perceive brands.[25] Online sentiment and constituency perspectives become increasingly important to manage given who customers trust.

For example, customers are more likely to trust peers. Eighty-three percent of consumers said that they completely trust the recommendation of a friend or family member. Two-thirds say they trust online reviews.[26] This means that companies *must* engage thoughtfully with constituencies online.

Constituencies are talking about brands and shaping narratives in public, online spaces. The question is not *does* it happen, but will firms passively stand by, or become active partners. Firms have the opportunity and imperative to shape the process by which constituents engage online. Companies set up guardrails and structures that support the narrative and overall goals of the brand. Companies will never have full control over constituencies, and research suggests that an authentic dialogue is more effective for customers,[27] but establishing a structure makes it more likely that the process moves in a positive way for firms.

Consistency and Authenticity Are Key

Regardless of the portfolio of strategies a firm deploys, engaging consistently and authentically with consumers is key. A recent BCG customer survey shows that customers are looking for more authentic engagement with brands and are put off by sales pitches (see Figure 4.3). This authentic engagement with constituents not only builds awareness and

FIGURE 4.3 Customers Seek Relationships with Brands That Are Authentic

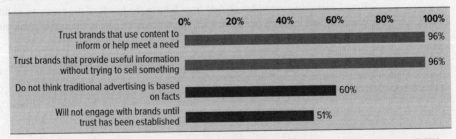

Source: Zuckerman et al. "Branded Content: Growth for Marketers and Media Companies." Boston Consulting Group, July 30, 2015, https://www.bcg.com/publications/2015/media-entertainment-branded-content-growth-for-marketers-and-media-companies.aspx.

[25] Anup Krishnamurthy and Ramesh Kumar, "Electronic Word-of-Mouth and Brand Image: Exploring the Moderating Role of Involvement through a Consumer Expectations Lens," *Journal of Retailing and Consumer Services* 43 (2018), pp. 149–156.

[26] "Global Trust in Advertising," Nielson, September 2015, https://www.nielsen.com/wp-content/uploads/sites/3/2019/04/global-trust-in-advertising-report-sept-2015-1.pdf.

[27] Shao et al., "Brandscapes: Contrasting Corporate-Generated versus Consumer-Generated Media in the Creation of Brand Meaning," *Marketing Intelligence and Planning* 33 (3), 2015, pp 414–443.

image, but also is as a way for brands to gather information to create a consistent, resonant narrative.[28]

Important is ensuring that firms are presenting the right message at the right time on the right channel.[29] A post that works on LinkedIn likely would not resonate on Instagram because each platform has its own distinctive personality, and firms must ensure that posts are congruent with the overall platform.

As firms plan messaging and communications strategies, they should come back to the strategic communications framework, and ask:

- Who are we attempting to reach?
  - Given that, what is the best communication channel?
  - What is the best way to structure the message?
- What do we want them to do?
- How have they responded?
- How must we adjust our message?

Building a Solid Reputation

We now turn our attention to corporate reputation, which represents the culmination of our framework. Charles Fombrun, New York University professor emeritus and author of the book *Reputation*, says that "in companies where reputation is valued, managers take great pains to build, sustain, and defend that reputation by following practices that (1) shape a unique identity and (2) project a coherent and consistent set of images to the public."[30]

Reputation differs from *perception* because it is built up over time and is not simply a perception at a given point in time. As the Reputation Framework illustrates, reputation is based on the perceptions of *all* of an organization's constituencies. Thus, reputation is an outcome, and as a result, cannot really be "managed" in any way.

Why Reputation Matters

The importance of reputation is evidenced by several prominent surveys and rankings that seek to identify the best and the worst among them: *Fortune*'s "Most Admired" list; *BusinessWeek* and Interbrand's "Best Global Brands" ranking; and Harris Interactive and the Reputation Institute's Reputation Quotient (RQ) Gold study, featured in *The Wall Street Journal*. And these rankings, among other measure of reputation more broadly, are viewed as some of the most important KPIs that CEOs turn to in tracking the success of their

---

[28] Zuckerman et al., "Branded Content: Growth for Marketers and Media Companies," *Boston Consulting Group*, July 30, 2015, https://www.bcg.com/publications/2015/media-entertainment-branded-content-growth-for-marketers-and-media-companies.aspx.

[29] Jen Hartmann, "How a 180-Year-Old Brand Made a Huge Social Media Pivot," Social Pros Podcast, https://www.convinceandconvert.com/podcasts/episodes/how-a-180-year-old-brand-made-a-huge-social-media-pivot.

[30] Charles J. Fombrun, *Reputation: Realizing Value from the Corporate Image* (Boston: Harvard Business School Press, 1996), pp. 5–6.

business. The ICCO recently published its World PR Report 2020, detailing the views of public relations companies for the forthcoming year. CEOs and other corporate leaders consistently ranked reputation as their most valuable asset and viewed it as a key area of growth over the next five years.[31]

According to the Hill & Knowlton Corporate Reputation Watch survey, almost all analysts agree that if a company fails to look after reputational aspects of its performance, then it will ultimately suffer financially.[32] In response to this demand, many public relations firms and consultancies now offer reputation measurement and management services to their corporate clients.

In 2020, the Axios-Harris Reputation survey of the U.S. ranked the following companies in their top five: Clorox, Hershey, Amazon, Publix, and General Mills. Notably, the top five had witnessed a considerable shake up in light of the COVID-19 pandemic, wherein Clorox topped the list for the first time in its history.[33] A strong reputation has important strategic implications for these and other firms, because, as Fombrun notes, "it calls attention to a company's attractive features and widens the options available to its managers, for instance, whether to charge higher or lower prices for products and services or to implement innovative programs."[34] As a result, the intangible entity of reputation is undoubtedly a source of competitive advantage. Companies with strong, positive reputations can attract and retain the best talent, as well as loyal customers and business partners, all of which contribute positively to growth and commercial success. As of late 2019, more than $21 trillion in market cap of the S&P500 could be attributed to intangibles, of which reputation is a top-ranking component.[35]

Reputation also can help companies weather crises more effectively. For example, strong reputations helped Johnson & Johnson (J&J) survive the Tylenol cyanide tampering crisis in the early 1980s and its recent quality control problems (see Chapter 10 for more on J&J's handling of the Tylenol crisis) and allowed Apple to weather its 2012 FoxConn labor scandal without measurable long-term damage to the company.

The changing environment for business, as discussed in Chapter 1, has implications for reputation. The proliferation of media and information, the demand for increased transparency, and the increasing attention paid to social responsibility (see Chapter 5) all speak to a greater focus by organizations on building and maintaining strong reputations. According to a recent survey, the vast majority of business leaders feel that it has become much more difficult to manage reputation as a result of digital and social media. The resulting rapid dissemination of information requires quick responses and internal alignment from companies.[36]

[31] Paul Blanchard, "The Importance of Brand Reputation: 20 Years to Build, Five Minutes to Ruin," *Forbes*, December 27, 2019, https://www.forbes.com/sites/forbesagencycouncil/2019/12/27/the-importance-of-brand-reputation-20-years-to-build-five-minutes-to-ruin.

[32] 2010 Hill & Knowlton Corporate Reputation Watch.

[33] "Corporate Reputation Rankings," The Harris Poll, https://theharrispoll.com/axios-harrispoll-100.

[34] David A. Aaker, *Building Strong Brands* (New York: The Free Press, 1996), p. 51.

[35] Bruce Berman, "$21 Trillion in U.S. Intangible Assets Is 84% of S&P 500 Value—IP Rights and Reputation Included," IP CloseUp, June 4, 2019, https://ipcloseup.com/2019/06/04/21-trillion-in-u-s-intangible-asset-value-is-84-of-sp-500-value-ip-rights-and-reputation-included.

[36] "Best Online Reputation Management Services of 2021," *Business News Daily*, November 16, 2020, https://www.businessnewsdaily.com/7901-best-reputation-management-services.html.

With this recent history, organizations are increasingly appreciating the importance of a strong reputation. How does an organization know where it stands? Because reputation is formed by the perceptions of constituencies, organizations must first uncover what those perceptions are and then examine whether they coincide with the company's identity and values. Only when perceptions and identity are in alignment will a strong reputation result.

Measuring and Managing Reputation

In assessing its reputation, an organization must examine the perceptions of *all* its constituencies. As mentioned earlier, many PR firms have developed diagnostics for helping companies conduct this research. Although one size does not fit all when it comes to measurement programs, all of them require constituency research.

Employees can be a good starting point, as they need to understand the company's vision and values and conduct themselves in every customer interaction with those in mind. An organization runs into trouble when it does not practice the values it promotes. As an example, Amazon ran into trouble when, during the COVID-19 crisis, it faced heat for sub-par safety standards. When workers from one warehouse protested, Amazon fired one of the protest leaders. As a result, Amazon faced public criticism and is embroiled in a lawsuit. That criticism extended to shareholders. At a shareholder call in 2020, shareholders pressed management on employee treatment.[37,38,39]

Customer perceptions of an organization also must align with the organization's identity, vision, and values. In the late 1990s, Burberry learned what can happen to corporate reputation when this is *not* happening, and how the reputation can be saved by taking aggressive steps to restore these connections.

When Rose Marie Bravo became CEO of Burberry in 1997, the company was facing a number of challenges. Profits were plummeting, and although some of it could be explained by the Asian economic crisis of the mid-1990s (by 1996, Asian consumers—at home and abroad—generated two-thirds of the company's revenues, causing the downturn to dramatically affect Burberry's sales),[40] internal factors were also at work. For one, prior to Bravo's arrival, instead of maintaining a cohesive Burberry brand across the globe, the company allowed each country's management team to develop the brand as it desired in the local market and allowed extensive licensing. As a result, when customers thought of Burberry, what came to mind depended on their geographic location. In the United States, it meant $900 raincoats and $200 scarves; in Korea it meant whiskey; and in Switzerland it meant watches. Bravo explained that, before her arrival, "[Burberry] had a disparate network of licensees marketing Burberry around the globe. It wasn't a coherent business. Each country was representing its own version of Burberry. Demand slowed. The business needed a clean up. The brand was over-exposed and over-distributed."[41]

[37] Kate Conger, "Senators Want to Know if Amazon Retaliated Against Whistle-Blowers," *The New York Times*, May 11, 2020, https://www.nytimes.com/2020/05/07/technology/amazon-coronavirus-whistleblowers.html.

[38] Josh Eidelson and Spencer Soper, "Amazon Warehouse Employees Sue Over Virus Brought Home From Work," *Bloomberg News*, https://www.bloomberg.com/news/articles/2020-06-03/amazon-warehouse-employees-sue-over-virus-brought-home-from-work.

[39] Denise Lee Yohn, "Amazon Faces a Crucible Moment with Employees," *Forbes*, June 2, 2020, https://www.forbes.com/sites/deniselyohn/2020/06/02/amazon-faces-a-crucible-moment-with-employees/#26f1c83f3822.

[40] Lauren Goldstein, "Dressing Up an Old Brand," *Fortune*, November 9, 1998, pp. 154–56.

[41] Quoted in Nigel Cope, "Stars and Stripes," *Independent*, June 6, 2001, Online Lexis-Nexis Academic, August 2001.

Not only was the company having trouble deciding what it was selling, but it was also struggling with how it was positioning its products. Burberry's inability to decide whether it was targeting upper or lower-end consumers in Asia, for example, led to its products being sold in bulk to discount retailers. This decision undermined the image the exclusive, high-end Burberry boutiques were trying to generate in that same market. Bravo realized that Burberry had to sharpen its focus and concentrate exclusively on high-end retailing to send a consistent message to consumers. Additionally, she recognized that by speaking primarily to older males as a high-end men's raincoat retailer, the company was not catering to a key consumer constituency—women—as effectively as it could.

Recognizing that the Burberry store portfolio needed to reflect the high-end focus of the brand, Bravo upgraded the flagship store in London and doubled the size of the New York store. Even more important, Burberry began to rein in its detached network of franchises to allow the company greater control over consistency of product and identity. The most visible turning point was a print advertising campaign featuring supermodel Kate Moss in a Burberry plaid bikini. These ads pushed Burberry's sales up dramatically and the average age of its customer down considerably by putting a fresh, playful face on a venerable fashion brand that, though esteemed for its nearly 150-year heritage, was looked upon by younger constituencies as stodgy and by many women as "not for me."

In many ways, Burberry's late-1990s refresh was so stunning that the brand became a victim of its own success. Estimated to be the world's most copied fashion logo, Burberry's grasp on the luxury market slipped, partly due to its own ubiquitousness. Under the leadership of Rose Marie Bravo's successor, Angela Ahrendts, Burberry once again aggressively sought to realign its brand. After taking the reins in 2006, Ahrendts focused on centralizing design and reviving core heritage products. Her efforts, from store renovations to a more unified product focus across all franchises, not only boosted company performance (sales more than doubled during her tenure), but helped to create a cohesive brand image and secure Burberry as a luxury brand, greatly enhancing its reputation around the world.[42] Since then, the company has continued to expend efforts in rebranding and trying to stay ahead of the curve in the fashion game. In fact, on the tail-end of the pandemic, the company enjoyed a historically high stock price, coming on the heels of introducing newer logoed products and efforts to better infiltrate the social media world.[43] The story of Burberry, then, applies to all corporations, not just luxury ones: continued attention to reputation must be applied day-in and day-out to continue to remain a success.

Conclusion

As we've seen in this chapter, brand and reputation are integral to an organization's success and credibility. Most managers who have not thought about corporate reputation tend to underestimate its value. This error is partly due to a lack of understanding about what corporate brand and reputation are all about and what they do for an organization,

[42] "Burberry's CEO on Turning an Aging British Icon into a Global Luxury Brand," *HBR*, January–February 2013, www.hbr.org.

[43] "Burberry Stock Price, https://www.google.com/search?q=burberry+stock+price&rlz=1C1CHBF_enUS860US860&oq=burberry+stock+price&aqs=chrome..69i57j0i13l3j0i22i30l6.2630j1j7&sourceid=chrome&ie=UTF-8.

but skeptics also should understand that an inappropriate or outdated identity can be as damaging to a firm as weak financial performance. Individuals seek consistency, and if perceptions about a corporation fail to mesh with reality, constituents take their business elsewhere.

No matter the strategy, an organization with a clear corporate identity that represents its underlying reality and is aligned with the images held by all of its constituencies will be rewarded with a strong reputation. Reputational success, in turn, matures into pride and commitment—among employees, consumers, and the general public—and these qualities are irreplaceable assets in an intensely competitive global business environment.

United Airlines Flight 3411

On April 9, 2017, United Express Flight 3411 was scheduled to fly its route from Chicago's O'Hare airport to Louisville, with a planned departure of 5:40 pm CDT and an arrival of 7:02 pm CDT. Seating capacity is limited to 70 passengers.

Before boarding, Flight 3411 was overbooked by one customer. Despite early attempts by United, via website/kiosk and multiple announcements at the gate asking for customers willing to take later flights, there were no volunteers. As a result, one customer who had not yet been given a seat assignment, was involuntarily denied boarding. This customer received a check as compensation and was booked on another United flight. The other customers were then called to board the plane.

At the same time, an earlier flight to Louisville originally scheduled to depart O'Hare at 2:55 pm CDT was experiencing a maintenance issue (it was unclear if this issue could be fixed, but regardless, it would depart after Flight 3411). Booked on this flight were four crew members, scheduled to operate an early Monday morning United Express flight from Louisville to Newark. Without this crew's arrival in Louisville, United worried that it might have to cancel at least one flight on Monday (if not more) while disrupting more than 100 customers. United then booked these four crew members on Flight 3411, creating the need to identify four customers who would not be able to take the flight.

United agents began to seek four volunteers while customers were already seated on this aircraft. The agent offered $800 travel credit plus the cost of meals and hotel accommodations for the evening, but no customers were willing to accept the offer. The agent then followed the *involuntary denial of boarding selection process* to determine which customers would be asked to leave the airplane.

Once the four customers on Flight 3411 were identified, the United supervisor spoke with two of the customers, a couple, who then departed the aircraft and received compensation. The next customers

approached were Dr. Dao and his wife, and Dr. Dao refused to leave the plane. The supervisor was unable to convince Dr. Dao to depart the airplane. Given Dr. Dao's unwillingness to deplane, the supervisor left the plane and spoke to the United zone controller, who indicated that authorities would be contacted. The supervisor went back on the plane to request again that Dr. Dao deplane and advised him that the authorities would be contacted. At this point, one customer onboard the aircraft volunteered to change flights for $1,000 but United needed two volunteers in order to avoid having to remove the Daos. No other customers would volunteer unless United could guarantee an arrival in Louisville later that night. Given the fact that the 2:55 pm CDT departure remained on a maintenance delay, with a possibility of cancelling, United could not make that commitment.

Officers from the Chicago Department of Aviation answered United's request for assistance. The security officers were unable to gain Dr. Dao's cooperation to depart the plane voluntarily.

At this time, the United supervisor left the airplane and attempted to call a manager about the situation, and Dr. Dao, as shown in video footage, was physically removed from his seat by the Chicago Department of Aviation Officers. After being forcibly removed from the aircraft, Dr. Dao ran back onto the airplane and Chicago Department of Aviation Officers removed him for a second time. He was later taken to the hospital.

Accounts of the incident quickly flooded social media. A fellow passenger, identified as Tyler Bridges, uploaded a video on his Twitter account that quickly went viral. Soon thereafter, additional passengers uploaded their own footage. Audra D. Bridges posted a video on Facebook, adding further context to her husband's video and showing an attempt by an officer to forcibly remove passengers from the plane. Jayse D. Anspach, of Louisville, posted a video on Twitter showing the unknown passenger in Tyler Bridges' video being dragged off the plane by a Chicago Department of Aviation officer.

After approximately 40 minutes, the flight reboarded without the Daos and departed for Louisville at 7:21 pm CDT, two hours and two minutes later than scheduled. It arrived at Louisville at 9:01 pm CDT, two hours behind schedule. During that time, however, the incident had exploded across social media channels, generating millions of impressions and demands for the airline to be boycotted.

With the incident quickly spiraling out of control on social media and lawyers pressuring him to proceed with caution, then-CEO Oscar Munoz faced a choice: How should he respond to the incident? How should he balance the need to avoid legal culpability with the potential additional reputational risk it would expose United to?

CASE QUESTIONS

1. Identify the key failures in United's initial response to the deboarding of Dr. Dao.

2. Consider the United CEO's initial response. How would you, as the United CEO, have responded differently to this crisis to avoid reputational damage?

3. Using the Corporate Communication Strategy Framework, how would you think about rebuilding the brand after this incident?

4. As the CEO of United, what corporate policy changes would you make to ensure that this type of incident does not happen again?

CHAPTER FIVE

Corporate Responsibility

In the previous chapter, we discussed the importance of corporate reputation—the sum of an organization's constituency perceptions built up over time. An increasingly significant contributor to corporate reputation is the notion of corporate responsibility (CR), which is a corporation's social and environmental obligations to its constituencies and greater society. This new lens is increasingly being used by constituencies ranging from the general public to investors to analyze and critique modern-day corporate behavior. In fact, some companies are fundamentally changing the way they conduct their operations to include responsible practices, and groups such as B Corporation and ISO 26000 are providing frameworks and guidelines on how companies can better manage their relationships with society.

When did society's expectations of corporations shift to include responsible and accountable behavior in addition to profit making? As recently as two decades ago, the general public viewed "do-gooding" as the primary domain of nonprofit organizations and good Samaritans. At the time, many considered businesses to be purely self-interested entities. Positioned in a corner directly opposite charities, the purpose of a corporation was profit maximization, with any efforts to give back to the community limited to check-writing and philanthropy at an arm's length. Milton Friedman, a University of Chicago economist, embodied the belief that businesses should be strictly economic, whereas governments and nonprofits should handle social and environmental issues. In the 1970s, Friedman's doctrines became famous through his *New York Times Magazine* article, "The Social Responsibility of Business Is to Increase Its Profits," in which he declared: "What does it mean to say that 'business' has responsibilities? Only people can have responsibilities. A corporation is an artificial person and in this sense may have artificial responsibilities, but 'business' as a whole cannot be said to have responsibilities, even in this vague sense."[1]

In the 1970s, society began to more actively question the means by which corporations generate profits, acknowledging for the first time that corporate practices and society's well-being are closely linked.[2] Corporations became more environmentally aware once

---

[1] Milton Friedman, "The Social Responsibility of Business Is to Increase Its Profits," *The New York Times Magazine*, September 13, 1970.

[2] Joshua Daniel Margolis and James Patrick Walsh, *People and Profits? The Search for a Link between a Company's Social and Financial Performance* (London: Lawrence Erlbaum Associates, 2001).

Mini Case Study

In October 2005, Lee Scott, Walmart's president, announced a large-scale strategy to reduce the company's impact on the global environment. The strategy was an effort to "become the most competitive and innovative company in the world" and had three goals: (1) to be supplied by 100 percent renewable energy, (2) to create zero waste, and (3) to sell resource-efficient and environmentally sustainable products.

Walmart wields significant influence—in 2014, it topped the *Fortune* 500 list as the world's largest company by revenue, bringing in $476 billion. It employs more than 2 million people and is the largest retailer in the world. Even in 2005, when Walmart's sustainability strategy was conceived, the company was a behemoth—it had 6,000 stores worldwide and 84 percent of Americans had shopped at a Walmart that year. Its power in the retail industry was derived from its strict supply chain efficiency, which allowed it to charge much lower prices than its competitors.

In general, Walmart addressed issues of environmental sustainability defensively, rather than proactively, in response to pressure by environmental groups. Thus, the 2005 sustainability strategy was a break from tradition. The strategy would be long-lasting, deeply embedded in Walmart's operations, and closely tied to the company's financial performance. Scott enlisted a consulting firm to conduct an environmental impact assessment that would enable Walmart to cut costs through an environmental strategy and differentiate from the competition. The environmental impact assessment, conducted in conjunction with the Environmental Defense Fund (EDF) and Conservation International (CI) identified five primary areas for improvement: greenhouse gas emissions, air pollution, water pollution, water use, and land use.

In June 2005, a team of Walmart executives, employees, and consultants identified three focus areas that would drive the goals for reducing Walmart's environmental impact: energy, waste, and products. The team defined 14 "Sustainable Value Networks" that drove Walmart's environmental agenda related to energy, waste, and products in the high-impact areas mentioned earlier. Each of these Value Networks was championed by an executive, and cross-functional teams were created to drive sustainability in different parts of the business. Importantly, sustainability became an added responsibility for existing roles, rather than a new functional group within the organization. It was a new paradigm for approaching the job. Additionally, Walmart sought sustainability ideas from outside stakeholders—it drew NGOs, suppliers, eco-friendly competitors, academics, and critics into the sustainability conversation.

The teams then executed a structured process to determine how Walmart could modify its business model to better meet the needs of the communities in which it operated. In sourcing seafood, for example, Walmart instituted several changes across the value chain.

In 2005, global fisheries were under severe pressure due to overfishing. Fishing was an inefficient activity in terms of fuel use and was getting worse as wild fish stocks continued to decline and boats had to venture further out to sea to catch fish. In addition, farmed fish typically had high concentrations of toxins and antibiotics, both of which are harmful to humans when consumed in large quantities. In an effort to secure its short-term and long-term seafood supplies (Walmart's seafood volume was growing 25 percent per year), Walmart engaged the Marine Stewardship Council (MSC) in certifying its suppliers for sustainably caught wild fish. Walmart aimed to have 100 percent of its seafood certified within three to five years.

Established in 1997 by Unilever and World Wide Fund for Nature (WWF), the MSC program developed a broad set of certification standards based on the UN Code of Conduct for responsible fishing. The certification is implemented through independent, MSC-accredited certifying agencies that audit fisheries and processors to ensure that marine resources are harvested sustainably "from boat to plate." Certified fisheries have their finished products labeled in with the MSC eco-label, thus raising consumer awareness. The MSC hoped that the certification process would pressure the industry to adopt more sustainable fishing practices.

In addition to working with MSC, Walmart developed other initiatives to address larger issues of fishery sustainability. These not only affected Walmart's suppliers, but also governments, customers, and NGOs. For example, Walmart worked with NGOs to establish marine reserves and no-fish zones to allow depleted fisheries to recover. By the end of 2006, 30 to 40 percent of Walmart's wild-caught fish were certified under MSC. By 2014, 90 percent of its wild-caught seafood received MSC certification.

Source: "WalMart's Sustainability Strategy," Stanford Graduate School of Business, April 2007 (revised June 2010), https://www.gsb.stanford.edu/faculty-research/case-studies/wal-marts-sustainability-strategy.

large-scale disasters such as Union Carbide's chemical leak in Bhopal, India, in 1984 and the Exxon *Valdez* oil spill in 1989 sparked widespread uproar about the irresponsibility of big business.[3] In the 1990s, a series of exposés in the mainstream media revealed to many consumers for the first time the "sweatshop" labor conditions and child labor used in garment and footwear supply chains by companies such as Nike. The exposés led to consumer outrage and boycotts, which prompted corporations to adopt codes of conduct to protect workers' rights.

Today, companies are increasingly aware of the impact that their operations have in their many communities, and beyond. We see companies forging into unprecedented territory by tackling issues ranging from income inequality and global pandemics to climate change and racial injustices—issues previously considered to be unrelated to their organizational mission but that can no longer be ignored. They are implementing community programs and partnerships with nongovernmental organizations (NGOs) and, most innovatively, are adapting their own business models to be more responsible and sustainable. In the new millennium, the for-profit and nonprofit sectors are no longer at odds; instead, the once-distinct lines between them are blurring. Notably, the 2020 Edelman Trust Barometer Report found that 81 percent of consumers looked to brands to "do what is right," viewing this attribute as a top five purchase criterion, right along with quality and value.[4] At no time was the importance of purpose highlighted than during the COVID-19 pandemic, when Edelman found that the number of consumers who were turning to brands to introduce higher purpose and contribution to society had increased to 89 percent of global consumers looking to companies to "help people meet pandemic related challenges."[5]

Many global executives today view corporate responsibility as being critical to their business strategy and operations. In April 2019, 181 heads of U.S. companies, including the CEOs of Amazon, American Airlines (the largest airline in the world), and J.P. Morgan Chase (the largest American bank), signed a statement of corporate purpose, declaring that a corporation's purpose is one that promotes "an economy that serves all Americans."[6] Such a statement represents a marked departure from earlier sentiment, present even just a decade, that a corporation's primary responsibility is to shareholders alone. Jamie Dimon, JPMorgan CEO and Chairman of the Business Roundtable, noted, however, that such a redefinition of corporate purpose is driven by more than just a philosophical awakening, but rather an increasing sense of the ways in which the fates of corporations are intertwined with the communities in which they work. He noted, "The American dream is alive, but fraying. Major employers are investing in their workers and communities because they know it is the only way to be successful over the long term."[7]

[3] "Just Good Business," *The Economist*, January 17, 2008.

[4] 2020 Edelman Brand Trust Barometer Report.

[5] Ibid.

[6] Elizabeth Dilts, "Top U.S. CEOs Say Companies Should Put Social Responsibility Above Profit," *Reuters*, August 19, 2019, https://www.reuters.com/article/us-jp-morgan-business-roundtable/top-u-s-ceos-say-companies-should-put-social-responsibility-above-profit-idUSKCN1V91EK.

[7] Ibid.

What Is Corporate Responsibility?

Corporate responsibility (often referred to as *corporate social responsibility*, *corporate citizenship*, *sustainability*, and even *conscious capitalism*) are some of the terms bandied about in the news media and corporate marketing efforts as companies jockey to win the trust and loyalty of constituents around the world.[8] The acronym *ESG,* which stands for environment, social, and governance, is also used to describe corporate responsibility initiatives. The term *triple bottom line*, popularized in 1994 by John Elkington, founder of British consulting firm SustainAbility, is also used in corporate responsibility conversations and refers to profit, people, and planet.[9] With such a wide array of terms actively in use in business lexicon, we will define corporate responsibility at the outset of the chapter to guide the rest of our discussion on its effects on corporate reputation.

Corporate responsibility (CR) describes an organization's respect for society's interests, as demonstrated by taking ownership of the effect its activities have on key constituencies—including customers, employees, shareholders, communities, and the environment—in all parts of its operations. In short, CR prompts a corporation to look beyond its traditional bottom line (economic profit or loss) to consider the greater social implications of its business. This accountability often extends beyond baseline compliance with existing regulations to encompass voluntary and proactive efforts to improve the quality of life for employees and their families as well as for the local community and society at large. A responsible company makes a concerted attempt to reduce the negative social and environmental footprint of its operations through a thoughtfully developed strategy implemented over the long term and not merely through temporary, stopgap measures such as monetary contributions to charitable causes.[10] For example, ExxonMobil donating $250 million over 32 years to sponsor Masterpiece Theatre qualifies as philanthropy, but it cannot be categorized as CR because it makes no effort to mitigate the lasting impact of the company's operations. In contrast, Starbucks' efforts to minimize the negative effects of its coffee supply chain and retail operations by purchasing beans from fair trade growers and paying its employees wages higher than industry averages serve as cornerstones of its CR strategy.[11]

Many times, a company's corporate responsibility efforts involve donations of time and expertise, as opposed to cash. As the *Financial Times* noted in 2017, companies are increasingly encouraging employees to donate their expertise and skillsets developed on the job, as opposed to volunteering in ways less related to their corporate work. Such skills-based volunteering seems to be yielding a high return, with *FT* finding that for every £1 a company spent on volunteer programs in London, there was a measurable social benefit return valued at £11. Importantly, however, charities are not the only entities that benefit from such corporate

---

[8] "Conscious Capitalism: Now *Creed* Is Good," BBC News, May 4, 2000.

[9] "Triple Bottom Line: It Consists of Three P's: Profit, People and Planet," *The Economist*, November 17, 2009, https://www.economist.com/node/14301663.

[10] "The ROI of CSR: Q&A with Geoffrey Heal," *Columbia Ideas at Work*, Columbia Business School, Spring 2008.

[11] Ibid.

actions; such engagement likewise builds trust among the local communities in which corporations operate and employees feel more connected to their employer's mission.[12]

As companies focus on organizing and prioritizing their CR efforts, they are increasingly connecting with other organizations to develop guidelines and standards. As of 2020, 11,593 companies in 156 countries around the world signaled their commitment to sustainability of human and environmental resources by participating in the "Global Compact" of the United Nations (UN).[13]

To help guide companies in their corporate responsibility efforts, the UN Global Compact drew upon several diplomatic human rights and sustainability documents when crafting its list of Ten Principles. Companies can use this list to guide their corporate responsibility initiatives.

The UN Global Compact Ten Principles

Human Rights

Principle 1: Businesses should support and respect the protection of internationally proclaimed human rights; and

Principle 2: make sure that they are not complicit in human rights abuses.

Labour

Principle 3: Businesses should uphold the freedom of association and the effective recognition of the right to collective bargaining;

Principle 4: the elimination of all forms of forced and compulsory labour;

Principle 5: the effective abolition of child labour; and

Principle 6: the elimination of discrimination in respect of employment and occupation.

Environment

Principle 7: Businesses should support a precautionary approach to environmental challenges;

Principle 8: undertake initiatives to promote greater environmental responsibility; and

Principle 9: encourage the development and diffusion of environmentally friendly technologies.

Anti-Corruption

Principle 10: Businesses should work against corruption in all its forms, including extortion and bribery.[14]

Similarly, the 2019 PwC CEO Survey showed that 72 percent of corporate leaders turn to the United Nation's Sustainable Development Goals in their reporting, recognizing that

---

[12] Sarah Murray, "Businesses Offer Their Expertise to Charity," *Financial Times*, April 25, 2017, https://www.ft.com/content/e2961964-1a29-11e7-a266-12672483791a.

[13] United Nations, "Global Compact," https://www.unglobalcompact.org.

[14] "The Ten Principles of the UN Global Compact," United Nations Global Impact, https://www.unglobalcompact.org/what-is-gc/mission/principles.

FIGURE 5.1
Strategy and
Society: The Link
between Competi-
tive Advantage
and Corporate
Social
Responsibility

Source: Michael E.
Porter and Mark R.
Kramer. Harvard
Business Review,
December 2006.

Generic Social Issues	Value Chain Impact	Competitive Context
• Social issues that are **not significantly affected** by the company's operations, nor materially affect its long-term competitiveness	• Social issues that are **significantly affected** by the company's activities in the ordinary course of business	• Social issues in the company's external environment that affect the **underlaying drivers of competitiveness** in the locations where the company operates

key constituencies ranging from shareholders to customers are looking to companies to wield their influence for good. At the same time, however, only 1 percent of leaders actually measure performance against these targets, underscoring just how nascent, in many ways, true, accountable corporate responsibility remains: companies recognize its importance but rigorously quantifying its impact is massively challenging.[15]

In shaping a CR strategy, a corporation ideally acknowledges and integrates the full spectrum of constituencies' "extra-financial" concerns—social, environmental, governance, and others—into its strategy and operations. The Global Reporting Initiative (GRI) describes five interdependent capital asset classes: financial, human, natural, social and technological.[16] *The Economist* has described CR as "part of what businesses need to do to keep up with (or, if possible, stay slightly ahead of) society's fast-changing expectations."[17] Developing an authentic CR strategy signals a corporation's intent to look beyond short-term financial returns and focus on long-term success and sustainability by managing those expectations. While this consideration often requires the executives of public companies to fight prevailing pressures to achieve strong quarterly results, increasing concrete data linking a commitment to CSR not only with bottom-line economic benefits, but also less tangible ones like increased innovation and greater talent retention, have made it far easier for business leaders to defend and remain committed to CSR principles.[18]

Despite these challenges, Harvard Business School guru Michael Porter and consultant Mark Kramer argue that CR is a strategy that, if implemented thoughtfully and thoroughly, can enhance a corporation's competitiveness. They analyze the interdependence of a company and society by using the same tools used to analyze overall competitive positioning and strategy development. In this way, CR can be used strategically to set an "affirmative [CR] agenda that produces maximum social benefit as well as gains for the business."[19] In 2011, Porter and Kramer published a seminal paper in the *Harvard Business Review* titled "Creating Shared Value". The problem, they say, lies in companies

---

[15] "PwC at The Davos Agenda 2021," PwC, https://www.pwc.com/gx/en/ceo-agenda/pwc-at-davos.html.

[16] "Carrots and Sticks: Promoting Transparency and Sustainability," Global Reporting Initiatives, 2010, https://www.globalreporting.org/resourcelibrary/Carrots-And-Sticks-Promoting-Transparency-And-Sustainability.pdf.

[17] "Do It Right," *The Economist*, Special Report: Corporate Social Responsibility, January 17, 2008.

[18] "CSR Performance and the Economic Value of Innovation," May 30, 2021, https://papers.ssrn.com/sol3/papers.cfm?abstract_id=3549827.

[19] Michael E. Porter and Mark R. Kramer, "Strategy & Society: The Link between Competitive Advantage and Corporate Social Responsibility," *Harvard Business Review*, December 2006.

that "view value creation narrowly, optimizing short-term financial performance in a bubble while missing the most important customer needs and ignoring the broader influences that determine their longer term success." In essence, they advocate for companies to espouse a broader definition of value—one that not only emphasizes profit, but also addresses the relationships that businesses have with the communities and environments they affect. A CR strategy should not be reactive but should *proactively* identify the social consequences of a company's entire value chain—the full spectrum of all of the activities it engages in when doing business—to pinpoint potential problems and opportunities wherever business and society intersect.[20]

KPMG's 2017 Survey on Corporate Responsibility found that businesses derived significant value from reporting on their CR initiatives through innovation, improved reputation, and improved communication within companies. Increasingly, companies have also begun reporting on such challenging topics as human rights and carbon footprints, denoting a shift in perspective that such topics are no longer the exclusive domain of governments or non-profits but rather also fall under the umbrella of corporate focus as well.[21]

To help companies with strong corporate responsibility platforms gain more credibility and recognition, an American nonprofit, B Lab, created the concept of the B corporation certification, with the "B" standing for "Benefit." B corporations are companies that meet "rigorous and independent standards of social and environmental performance, accountability, and transparency." Companies can apply to B Lab for B corporation status much in the same way that companies can apply to certifying bodies to achieve fair trade, organic, or LEED certification. In 2020, B Lab reported that more than 3,500 applicants across 70 countries had become B corporations, representing a 350 percent increase in certified B-corp companies in just six years. These companies represent 60 industries and include investment groups and construction firms. Consumer product companies such as King Arthur Flour, Patagonia, Method, Seventh Generation, Guayaki, EO Products, and Numi Organic Tea have achieved B corporation status.

On its website, B Lab lists the following reasons that companies may want to become a B corporation: "Differentiate your brand, maintain mission, save money [particularly via partnerships and discounts negotiated for members by B Lab], generate press, attract investors, improve and benchmark performance, and build a movement."[22]

In addition to its own certification, B Lab has taken its mission a step further and is working with state governments to legitimize the B corporation as a legal incorporation option. Similar to the C corporation, S corporation, limited liability company (LLC), and limited liability partnership (LLP), B corporation status reflects the organizational structure of a company, as well as the tax laws that affect it. As of 2020, 37 states, including Delaware, California, Hawaii, Virginia, Maryland, and Vermont recognized B corporations, and 4 states were considering legislation for recognizing them.[23] B Lab is pursuing this agenda because it believes that "current corporate law makes it difficult for businesses to consider employee, community, and environmental interests when making decisions."

[20] Michael E. Porter and Mark R. Kramer, "Creating Shared Value," *Harvard Business Review*, January–February 2011.

[21] "The KPMG Survey of Corporate Responsibility Reporting 2017," KPMG, https://home.kpmg/xx/en/home/insights/2017/10/the-kpmg-survey-of-corporate-responsibility-reporting-2017.html.

[22] www.bcorporation.net/.

[23] www.bcorporation.net/.

With the vast majority of states, either having already implemented or currently review-ing B corporation legislation, and with consumers agitating for more corporate responsibil-ity, it seems increasingly likely that corporations that do not make an effort to carve out their own CR niche will be left trailing their competition.

The Twenty-First Century's CR Surge

Corporations are increasingly aware that as they look out for society's best interests, they are actually looking out for their own interests, too, particularly in the long run. As Charles Handy notes, "business needs a sustainable planet for its own survival, for few companies are short-term entities; they want to do business again and again, over decades."[24] Businesses do not exist in a vacuum—they inevitably intersect with society and are mutually dependent for their survival. As *Financial Times* Assistant Editor Michael Skapinker argues, "companies cannot thrive in collapsing societies. Without political sta-bility, the future of business is grim. . . . Even in the most stable countries, companies need the community's approval to function. Opinion can turn against them fast: witness European consumers' distaste for genetically modified food, or the attacks on pharmaceu-tical companies over the pricing of AIDS drugs in Africa."[25] This argument includes corporations' need for an environmentally stable context in which to operate. Pressing environmental and social issues today—from climate change to income inequality—pose serious threats to "business-as-usual" operations. Sal Palmisano, Chairman of the Board and former CEO of IBM, describes the new expectations corporations must meet to survive in light of these risks: "All businesses today face a new reality. . . . Businesses now operate in an environment in which long-term societal concerns—in areas from diversity to equal opportunity, the environment and workforce policies—have been raised to the same level of public expectation as accounting practices and financial performances."[26]

Corporations slow to adapt to this new reality pay a price. An often-cited example is Walmart's 2004 discovery of a report prepared by McKinsey & Co., subsequently made public by walmartwatch.com, of a public education campaign devoted to challenging Walmart to become a better corporate citizen. The report revealed that up to 8 percent of Walmart consumers surveyed at the time had ceased shopping at the chain because of its reputation, which at the time included a perceived CR deficit.[27] Walmart's CEO at the time, Lee Scott, reacted with the comment: "We thought we could sit in Bentonville, take care of customers, take care of associates—and the world would leave us alone. It doesn't work that way any-more."[28] In a published statement, Scott also admitted Walmart had been caught off-guard by its entanglement in social and environmental issues: "To be honest, most of us at Walmart have been so busy minding the store that the way our critics have tried to turn us into a political symbol has taken us by surprise. But one thing we've learned from our critics . . . is

[24] Charles Handy, "What's a Business For?" *Harvard Business Review*, December 2002.

[25] Michael Skapinker, "Corporate Responsibility Is Not Quite Dead," *Financial Times*, February 12, 2008.

[26] Daniel Yankelovich, *Profit with Honor: The New Stage of Market Capitalism* (New Haven: Yale University Press, 2006), p. 9.

[27] Marc Gunther, "The Green Machine," *Fortune*, August 7, 2006.

[28] "The Debate over Doing Good," *BusinessWeek*, August 15, 2005.

that Walmart's size and industry leadership mean that people expect more from us. They're right to, and when it comes to playing our part . . . we intend to deliver."[29]

People today are expecting more. *The Economist* noted that shareholders, employees, and the public at large all now are turning to the business world to help solve problems that either governments are failing to address or businesses themselves helped create in the first place.[30] In 2010, IBM surveyed 1,500 global CEOs and found that 76 percent of the CEOs believed that they are expected by customers to increase their focus on social responsibility initiatives.[31] In today's world of heightened awareness of climate change, human rights, and scarcer resources, a corporation's "extra-financial" behavior—how well it treats its stakeholders and the world in which it operates—contributes greatly to its trust worthiness. Trust is not an abstract notion; it can have a significant impact on a company's bottom line. For example, the 2020 Trust Barometer Report published by the international public relations firm Edelman revealed that 64 percent of consumers viewed their "wallet as their vote" and would therefore not purchase a brand whose values did not align with their own—a 13 percent increase from 2017 survey participants. Moreover, the survey also found that trust was far more closely tied with ethics than with competence and, in fact, found that ethical drivers were three times more important to company trust than was competence.[32]

Notably, trust in major institutions and leaders generally is lower today than it was several decades ago, and the global coronavirus pandemic of 2020 and contentious political elections only further contributed to such instability. Notably, the 2020 Trust Barometer Report found that 66 percent of respondents did not have confidence that "current leaders will be able to address our country's challenges," though trust in CEOs stood slightly higher (at 51 percent) than trust in government leaders (42 percent).[33] Clearly, significant challenges persist with trust in general in today's society, though this also presents significant opportunity for business leaders to become even more influential change leaders by filling voids left by other traditional agents of change.

Corporate Responsibility and the Media

At the same time, widespread Internet access—with more than 4.6 billion people online as of 2020[34]—has redefined the notion of transparency for corporations. The Internet and social media platforms such as Twitter and Facebook now serve as powerful forums for like-minded people to educate and organize themselves. Individuals also now have a powerful tool for spreading once proprietary company information. It is easier than ever for constituents to monitor companies and to criticize them for everything from human rights

[29] Yankelovich, *Profit with Honor*, p. 10.

[30] "Big Business Is Beginning to Accept Broader Social Responsibilities," *The Economist*, August 24, 2019, https://www.economist.com/briefing/2019/08/22/big-business-is-beginning-to-accept-broader-social-responsibilities.

[31] "Capitalizing on Complexity: Insights from the Global Chief Executive Officer Study," IBM, 2010, www.935.ibm.com/services/c-suite/series-download.html.

[32] Edelman Trust Barometer 2020, https://www.edelman.com/sites/g/files/aatuss191/files/2020-01/2020%20Edelman%20Trust%20Barometer%20Global%20Report_LIVE.pdf.

[33] Ibid.

[34] "Global Digital Population as of January 2021," Statista, https://www.statista.com/statistics/617136/digital-population-worldwide.

violations that take place in a distant corner of a company's supply chain to carbon emissions that are in excess of local regulatory limitations. Perhaps most notably, social media platforms have enabled the sharing of nearly real-time videos and photo and audio evidence of all kinds of instances of corporate "irresponsibility." A passenger being violently dragged off an overbooked Delta Airlines flight, a woman humiliated and refused boarding access on American Airlines due to her clothing of choice, and two men arrested in a Starbucks for "trespassing" all prompted immediate backlash across Twitter, Facebook, and then more traditional media forums, spilling out into boycotts and even protests.[35] Thus, this era of transparency makes it nearly impossible for companies to hide any instance of unethical or ethically ambiguous action, compelling them to take a more proactive approach to how they manage their reputation and day to day activities.

Further attention is paid to corporations' CR efforts through a proliferation of socially responsible indices and rankings, such as the "Best in Social Responsibility" category on *Fortune*'s Most Admired Companies list. In 2009, *Newsweek* began publishing its annual Green Rankings to evaluate corporate responsibility initiatives. Many corporations today vie for inclusion on widely admired indices including the FTSE4Good Index—an index created by benchmarking company FTSE and designed specifically to help measure the performance of companies meeting globally recognized corporate responsibility standards.[36] Another index of such companies is the Dow Jones Sustainability World Index, which is comprised of the top 10 percent of 2,500 companies worldwide according to long-term economic, environmental, and social sustainability criteria.[37]

These communication channels and points of engagement directly influence constituencies' impressions of a corporation. A corporation lacking a CR strategy and a clear communication plan for its CR strategy runs the risk of losing control of its reputation in today's highly networked and highly scrutinized business environment.

The Upside of CR

Although CR is taking center stage thanks to a business environment of proliferating risks, adopting a socially responsible strategy can offer a compelling upside to corporations. Contrary to Friedman's claims, responsible business practices do not necessarily undermine a corporation's profit motive. In fact, many CEOs today describe acting responsibly as pragmatic—it makes good business sense. A well-executed CR strategy can translate into an array of benefits, including attracting and retaining customers, identifying and managing reputational risks, attracting the best-quality employees, and reducing costs. Lee Scott, former CEO of Walmart, explains the benefits to Walmart as follows: "By thinking about sustainability from our standpoint, it is really about how do you take the cost out, which is waste, whether it's through recycling, through less energy use in the store, through

[35] Lindsey Bever, "Doctor Who Was Dragged, Screaming, from United Airlines Flight Finally Breaks Silence," *The Washington Post*, April 9, 2019, https://www.washingtonpost.com/transportation/2019/04/09/doctor-who-was-dragged-screaming-united-airlines-flight-finally-breaks-silence.

[36] www.ftse.com/Indices/FTSE4Good_Index_Series/index.jsp.

[37] www.sustainability-index.com.

construction techniques we're using, through the supply chain. All of those things are simply the creation of waste."[38] Cutting costs allows Walmart to charge even lower prices, which supports its mission of helping customers to "Save Money. Live better." At the same time, however, companies ought to be wary of so obviously embracing CR initiatives for purely bottom line benefit, as this can actually detract from and even eliminate some other benefits otherwise realized when attention to CR comes from a more authentic, less profit-motivated position. Describing their research in a January 2019 HBR piece, Stephen Meier and Lea Cassar noted that, "If employees think their company is using CSR initiatives instrumentally—trying to engage in prosocial activities only to benefit from it—then they'll react negatively and put in less effort. In other words, while these initiatives will benefit society, they will backfire for companies if people think they're being used for the wrong reasons."[39]

The scale and nature of the benefits from CR activities for an organization can vary depending on the business and are often difficult to quantify, though increased efforts are being made to link CR initiatives directly to financial performance. In the meantime, a strong business case exists that CR positively affects the bottom line.

Reputation Risk Management

Managing reputational risk is a central part of any robust corporate communication strategy. As Berkshire Hathaway CEO Warren Buffett once famously noted: "It takes 20 years to build a reputation and five minutes to ruin it. If you think about that, you'll do things differently." Corruption scandals or environmental accidents can devastate a carefully honed corporate reputation in a matter of days. These events can also draw unwanted attention from regulators, courts, governments, and media. Building a genuine culture of "doing the right thing" within a corporation—the foundation of any genuine CR strategy—can help offset these risks.

Brand Differentiation

In crowded marketplaces, companies strive for a unique selling proposition that can separate them from the competition in consumers' minds. Corporate responsibility can help build customer loyalty based on distinctive ethical values. Several major brands, such as Stonyfield, Seventh Generation, TOMS shoes, and The Body Shop, are built on such ethical values. Former GE CEO Jeffrey Immelt emphasized the importance of differentiating a brand by staying ahead of issues and evolving with ever-changing constituency concerns: "When society changes its mind, you better be in front of it and not behind it, and [sustainability] is an issue on which society has changed its mind. As CEO, my job is to get out in front of it because if you're not out in front of it, you're going to get [ploughed] under."[40]

---

[38] "Alan Murray," *The Wall Street Journal*, March 24, 2008.

[39] Stephan Meier and Lea Cassar, "Stop Talking About How CSR Helps Your Bottom Line," *Harvard Business Review*, January 31, 2018, https://hbr.org/2018/01/stop-talking-about-how-csr-helps-your-bottom-line.

[40] Morgen Witzel, "A Case for More Sustainability," *Financial Times*, July 2, 2008.

Talent Attraction and Retention

As we discuss in more detail later in the chapter, a CR program can aid in employee recruitment and retention. It can also help improve the image of a company among employees, particularly when they become involved through fundraising activities, community volunteering, or helping shape the company's CR strategy itself. Using these tactics to strengthen goodwill and trust among present and future employees can translate into reduced costs and greater worker productivity. According to a 2016 Cone Communications study, 75 percent of millennials are willing to take a pay cut to work for a socially responsible company, with 55 percent of the general workforce also citing their willingness to trade pay for purpose.[41]

License to Operate

Corporations want to avoid interference in their business through taxation or regulations. By taking substantive voluntary steps, they may be able to persuade governments and the wider public that they are taking current issues such as health and safety, diversity, or the environment seriously and thus avoid intervention. Expenses today can result in future cost savings or increased revenue streams from new, socially responsible products and services. Consider DuPont saving more than $2 billion from energy use reductions since 1990—an upfront investment that, years later, continues to pay in spades.[42] In the words of Abby Joseph Cohen, formerly chief investment strategist at Goldman Sachs, "Companies are taking a broader view that allows them to see that a cost today may reduce future liabilities, and the reduction of those future liabilities in turn has a positive impact on their cost of capital."[43] Acting before regulations force them to can position corporations as well-respected leaders in responsibility and sustainability.

CR Critics

Despite mounting evidence in support of CR's benefits, followers of Milton Friedman and others continue to argue there is no place for social responsibility in business. These critics rail against CR as detracting from a corporation's commercial purpose and effectiveness, thereby inhibiting free markets. In this view, responsibility and profitability constitute a zero-sum game; corporations are for-profit institutions whose primary purpose is profit and who lose competitiveness through altruistic, profit-diminishing behavior. Some critics claim CR is little more than a public relations strategy, in which companies cherry-pick their good activities to showcase and ignore the others, creating an inaccurate image of a socially or environmentally responsible company. Others contest that CR programs are often undertaken in an effort to distract the public from the ethical questions posed by their core operations. In general, however, constituencies are increasingly calling for more corporate responsibility and demanding that companies rise to the occasion.

---

[41] "Three-Quarters of Millennials Would Take a Pay Cut to Work for a Socially Responsible Company, According to Research From Cone Communications," Cision, November 2, 2016, https://www.prnewswire.com/news-releases/three-quarters-of-millennials-would-take-a-pay-cut-to-work-for-a-socially-responsible-company-according-to-research-from-cone-communications-300355311.html.

[42] Porter and Kramer, "Strategy & Society."

[43] Stephanie Strom, "Make Money, Save the World," *The New York Times*, May 6, 2007.

CR and Corporate Reputation

As we move on from our overview of CR and its general benefits, we will focus our discussion on one central question: what kind of contribution can responsible business practices make to the strengthening of a corporation's reputation? Research from MIT Sloan has found that investment in corporate responsibility can serve as a greater "insurance policy" regarding corporate reputation more than almost any other investment. Researchers noted, "The results of our survey showed that the company's reputation for corporate social responsibility had a greater effect on consumers' willingness to overlook negative information about the company than the company's reputation for being customer-oriented (defined as the extent to which a business is viewed as being caring and attentive to customer needs) or for being oriented toward service quality. These results suggest that a dollar invested in corporate social responsibility initiatives would buy greater insurance against negative information than a dollar invested in either service-quality orientation or customer orientation."[44] Studies have also confirmed that the average person's decisions about what to buy and with whom to do business are influenced by a company's reputation for social responsibility. In turn, CR has become a critical means to build trust with corporate constituents. College-educated Americans today have begun viewing social responsibility as more important than an overall corporate brand or financial performance, second only to the quality of their products and services when deciding which companies to trust.

Although the evidence for engaging in corporate responsibility initiatives is compelling, companies should be aware that instituting and publicizing CR activities in an effort to boost reputation can backfire. A *McKinsey Quarterly* article presented research that found that companies with poor perceived product quality can actually be *hurt* by publicizing their CR efforts because consumers then assume that the company is focusing on the wrong issues. The study's authors recommend that companies follow these three steps: (1) "don't hide market motives" (consumers understand a need for profit), (2) "serve stakeholders' true needs," and (3) "test your progress."[45]

We now examine several key corporate constituencies—customers, investors, employees, NGOs, and environmentalists—to take a closer look at each group's evolving expectations of corporate responsibility and what corporations can and should be doing in response to strengthen their reputations.

Consumer Values and Expectations: Taking Matters into Their Own Hands

Millions of everyday consumers possess the unprecedented power to determine the fates of corporations. In his book *Supercapitalism*, former U.S. Labor Secretary Robert Reich contends that the average person had an easier time expressing values as citizens through democracy 30 years ago.[46] He argues that today many use their role as consumers to

---

[44] "Does Social Responsibility Help Protect a Company's Reputation?" MIT Sloan, March 23, 2011, https://sloanreview.mit.edu/article/does-social-responsibility-help-protect-a-companys-reputation.

[45] CB Bhattacharya, Daniel Korschun, and Sankar Sen, "What Really Drives Value in Corporate Responsibility," *McKinsey Quarterly*, December 2011, www.mckinseyquarterly.com/What_really_drives_value_in_corporate_ responsibility_2895.

[46] Matt Woolsey, "Supercapitalism: Transforming Business," *Forbes*, September 6, 2007.

communicate those same values at the cash register, and we have seen this reflected in the way consumers perceive their purchase decisions, with 64 percent respondents to the 2020 Trust Barometer survey agreeing with the sentiment that "My wallet is my vote."[47] We also see more individuals taking matters of philanthropy into their own hands. Founded in 2005, Kiva—a California-based company that connects lenders and borrowers from around the world—has amassed some 1.9 million lenders who make online donations in $25 increments. These lenders have funded more than 3.7 million borrowers from Tanzania to Tajikistan with $US 1.489 billion lent thus far. On its website, Kiva boasts a 95 percent repayment rate. Their work has sparked a new model of philanthropy, connecting donors and recipients, eliminating the middleman, and, in the process, empowering individuals.[48] At the same time, consumers' personal values are reflecting a greater individual commitment to responsibility. In 2018, Americans gave over $US 410 billion to charities, an historic high.[49]

Compelling evidence exists that consumers are willing to use this individual empowerment to act on their values—reaching into their pocketbooks to pay more for the sake of corporate responsibility. Consider fair trade coffee, which is priced at a premium compared with regular, noncertified coffee. The International Fair Trade Association defines fair trade as incorporating "concern for the social, economic and environmental well-being of marginalized small producers . . . not maximiz[ing] profit at their expense."[50] Despite the higher price tag, demand for fair trade products continues to grow; global sales reached €9.8 billion in 2018, up nearly €7 billion from a decade earlier in 2008.[51]

Organic food—viewed by many as better for their health, for the health of farm workers, and for the environment—has experienced a similar explosion, benefiting organic food retailers such as Whole Foods. The U.S. sales of organic food and beverages have grown from $US 1 billion in 1990 to $US 50 billion in 2019.[52] The United States had over 14,000 certified organic farms in 2016, representing a 56 percent increase from 2011, according to the latest data available from the U.S. Department of Agriculture.[53]

In addition to going the extra mile to pay more for socially responsible products, consumers have been willing to punish corporations for their lack of corporate responsibility. Though research is inconclusive regarding the efficacy of boycotts and avoiding products due to a company's (real or perceived) lack of commitment to CR, the frequency of consumer participation in these practices has increased over the years.[54] The practice dates

[47] Edelman Trust Barometer 2020, https://www.edelman.com/sites/g/files/aatuss191/files/2020-01/2020%20Edelman%20Trust%20Barometer%20Global%20Report_LIVE.pdf.

[48] Kiva, https://www.kiva.org.

[49] *Giving USA 2018*, https://givingusa.org.

[50] Andrew Downie, "Fair Trade in Bloom," *The New York Times*, October 2, 2007.

[51] "Revenue of Fairtrade International Products Worldwide from 2004 to 2018 (in billion euros)," Statista, October 2019, https://www.statista.com/statistics/271354/revenue-of-fair-trade-products-worldwide-since-2004.

[52] Organic Food Sales in the United States from 2005 to 2019," Statista, June 2020, https://www.statista.com/statistics/196952/organic-food-sales-in-the-us-since-2000.

[53] Kristen Bialik and Kristi Walker, "Organic Farming Is on the Rise in the U.S.," Pew Research Center, January 10, 2019, https://www.pewresearch.org/fact-tank/2019/01/10/organic-farming-is-on-the-rise-in-the-u-s.

[54] "When Do Consumer Boycotts Work?" *The New York Times*, February 7, 2017, https://www.nytimes.com/roomfordebate/2017/02/07/when-do-consumer-boycotts-work.

back to 1830, if not earlier, when the National Negro Convention called for a boycott of slave-produced goods and has prompted shifts in corporate behavior throughout the past two centuries.[55] The Rainforest Action Network established its influence as an NGO by orchestrating a boycott of Burger King in 1987 for importing beef from countries where rainforests are destroyed to provide pasture for cattle.[56] Burger King's sales subsequently declined by 12 percent, prompting Burger King to cancel $35 million worth of beef contracts in Central America and announce an end to rainforest beef imports.[57] Or consider Shell reeling from its poor handling of its 1995 decision to dispose of an oil storage platform that it no longer needed, the Brent Spar, by simply sinking it in the Atlantic Ocean. Environmental NGO Greenpeace staged protests, using vivid and emotional language, prompting a widespread boycott of Shell stations in northern Europe, with sales volumes in Germany dropping as much as 40 percent in June 1995.[58]

Not only must corporations be aware of the changing values and behavior of consumers, they also must remember that expectations of corporate responsibility are far from homogeneous across the globe, differing to a sometimes large degree across countries, regions, and hemispheres. Monsanto, the world's largest seed company, suffered for failing to recognize the strong opposition to genetically modified (GM) foods prevailing in Europe, based on fears that GM crops can create animal and human health issues and take a negative environmental toll. Despite soaring food prices, Europeans appear to be particularly apprehensive about the use of such crop technologies,[59] whereas similar concerns are far less prevalent in Monsanto's home base in the United States.

Investor Pressures: The Growth of Socially Responsible Investing

Earlier in the chapter, we discussed Milton Friedman's argument that there is no place for social responsibility in for-profit entities. In this view, executives are merely agents of investors, the individuals who own the corporation.[60] How does Friedman's argument reconcile with investors' increased use of capital markets as a mechanism to encourage socially responsible corporate behavior? Investors today are demonstrating an increased interest in socially responsible companies, rewarding them by using CR more frequently as part of their criteria to invest. Almost two-thirds of Americans cite a company's record of social responsibility as "an influential factor when making a decision to purchase stock or invest in a company."[61] As a result, approximately 25 percent of money professionally managed in the United States today can be categorized as socially responsible investing (SRI),[62] including social or environmental goals and an investment strategy that employs screening, divesting, or shareholder activism. As *Fortune* magazine describes, this

[55] Leo Hickman, "Should I Support a Consumer Boycott?" *The Guardian* (UK), October 4, 2005.

[56] Rainforest Action Network, www.ran.org.

[57] Ibid.

[58] David P. Baron, "Facing-Off in Public," *Stanford Business*, August 2003.

[59] Sam Cage, "High Food Prices May Cut Opposition to Genetically Modified Food," *Reuters*, July 8, 2008.

[60] Friedman, "The Social Responsibility of Business."

[61] "Rethinking Corporate Social Responsibility."

[62] Karen Demasters, "SRI Used in 25% of Professionally Managed U.S. Assets, Report Says," *Financial Advisor*, October 31, 2018, https://www.fa-mag.com/news/sri-strategies-affect-one-quarter-of-investments--us-sif-said-41640.html.

development constitutes a multitrillion-dollar "wager that socially responsible companies will outperform companies that don't engage a wide array of stakeholders, from shareholders and customers to employees and activists, in an ongoing conversation about what can be done better."[63] High-profile investment management shops driven by socially responsible missions are springing up, even from within more traditional, non-social impact investing firms, such as TPG's $4 billion Rise Fund, which includes involvement from the likes of Jeff Skoll and John Kerry. Notably, the fund is pursuing "market rate" returns in conjunction with social benefits, viewing impact investing not as a merely altruistic strategy but one that can achieve top quartile returns. Perhaps most importantly, they have also begun to tackle the challenge of quantifying impact—a massive task in large part due to the very philosophical nature of defining impact. The firm implemented a framework that generates an "impact multiple of money" (IMM), a measure of social value created by a company per equity dollar invested, with a commitment to pass on those companies that do not reach the appropriate projected IMM.[64]

Impact investing as a field has grown considerably over the past decade, reaching a total global market size of nearly $720 billion. Importantly, impact investing itself is an umbrella term, representing investors pursuing a range of returns (from market rate to sub-market) and utilizing a range of financial tools (from private debt to publicly traded equity to private equity). Similarly, the range of participants in impact investing is broad, encompassing firms from JP Morgan to UBS to Goldman Sachs. In their 2020 annual report, the Global Impact Investing Network, whose members collectively manage nearly $500 billion in assets, affirmed that the primary motivations for investors making impact investments stand rooted in impact, with nearly all respondents (87 percent) to their survey considering both impact to be "central to their mission" and their "commitment as responsible investors" as "very important" motivators. At the same time, however, two-thirds of respondents noted that they sought risk-adjusted, market-rate returns for their assets, providing further evidence that the perceived tradeoff between profit and purpose is fading away.[65]

Responsibility Inside and Out: Employee Involvement in CR

In Chapter 7 on internal communications, we underscore the essential role employees play as brand ambassadors for a corporation. The same holds true in the implementation of a CR strategy. The next generation of corporate leaders is actively searching for responsible practices in corporate track records as they recruit and pick a place to start their careers. Top business schools around the world are offering a greater number of corporate responsibility, values-based leadership, and sustainable enterprise courses and programs, addressing business students' desire not just to work hard but to do some good at the same time.[66] Net Impact, an association of 130,000 business professionals working to improve corporate responsibility, reports that it has active chapters at 90 percent of top MBA campuses.

[63] Telis Demos, "Beyond the Bottom Line," *Fortune*, October 23, 2006.

[64] Vikram Gandhi, "The Rise Fund: TPG Bets Big on Impact," Harvard Business School Case, February 2018, https://www.hbs.edu/faculty/Pages/item.aspx?num=54014.

[65] "Annual Impact Investor Survey 2020," GIN, https://thegiin.org/assets/GIIN%20Annual%20Impact%20Investor%20Survey%202020.pdf.

[66] Strom, "Make Money, Save the World."

Once a corporation has attracted top talent, engaging those employees from all levels of the organization in a company's CR efforts is imperative. Employees are often the primary spokespeople for a corporation, responsible for much word-of-mouth information shared and impressions formed. Furthermore, making employees central to a CR strategy can boost employee goodwill and morale, decrease turnover, and increase operational efficiencies by encouraging employees to identify opportunities for sustainability and cost-savings.[67] Many corporations are missing out on this upside—though more than three-quarters of executives say corporate citizenship fits their companies' traditions and values, only 36 percent report talking to their employees about corporate citizenship.[68] IBM serves as an example of a company successfully engaging its employees in CR issues, hosting regular brainstorming sessions focused on corporate responsibility and sustainability. It often refers to its now famous, and still largest, first "InnovationJam" held in 2006.[69] During this InnovationJam, more than 150,000 IBM employees, family members, clients, and partners in 104 countries joined in an online conversation on IBM's global intranet (www.ibm.com/ibm/think-2007). Driven primarily by IBM employees, more than 46,000 observations and ideas were posted on how to translate IBM's technologies into economic and broader societal value. IBM allocated $100 million to exploring 10 promising business opportunities suggested, including creating access to branchless banking for the underprivileged masses around the world and working with utility companies to increase power grid and infrastructure efficiency.

Stanley Litow, IBM's vice president of corporate citizenship and corporate affairs and president of IBM's Foundation, further explains IBM's approach to corporate responsibility: "In the *Harvard Business Review*, Rosabeth M. Kanter described the IBM approach as going from 'spare change to real change.' With the spare change approach, the company makes X amount of dollars and it gives its spare change back to the community, with the goal being generosity. But with the real change approach, you take what is most valuable to the company—in our case, our innovation technology, and the skill and talent of our people—and contribute it into the community. The real change approach is strategic, it's a systemic part of the way we operate as a company, and that is the case for tie-in to business strategy. In the end, it's even more generous to do it that way."[70]

Strong evidence exists that the general public now views genuinely responsible behavior as starting *inside* the four walls of an organization. A year after leaders from the Business Roundtable redefined the purpose of a corporation as one extending beyond responsibility to shareholders but to society more generally, participants in a Harris Poll noted progress in the way corporations treat their employees, but with considerable room for improvement. When asked how much responsibility companies have when it comes to impact on a range of constituencies (ranging from shareholders to the general public), nearly eight in ten respondents reported that companies have equal responsibility to all stakeholders;

---

[67] Gabrielle McDonald, "In-house Climate Change: Use Communication to Engage Employees in Environmental Initiatives. (The Green Revolution)," *Communication World*, November–December 2007.

[68] "Time to Get Real: Closing the Gap between Rhetoric and Reality, The State of Corporate Citizenship 2007," Boston College Center for Corporate Citizenship, December 2007.

[69] www.collaborationjam.com.

[70] "From Spare Change to Real Change: An Interview with Stanley Litow," *LEADERS*, April 2010, www.leadersmag.com/issues/2010.2_Apr/Making%20a%20Difference/Litow.html.

and additionally, when forced to rank-order the constituencies to which companies are most beholden, the health and well-being of workers was consistently ranked first.[71] At the same time, however, 72 percent of those surveyed believed companies had a positive impact on shareholders, but only 47 percent believed companies had a positive impact on the financial well-being of their employees.[72] Clearly considerable room remains for improvement, then, not only in the treatment of employees but also in communicating the steps taken to take care of one's workforce with the public.

Building a Values-Based Culture

A critical element of valuing employees is codifying corporate beliefs—including those pertaining to employees and other constituencies—in a set of corporate values for each employee to embody. A clear and prominent set of values or code of ethics instilled in employees should ideally serve as a navigational compass for everyday work activities. Employees who live and breathe their company's values are far less likely to engage in legal or ethical breaches. A strong, values-based culture can also contribute to an organization's competitive edge, increasing employee pride, loyalty, and willingness to go the extra mile for the sake of the corporation's mission.[73] Former IBM chairman Thomas J. Watson described the importance of corporate values and strong employee faith in them in this way:

> Consider any great organization—one that has lasted over the years—and I think you will find that it owes its resiliency, not to its form of organization or administrative skills, but to the power of what we call beliefs and the appeal these beliefs have for its people. This, then, is my thesis: I firmly believe that any organization, in order to survive and achieve success, must have a sound set of beliefs on which it premises all its policies and actions. Next, I believe that the most important single factor in corporate success is faithful adherence to those beliefs. And finally, I believe that, if an organization is to meet the challenges of a changing world, it must be prepared to change everything about itself except those beliefs as it moves through corporate life.[74]

For a values-based corporate culture to take root and thrive, the tone must be set from the top. Warren Buffett, CEO of Berkshire Hathaway and noted philanthropist, is adamant about this, taking an active role in clearly communicating his ethical expectations to his employees. Using blunt, everyday language—and analogies that any employee can easily identify with—he explicitly states intolerance for ethical wrongdoings, citing ethics as more important than profits. Most important, Buffett creates a clear connection between the individual actions of employees and corporate culture, in turn shaping the organization's overall reputation. Buffett emphasized this personal accountability in a now legendary September 2006 memo to Berkshire Hathaway employees: "Your attitude on such matters,

---

[71] "A Year After the Business Roundtable Redefined the Purpose of a Corporation, Americans See Progress But Opportunity for Treating Workers Better," The Harris Poll, https://theharrispoll.com/a-year-after-the-business-roundtable-redefined-the-purpose-of-a-corporation-americans-see-progress-but-opportunity-for-treating-workers-better.

[72] Ibid.

[73] Francis Joseph Aguilar, *General Managers in Action: Policies and Strategies*, 2nd ed. (Oxford: Oxford University Press, 1992).

[74] Ibid.

expressed by behavior as well as words, will be the most important factor in how the culture of your business develops. And culture, more than rule books, determines how an organization behaves. Thanks for your help on this. Berkshire's reputation is in your hands."

Research underscores the enormous impact corporate leaders have on the atmosphere of a workplace and the values and behavior encouraged within it. The 2020 Global Business Ethics Survey found that globally more than one in five workers have felt pressure to compromise their organization's ethics standards, policies or the law. Notably, top-down leadership appears to have a strong impact on the behavior of those in the workplace. Those in workplaces where leadership's commitment to values and ethical behavior was viewed as weak were three times more likely to report pressure to act unethically or illegally.[75]

Ensuring that employees are striking a healthy balance in their lives is another important piece of building an ethical culture. Deloitte's Ethics & Workplace survey also found that an overwhelming 91 percent of employed adults polled claim they are more likely to behave ethically in the workplace when they maintain a good work–life balance.[76] A positive working environment reduces stress and frustration levels, thereby diminishing the likelihood of cutting corners to meet unrealistic demands. It is disturbing to consider research by corporate trend-tracking service DYG SCAN pointing to a pattern of employees no longer believing in employer loyalty, concern, and personal commitment.[77] Investing in employees to foster a sense of mutual accountability and encouraging the free airing of issues without fear of reprimand or retaliation can go a long way toward strengthening an ethical culture.[78] Taking another step to provide employees with resources—such as ethics training to prepare them for dilemmas or a hotline to call if one occurs—can be critical to keep a corporate culture aligned with the strong values that must underpin all successful corporate citizenship efforts.

Strategic Engagement: The Continued Influence of NGOs

In today's business context of precarious trust in corporations, nongovernmental organizations continue to rank among the most trusted institutions in the world. Edelman's 2020 Trust Barometer reveals the gap between the level of global trust in NGOs (70 percent) and trust in government (59 percent).[79] As Edelman describes: "NGOs have moved quickly into the 'trust-void' and have taken advantage of the downward spiral in public perceptions of government, media, [and] corporations . . . 'thought-leaders' are two to three times as likely to trust an NGO to do what is right compared to large companies because they are seen as being motivated by morals rather than just profit."[80] Making

[75] "Global Business Ethics Survey," ECI, 2020, https://www.ethics.org/wp-content/uploads/Global-Business-Ethics-Survey-2020-Report-1-Final.pdf.

[76] Allen, "Creating a Culture of Values."

[77] Yankelovich, *Profit with Honor*, p. 43.

[78] David Gebler, "Is Your Culture a Risk Factor?" *Working Values Ltd.*, September 2005.

[79] Edelman Trust Barometer 2020, https://www.edelman.com/sites/g/files/aatuss191/files/2020-01/2020%20Edelman%20Trust%20Barometer%20Global%20Report_LIVE.pdf.

[80] "Non-Government Organizations More Trusted Than the Media, Most-Respected Corporations or Government," http://developmentgateway.org, p. 2.

active use of social networking sites including Facebook and video-sharing sites such as YouTube has enabled NGOs to recruit thousands if not millions of new supporters on the Internet in recent years to spread their agendas with unprecedented speed and volume.

In recent years, the public has come to trust NGOs more than they trust corporations or governments, particularly pertaining to CR issues such as health, the environment, and human rights.[81] According to one global advocacy group focused on sustainability: "[NGOs] are the moral compass and ethical watchdogs against the forces of government and capitalism that seek to despoil the planet and crush the faceless majority."[82] These voluntary organizations rally around a particular cause and hold corporations accountable for their behavior, launching campaigns against them whenever they fall short of expectations. The pervasive use of the Internet and its communication tools such as Twitter and Facebook has only strengthened and lengthened the reach of NGO communications, enabling local organizations to voice their messages to a global audience and pose an even greater threat to corporate reputations. Organizations including Amnesty International, Greenpeace, the National Wildlife Federation, Oxfam, the Rainforest Action Network, Friends of the Earth, Sierra Club, and Public Citizen maintain active blogs to spread messages and engage new supporters on CR and sustainability.[83] As a result, the chairman of Goldman Sachs International and former chairman of BP, Peter Sutherland, places NGOs alongside multinational corporations in terms of world influence: "The only organizations now capable of global thought and action—the ones who will conduct the most important dialogues of the 21st century—are the multinational corporations and the NGOs."[84]

For the most part, NGOs have achieved great success in controlling this dialogue, proactively engaging corporations to effect the change they seek. As Randall Hayes, founder of the Rainforest Action Network (RAN), explains: "If you [as an NGO] are not talking to business, you are just preaching to the choir. The real change to protect the environment is going to come from the business sector; we can't depend on government regulation to solve our problems."[85] Therefore, NGOs pick their targets with great care and in recent years have recognized the rising power of the capital markets to influence responsible corporate behavior. In 2000, RAN launched an ongoing advocacy campaign against Citigroup and its environmental record, staging visible demonstrations at corporate headquarters in New York, organizing consumer boycotts, and running a full-page ad in the *International Herald Tribune* that depicted then CEO Sandy Weill as an environmental villain.[86] In 2003, Citigroup agreed to meet with RAN to discuss environmental strategy, resulting in what RAN dubs the most far-reaching commitment made by any bank to date.[87] Mounting pressure from RAN and other NGOs has served as the catalyst for more than 80 financial institutions to sign on to

---

[81] Edelman Trust Barometer 2015.

[82] International Foundation for the Conservation of Natural Resources Fisheries Committee, "IFCNR Special Report: How NGOs Became So Powerful," February 20, 2002.

[83] "Corporate Social Responsibility and Sustainability in the Blogosphere," Edelman, 2006.

[84] Speech by David Grayson, "The Public Affairs of Civil Society," January 26, 2001.

[85] SustainAbility, Global Compact, and United National Environment Programme, "The 21st Century NGO: In the Market for Change," June 2003, p. 30.

[86] Matthew Yeomans, "Taking the Earth into Account," *Time Europe* 165, no. 19 (May 9, 2005).

[87] Christopher Wright, "For Citigroup, Greening Starts with Listening," *Ecosystem Marketplace*, April 4, 2006.

the Equator Principles—a clear and consistent standard for assessing and managing environmental and social risk in project financing—since June 2003.[88] Various NGOs targeting a number of banks simultaneously was a highly effective tactic, breeding a sense of CR competition among leading financial institutions to trump one another's commitments, thereby making it much more difficult for any socially or environmentally damaging project to slip through the cracks and gain financing.

The widespread influence of NGOs reaffirms the need for corporations to think strategically about relationships with these organizations when building and executing a CR strategy. NGOs have the power to wreak havoc with eye-catching, direct, and powerful communication campaigns. As a result, corporations must identify opportunities to collaborate with NGOs and establish relationships before a crisis strikes or negative press airs. The CR team within a corporation should attempt to anticipate the mind-set of NGOs, pinpointing issues of mutual concern from their critical vantage point. Companies must not only be poised to discuss these issues with their NGO critics but should also foster ongoing dialogues on CR topics with all constituents to gauge existing concerns and communicate the efforts they are making to address them. Finally, and perhaps most critically, a company's corporate communication team should be actively involved in crafting the NGO and overall CR communication strategy to ensure consistency across all messages shared with internal and external constituents.

Being Green: The Corporation's Responsibility to the Environment

Earlier in the chapter, we described corporations as requiring a healthy and prosperous society to exist. In 2006, former U.S. Vice President and Nobel Peace Prize recipient Al Gore's highly acclaimed documentary *An Inconvenient Truth* revealed that environmental stability is not something to be taken for granted. The film vividly depicted the environmental concerns of this century and bred increasing anxiety over climate change among millions of consumers. In turn, increasing evidence exists that constituents are rewarding companies that are environmentally responsible, doing their bit to preserve the planet. A recent study found that 72 percent of global consumers expect corporations to take action to preserve and sustain the environment.[89] Importantly, those in the C-suite no longer seem to view environmental responsibility as a "nice to have" but rather as a "need to have," increasingly recognizing that the futures of their companies are tied with the future of the environment. According to the 2019 United Nation Global Compact-Accenture CEO Survey on Sustainability, 44 percent of CEOs see a carbon net-zero future for their company in the next 10 years. Notably, movement toward a net-zero future is considerably technologically driven, with such actions as migrating to the cloud considerably reducing carbon emissions while resulting in 30–40 percent total cost of ownership savings, further underscoring the bottom-line links between ESG and profitability.[90]

Those companies that act as environmental leaders can seize an opportunity to truly differentiate their brands in a sea of corporations claiming corporate responsibility. Coca-Cola is assuming such a leadership position in the water conversation arena and in the

---

[88] www.equator-principles.com, retrieved July 2, 2015.

[89] 2010 Edelman goodpurpose Study.

[90] "UN Global Compact-Accenture Strategy 2019 CEO Study," UN, 2019, https://www.unglobalcompact.org/library/5715.

process is protecting the resource most critical to its production process and future profitability. In June 2007, Coca-Cola announced its investment of $US 20 million over five years to improve global water conservation, partnering with the World Wildlife Fund to preserve seven of the world's major rivers.[91] Since then, Coca-Cola's commitment to water conservation, and the returns on its efforts, have only increased, with the company now having reached its goal of returning 100 percent of the water they use to create their drinks, ultimately regenerating more drinkable water in the process.[92] By 2025, the World Wildlife Fund anticipates two-thirds of the world's population will face water shortages,[93] a dangerous prospect for Coke. As Neville Isdell, then CEO of Coca-Cola, stated bluntly during his announcement of the company's long-term goal to become "water neutral" by returning all water used in its beverages and their production to nature and communities through conservation, recycling, and other programs: "Water is the main ingredient in nearly every beverage that we make. Without access to safe water supply, our business simply cannot exist."[94]

Coca-Cola is also making efforts to repair the trust of certain stakeholders damaged by prior water controversies, most notably when the NGO Centre for Science and Environment alleged that certain company products contained trace amounts of pesticide residues in India in 2003. Jeff Seabright, Coca-Cola's Vice President of Environment and Water Resources, admits that the company's initial public relations during the crisis was ineffective and that the company has used the episode as a valuable lesson that perception is just important as reality in successfully running a responsible and sustainable operation. In Seabright's words: "If people are perceiving that we're using water at their expense, that's not a sustainable operation. We sell a brand. For us, having goodwill in the community is an important thing."[95] Looking to the future, Chinese consumption represents significant revenue opportunities for Coca-Cola and countless other multinational corporations. To protect the opportunities in this market—riddled with environmental problems—Coke has partnered with NGOs to boost environmental education and encourage river conservation and rainwater harvesting in the country.

With increased attention to corporations' environmental efforts, NGOs and the general public will be watching to see whether companies deliver on their lofty promises. Consider FedEx—an environmental leader awarded a Clean Air Excellence prize by the Environmental Protection Agency in 2004 for its plans to replace its 30,000 medium-duty trucks over the next 10 years with clean-burning hybrid trucks, sparing the atmosphere 250,000 tons of greenhouse gases annually.[96] The overnight shipping leader has not fully delivered on its commitment; by 2013, FedEx reported that only 577 all-electric and hybrid vehicles were in use, representing a tiny percentage of its fleet.[97] As of October 2020, the company continued

[91] Dune Lawrence, "Coca-Cola to Spend $20 Million on Water Conservation," *International Herald Tribune*, June 6, 2007.

[92] "Water Stewardship," The Coca-Cola Company, https://www.coca-colacompany.com/sustainable-business/water-stewardship.

[93] Ling Woo Liu, "Water Pressure," *Time*, June 12, 2008.

[94] Ibid.

[95] Ibid.

[96] Ibid.; Elgin, "Little Green Lies."

[97] http://about.van.fedex.com/2013-environment-efficiency.

to only report 2012 data regarding its success in meeting its sustainability objectives regarding electric and hybrid vehicles, further underscoring the gap between the company's public commitments and their actions. As FedEx VP for environmental affairs and sustainability Mitch Jackson explained, profitability is the underlying reason for the lack of follow-through: "We do have a fiduciary responsibility to our shareholders. We can't subsidize the development of this technology for our competitors."[98]

As we move on to discussing best practices in CR communications, we will highlight the importance of backing promises and claims of responsibility with bona fide action to maintain and strengthen trust and goodwill with increasingly conscious constituents.

Communicating about Corporate Responsibility

The strongest of CR strategies are lacking if they do not include a clear communications component. Although CR may be housed in varying areas of an organization—within the human resources, business development, or corporate communication departments of an organization, for example—corporate communicators must be actively engaged in CR messaging to ensure consistency and integration with the overall communication and reputation management strategy. We now review a number of key considerations a corporation should keep in mind when building and communicating its CR strategy.

A Two-Way Street: Creating an Ongoing Dialogue

As we discussed earlier in the chapter, tracking and responding to constituency expectations is a key component of a CR strategy's success, enabling a company to stay ahead of the changing ethos and, in the process, strengthen its reputation. A primary way to monitor constituency expectations is by fostering an ongoing and active dialogue with consumers, shareholders, and the general public about the social and environmental role companies should play. The 2018 Edelman Earned Brand study found that nearly two-thirds (64 percent) of consumers will buy or boycott a brand because of its position on a social or political issue. A lack of dialogue can lead to a lack of awareness of external opinions on issues of corporate responsibility, and corporations similarly need to be proactive in understanding the social and environmental concerns of their consumers, as opposed to prioritizing communication just their own areas of focus.[99]

The Dangers of Empty Boasting

Given the array of potential benefits CR brings to the table—including loyal workers and customers—many companies are eager to position themselves as responsible. Unfortunately, this eagerness has produced a wave of companies trumpeting actions that are not necessarily backed by substance. As noted earlier in the chapter, pursuing CSR initiatives solely to benefit the bottom line may actually destroy many of the benefits such initiatives are intended to create internally, with employees less likely to trust and therefore less likely to engage with and put in their best effort for those companies whose efforts seemed

---

[98] Ibid.

[99] FedEx and the Environment, http://www.fedex.com/sc/about/sustainability/environment.html.

less than authentic. In many ways, this consequence makes sense in that it mirrors how many people care about individual's intentions *as well as* their actions; the absence of authenticity in either arena can negate any otherwise good results. If companies ignore the importance of authenticity and trust, they are likely to face repercussions in terms of consumer purchasing decisions, with consumers now ranking trust in a brand as the second most important purchase and loyalty criterion, behind only price.[100]

In this environment of watchfulness and skepticism, corporations need to work hard to bridge the divide between rhetoric and reality. As the Natural Marketing Institute (NMI) explains regarding corporate environmentalism: "[T]he future of the green movement will require a new level of sophistication and clarity as consumers increasingly discern between those companies that are truly sincere versus those that are perceived as participating for superficial reasons."[101] Even the leading hybrid car manufacturer Toyota has not been immune to the criticism of false advertising. The environmental community has expressed dissatisfaction with Toyota over its efforts to block legislation before Congress to boost fuel economy for all new vehicles from 25 to 35 miles per gallon by 2020, claiming the target is technologically unrealistic. In response, a "How Green is Toyota?" campaign was launched by a number of environmental groups, resulting in more than 100,000 e-mails sent to Toyota's top U.S. executive.[102] In October 2007, protesters draped a Toyota dealership in Detroit with images of flag-wrapped coffins and the tagline "Driving War and Warming."[103] Toyota answered by launching its biggest advertising campaign to date, featuring a commercial of the Prius constructed using grass, twigs, and earth and asking: "Can a car company grow in harmony with the environment? Why not? At Toyota, we're not only working toward cars with zero emissions. We're also striving for zero waste in everything else we do." The ads unleashed new criticism of Toyota's eco-awareness as little more than a slick PR effort, sparking a new round of protests using Toyota's own slogan, "Why not?"[104]

The Transparency Imperative

With the Internet granting NGOs and average consumers unprecedented corporate access, pressure is mounting for companies to reveal proactively both the good and the bad elements of their operations. Companies have achieved success in turning a critical eye on themselves and citing where they can be doing better on the CR front. For example, Nike and The Gap became the first to reveal the names of their overseas factories—acknowledging the shortcomings in their respective global supply chains—and set a new benchmark several years ago.[105] In much the same manner as mystery shoppers gauge the quality of in-store customer service, Nike conducts surprise inspections of its global manufacturers to ensure they meet worldwide standards.[106] Patagonia has taken transparency a step

[100] Edelman Trust Barometer 2020, https://www.edelman.com/sites/g/files/aatuss191/files/2020-01/2020%20Edelman %20Trust%20Barometer%20Global%20Report_LIVE.pdf.

[101] Lifestyles of Health and Sustainability 2007, Consumer Trends Database, www.nmisolutions.com.

[102] Keith Naughton, "Toyota's Green Problem," *Newsweek*, November 19, 2007.

[103] Ibid.

[104] Ibid.

[105] Jeffrey Hollender and Bill Breen, "Can You Be Green without Also Being Transparent?" *Harvard Business Online*, June 19, 2008.

[106] William J. Amelio, "Worldsource or Perish," *Forbes*, August 17, 2007.

further through its interactive website "The Footprint Chronicles," tracking the negative impact of its products on the environment "from design to delivery."[107] The site highlights Patagonia's environmental shortcomings and emphasizes its willingness to keep improving: "We're keenly aware that everything we do as a business—or have done in our name—leaves its mark on the environment. As yet, there is no such thing as a sustainable business but every day we take steps to lighten our footprint and do less harm."[108] Such self-critical transparency can help build trust with constituencies. Transparency is also important for companies seeking favorable media coverage for their CR reporting and CR initiative updates. In a recent online post entitled, "I Published My Sustainability Report . . . So, Where's My Media Coverage?" on the Fleishman-Hillard website, the highly regarded PR and marketing communications consulting firm provides the following advice to companies: (1) "don't sugarcoat your story," (2) "be real," and (3) "be detailed." The blog posting goes on to quote a sustainability reporter for *Fortune*, Marc Gunther, who shares the following insight: "Sustainability reports arrive almost daily now. A company's report needs to stand out from the crowd. Ideally, by pushing the envelope in some way—being forward-thinking, or unusually transparent, or willing to talk honestly about setbacks and frustrations as well as accomplishments and points of pride."[109] Positioning oneself as fallible—and determined to do better—can go a long way in winning the hearts of story-seeking journalists and skeptical consumers who are now armed with unprecedented insights into companies' business practices via the Internet and the widespread voices of critical NGOs. Consumers today are savvy enough to recognize that identifying a problem is the first necessary step toward solving it.[110]

Getting It Measured and Done: CR Reporting

Providing metrics—hard-and-fast evidence of CR efforts and results—will become increasingly important as more stakeholders pay close attention to the claims and realities of corporate behavior.

In such a metrics-conscious environment, the demand for corporations to issue crisp and clear CR reporting will only continue to increase. In 2019, 90 percent of companies on the S&P500 published sustainability reports, growing exponentially from the mere 27 reports produced in 1992.[111]

The 2017 KPMG Study found that nearly three-quarters of companies surveyed report on CR efforts to varying degrees, and most of the world's biggest companies now integrate financial and non-financial data in their annual reports.[112]

[107] "The Footprint Chronicles," Patagonia, https://www.patagonia.com.

[108] Ibid.

[109] Elin Nozewski, "I Published My Sustainability Report . . . So, Where's My Media Coverage?" Fleishman-Hillard Sustainability blog, December 15, 2011, http://sustainability.fleishmanhillard.com/2011/12/15/i-published-my-sustainability-report-so-where%E2%80%99s-my-media-coverage/#.

[110] Hollender and Breen, "Can You Be Green without Also Being Transparent?"

[111] "90% of S&P 500 Index Companies Publish Sustainability Reports in 2019, G&A Announces in its Latest Annual 2020 Flash Report," Intrado, July 16, 2020, https://www.globenewswire.com/news-release/2020/07/16/2063434/0/en/90-of-S-P-500-Index-Companies-Publish-Sustainability-Reports-in-2019-G-A-Announces-in-its-Latest-Annual-2020-Flash-Report.html.

[112] "The Road Ahead," KPMG, 2017, https://assets.kpmg/content/dam/kpmg/xx/pdf/2017/10/kpmg-survey-of-corporate-responsibility-reporting-2017.pdf.

What makes a CR report effective? First, it should appeal to the full range of a corporation's constituencies, providing both quantitative and qualitative evidence of CR efforts. Other important traits of a CR report include the disclosure of the bad as well as the good, acknowledging room for improvement, relevant and direct content (without burying truths in dense reports), creative and engaging delivery of facts, and the engagement of employees and other constituencies in the creation of the reports.[113] Starbucks uses its CR reporting as an opportunity to engage with groups ranging from environmentalists and coffee suppliers to academics and board members to ensure content is relevant and meaningful.[114] More creative formatting, such as storytelling through video, can also be an effective way for organizations to humanize their CR reporting. Finally, much like an audited annual report, an external verification statement from a neutral third party can increase a CR report's credibility. In 2009, however, only 25 percent of CR reports included such external verification, but as of 2020, all big four auditing firms (E&Y, KPMG, PwC, and Deloitte) offered CSR auditing services in addition to their traditional financial auditing services, signally an increased market demand for more formal reviews of CR efforts.[115]

Quantifying CR efforts can pose significant challenges given the many intangible aftereffects of responsible behavior, many of which take years to accrue. Environmental impact is much easier to quantify than social impact, but companies should make efforts to measure wherever and however possible. Columbia Business School Professor Geoffrey Heal argues that environmental reporting could also be improved by standardizing it in a format similar to the Generally Accepted Accounting Principles (GAAP) to enable cross-company comparisons[116] and possibly even fuel CR competitiveness among companies. The Global Reporting Initiative (GRI) produces a global standard in sustainability reporting, which more than 1,000 organizations from 60 countries use, but its guidelines do not include quantification.[117] Although critics can easily ignore or discount anecdotal evidence of CR successes, crisp numbers—backed by a clear methodology and explanation—are far more difficult to dispute.

Conclusion

With a record number of companies devoting significant budgets and human capital to CR efforts, there is more CR chatter to compete with, which makes it difficult to differentiate a company as responsible. In this environment, responsibility is no longer an option; it is a necessary condition that a corporation must meet to maintain positive relationships with its constituents and ensure its ongoing survival. The following list of key takeaways can ensure a thoughtful communication strategy is properly integrated to fuel the success of a corporation's CR program.

---

[113] "International Survey of Corporate Responsibility Reporting 2013," KPMG, 2013, www.kpmg.com/Global/en/IssuesAndInsights/ArticlesPublications/corporate-responsibility/Documents/corporate-responsibility-reporting-survey-2013.pdf.

[114] Amy Anderson, Starbucks Communications Program Manager, 2008 International Association of Business Communicators International Conference, June 23, 2008.

[115] "CR Reporting Awards 07."

[116] "The ROI of CSR."

[117] Ibid.; Global Reporting Initiative, www.globalreporting.org.

1. It Starts on the Inside

Throughout the chapter, we have emphasized the importance of engaging employees in a CR strategy. Walmart cites employee engagement in its CR efforts as a critical part of its green plan's success. Each employee is encouraged to make voluntary changes in his or her life to make a positive individual contribution to the environment—from using compact fluorescent lights to riding a bike to work—which helps them rally more personally around Walmart's corporate environmental efforts and share those messages in-store with consumers.[118] At Walmart Canada, vice presidents draw from the lower ranks of the company's 75,000-employee pool to pull together 14 "Sustainability Value Networks," teams that submit proposals and action plans on topics including greenhouse gas reduction and operational waste reduction.[119] Ensuring a CR strategy resonates strongly with employees can help drive greater efficiencies and positive feelings of ownership and membership in a company that stands for something greater than profits alone.

2. Collaborate with Friends and Foes

The old adage holds true in CR communications: keep your friends close and your enemies even closer. The continued influence of NGOs presents an opportunity for corporations to forge partnerships to defend against attacks and build credibility with the millions of consumers who hold these cause-driven organizations in high regard. McDonald's, for example, worked closely with the Environmental Defense Fund in the early 1990s to change from plastic, foam packaging to paper through a collaborative effort, which helped to stave off some critiques of their approach to sustainability.

3. Present the Bad with the Good

The importance of transparency cannot be overstated in the implementation of a CR strategy. Companies that do not disclose or downplay the negative attributes or effects of their operations do so at their own peril. Given the sophistication and vigilance of NGOs and the average consumer with a Twitter account, today, a company's constituents will likely find out the truth whether or not the company proactively tells them. Being transparent means being clear in CR communication and not clouding realities with vague or verbose prose. Admitting mistakes and missteps is the first, necessary step to correcting them. Constituents will be more forgiving and trustful of a company that openly discusses its challenges in implementing CR initiatives than they will be of companies that attempt to mask or misrepresent shortcomings. Clarity also means using metrics and quantifying CR efforts wherever possible and, just as important, explaining the methodology. Constituencies will only appreciate and engage with a company's CR strategy if they are able to understand what it is and how the results are being measured.

4. Stay One Step Ahead of Antagonists

Corporations should keep a finger on the pulse of influencers, critics, and all constituents to gauge existing opinions and spot potential trouble brewing well in advance of a CR crisis erupting. This monitoring will enable a company to tell its own story and maintain

[118] David Dias, "Giant Steps," *Financial Post Business* (Canada), July/August 2008.
[119] Ibid.

a strong grasp on its reputation. In the words of Mary Jane Klocke, Director of North American Shareholder Marketing at BP: "Engagement raises brand awareness, offers valuable insights and perspectives from key stakeholders and gives us avenues of influence and opportunity to get the facts out . . . rather than have the [socially responsible investment or SRI] community receive its information from the media or other third parties."[120]

5. *Match Rhetoric with Action*

Constituencies today have little patience for self-aggrandizing corporations that inaccurately inflate their CR efforts or do not deliver on promises made. The greater the number of corporations that vie to win approval through CR efforts, the more savvy and discerning constituencies will be in separating hollow rhetoric from bona fide results. Companies should also be careful to never express complacency in their efforts to be responsible. Just as the business environment—and a corporation's intersection with social, environmental, and governance issues—is constantly in flux, so a CR strategy must be continually reshaped.[121] David Douglas, Vice President of Applied Innovation at the Breakthrough Institute, explains: "A big mistake is to send the message that your company believes it has done all it can do. There is always room for improvement when it comes to developing business practices that create social and business value. To indicate otherwise brings the credibility of your company's entire [CR] program into question."[122]

[120] Garrett Glaser, "Lessons Learned in Promoting CSR," *Corporate Responsibility Officer*, 2007.

[121] Porter and Kramer, "Strategy & Society."

[122] Glaser, "Lessons Learned in Promoting CSR."

Case 5-1

Starbucks Coffee Company

On an overcast February afternoon in 2000, Starbucks CEO Orin Smith gazed out of his office window in Seattle and contemplated what had just occurred at his company's annual shareholder meeting. In prior years, the meeting had always been a fun, all-day affair where shareholders from around the country gathered to celebrate the company's success. This year, however, Smith and other senior Starbucks executives heard an earful from the activist group Global Exchange at the meeting. Global Exchange, a human rights organization dedicated to promoting environmental, political, and social justice around the world, criticized Starbucks for profiting at the farmers' expense by paying too little for beans and not buying "fair trade" beans. Not only did the activists disrupt the company's annual meeting to the point that the convention hall security police asked the activists to leave, but they also threatened a national boycott if the company refused to sell and promote fair trade coffee. Although Smith strongly disagreed with using the shareholders meeting as a public forum, he knew there was a strong likelihood his company could face serious reprisals if it did not address the issues raised by Global Exchange.

FAIR TRADE COFFEE

Fair trade began after World War II as religiously affiliated nonprofit organizations purchased handmade products for resale from European producers. Fair trade was an economic model based on fair labor compensation and mutual respect between producers and consumers. By the late 1990s, the fair trade movement had gained a foothold in the United States, and in early 1999, TransFair USA, a third-party certification agency, launched its Fair Trade Certified coffee label. During that summer, Global Exchange began a campaign to educate consumers and the media about labor conditions in the coffee industry, focusing on getting the message out to specialty coffee consumers. Although the activists were

successful in educating pockets of consumers, they knew their effectiveness was limited without directing blame for the farmers' woes. Global Exchange decided to take an anticorporation stance and focused its attention on the most visible brand in specialty coffee: Starbucks.

At this time, fair trade coffees were coffees that were purchased directly from cooperatives of small farmers at a guaranteed floor price. Unlike shade and organic coffees, fair trade coffee focused on the workers' economic sustainability. Fair trade coffee attempted to cut out or limit the middlemen and provided much-needed credit to small farmers so that they could end their poverty cycle. Licensing organizations in individual importing countries certified fair trade coffee from farmers listed on the Fair Trade Registry. Consequently, there was a host of different certifying agencies, and fair trade coffee accounted for different market share in each country.[1]

STARBUCKS' ISSUES WITH FAIR TRADE COFFEE

For Starbucks, the real issues were brand perception and the consumer proposition. Starbucks hesitated to sign a fair trade license, not wanting to commit until it had carefully weighed all of the implications.[2] According to Starbucks executives, their chief concern with fair trade coffee was finding top-quality beans from cooperatives that had not demonstrated an ability to produce quality beans to Starbucks

[1] Rice & McLean, p. 78.

[2] Smith, personal interview.

Source: This case was sponsored by the Allwin Initiative for Corporate Citizenship and prepared by Alison Stanley, T'02, under the direction of Professor Paul A. Argenti, with the cooperation of Starbucks Coffee Company. © 2002 Trustees of Dartmouth College. All rights reserved.

standards. From earlier cupping analyses, Starbucks had little evidence that fair trade coffee met its quality standards. Starbucks was beginning to move toward purchasing more of its coffee through direct relationships with exporters or farmers and negotiated a price based on quality. The company was willing to pay higher prices for great-quality beans and had developed long-term contracts with many of its suppliers.

Mary Williams, senior vice president (VP) of the coffee department, was known throughout the coffee industry as a "tough cupper" who would not settle for anything less than top-quality beans and explained, "the relationships I have with farmers were built over the last 20 years. It's taken some of them years before I would use their beans consistently and pay them $US 1.26 or more. Now I was being asked to use another farmer who I didn't know and pay him the same price without the same quality standards?"[3] On average, farmers sent samples and met with Starbucks coffee buyers at their farms for at least two years before Starbucks accepted their beans. In weighing the fair trade coffee issue, Williams had secondary concerns with how the farmers she worked with would react when they discovered that other farmers received the same price without being held to the Starbucks quality standards. This was not a trivial issue because it was more expensive to grow high-quality beans. Further, she feared that the smaller cooperatives would not be able to guarantee that they could take back a low-quality shipment and replace it based on Starbucks' volume and quality needs.

Starbucks was also concerned about its brand exposure if the quality of fair trade coffee turned out to be very different from the rest of its 30 whole bean coffee line. Coffee quality was a critical component of the Starbucks brand, and if it was compromised the value of the brand could be seriously diminished. "Honestly, we didn't want to put our brand at risk," said Tom Ehlers, VP of the Whole Bean department. "This was an uncharted category and as marketers,

we were concerned about endorsing a product that didn't meet our quality standards."[4] The Whole Bean department would face several challenges in introducing fair trade coffee to 3,200 stores in the United States. First, it would have to come up with a good story for fair trade coffee. "A lot of our business is about the romance of coffee—where it comes from and how to make it come alive for the customer. We weren't really sure where fair trade beans would be coming from because of the quality," explained Tim Kern, Whole Bean product manager.[5]

And how would fair trade coffee be priced? Starbucks coffee was a high-margin business, but if the company were to charge a premium for fair trade, how would customers perceive this? Although pricing was a secondary issue to consider, it was not a reason for Starbucks to abandon fair trade coffee. Orin Smith recalled, "In fact, a number of people believed that the sale of low quality Fair Trade coffee undermined their entire business proposition with customers: Starbucks and other specialty coffee companies had persuaded customers to pay high prices for quality coffee. This enabled roasters to pay the highest prices in the industry to coffee sellers." If quality was reduced, specialty coffee would be no different than mass market coffee and the consumer would be unwilling to pay premium prices. This would destroy the industry's ability to pay price premiums to producers.

THE STARBUCKS CULTURE

In 1990, Starbucks' senior executive team drafted a mission statement laying out the guiding principles behind the company. The team hoped that the principles included in this mission statement would help partners (Starbucks' term for employees) to gauge the appropriateness of their decisions and actions. As Orin Smith explained, "Those guidelines are part of our culture and we try to live by them every day." After drafting the mission statement, the executive

---

[3] Mary Williams, Starbucks SVP Coffee Department, July 24, 2002.

[4] Tom Elhers, personal interview, Starbucks VP Whole Bean, July 25, 2002.

[5] Tim Kern, personal interview, Starbucks Whole Bean product manager, July 25, 2002.

EXHIBIT 5.1   Starbucks Mission Statement

Establish Starbucks as the premier purveyor of the finest coffee in the world while maintaining our uncompromising principles as we grow. The following six guiding principles will help us measure the appropriateness of our decisions:

- Provide a great work environment and treat each other with respect and dignity.
- Embrace diversity as an essential component in the way we do business.
- Apply the highest standards of excellence to the purchasing, roasting, and fresh delivery of our coffee.
- Develop enthusiastically satisfied customers all the time.
- Contribute positively to our communities and our environment.
- Recognize that profitability is essential to our future success.

team asked all Starbucks partners to review and comment on the document. Based on their feedback, the final statement (see Exhibit 5.1), put "people first and profits last." In fact, the number one guiding principle in Starbucks' mission statement was to "provide a great work environment and treat each other with respect and dignity."

Going forward, Starbucks did three things to keep the mission and guiding principles alive. First, it provided all new partners with a copy of the mission statement and comment cards during orientation. Second, when making presentations, Starbucks' leadership continually related decisions back to the appropriate guiding principle or principles they supported. And third, the company developed a "Mission Review" system through which any partner could comment on a decision or action relative to its consistency with one of the six principles. The partner most knowledgeable on the comment had to respond directly to such a submission within two weeks, or if the comment was anonymous, the response appeared in a monthly report. As a result of this continual emphasis, the guiding principles and their underlying values had become the cornerstones of a very strong culture.

After buying Starbucks, CEO Howard Schultz had worked to develop a benefits program that would attract top people who were eager to work for the company and committed to excellence. One of Schultz's key philosophies was to "treat people like family, and they will be loyal and give their all." Accordingly, Starbucks paid more than the going wage in the restaurant and retail industries, granted stock options to both full- and part-time partners in proportion to their level of base pay, and offered

health benefits for both full- and part-time partners. As a result of its commitment to its employees, Starbucks enjoyed a low annual employee turnover (60 percent versus the restaurant industry average of 200 percent) and employees reported high job satisfaction. All of this satisfaction had fostered a strong culture that employed a predominately young and educated workforce of individuals who were extremely proud to work for Starbucks. Their pride came from working for a very visible and successful company that tried to act in accordance with the values they shared. According to Smith, "It's extremely valuable to have people proud to work for Starbucks and we make decisions that are consistent with what our partners expect of us."

CORPORATE RESPONSIBILITY AT STARBUCKS

Just as treating partners well was one of the pillars of Starbucks' culture, so too was contributing positively to the communities that it served, and to the environment. Starbucks made this commitment not only because it was the right thing to do but also because its workforce was aware and concerned with global environmental and poverty issues. In addition to sustaining and growing its business, Starbucks supported causes "in both the communities where Starbucks stores were located and the countries where Starbucks coffee was grown."

On the local level, store managers were granted discretion to donate to local causes and provide coffee for local fundraisers. One Seattle store donated more than $500,000 to Zion Preparatory Academy, an African-American school for inner-city youth. CEO Howard Schultz used his own money to start the Starbucks Foundation, which provided "opportunity grants" to nonprofit literacy groups, sponsored young writers programs, and partnered with Jumpstart, an organization helping Headstart children. Although the Starbucks Foundation was technically separate from the company, Starbucks made an annual donation to the foundation.

On the international level, in 1991, Starbucks began contributing to CARE, a worldwide relief and development foundation, as a way to give back to coffee-origin countries. By 1995, Starbucks was CARE's largest corporate donor, pledging more than $100,000 a year and specifying that its support go to coffee-producing countries. The company's donations helped with projects such as clean-water systems, health and sanitation training, and literacy efforts. By 2001, Starbucks had contributed more than $1.8 million to CARE.

In 1998, Starbucks partnered with Conservation International (CI), a nonprofit organization that helped promote biodiversity in coffee-growing regions, to support producers of shade-grown coffee. The coffee came from cooperatives in Chiapas, Mexico, and was introduced as a limited edition in 1999. The cooperatives' land bordered the El Triunfo Biosphere Reserve, an area designated by CI as one of the 25 "hot spots" that were home to over half of the world's known plants and animals. Since 1999, Starbucks had funded seasonal promotions of the coffee every year, with the hope of adding it to its lineup of year-round offerings. The results of the partnership had proven positive for both the environment and the Mexican farmers. Shade acreage increased by 220 percent, and farmers received a price premium of 65 percent above the market price and increased exports by 50 percent. Since the beginning of the partnership, Starbucks made loan guarantees that helped provide over $750,000 in loans to farmers. This financial support enabled these farmers to nearly double their income.

In 1992 Starbucks developed an environmental mission statement to articulate more clearly how the company interacted with its environment, eventually creating an Environmental Affairs team tasked with developing environmentally responsible policies and minimizing the company's "footprint." Additionally, Starbucks was active in using environmental purchasing guidelines, reducing waste through recycling and energy conservation, and continually educating partners through the company's "Green Team" initiatives. In 1994, Starbucks hired Sue Mecklenburg as the first director of Environmental Affairs. Although Starbucks had supported responsible business practices virtually since its inception, as the company grew, it felt more pressure to protect its image. It was Mecklenburg who developed the idea of using paper sleeves instead of double cupping.

At the end of 1999, Starbucks created a Corporate Social Responsibility department, and Dave Olsen was named the department's first senior vice president. According to Sue Mecklenburg, "Dave really is the heart and soul of the company and is acknowledged by others as a leader. By having Dave be the first Corporate Responsibility SVP, the department had instant credibility within the company." Between 1994 and 2001, Starbucks' CSR department grew from only one person to fourteen.

THE FAIR TRADE DECISION

Starbucks had defined being a socially responsible corporation "as conducting our business in ways that produce social, environmental and economic benefits to the communities in which we operate." Starbucks knew that consumers were increasingly demanding more than just a "product," at the same time that employees were increasingly electing to work for companies with strong values. In a 1999 survey by Cone Communications, 62 percent of respondents said they would switch brands or retailers to support causes they cared about. Another survey conducted in 2001 showed that 75 to 80 percent of consumers were likely to reward companies for being "good corporate citizens," and 20 percent said they'd punish those who weren't.[6] The company cared about being a responsible corporation for a variety of reasons: increasing employee satisfaction,

---

[6] Alison Maitland, "Bitter Taste of Success," *Financial Times*, March 11, 2002, p. 2.

maintaining quality supply sources, obtaining a competitive advantage through a strong reputation, and increasing shareholder value.[7]

As he looked out over the busy port in Seattle's South of Downtown district, Orin Smith pondered all of these issues. Although offering fair trade coffee was a good objective and consistent with the company's aims of being a socially responsible organization, Smith knew he could not base his decision on this factor alone. Even though Smith had a rough idea of which issues his executive team would bring up during the discussion, as the CEO he had to consider the larger picture. He drummed his fingers on the desk and asked himself how Starbucks could support fair trade coffee given that the company had limited resources, a strong reputation to protect, and shareholders who were willing to support causes only so much.

CASE QUESTIONS

1. What are the key issues for Starbucks?
2. What are the problems associated with the decision to offer fair trade coffee from a communications perspective? What are the problems associated with not offering fair trade coffee?
3. What should Smith do?

---

[7] Packard, "Sustainability Practices Presentation."

CHAPTER SIX

Media Relations

One of the most critical areas within any corporate communication function is the media relations department. The media are both a constituency and a conduit through which investors, employees, customers, and community members receive information about and form images of a company. Consumers, for instance, might see a *60 Minutes* segment on a particular firm or read an article about it in *Bloomberg Businessweek* or *The Wall Street Journal*. With the growth of digital communications platforms, the media's role as disseminator of information to a firm's key constituencies, including the general public, has changed dramatically in recent years. Virtually every company now has some kind of media relations department that covers the many wide ranges of media, whether it is one part-time consultant or a large staff of professionals.

In this chapter, we look at what media relations professionals do, and also how companies should approach the different members of the now expanded "press." We examine who the media are, how firms communicate with the media through relationship building, and what constitutes a successful media relations program in today's changing business environment.

The Evolution of the News Media

The news media are omnipresent in our society. With the advent of television in the late 1940s and early 1950s, the tremendous growth of the Internet since the 1990s, and the explosion of social media in the 2010s, what had once been the exclusive domain of the print medium in newspapers as well as radio increasingly has become part of the visual realm through televisions, computers, and mobile.

The arrival of television moved the "headline news" that had formerly been found in newspapers to a new, nearly instantaneous medium. Newspapers adapted by taking over the kind of analysis that had previously appeared in weekly news magazines such as *Time* and *Newsweek*. The news magazines, in turn, took over the feature writing and photo journalism that used to appear in older monthlies such as *Life Magazine* and the *Saturday Evening Post*.

Referred to as "the press" in earlier times, the expanded media are a powerful part of American society. The First Amendment of the Constitution guarantees the right of free speech in the United States, and over the years, the media have helped shape attitudes in this country on issues as diverse as gun control and hemlines, abortion and corporate pay. A free press also attempts to hold politicians accountable for their actions in both public and private life, and though the relationship between politicians and the media have become particularly tense of late, their role is perhaps more pivotal than ever.

Today, with the rise of social media platforms, from Facebook to Twitter to TikTok, the average citizen has actually *become* part of the media. These digital platforms have empowered nearly anyone to act as a journalist of sorts, hence the term *citizen journalism*. These stakeholders can have an incredible impact on businesses, politicians, and global political events, as we shall discuss later.

Business historically had a bit of an antagonistic relationship with the press. This relationship stems in part from the privacy that corporations enjoyed in the early part of the last century. Unaccustomed to dealing with the media, most companies simply acted as if the media didn't matter. Later in the twentieth century, companies were forced to rethink this isolationist approach due to a number of developments, including laws governing the disclosure of certain information by public companies at regular intervals, a Supreme Court ruling in 1964 that required proof of malicious intent to win libel cases against the media, more public interest in business (see Chapter 1), and more media interest in business.

These last two events in particular—increased public and media interest—had a profound effect on business and its dealings with the media. Which came first? Although it is difficult to determine whether the media generated heightened interest in business or were simply responding to changes in public attitudes, what is certain is that sometime in the 1970s, business coverage started to change. Since then, the private sector has become much more public.

Part of what perpetuated this shift in attitudes was the public's realization that business had a tremendous effect on their lives. Incidents like the oil embargo, environmental problems at Love Canal, and questionable advertising on children's television programs all became enmeshed in other controversies in the 1970s, such as Watergate and the Vietnam War. People began to see companies as entities controlling important parts of their lives that did not have to answer to anyone in the way that government did to voters. Special interest watchdog groups emerged to deal with this problem and to make business more accountable.

Business leaders were used to the privacy that they had maintained for decades and were reluctant to admit that times had changed. Even today, some older business professionals resist accepting the importance of communicating through the media, and are especially wary of embracing social media. This kind of attitude is increasingly risky and less common, however, as each industry—from oil and gas, to financial services, to pharmaceuticals—has found itself the subject of some level of public scrutiny, and many companies have learned the hard way that when a crisis hits, having poor or nonexistent relationships with the media, or lacking an effective online communications strategy, will only make the situation worse.

Companies have also had to adapt to a 24/7 news cycle, and to media that include an expanded set of voices. The media, once a powerful conduit of information exchange between businesses and stakeholders, now find themselves competing not only with other news outlets, but also with companies and their stakeholders. The ability to create content has been democratized by the broad range of social media platforms, thus redefining media relations in a profound way. This new media reality doesn't just challenge news outlets; businesses that once depended on their outbound press releases to be interpreted by reporters and then communicated to stakeholders are now forced to engage directly with audiences in two-way conversations rather than one-sided monologues.

The Growth of Business Coverage in the Media

Before the 1970s, business news was relegated to a few pages toward the back of the newspaper (consisting mostly of stock quotations) and to a handful of business magazines; it received virtually no coverage at all in national and local television news broadcasts. As public attitudes changed, however, the business news sections in newspapers gained recognition and began to expand. Because the media are interested in satisfying the needs of readers and viewers, they had to meet the public's growing interest in the private sector and its participants.

Around the same time that *The New York Times* developed Business Day, a separate section published every day devoted to business issues, *The Wall Street Journal* became the number-one selling newspaper in the United States. Business magazines started to become profitable, and television networks and their local affiliates began to devote segments to business news.

Today, so many magazines and websites are devoted to business news that it is nearly impossible to find a topic not thoroughly covered by one media outlet or another. In recent years, news of corporations, the stock market, and business personalities has often become the lead story on national news television and radio broadcasts. With near instantaneous reporting on social media platforms, and 24-hour business networks such as CNBC and Fox Business Network, corporate news is now virtually impossible to ignore.

Compared to decades past, business news today is actually exciting. The large-format *Fortune* magazine found in doctors' offices in the 1950s and 1960s was a dull vehicle for companies to express their points of view. *Fortune* was more successful than others, however, because it allowed executives to check quotes—a practice then unknown anywhere other than this one magazine. Today its cover stories appeal to a wider audience. *Forbes* gains attention from a broad readership by publishing salaries of top entertainers; *Bloomberg Businessweek* attracts an audience through features such as its widely read rankings of business schools and corporate boards.

As coverage of business increased, however, the media industry was consolidating. Fifty corporations controlled the vast majority of all news media in the United States in 1983. As of 2019, only six corporations owned and operated 90 percent of this country's "mass media."[1] Thus, economics plays a big part in what gets covered, as major industrial companies worry more about the bottom line at their media subsidiary (for instance, ComCast and its NBC Universal network). Media conglomerates, including Rupert Murdoch's News Corp, have also increasingly been accused of allowing politics to shape their coverage. According to its critics, News Corp's Fox News has changed the old model of television news, which was pitched toward a mass audience across the political spectrum and aspired to standards of fairness in reporting, and replaced it with an aggressive drive toward partisan coverage. Fox News is the most watched cable news network in America, continually outpacing competitors like CNN and MSNBC.[2]

---

[1] Nicolas Rapp and Aric Jenkins, "Chart: These 6 Companies Control Much of U.S. Media," *Fortune*, July 24, 2018, https://fortune.com/longform/media-company-ownership-consolidation.

[2] Michael Grynbaum, "Boycotted. Criticized. But Fox News Leads the Pack in Prime Time." *The New York Times*, August 9, 2020, https://www.nytimes.com/2020/08/09/business/media/fox-news-ratings.html.

Most executives today recognize that the media are more likely to cover the mistakes rather than the companies. In general, the worse the news is about a company or its CEO, the more likely it is to become a major news story that will capture the media's (and the public's) attention, if only briefly. With the rise in corporate scandals, beginning most notably in 2001 with the infamous dissolution of the energy company Enron, the public developed a stronger appetite for corporate exposés. The traditional model of media as mouthpiece for corporate news seemed outdated in a time when people craved authenticity and engagement. At the same time, while social media platforms have risen in influence, Americans are still skeptical of turning to them for news sources, with a recent Edelman Trust Barometer report noting that 60 percent of respondents felt social media sites were not doing enough to control the spread of "fake news" and 30 percent turning to the government to regulate these platforms more.[3]

Building Better Relations with the Media

To build better relationships with members of the media, organizations must take the time to cultivate relationships with the right people. This task might be handled by employees within the company's media relations department (if one exists) or given to a public relations firm to handle. Either way, companies should be sure to avoid falling into some of the common pitfalls of what has historically been media relations "standard practice."

For example, most old-style public relations experts rely on a system of communication with the media that no longer works. That system sends out press releases (or video news releases) to a mass audience and hopes that someone will pick up the story and write about it. Why is this system no longer valid? The vast majority of press releases go unread by reporters in the United States—due to both the massive quantities of releases these reporters receive daily and the time constraints under which reporters work. The same is true for many of the mailings, e-mails, and voicemails from public relations agencies. Overall, journalists prefer receiving emails with hi-res images and links to press/media rooms, along with relevant contact information. According to a 2018 survey conducted by *PWR New Media*, 87 percent of journalists prefer email.[4] Journalists have also shifted to considering an article's performance on social media first and foremost when publishing items. As of 2020, 63 percent of journalists in the United States track the number of times their stories are shared on social media platforms, and 41 percent consider a story's "share potential" before deciding to pursue it.[5] As stated by one respondent to *PWR*'s survey, "My coverage of topics or the direction we take in stories is often now driven by analytics from our website and from Facebook. Analytics is used as a weekly and monthly ongoing reader survey to make business and coverage decisions and rapid changes in how we cover our news."[6]

[3] "People Don't Trust Social Media—That's a Growing Problem for Businesses," CBS, June 18, 2018, https://www.cbsnews.com/news/edelman-survey-shows-low-trust-in-social-media.

[4] "Journalists Speak Out," PWR, 2018, https://pwrnewmedia.com/2018/powerlines/jan9/downloads/journ-survey-whitepaper-1-18.pdf.

[5] Beki Winchel, "Report: Journalists Are Ditching the Press Release," PR Daily, May 29, 2018, https://www.prdaily.com/report-journalists-are-ditching-the-press-release.

[6] "Journalists Speak Out," PWR.

Part of the problem is that the measure of success in the media relations business has for years been the amount of "ink" (or coverage) that a company gets, whether aided by in-house professionals or an outside consultant. Yet few companies try to figure out what value a "hit" (as it is called in the business) in a relatively unimportant publication has in terms of a firm's overall communication strategy. Getting lots of ink, which means lots of articles written about a company, may not have any value if it doesn't tie back to the company's strategic communication objectives (see Chapter 2) it started out with in the first place.

As discussed later in this chapter, most communication measures to date have focused on the quantity or efficiency of communication output. Although the majority of communications professionals still judge success on their ability to place material in the media rather than on the impact such coverage might have on shifting opinion, awareness, or moving markets, there is evidence that this is changing. Senior executives within companies are increasingly interested in demonstrating return on investment (ROI) from their public relations (PR) and marketing efforts. One benefit of much of news being shared online so frequently has been the ability to deliver quantified benefit of news and PR impact with the C-suite, with companies increasingly turning to media impressions, number of media placements, and finally Google Analytics to assess efficacy.[7]

The message to companies about press releases is thus: mass-mailed releases largely do not work. As of 2019, only 3 percent of journalists rely on them heavily, with 53 percent of journalists ignoring them entirely.[8]

Conducting Research for Targeting Traditional Media

The way a typical media research operation might unfold for a company is as follows: first, senior managers working with the members of the corporate communication department determine what objectives they have for a certain story. Let's assume, for example, that the story is about a major company that is moving into a new foreign market. The managers' objective might be to create awareness about the move into the new market and also to discuss how the firm has changed its global strategy. Thus, this story is part of an overall trend at the company rather than a one-shot, tactical move. Given these considerations, the company would begin to search for the right place to pitch the story.

To do this, the corporate communications professionals conduct research to find out who covers their industry and the company specifically. Identifying online, print, and TV reporters is relatively easy for most companies because the same reporters typically cover the same topic for a period of time and have established relationships with the company either directly or indirectly in that process. Some of these reporters—typically those from print journalism—would definitely be interested in the story. If the company is maintaining its records properly, it can determine at a glance which reporters will most likely cover the story and, more important, who will be likely to write a "balanced story" (code words for a positive piece) about this strategic move.

[7] Katie Bouwkamp, "Stop the Spin: 3 Ways to Measure the ROI of PR," HubSpot, https://blog.hubspot.com/agency/measure-roi-pr.

[8] "Report: Journalists Are Ditching the Press Release," PR Daily.

How do companies determine who is going to write a positive piece before rather than after pitching the piece? This point is where ongoing research pays off. Each time a journalist covers a firm in the industry, the corporate communications professionals need to determine what *angle* the reporter has taken. To continue with our example, suppose a look at the records shows that *The Wall Street Journal* reporter who covered the company's beat has recently written a piece about a competing firm moving into a different market as part of its new global strategy. Chances are, this reporter will not be interested in writing the same story again about another company.

By conducting this kind of research, companies can avoid giving reporters information that they are not interested in, and communications need only occur when a company's media audience is most likely to be receptive. Although this system is not foolproof, it generally yields better results than sending out a story to 300 reporters hoping that four or five may pick it up, with no idea who they are or what angle they are likely to take on the story.

Today, companies can easily access information about the journalists who cover them. Consultants generate computer analyses of reporters' articles, ask industry sources to provide critiques of writers they know, and find out personal information about targeted journalists. Earlier generations of PR professionals worked hard to get such information at long lunches with reporters, but new technology allows corporate communications professionals to access such information through electronic databases, such as Cision's PR software or Agility Pro's MediaPro.

In addition to figuring out who is covering a company's beat, the firm's corporate communication team needs to determine what kind of a reporter it is dealing with. For a television network, such as CNN, this determination means knowing who the producer for the piece will be. Many producers' past segments can be found online, via their own social media feeds or online newsrooms. Alternatively, a communications professional from the company can call the head office in Atlanta and purchase the producer's last two or three stories. For a business magazine such as *Forbes*, electronic databases—such as LexisNexis or Factiva—contain stories that reporters have written over a period of time. Those written in the last two years are most likely to be useful to your company.

What can corporate communications professionals learn by looking at previous stories the producer at CNN has filed and earlier stories that the *Forbes* reporter has written? An individual tends to write about things or put together reports in a particular way. Very few reporters change their style from one story to the next. They have found an approach that works for them—a formula, so to speak—and they tend to stick with formulas that work.

What this kind of analysis usually reveals is that the journalist tends to write or present stories with a particular point of view. One such analysis performed for a company on a *Forbes* reporter's work showed that he liked to write "turnaround" stories. That is, he liked to present the opposite point of view from what everyone else had written about. So, if a company, for example, is trying to make a case for such a turnaround, this reporter would be more likely to write the kind of article that would be helpful for the company despite his negative tone.

Watching the CNN producer's work could help determine how this individual conducts interviews, how the stories are edited, whether he or she likes to use charts and graphs as part of the story, and so on. Let's say that the producer, for example, seems to present balanced interviews, as opposed to antagonistic ones, and likes to use charts and graphs. Again, this makes it seem as if such a producer could easily turn out a positive story for the company—a goal that should be pursued.

Corporate communication departments should perform this type of analysis for each call that comes in. Many executives complain about the amount of time such analysis takes, but the benefits of handling an interview with this kind of preparation make the effort involved well worthwhile.

Researching and Engaging the Expanded "Press"

Imagine, as in the story above, that the company preparing for its launch into a new foreign market must go about identifying influential media in the online space. Identifying these members of the expanded "press," namely online communities, social media outlets, and citizen journalists, is more complicated. Those who function solely online, unlike print journalists, can provide commentary on a wider range of topics, and may not be governed by formal training, long-established standards, or official affiliations. While many in the social media world are merely exercising their right to free speech, others offer insightful commentary about issues and, in turn, have influence over large audiences. Arianna Huffington, for example, is an incredibly influential media representative who built an empire that lives and works solely in the online space. The Huffington Post, her left-wing online news and commentary site, is the first online news outlet to win a Pulitzer Prize. Even BuzzFeed, which publishes an array of online content, has been nominated for two Pulitzer prizes.[9]

Understanding which online observers are influential to a particular company's constituencies is the first step in research and engagement. There are strategies for identifying those online who influence a specific audience, and most, not surprisingly, come in the form of online monitoring and tracking devices. The ever-growing list of applications that help executives wrap their arms around the massive volume of online conversations includes Google Alerts, HubSpot's PR Kit, and Prowly. But more than being reactive and simply waiting for a blogger to praise or pummel their company, corporate communications executives must court bloggers proactively for coverage. Best in class companies, such as HP, successfully identify the bloggers who exercise significant influence over their stakeholders by having a stable of employees charged with actively surveying cyberspace (HP has more than 50 corporate blogs alone).

HP learned early on that bloggers are the greatest sales reps they never had on payroll: In September 2008, HP made an announcement that it had increased personal computer sales by 10 percent the previous May simply by leveraging the blogging community to promote HP's recently released HDX Dragon computer system. Skeptics immediately assumed that the company had paid off bloggers to build buzz around the product, but according to HP's Vice President and General Manager for the Personal Systems Group, bloggers weren't given a cent. All HP executives did was send 31 new computer systems

---

[9] "20 Facts You Probably Didn't Know About BuzzFeed News," BuzzFeed, November 19, 2018, https://www.buzzfeed-news.com/article/buzzfeednews/buzzfeed-news-facts.

to 31 influential bloggers in the tech space, offering to let them give them away in competitions to their readers.[10]

Investing in web-based communications platforms is another way to bring bloggers and online commentators directly to you. There are many examples of companies that are successfully harnessing online tools to reach the expanded media. For example, Microsoft has built an online newsroom called "PressPass" within its main website that brings corporate information, news, fast facts, PR contact information, image galleries, and broadcasts into one central location for journalists to access. Likewise, General Motors' European arm built a social media newsroom to archive news, aggregate recommended blogs, offer multimedia downloads, and consolidate RSS feeds.

Blogger outreach is not only for the biggest, most tech-savvy corporate players; on the contrary, organizations of any size can identify influential blogger communities and effectively engage with them. The first thing any communications executive must do is resist the urge to send press releases and pitches to the bloggers they identify. True to almost all "digerati," bloggers are extremely conscious of maintaining authenticity, which means that communications executives must learn to listen if they have any hope of successfully targeting them.

As when working with traditional print journalists and TV producers, communications executives must review a substantial backlog of the blogger's posts along with the comment threads before reaching out and pitching a story. Katie Paine, CEO of communications firm KDPaine & Partners, recommends "reading as much as six months' worth of posts before ever engaging the blogger. Listen until you understand the tone and nature of the conversation."[11] This level of reconnaissance gives executives a thorough understanding of the blogger's interests, as well as the audience's level of engagement with the blog.

Pitching bloggers is in many ways more complicated than pitching their traditional counterparts: because online media are so much about customization and individual engagement, bloggers can be flippant with communications executives who "corrupt" the code of authenticity with generic press releases and hand-spooned media pitches. Beyond making sure that the approach is entirely germane to a blogger's audience, the pitch itself must be as concise as possible. "You certainly can't spin your way to a blogger's heart," claims Sir Martin Sorrell, Chief Executive of Advertising at marketing giant WPP. "Respect and engagement are essential. Handing product over to bloggers wouldn't be enough. If, however, you invite bloggers in to get their ideas on a brand, you might succeed. Get them involved; give them something of value. The prize for getting it right? The stakeholder becomes a brand loyalist and tells other people."[12]

Responding to Media Calls

In addition to doing their homework on reporters, companies can strengthen their relationships with the media through the way they handle requests for information. Many

---

[10] Matt Marshall, "HP Announces an (Almost) Unbelievable Blogger Campaign," *VentureBeat Digital Media*, September 24, 2008.

[11] Katie Paine's Measurement Blog, https://painepublishing.com.

[12] Sir Martin Sorrell, "Public Relations: The Story Behind a Remarkable Renaissance," Institute for Public Relations Annual Distinguished Lecture, New York, November 5, 2008.

companies willingly spend millions of dollars on advertising but are unwilling to staff a media relations department with enough personnel to handle incoming calls from the media.

This refusal can be a costly mistake, as responding to such requests carefully, and timely, can make a powerful difference in how the company appears in the story. Let's say that a company has gotten negative press over the last couple of years because it has not kept up with the times, but it is now working on a campaign to change its image. A call comes in from a reporter at CNN, and another call comes in from a reporter at *Forbes*. What should the communications staff do to ensure that both of these requests are met in a timely manner and one that will reflect best on the company?

To begin with, calls should come into a central office that deals with all requests for information from important national media. Although this sounds like common sense, calls are often answered by an administrative assistant who cannot distinguish between important and unimportant calls from the media. Many an opportunity has been lost because someone failed to get the right message to a media relations expert in the corporate communications department.

Next, the person who takes the call should try to find out what angle the reporter is taking on the story. In our example, the CNN reporter may or may not have a particular point of view, but the *Forbes* reporter probably does, as that publication prides itself on taking a particular approach to its stories. The company needs to find out what that approach is before responding to the request. Let's assume that the CNN reporter wants to look at the company's activities as part of an industry trend toward more upscale positioning. The *Forbes* reporter, on the other hand, seems to imply from the conversation that she sees the company's new approach in a less-than-positive light.

The person responsible for that telephone call should try to get as much information as possible while being careful not to give in return any information that is not already public knowledge. The tone of the conversation should be as friendly as possible, and the media relations professional should communicate honestly about the possibilities of arranging an interview or meeting other requests. At the same time, he or she should find out what kind of deadline the reporter is working under.

This issue is often a point of contention between business and the media. Particularly with senior executives who are accustomed to arranging schedules at their own convenience, a call from the media at an inconvenient time can be an annoyance. But all reporters must meet deadlines. They have to file their stories—whether on television or radio, in print, or on the web—on a certain date, by a certain time. These deadlines usually have little flexibility, so knowing in advance what the deadline is allows you to respond within the allotted time. Being aware of deadlines is similarly critical when proactively pitching a story to avoid irritating reporters under deadline crunches and, by doing so, leaving them with a negative impression of the company. Responding to media calls in a timely manner is especially critical today given the speed at which news can travel online. Politicians from Eliot Spitzer to Congressman Anthony Weiner and sports personalities such as Tiger Woods have learned that in the age of texting and Twitter, not communicating is communicating. Any brand that does not have an online communications strategy in place when called on for comment, or worse, when a crisis hits, risks its reputation. (See Chapter 10 for more on crisis communication.)

Preparing for Media Interviews

Once the research and analysis are complete, the employee who will be interviewed, whether at the executive level or more junior, needs to be prepared for the actual meeting with the reporter. If the interview is to be conducted by phone, as is often the case for print articles, a media relations professional should plan to sit in on the interview. The following approach works best.

First, the employee should be given a short briefing on the reporter's or producer's prior work, using examples gathered in the research phase discussed earlier, so that he or she develops a clear understanding of the reporter's point of view. For example, if the reporter tends to write turnaround pieces, the appropriate passages from relevant stories should be shown to the employee.

One *Fortune* 500 CEO prepared for an interview with CNN by watching the last two or three major stories the producer had filed. Having done so, he was able to begin the conversation with the producer by saying how much he liked one of the stories. This positive beginning set the tone for the rest of the interview. Additionally, after learning that the producer always used a list of bullet points as part of each story, the CEO developed a list of points he wanted to communicate about the company in bullet-point form and handed it to him before he left. When the story was broadcast, it was positive about the company, and the list of bullet points was right up there on the television screen, which delighted the CEO, who had worried for days about the interview.

Once the employee has been briefed on the reporter's background and likely angle, he or she should be given a set of questions that the reporter is likely to ask. These questions can be developed from what the communications staff member working on this interview has gleaned in previous conversations with the reporter, from an analysis of the reporter's work, and from what seem to be the critical issues on the subject. If possible, the communications specialist should arrange a trial run with the employee to go over answers to possible questions. The employee also should understand that the agenda for a news story is hard to change—once the reporter has decided to write or produce a particular kind of story, it is difficult to introduce a new topic into the discussion.

In preparing for a television interview or webcast, a full dress rehearsal is absolutely essential. The interview should look as if it is totally natural and unrehearsed when it actually occurs, but the employee should be prepared well in advance. This requirement means thinking about what to communicate to the reporter, no matter what he or she asks during the interview. While the employee cannot change the agenda for the interview, as discussed earlier, he or she can get certain points across as the dialogue moves from one idea to the next.

In addition to thinking about what to say, the employee needs to think about the most interesting approach to expressing these messages. Using statistics and anecdotes can help bring ideas alive in an interview. What is interesting, however, depends on the audience. Many people mistakenly assume that the reporter is their audience, but it is the people who will watch the interview with whom they are really communicating. Communications professionals and executives must keep this in mind in determining the best approach for a television or online interview. Know your audience: the tone and tenor for an appearance on an evening news hour are different from those of a Zoom chat with a site for new mothers. (See Chapter 2 for more on communication strategy, especially analyzing constituencies.)

INTERVIEW TIPS

Communications expert Mary Munter suggests the following tips when preparing for a media interview:*

- Keep answers short; think in 10-second sound bites.
- Avoid saying "no comment"; explain why you can't answer and promise to get back to the reporter when you can.
- Listen carefully to each question; think about your response; only answer the question you were asked.

- Use "bridging" to move the interviewer from his or her question to your communication objective.
- Use anecdotes, analogies, and simple statistics to make your point.
- Keep your body language in mind throughout the interview.

*Adapted from Mary Munter, "How to Conduct a Successful Media Interview," *California Management Review*, Summer 1983, pp. 143–150.

Finally, the employee needs to be prepared to state key ideas as clearly as possible at the beginning of the interview. Answers to questions need to be as succinct as possible. Especially in television, where sound bites of three or four seconds are the rule rather than the exception, as well as online, where platforms like Twitter offer just 280 characters for a single tweet, executives need training to get complicated ideas into a compact form that the general public can easily understand.

Gauging Success

Measurement has been transformed thanks to the ease with which communications campaigns conducted using digital platforms can be tracked. Although most communications professionals still believe that media placements are the strongest indicators of a campaign's success, most PR professionals agree that knowledge and insight about those placements is equally as important. To meet this demand, a wide array of analytical services and techniques have emerged. These range from relatively inexpensive basic quantitative analyses to highly customized qualitative interpretations that tell clients whether their placements are being received by the right audience, in the right places. Various other deliverables, including advertising value equivalent (AVEs), Canada's Media Relations Rating Points System (MRRP), internal reviews, benchmarking, opinion polling, and specialist media evaluation tools, also help measure success and in turn, ROI, but there is no standard system of measurement adopted by all communications professionals.[13] The expansion of online platforms as ways of disseminating information about a business has also changed the metrics that businesses use to track the success of online pieces. Earned media, which is content covering a business that the business did not itself try to place, is another measure that is becoming increasingly important for businesses to track.[14] Large tech companies, such as Facebook and Google, have offered their own solutions for

[13] Edelman.com, www.edelmandigital.com/2013/05/24/friday-five-reasons-to-look-beyond-advertising-value-equivalency.
[14] Lindsay Kolowich Cox, "Earned Media, Explained in 400 Words or Less [Examples]," HubSpot, https://blog.hubspot.com/marketing/what-is-earned-media-faqs.

tracking online engagement, and a wide range of startups, from Hootsuite to Agorapulse, have emerged to similarly help track the impact of companies' online presence.[15]

Companies have also discovered that they can turn to social media to test new product ideas and marketing campaigns before launching more broadly. For example, if a company is considering selling a new line of suitcases, they may reach out to loyal customers and influencers to gauge their reaction to a new product makeup. Startups have even sprung up to help manage this online test market. For example, PowerReviews helps companies identify the best online "product testers" and collates data to streamline this online test process.[16] This process is a far cry from the old days of bringing in a group of potential consumers to a room in person and attempting to collect feedback in that way.

In addition to this sort of media monitoring and analysis, more sophisticated approaches to the measurement of media relations, referenced earlier, have the power to:

- Identify which communications activities create the most value in terms of a specific business outcome.
- Evaluate how well an organization's various communications functions perform against an industry average.
- Demonstrate the total value created by a communications department in terms of one or more business outcomes.
- Drive strategic and tactical decision making in the communications function, hedging reputational risk and managing major events such as mergers and top management changes.
- Highlight actual corporate value created by communications activities.[17]

Maintaining Ongoing Relationships

By far the most critical component in media relations is developing and maintaining a network of contacts with the media. Building and maintaining close relationships is a prerequisite for generating coverage. A company cannot simply turn the relationship on and off when a crisis strikes or when it has something it would like to communicate to the public. Instead, firms need to work to develop long-term relationships with the right journalists for their specific industry. This effort usually means meeting with reporters just to build goodwill and credibility. The media relations director should meet regularly with journalists who cover the industry and also should arrange yearly meetings between key reporters and the CEO. The more private and privileged these sessions are, the better the long-term relationship is likely to be. Most communications professionals now recognize that nothing can match face-to-face meetings when it comes to building relationships with key editors and journalists. Online influencers, as well, need to be proactively courted at times when the company recognizes their work will overlap with what those with an online presence cover.

One example of a company's successful efforts to build strong media relations is Matalan Clothing Retailers in the United Kingdom. The company offers journalists tours of its

[15] Eric Siu, "10 Ways to Measure Social Media Engagement (Plus 7 Tools to Track It!)" Single Grain, https://www.sin-glegrain.com/blog-posts/10-ways-to-measure-social-media-engagement.

[16] Russ Banham, "New Product Launch: Testing The Waters With Social Media," *Forbes*, November 28, 2016, https://www.forbes.com/sites/centurylink/2016/11/28/new-product-launch-testing-the-waters-with-social-media.

[17] Quoted in "How Do Your PR Efforts Measure Up in the Wired World?" *Interactive PR and Marketing News*, November 26, 1999, p. 1.

headquarters, including opportunities to try on its clothing in changing rooms and, most surprising, to fully analyze its distribution network. Chris Lynch, formerly of Ludgate Communications, a representative of Matalan, explains, "We tactically avoid granting phone interviews in order to get journalists to meet us face-to-face. Otherwise it ends up being just about the numbers."[18] By taking such a personalized approach, Matalan quickly became a favorite company among journalists. This success has continued, with Matalan recently winning "Home Retailer of the Year" in the National Home Awards sponsored by the *Daily Telegraph*.[19]

Many companies take a less "integrated" approach than Matalan and use the more typical venue of a meeting between a member of the media and a company executive. Because these meetings often have no specific agenda, they can be awkward for all but the most skilled communicators. Within organizations, people assigned to handle media relations should enjoy "meeting and greeting," should be tapped into the company's top-line strategic agenda, and should be able to think creatively.

Often these kinds of meetings occur at lunch or breakfast. They should be thought of as a time to share information about what is going on at the company, but with no expectation that a story will necessarily appear anytime soon. In the course of such a conversation, the skillful media relations professional will determine what is most likely to interest the reporter later as a possible story. Without being blatant about it, he or she can then follow up at the appropriate time with the information or interviews that the reporter wants.

Media relations professionals should expect to be rebuffed from time to time. They may get turned down for lunch several times by reporters who are particularly busy, only to find them very receptive to a long telephone conversation. As is true with personal relationships, media relations professionals will find that they simply do not get along with every journalist they come into contact with. Unless the reporter is the only one covering a company's beat at an important national media outlet, this awkwardness should not be an insurmountable problem. When personality conflicts do occur, professionals can and should work around them to ensure that the overall relationship of the company with that media outlet is not jeopardized and media opportunities are not missed.

One hotel executive at a major chain didn't think that he needed to have any sort of relationship with the reporter covering his beat at *The Wall Street Journal*. After almost two years of being left out of nearly every major story on the industry, a consultant persuaded him to try again to establish a relationship with this reporter. The reporter was only too happy to make amends as well, as she needed the company's cooperation as much as it needed her. Nonetheless, that attitude cost the company nearly two years of possible coverage that it would not get back.

Building a Successful Media Relations Program

What does it take, then, to create a successful media relations program? First, organizations must be willing to devote resources to the effort. This rule does not necessarily have to mean huge outlays of money; an executive's time can be just as valuable.

[18] Paul Argenti and Courtney Barnes, *Digital Strategies for Powerful Corporate Communications*, p. 71.

[19] Matalan website, www.matalan.co.uk.

Jim Koch, cofounder and chairman of the company that makes Sam Adams beer, brought his beer into the national limelight through the skillful use of media relations with the help of one outside consultant at a fraction of the cost of a national advertising program. Warby Parker's success is thanks in part to its founders taking the time to get coverage in GQ, which ultimately led to them being dubbed "the Netflix of eyeware" and nearly crashing their site due to all the incoming traffic.[20] The moral remains for both examples: high-level executive involvement on strategic pieces can have huge ROI.

For many larger companies, the media relations effort will involve more personnel and often the use of outside counsel. What follows is what is needed, at a minimum, for the effort.

Involve Communications Professionals in Strategy

In the age of reputation management, companies have increasingly realized that communications must have a seat at the table when it comes to setting strategy. The extent to which this occurs frequently, however, is not entirely clear. Per a 2018 Spencer Stuart report, only 16 Chief Communications Officers serve on the boards of Fortune 500 companies, despite increasing awareness that this function is not just central to communicating a company's business strategy but also to actually building it.[21]

Although the communications point of view will not always win in the discussions that take place at top management meetings, having these individuals involved will at least allow everyone to be familiar with the pros and cons of each situation and decision. Communications professionals who are involved in the decision-making process also feel more ownership for the ideas that they need to present to the media.

Develop In-House Capabilities

Using consultants and public relations firms may be beneficial in some cases, but most companies choose to develop an in-house media relations staff. Companies can save thousands of dollars a month by using internal staff and investing in the right tools to conduct research for analyzing the media. Often, the best communicator for a brand is an employee; firsthand knowledge is difficult to outsource.

One problem for many companies, however, is that they do not consider media relations to be important enough to hire professional staff in this area. Lawyers, executive assistants, and even accountants often handle communications because of the unfortunate assumption that, because "anyone can communicate," it doesn't matter whom you put on this assignment. Companies must recognize that building relations with the media is a skill and that individuals with certain personalities and backgrounds are better suited to the task than others.

Use Outside Counsel Strategically

For many companies, including those with limited budgets and resources, outsourcing media relations often makes more sense than hiring an internal communications team.

[20] Graham Winfrey, "The Mistake That Turned Warby Parker Into an Overnight Legend," *Inc.*, May 2015, https://www.inc.com/magazine/201505/graham-winfrey/neil-blumenthal-icons-of-entrepreneurship.html.

[21] Alexis Gorman and George Jamison III, "Chief Communications Officers in the Boardroom," Spencer Stuart, June 2018, https://www.spencerstuart.com/research-and-insight/chief-communications-officers-in-the-boardroom.

Companies that do decide to look externally for media relations support have a wealth of options, from industry-specific consultancies to global communications agencies such as Edelman that have in-house digital capabilities. One of the chief arguments for hiring external agencies is that PR professionals have influence with press in a given space: they specialize in maintaining relationships with specific journalists and editors and are in constant dialogue with the media.

Many companies choose to outsource only part of their media relations strategy. Many, for example, choose to outsource aspects of their digital media needs, including search engine optimization (SEO), social media measurement, and content production. Even the most experienced press release writer may struggle to capture the clipped, casual tone of a Twitter account. As media relations evolves under the influence of social media, large, integrated campaigns will become more popular, and they will require the skillsets of many different kinds of media agencies, from a team to manage the Facebook account to a production house that can produce video content.

Developing an Online Media Strategy

Until recently, media coverage—newspaper headlines or more in-depth profiles on television news shows like *60 Minutes*—has been the primary means for exposing corporate flaws. Accordingly, companies with well-managed media relations programs have had some leverage to get their own side of the story communicated to the public. Over the last two decades, however, the rise of the Internet, social media, and mobile have transferred an enormous amount of power into the hands of individuals. We will see in Chapter 10 that one disgruntled Dunkin' Donuts customer created a crisis situation for the company by launching his own anti-company website. This same occurrence has happened on a massive level for retail behemoth Walmart, which is the target of countless sites and blogs created solely to trash its reputation. Digital communications platforms have enabled consumers to seize control of corporate messages and reputations and, in effect, have their way with them.

Thus, the Digital Age has many implications for business, including an expansion to individuals of powers that were previously concentrated in the hands of the organized media. Accordingly, companies' media strategies need to be augmented with tactics for dealing with this new dimension of coverage, including, for instance, establishing a forum for constituencies to share opinions, concerns, and complaints about the company, and a proactive effort to monitor information circulating about the company in various media channels.

As much as digital communications platforms present the threat of the unknown, so too can they provide incredible opportunities to communicate messaging in new, more creative and effective ways. Media relations has transformed into an almost unrecognizable rendition of its former self, with much of the messaging about a brand coming not from the one-way pipeline of company to press to shareholder, but from content created directly by the consumer. Social media and instant reporting by "on-scene" witnesses means that much of what is being communicated about companies is actually the product of individuals in addition to the mainstream media. By creating integrated media campaigns that tie together strong online and offline channels, companies can increase visibility and brand awareness. The vast majority already have: 96 percent of Fortune 500 Companies maintain an active Twitter feed, 95 percent have Facebook pages, and 99 percent are on LinkedIn.[22]

The most sophisticated companies understand that in the new media relations environment, control over who sees content is as much in the hands of customers as journalists, editors, and advertisers. Richard Edelman, president and CEO of the world's largest PR firm, describes the current environment as one in which "companies who wish to build relationships with potential customers must now do so on readers' terms. That means communicating meaningfully *before* selling to them. It means sharing useful and entertaining information as a primary objective, with the understanding that relationships and sales will eventually flow if done appropriately." Early adopters of integrated marketing, like Red Bull, understood this well and created creative content that focused on storytelling, not selling. Such an approach can be particularly efficacious when used appropriately, since storytelling can be up to 22 times more memorable than just facts.[23] Many companies have taken their storytelling one step further, engaging in what has become known as stunt marketing. Red Bull's Stratos campaign is one of the most sensationalist stunts in recent years. In 2012, Red Bull sponsored world champion skydiver Felix Baumgartner to break the sound barrier with a 24-mile jump from space, which was aired live online. Millions of people watched the sponsored jump. Red Bull sold an interesting and compelling story that hit what Edelman describes as the new paradigm of communications marketing: the concept was built for consumption, emotion, and sharing, and it was supported by data and insight.[24]

One of the best integrated media campaigns of the past decade is Dove's Real Beauty campaign. The campaign started in 2004, growing out of a photography exhibit in Toronto titled "Beyond Compare: Women Photographers On Real Beauty." The show was organized by Dove and Ogilvy & Mather and featured work from 67 female photographers. It marked the beginning of Dove's brand proposition to understand how women think about beauty. Following the exhibit, Dove launched a series of ads featuring real women whose appearances were outside the stereotypical norms of beauty. The ads asked viewers to judge the women's looks and invited them to cast their votes at a Dove microsite. Dove also authored a study on women and beauty, which drove the ideology behind the campaign and lent credibility: the study found that only 2 percent of women around the world would describe themselves as beautiful. Dove established a mission to use the campaign "to challenge beauty stereotypes and invite women to join a discussion about beauty."

Over 15 years later, the Real Beauty campaign continues to be one of marketing's most talked about success stories. Sales for Dove jumped from $2.5 billion to $4 billion during the campaign's first 10 years, and in 2019, *PRWeek* named the campaign the Best U.S. Campaign of the past 20 years.[25] This is not to say that the campaign has been without

---

[22] Nora Barnes, "Winners and Losers as the 2019 Fortune 500 Approach Social Media Saturation," The Conference Board, December 20, 2019, https://www.conference-board.org/blog/marketing-communications/Social-Media-and-Fortune-500.

[23] Celinne Da Costa, "3 Reasons Why Brand Storytelling Is the Future of Marketing," *Forbes*, January 31, 2019, https://www.forbes.com/sites/celinnedacosta/2019/01/31/3-reasons-why-brand-storytelling-is-the-future-of-marketing.

[24] Shane Snow, "Richard Edelman: Traditional Marketing Is Broken," LinkedIn, June 26, 2014, https://www.linkedin.com/pulse/20140626210241-7374576-richard-edelman-traditional-marketing-is-broken.

[25] Olivia Zed, "How Dove's Real Beauty Campaign Won, and Nearly Lost, Its Audience," *PRWeek*, April 16, 2019, https://www.prweek.com/article/1582147/doves-real-beauty-campaign-won-nearly-lost-its-audience.

its share of missteps over the years. For example, an ad ran depicting a black woman transforming to white through their soap, resulting in an unwitting nod to racist sentiments. Unsurprisingly, a swift wave of criticism came across social media, denouncing Dove's actions and resulting in the company retracting the ad and issuing an apology. This, in part, has driven the campaign's evolution to the use of the hashtag #ShowUs, where Dove sought to turn to a crowd-sourced approach to even further broaden the ways in which the company displayed "Real Beauty."[26]

Other companies have sought to use social media platforms to not only reach customers but also to promote broader messages. In March 2020, Proctor & Gamble launched the #DistanceDance hashtag via TikTok to encourage consumers to stay home and remain socially distant. P&G also committed to donating to Feeding America for each of the first 3 million views, which occurred well within the first few days of launch. In fact, in the first week alone, the #DistanceDance garnered 8 billion views and 1.7 million iterations, with sports teams and celebrities joining in on the trend.[27] P&G's campaign demonstrated that smart partnering with the correct influencers can not only increase the chance of virality, but it can also promote brand awareness in a way that also produces some social good.

Socialize Your Media Relations Strategy

Studies have shown that the public is often far more trusting of other consumers than it is of traditional institutions, including corporations. According to the 2020 Edelman Trust Barometer, 59 percent of all respondents trust "a person like yourself" to relay credible information about a company.[28] This response helps explain the phenomenal rise of social media, where people can not only converse easily with others who have interacted with a brand but where a brand itself can feel more approachable and less "corporate." The statistics on social media adaption are staggering: as of January 2019, 83 percent of the world's Internet users have a presence on social media sites,[29] with over 2.7 billion monthly active users on Facebook, 330 million monthly active users on Twitter, and 1.1 billion users on Instagram.[30]

Tapping into the information circulating on the Internet can give companies extraordinary access to information about customer needs and complaints. Monitoring social media sites such as Twitter and Facebook can enable companies to learn about current constituency needs and tailor actions to meet those that are most vital to the company's reputation and bottom line. As leading reputation strategist Leslie Gaines Ross warns, "[C]orporations now operate in a landscape rife with new threats to their reputations. Equipped to do battle with large competitors, they may be caught unawares by small-scale adversaries in command of a surprisingly potent new-media and social network arsenal: blogs, tweets,

[26] Ibid.

[27] Michelle Cyca, "7 of the Best Social Media Campaigns (and What You Can Learn From Them)," Hootsuite, August 19, 2020, https://blog.hootsuite.com/social-media-campaign-strategy.

[28] 2020 Edelman Trust Barometer.

[29] "Social Media Statistics and Facts," market.us, November 11, 2020, https://market.us/statistics/social-media.

[30] "Number of Monthly Active Facebook Users Worldwide," Statista, https://www.statista.com/statistics/264810/number-of-monthly-active-facebook-users-worldwide.

text messages, online petitions, Facebook protest sites, and digital videos."[31] By using the Internet proactively, companies can glean valuable insights about constituency attitudes, sentiments, and reactions to which they might otherwise not have access. In many ways, a company should view the Internet as an unprecedented and ideal survey group. Without a doubt, online monitoring can help companies gauge the sentiments of constituencies, allow them to respond effectively, and help them stay on top of today's information surge. However, companies should not become so consumed by the power of the Internet that they neglect other important media channels.

Handle Negative News Effectively

Although negative news reporting has existed as long as the press itself, its frequency and severity has increased exponentially in the context of the changing business environment for all of the reasons discussed in this chapter. Now more than ever, organizations' reputations are vulnerable to the innumerable unknowns that infiltrate the press due to digital communications platforms. Corporate leaders have seen their peers crumble under the glare of unanticipated negative press and are changing their business strategies and response mechanisms accordingly.

Because of the widespread reach of the Internet, companies must keep their proverbial fingers on the pulse of the ever-changing news landscape and constantly work to build the goodwill that will help them to weather any negative press. (See Chapter 4 for more on reputation management.) Bad publicity online can legitimately threaten the bottom line. Many companies assign employees or obtain external specialists to search for negative stories about the company. Others take advantage of low-cost tools, such as turning to Google Alerts.

When companies carefully monitor web activity, they are better positioned to respond in a timely manner to negative comments. Oreo recently won praise as the talk, or tweet, of the 2013 Super Bowl. When power went out during the game, Oreo seized the opportunity, tweeting "You can still dunk in the dark" during the 34-minute hiatus. The tweet was retweeted almost 15,000 times, and Oreo's Twitter following increased by about 8,000. The post garnered nearly 20,000 likes on Facebook and earned Oreo more than 34,000 new Instagram followers. The positive reaction left many media analysts wondering whether the tweet had an even greater payoff than Oreo's actual Super Bowl ad, which cost millions more to create. What was seemingly a spontaneous message, however, was actually the result of months-long marketing planning. Lisa Mann, Oreo's VP of Cookies, explained that it was the result of a carefully built social-media strategy that made the brand ready to respond to whatever opportunity was thrown its way. Having already committed to a Super Bowl ad spot, "[W]e decided to have a social media command center, so that we could respond real time to buzz," Mann said. "Of course we couldn't have anticipated the blackout, but in that command center we had brand people, agency people." In the command center were representatives from all of Oreo's creative agencies—Wieden + Kennedy, Mediavest, and Weber Shandwick as well as 360i. Oreo executives were dialed in, and emails circulated between senior marketing leaders. Oreo was able to execute in real time.[32]

---

[31] "Reputation Warfare," *Harvard Business Review*, December 2010, http://hbr.org/2010/12/reputation-warfare.ar/1.

[32] Jenny Rooney, "Behind the Scenes of Oreo's Real-Time Super Bowl Slam Dunk," *Forbes*, February 4, 2013, https://www.forbes.com/sites/jenniferrooney/2013/02/04/behind-the-scenes-of-oreos-real-time-super-bowl-slam-dunk.

Many companies recognize that the best way to prevent negative news is to ensure that inside information does not leak. Companies are getting smarter about creating social media guidelines and policies that regulate the flow of sensitive information from within. Any corporate employee, whether a CEO with a LinkedIn Profile or a recent MBA hire with a Twitter account, can potentially make "news" without proper guidance. Ever the innovator, IBM was one of the first companies to introduce guidelines for social platforms. In the spring of 2005, the company created a wiki and asked employees to contribute advice and fair restrictions in terms of authoring blogs. This wiki became the first iteration of the company's blogging policy, and evolved into what is now IBM's comprehensive "Social Computing Guidelines," authored by the employees themselves.[33]

When a company does stumble upon bad news circulating about itself—be it a condemning attack online or a hostile op-ed article in a daily newspaper—the communications department should quickly assess the potential damage that the news might cause. Who is the person who has issued the complaint? Are the comments valid? Is the person speaking only as an individual, or does she or he represent a broader constituency, such as investors or employees? If a broader constituency, how widespread are the complaints? If a rogue website has been constructed, how many hits per day has it received, and how have people generally responded to the negative message? If an unflattering newspaper article has been printed, how wide is the paper's circulation?

Once these questions are answered, a company's task force or permanent crisis communication team—including members of senior management—must brain-storm some potential actions. Company lawyers should be consulted to discuss what legal stance the company might need to take. Lawyers will be able to offer advice about whether newspaper articles or sites are defamatory, warranting a lawsuit against the perpetrator.

Conclusion

As technology develops new mechanisms for disseminating information, the media relations function will continue to evolve away from the old PR flak model into a professional group that can help organizations get their message out quickly, honestly, and to the right media.

Companies today are under constant scrutiny from many of their constituencies. A demand for instantaneous information accompanies this public watchfulness, and the pressure is increasing with each new technological innovation. Managers must be prepared to answer this demand by considering all constituencies in dealing with the media agents who inform them. By crafting messages with care and then using proper media channels, companies can tap into this powerful "conduit constituency," the media, to ensure that the best possible message is disseminated and heard.

---

[33] IBM Social Computing Guidelines, www.ibm.com/blogs/zz/en/guidelines.html.

Adolph Coors Company

Shirley Richard returned from lunch one April afternoon in 1982 and found a message on her desk that Allan Maraynes from CBS had phoned while she was out. "God, what's this?" was all she could say as she picked up the phone to discuss the call with her boss, John McCarty, Vice President for Corporate Public Affairs. In her second year as Head of Corporate Communication for what was then the nation's fifth-largest brewer, Richard was well aware of the Adolph Coors Company's declining popularity—a decline that she partially blamed on an ongoing conflict with organized labor. But the conflict was hardly breaking news, and she was almost afraid to ask why CBS was interested in the company.

Richard found out from her boss that Maraynes was a producer for the network's news program "60 Minutes." Reporter Mike Wallace had already phoned McCarty to announce plans for a "60 Minutes" report about the company. Program executives at CBS were aware of accusations of unfair employment practices that the AFL-CIO had raised against Coors and wanted to investigate the five-year battle between the brewery and organized labor.

Once McCarty explained the message from Maraynes, Shirley Richard sank into her chair. She had spent the last year working hard to understand organized labor and its nationwide boycott of Coors beer, and she was convinced that the company was being treated unfairly. She believed the union represented only a small subset of Coors's otherwise satisfied workforce. But Richard also doubted whether the facts could speak for themselves and was wary of the AFL-CIO's ability to win over the media. She was well aware of Mike Wallace's reputation for shrewd investigative reporting.

On the other hand, "60 Minutes" was considered by many corporations as anti-big-business, and Richard had no idea how corporate officials would respond under the pressure of lights, camera, and the reporter's grilling questions. McCarty and Richard met with the two Coors brothers to discuss the

network's proposal and to determine whether producer Maraynes should even be allowed to visit the Coors facility. Company President Joseph ("Joe") Coors and Chairman William ("Bill") Coors were skeptical of the prospect of airing the company's "dirty laundry" on national television. But McCarty was interested in the opportunity for Coors to come out into the public spotlight. Richard knew that granting interviews with Wallace and permission to film the Coors plant came with enormous risk.

Richard was frustrated by growing support for the boycott, and her own strategies to deal with the problem had been unsuccessful. She believed the interview with CBS might only exacerbate an already difficult situation. Her own public relations effort had been an attempt to portray the circumstances as she believed them to be: good management harassed by disgruntled labor organizers. She was convinced that her job was not an effort to cover up Coors's employment practices.

Richard debated how the company should handle the proposal from CBS. Any decisions about approaching "60 Minutes" also would have to be approved by the Coors brothers. Richard felt uncertain about how much control she would ultimately have over the communications strategy. Joe Coors, an ardent conservative and defender of private enterprise, would undoubtedly resist an open-door policy with the network. At the same time, Richard wondered if she should attempt to convince the management of this traditionally closed company to open itself to the scrutiny of a "60 Minutes" investigation or whether the best defense would be a "no-comment" approach. But with no comment from Coors, anything organized labor was willing to say on camera would go uncontested.

Source: This case was prepared by Professor Paul A. Argenti, Tuck School of Business at Dartmouth. © 2001 Trustees of Dartmouth College. All rights reserved.

HISTORY OF THE ADOLPH COORS COMPANY

The Coors brewery was established in 1880 by Adolph Coors, a Prussian-born immigrant who came to the United States in 1868. Having trained as an apprentice in a Prussian brewery, 22-year-old Adolph Coors became a foreman at the Stenger Brewery in Naperville, Illinois, in late 1869. By 1872, Coors owned his own bottling company in Denver, Colorado. With his knowledge of brewing beer and the financial assistance of Joseph Schueler, Coors established his own brewery in Golden, Colorado. His product was an immediate success. In 1880, Adolph Coors bought out Joseph Schueler and established a tradition of family ownership that was maintained for almost a century.

Famous for its exclusive "Rocky Mountain spring water" system of brewing, the Adolph Coors Company soon became something of a legend in the beer industry. The Coors philosophy was one of total independence. A broad spectrum of Coors subsidiaries combined to create a vertically integrated company in which Coors owned and managed every aspect of production: The Coors Container Manufacturing plant produced aluminum and glass containers for the beer; Coors Transportation Company provided refrigerated trucks to haul the beer to its distribution center as well as vehicles to transport coal to fuel the Golden brewery; Coors Energy Company bought and sold energy and owned the Keenesburg, Colorado, coal mine; the Golden Recycle Company was responsible for ensuring a supply of raw materials for aluminum can production. By 1980, the recycling plant was capable of producing over 30 million pounds of recycled aluminum a year. Other subsidiaries fully owned by Coors included Coors Food Products Company, Coors Porcelain Company, and the American Center for Occupational Health.

THE COORS MYSTIQUE

A certain mystique surrounding the Golden, Colorado, brewery, and its unique, unpasteurized product won the beer both fame and fortune. Presidents Eisenhower and Ford shuttled Coors to Washington aboard Air Force jets. Actors Paul Newman and Clint Eastwood once made it the exclusive beer on their movie sets. Business magazines lauded Coors as "America's cult beer." As Coors expanded its distribution, the mystique appeared irresistible; Coors moved from 12th to 4th place among all brewers between 1965 and 1969 with virtually no advertising or marketing.

Part of the Coors mystique was attributed to its family heritage. For over a century of brewing, company management had remained in the hands of Adolph Coors's direct descendants. Reign passed first to Adolph Coors Jr., then to his son William Coors. In 1977, Bill Coors turned over the presidency to his younger brother Joseph but continued as Chairman and Chief Executive Officer. The company's newest President, Joe Coors, was a well-known backer of right-wing causes such as the John Birch Society; a founder of a conservative think-tank, the Heritage Foundation; and a member of President Ronald Reagan's so-called Kitchen Cabinet. The family name was closely associated with strong conservatism by consumers, labor, and the industry.

The Coors Company was built on a tradition of family and, even after going public in 1975, remained an organization closed to active public relations. Bill Coors recalled that his father, Adolph Coors Jr., was a shy man, and throughout its history the company was reluctant to attract any public attention. In 1960, the sensational kidnapping and murder of brother Adolph Coors III focused the public eye on the family and the business, but Coors maintained a strict "no-comment" policy.

THE NATURE OF THE BREWING INDUSTRY

From the mid-1960s through the 1970s and into the 1980s, the brewing industry was characterized by a shrinking number of breweries coupled with a growing volume of production and consumption. In 1963, Standard and Poor's Industry Surveys reported 211 operating breweries. Ten years later that number had dropped to 129, and by 1980 there were only 100 breweries in operation. On the other hand, per capita consumption of beer rose from 15 gallons a year in 1963 to 19.8 gallons in 1973. By 1980, per capita consumption had jumped to 24.3 gallons a year.

Until the mid-1970s, beer markets were essentially local and regional, but as the largest breweries expanded, so did their share of the market. Combined, the top five brewers in 1974 accounted for 64 percent of domestic beer production, up from 59 percent in 1973. Previously strong local and regional breweries were either bought by larger producers or ceased operations.

A notable exception, however, was the Adolph Coors Company, which dominated the West. Until 1976, the company's 12.3-million-barrel shipment volume was distributed only in California, Texas, and 10 other western states. Coors's share of the California market alone was well over 50 percent in 1976. Coors dominated its limited distribution area, capturing at least 35 percent of the market wherever it was sold statewide. The Coors Company ranked fifth in market share nationally throughout the 1970s, trailing giants Anheuser-Busch, Joseph Schlitz, Phillip Morris's Miller, and Pabst, all of which had much broader distribution areas.

Competition for market share among the top five brewers was intense during the 1970s and led producers to more aggressive attempts to win consumers. According to compilations by Leading National Advertisers, Inc., advertising expenditures for the first nine months of 1979 were up 37 percent from the previous year for Anheuser-Busch, 18 percent for Miller, 14 percent for both Schlitz and Pabst, and 78 percent for Adolph Coors.

MARKETING AND DISTRIBUTION AT COORS

Industry analysts criticized the Coors Company's sales strategy for stubbornly relying on its product's quality and image rather than marketing. In 1976, the Coors mystique appeared to be losing its appeal to strong competitors—for the first time since Prohibition, Coors could not sell all of its beer. The company finally responded to competition by intensifying its marketing and development operations. Between 1976 and 1981, the company attempted to revive sales by adding eight new states to its distribution. In May 1978, Coors began to market its first new product in 20 years: Coors Light. In 1979, Coors began the first major advertising campaign in its history to defend itself against aggressive competitors such as Philip Morris's Miller Brewing Company and Anheuser-Busch. The company's 1981 annual report pictured Coors's newest product—George Killian's Irish Red Ale—along with a newly expanded package variety designed to "keep pace with consumer demand."

The Coors Company went public in 1975, but investors did not fare well as stock prices declined for the rest of the decade. Coors entered the market at a share price of $31 but by 1978 had fallen to $16—a loss of about 50 percent for the first public stockholders. Net income, according to the company's annual report, was $51,970,000 in 1981, or $1.48 per share. That figure reflected a 20 percent drop from $64,977,000, or $1.86 per share, in 1980.

MANAGEMENT–LABOR RELATIONS AT COORS

During pre-Prohibition years, breweries, including Coors, were entirely unionized. In 1914, the first vertically integrated industrial union in the country established itself at Coors. When the country went dry, Coors remained viable through alternative operations, but the workforce still had to be reduced. Coors offered older workers employment but fired younger employees. A strike of union employees resulted and remained in effect until 1933, when Prohibition was repealed. The company, however, continued to operate without a union until 1937 when Adolph Coors Jr. invited the United Brewery Workers International (UBW) into the Coors Company.

In 1953, the company experienced an abortive strike by the UBW to which a frightened management immediately gave in. In 1955, Coors's organized porcelain workers struck because their wages were less than those of brewery workers. Although the plant continued to operate, all of Coors's unionized workers engaged in a violent strike that lasted almost four months. The union ultimately lost the battle 117 days after the strike, when workers returned to the plant on company terms.

Negotiations over a new union contract in 1957 ended in a stalemate between labor and management, and workers again decided to strike. For another four months, workers were torn between paternalistic and small-town personal ties to management and the demands of the union. Bill Coors, who was then the plant manager, recalled that during the strike, management had wanted to show the union it was not dependent on union workers. Coors hired college students during the summer of 1957 as temporary replacements for the striking brewers. When the students left, the picketers were threatened by management's vow to hire permanent replacements and returned to the plant. The strike was a clear defeat of the union's demands and ultimately left international union leaders with an unresolved bitterness toward Coors. Back in full operation by the fall of 1957, Coors management believed it had won complete control.

By the end of the 1950s, 15 local unions were organized at Coors. Management tolerated the unions but claimed they did not affect wages or employment practices. The Coors family firmly believed that good management removed the need for union protection and that management could win workers' loyalty. In 1960, the plant's organized electricians went on strike but failed to garner the support of other unions, and the plant continued to operate with nonunion electricians hired to replace the strikers. Similar incidents occurred with Coors's other unions. A 1968 strike by building and construction workers ended with Coors breaking up 14 unions. By 1970, Coors's workforce was predominantly nonunion.

A contract dispute between Coors's management and UBW Local 366 erupted in 1976. Workers demanded a 10 percent wage increase and better retirement benefits. After more than a year of negotiations, union officials rejected management's compromise offer, which labor contended would erode workers' rights. In April 1977, over 94 percent of UBW workers voted to strike. Production at the plant continued at 70 percent of normal capacity, however, and management boldly announced plans to replace striking workers. In defense of the union, AFL-CIO

officials declared a nationwide boycott of the beer until a new contract settlement was reached. But within five days of initiating the strike, 39 percent of the union members crossed the picket lines to return to work.

In 1978, Coors management called an election for decertification of UBW Local 366. Because more than a year had passed since the strike began, National Labor Relations regulations restricted striking union members from voting. Only workers remaining at the plant, including "scabs" hired across the picket lines, could vote on whether to maintain the UBW Local. In December of that year, Coors employees voted a resounding 71 percent in favor of decertifying the Local UBW.

Since 1957, the Coors brewery had been a "closed shop," in which workers were required to pay union dues if they were to benefit from union action. But company officials called the 1978 decertification vote a victory for the "open shop," wherein workers could enjoy union benefits without paying dues as members. Union officials, frustrated over the lack of a new contract and the decertification vote, publicly charged Coors with "union busting."

In fact, according to AFL-CIO officials, the UBW was the 20th Coors union decertified since the mid-1960s. Management consistently argued that employees simply rejected union organization because they didn't require it; good management eliminated the need for a union to protect workers. But organized labor maintained that all 20 unions had been "busted" by votes called while members were on strike and scabs were casting the ballots. By the end of the decade, only one union representing a small group of employees remained active at Coors.

NATIONWIDE BOYCOTT

The AFL-CIO was determined not to be defeated by the ousting of the UBW Local from the Golden plant. In defense of the union, AFL-CIO officials declared a nationwide boycott of Coors beer until a new contract settlement could be reached and soon began to claim that their efforts had a significant effect on sales. In fact, 1978 figures reported a 12 percent profit decline for the brewery during fiscal

1977 and predicted that 1978 figures would fall even lower. Corporate officials conceded the boycott was one factor influencing declining sales but refused to admit the drop was consistent or significant.

The defeat of the Coors local brewers' union fueled the boycott fire, but the protest focused on issues beyond the single contract dispute begun in 1977. The other issues of protest related to Coors's hiring practices. Labor leaders claimed that a mandatory polygraph test administered to all prospective employees asked irrelevant and personal questions and violated workers' rights. In addition, the protesters claimed that Coors discriminated against women and ethnic minorities in hiring and promotion. Finally, boycotters argued that Coors periodically conducted searches of employees and their personal property for suspected drug use and that such search and seizure also violated workers' rights. The boycott galvanized organized labor as well as minority interest groups that protested in defense of blacks, Hispanics, women, and gays.

The boycott's actual effect on sales was the subject of dispute. Coors's sales had begun to fall by July 1977, just three months after the boycott was initiated. Some analysts attributed the drop not to protesting consumers but rather to stepped-up competition from Anheuser-Busch, which had begun to invade Coors's western territories. Despite a decline, Coors remained the number-one seller in 10 of the 14 states in which it was sold. Labor, on the other hand, took credit for a victory at the end of 1977 when Coors's fourth-quarter reports were less than half of the previous year's sales for the same period. Dropping from $17 million in 1976 to $8.4 million in 1977, Coors was faced with a growing challenge. There was no doubt that management took the AFL-CIO protest seriously and began attempts to counter declining sales through more aggressive advertising and public relations.

FEDERAL LAWSUIT

The AFL-CIO boycott gained additional legitimacy from the federal government. In 1975, the federal Equal Employment Opportunity Commission (EEOC) had filed a lawsuit against Coors for discrimination in hiring and promotion against blacks, Mexican Americans, and women. The suit charged Coors with violating the 1964 Civil Rights Act and challenged Coors's hiring tests, which the EEOC said were aimed at revealing an applicant's arrest record, economic status, and physical characteristics. The lawsuit stated that the company used "methods of recruitment which served to perpetuate the company's nonminority male workforce."

In May 1977, one month after the initiation of the AFL-CIO boycott, Coors signed an agreement with the EEOC, vowing that the brewery would not discriminate in hiring. But according to media reports, Coors still refused to admit any past bias toward blacks, Mexican Americans, and women. Coors said it would continue a program begun in 1972 designed to increase the number of women and minorities in all major job classifications. Striking brewery workers refused to sign the agreement, although the Coors's Operating Engineers Union entered into the agreement.

DAVID SICKLER AND THE AFL-CIO

The principal organizer of the AFL-CIO boycott against the Adolph Coors Company was the former President of the company's Local UBW. David Sickler had been employed by Coors for 10 years, acting as a Business Manager from 1973–1976. Sickler left the plant in 1976 to take a job with the AFL-CIO in Montana. In April 1977, the AFL-CIO decided to put Sickler in charge of coordinating the national boycott against Coors. Sickler moved to Los Angeles, where he also served as Director of the Los Angeles organizing committee and the subregional office of the AFL-CIO.

Sickler initially resisted the AFL-CIO's request to put him in charge of organizing the boycott. He believed that his past employment at the company made him too close to the situation to offer a fair position on the issues at stake. But the AFL-CIO felt that Sickler's tenure with Coors made him an ideal choice; according to Sickler, his personal reports of abuse by the company in hiring and employment practices were shared by numerous Coors employees and were the central issues of the boycott.

Sickler contended that when hired by Coors, he had been subjected to questions on a lie detector test regarding his personal life and sexual preference. In addition, he reported the company's practice of searching individuals or entire departments for suspected drug use. Despite corporate officials' insistence that the accusations were false, Sickler was convinced that Coors employees were generally "unhappy, demoralized."

Coors management was determined to fight back against the boycott and filed a breach of contract suit against the Local 366. The company charged that any boycott was prohibited under contract agreements. Management also made clear to the public its outrage over the boycott, as chairman Bill Coors began to speak out in the national media. In a 1978 interview with *Forbes* magazine, Coors stated about the AFL-CIO: "No lie is too great to tell if it accomplishes their boycott as a monument to immorality and dishonesty." Earlier that year, Bill Coors defended the company against charges of being anti-union. A *New York Times* report on the dispute quoted the CEO as saying: "Our fight is not with Brewery Workers Local 366. Our fight is with organized labor. Three sixty-six is a pawn for the AFL-CIO; that's where they're getting their money."

CORPORATE COMMUNICATION AT COORS

The 1977 boycott forced company officials to reexamine the area of corporate communication. Because labor leaders set out to "destroy the company," Bill Coors, now Chairman and CEO of the company, believed management must relate its side of the story. "There was no lie they wouldn't tell," the CEO recalled. "No one knew about Coors, and we had no choice but to tell the story."

In 1978, John McCarty, responsible for fundraising at Pepperdine University, was hired as the Vice President of Corporate Public Affairs. McCarty brought to Coors expertise in minority relations and set out to repair the company's damaged reputation among minority groups. McCarty established a staff of corporate communication officers. The division was organized into four branches under McCarty's

leadership: corporate communication, community affairs, economics affairs, and legislative affairs.

In response to the boycott and declining sales, McCarty enlisted the expertise of J. Walter Thompson's San Francisco office to help the company improve its corporate image. Coors launched what analysts termed a strong "image-building" campaign in 1979, with messages aimed at ethnic minorities, women, union members, and homosexuals. The theme throughout the late 1970s was clearly a response to labor's accusations against the company: "At Coors, people make the difference."

Another component of the new image campaign, according to media reports, was to condition company managers to project charm and humility in dealing with reporters. Coors executives participated in a training course designed to help them overcome a traditional distrust of the media.

SHIRLEY RICHARD

Shirley Richard was hired along with McCarty in 1978 to direct the company's legislative affairs function but was familiar with the Coors Company long before joining its staff. From 1974 to 1978, Richard worked on the Coors account as a tax manager for Price Waterhouse. One important issue for the Coors account, Richard recalled, was the deductibility of lobbying expenses and charitable donations. As part of her job, Richard became involved in the political arena, helping Coors set up political action committees. When Richard decided to leave Price Waterhouse in 1978, she asked Coors's Vice President of Finance for a job and was hired to head the legislative affairs department, a position she held until 1981.

Richard recalled her first year with the company as a time when Coors was "coming out of its shell"; Philip Morris's purchase of Miller Brewing Company meant increased competition for Coors and a demand for more aggressive advertising. In 1975, the company sold its first public stock. The bad publicity from the 1977 strike and its aftermath combined with greater competition led to a serious decline in sales and disappointed shareholders. Clearly, the Coors mystique alone could no longer speak for itself, and an aggressive public relations campaign was unavoidable.

One year before the "60 Minutes" broadcast of the Coors story, Richard became Adolph Coors Company's Director of Corporate Communications. In that position, she managed 25 people, covering corporate advertising, internal communications, distribution communications, training programs, and public relations personnel.

CONFRONTATIONAL JOURNALISM

The challenge of CBS's "60 Minutes" to any company under its investigation was formidable. The 14-year-old program was consistently ranked in Nielsen ratings' top 10 programs throughout the 1970s. Media critics offered various explanations for the success of this unique program, which remarkably combined high quality with high ratings. A *New York Times* critic summarized the sentiment of many within the broadcast profession when he called "60 Minutes," "without question, the most influential news program in the history of the media."

The program had earned its popularity through consistently hard-hitting investigative reporting. Executive producer Don Hewitt proclaimed "60 Minutes" the "public watchdogs." In his book about the program, Hewitt recalled, "I became more and more convinced that a new type of personal journalism was called for. *CBS Reports, NBC White Papers*, and *ABC Closeups* seemed to me to be the voice of the corporation, and I didn't believe people were any more interested in hearing from a corporation than they were in watching a documentary." Stories revealing insurance executives taking advantage of the poor with overpriced premiums, companies polluting streams and farmlands by irresponsibly dumping, or physicians gleaning profits from unnecessary surgery had all worked to rally public support and faith in CBS as a sort of consumer protection agency.

The program's success in uncovering scandal was due in large part to the aggressive and innovative technique of Mike Wallace. Wallace had been with the program throughout its history and was responsible for shaping much of the "60 Minutes" image. His reporting was always tough, sometimes

theatrical, and was commonly referred to within the media as "confrontational journalism."

Allan Maraynes was assigned to produce the Coors segment. His experience with "60 Minutes" was highlighted by some significant clashes with big business. He had produced stories on the Ford Pinto gasoline tank defects, Firestone tires, I. Magnin, and Smith-Kline. Maraynes was alerted to the Coors controversy when "60 Minutes" researchers in San Francisco told him they suspected bad things were happening at Coors. The research group told Maraynes that the AFL-CIO was calling Coors a "fascist organization," which sounded to the producer like good material for a story.

Maraynes first flew to California to interview David Sickler. "We said we were setting about to do a story explaining that a fascist state exists at Coors," Maraynes recalled about his conversation with Sickler. "If it's true, we'll do it." Maraynes wanted Sickler to give him as much information about the boycott as he had. Maraynes wanted the angle of the story to be a focus on case histories of the people who had experienced Coors's unfair treatment.

OPEN OR CLOSED DOOR?

With the phone call from Maraynes, all of the pressures from David Sickler, the AFL-CIO, and the boycott were suddenly intensified. Shirley Richard had worked hard in the last year to focus public attention away from the boycott, but now her efforts to project a positive corporate image were threatened. Thinking ahead to the next few months of preparation time, she felt enormous pressure in the face of such potentially damaging public exposure.

Shirley Richard was not naive about Mike Wallace or the power of television news to shape a story and the public's opinion. Richard, along with other Coors executives, believed that the company was not at fault, but that did nothing to guarantee that its story would be accurately portrayed in a "60 Minutes" report. Mike Wallace himself had voiced the reason for a potential subject to fear the program's investigative report. In a *New York Times* interview, Wallace stated: "You (the network) have the power to convey any picture you want."

Richard knew that a big corporation's abuse of employees was just the kind of story "60 Minutes" was built on, and she didn't want Coors to be part of enhancing that reputation, especially when she believed organized labor had fabricated the controversy about Coors. Given Mike Wallace's desire to get the story, Shirley Richard guessed the company would automatically be on the defensive.

"60 Minutes" was determined to do the story, with or without cooperation from Coors. Richard wondered, however, whether an interview with Mike Wallace would do the company more harm than good. On the other hand, she considered the possibility that the company could somehow secure the offensive and turn the broadcast into a final clarification of Coors's side of the boycott story.

Richard was clearly challenged by an aggressive news team, and she was uncertain about cooperation from the conservative Coors brothers. Even if she could convince them that an open door was the best policy, would corporate officials be able to effectively present the facts supporting Coors's position? The national broadcast would reach millions of beer drinkers, and Richard knew that the "60 Minutes" report could either make or break the future success of Coors beer.

CASE QUESTIONS

1. What problems should Richard focus on?
2. What kind of research should she do?
3. What would her communication objective be if Coors agreed to the interview? If the brothers did not do the interview?
4. Should Shirley Richard encourage or discourage the Coors brothers to go on "60 Minutes"?
5. What suggestions would you have for improving media relations at Coors?

Source: This case was researched and written by Professor Paul A. Argenti in 1985 and revised in 1994, 1998, 2002, and 2005.

CHAPTER SEVEN

Internal Communications

For years, managers have focused on "customer care." More recently, they have begun to dedicate the same kind of attention to their own employees, recognizing that employees have more to do with the success of a business than virtually any other constituency. According to a 2019 study in which consulting firm Willis Towers Watson analyzed data from 500 global companies, separating them into high-, average-, and low-employee experience (EX), companies in the high-performing category outperformed their low-performing peers across a broad range of metrics, from return on equity to one-year change in gross profit margin to three-year revenue growth.[1] Moreover, evidence exists to suggest that strong employee engagement is a *cause* of strong financial performance and not merely correlated with it (or perhaps even a consequence of it). A longitudinal study from Gallup and the University of Iowa examined the responses of nearly 150,000 individuals in over 2,000 business units and found evidence supporting the causal relationship between employee satisfaction and financial performance. While better financial performance did seem to increase employee satisfaction, employee satisfaction had a considerably stronger impact on the latter.[2] The implications, then, are clear: employee engagement is no longer something that can be categorized as a "nice-to-have" but rather must be viewed as a "need-to-have." Strong financial performance is very much so predicated upon it.

In this chapter, we examine how organizations can strengthen relationships with employees through internal communications. Internal communications today is more than memos, e-mails, Slack messages, and Zoom meetings that comprise it; it's about building a corporate culture based on values and having the potential to drive organizational change. We start by looking at how the changing environment for business has created the need for a stronger internal communications function. Then we explore ways to organize internal communications through planning and staffing and how to implement a strong program using various communication channels. Finally, we discuss management's role in internal communications.

---

[1] Ed Emerman, "Better Employee Experience Proven to Drive Financial Success," Willis Towers Watson, November 4, 2019, https://www.willistowerswatson.com/en-US/News/2019/10/better-employee-experience-proven-to-drive-financial-success.

[2] James K. Harter, Frank L. Schmidt, James W. Asplund, Emily A. Killham, and Sangeeta Agrawal, "Causal Impact of Employee Work Perceptions on the Bottom Line of Organizations," *Perspectives on Psychological Science* 5, no. 4 (August 2010), https://journals.sagepub.com/doi/full/10.1177/1745691610374589.

Internal Communications and the Changing Environment

As discussed in Chapter 1, the environment for business has changed dramatically over the last 50 years. Today's employee is a different person in terms of values and needs than his or her counterpart in earlier decades. Most of today's employees are well-educated individuals, have higher expectations of what they will get out of their careers than their parents did, and want to understand more about the companies for which they work. Millennials and Gen Z-ers, in particular, have the unique expectation of ethical and socially responsible employers.[3]

The workplace of today is also different—tighter staffing, longer hours, greater workloads, and more emphasis on performance are the norm. Over a decade later, scars from the Great Recession remain. As Wharton management professor Peter Cappelli notes, "One in five employees lost their jobs at the beginning of the Great Recession. Many of those people never really recovered; they never got real work again." For those who did return to normal work (or who were able to remain employed), prospects were necessarily considerably better. While unemployment hit a historic low of 3.5 percent in 2019,[4] wages, benefits, and job conditions did not improve at a comparable rate.[5] The COVID-19 global pandemic did much to disrupt once again, with unemployment in the United States reaching a historic high of 14.7 percent in April of 2020.[6] While that number dropped to 6.8 percent by year's end,[7] these numbers were still considerably higher for women and people of color, who bore the brunt of the pandemic.[8] All told, these factors are causing employees to look more critically at how senior management is communicating with them, what is being communicated, and whether or not they feel engaged in and aligned with the company's direction.

The increasingly complex and highly competitive nature of today's business environment puts greater pressure on employees and also calls for a more concerted effort in the area of internal communications. "There's a tremendous anxiety in the workplace," says Rick Hodson, a longtime practitioner of employee communications. "When internal communications programs shrink, or disappear, rumor and gossip fill the vacuum. If you keep information from employees, they'll keep their ideas and feelings from you, states Hodson."[9]

[3] "Welcome to Generation Z," Deloitte, https://www2.deloitte.com/content/dam/Deloitte/us/Documents/consumer-business/welcome-to-gen-z.pdf.

[4] Roxanna Edwards and Sean M. Smith, "Job Market Remains Tight in 2019, as the Unemployment Rate Falls to Its Lowest Level Since 1969," BLS, April 2020, https://www.bls.gov/opub/mlr/2020/article/job-market-remains-tight-in-2019-as-the-unemployment-rate-falls-to-its-lowest-level-since-1969.htm.

[5] "How the Great Recession Changed American Workers," Knowledge at Wharton, September 10, 2018, https://knowledge.wharton.upenn.edu/article/great-recession-american-dream.

[6] Rakesh Kochhar, "Unemployment Rose Higher in Three Months of COVID-19 Than It Did in Two Years of the Great Recession," Pew Research Center, June 11, 2020, https://www.pewresearch.org/fact-tank/2020/06/11/unemployment-rose-higher-in-three-months-of-covid-19-than-it-did-in-two-years-of-the-great-recession.

[7] Nelson D. Schwartz, "Unemployment Claims Remain High as Millions Still Struggle to Find Work," *The New York Times*, December 31, 2020, https://www.nytimes.com/2020/12/31/business/economy/unemployment-claims.html.

[8] Tori Bedford, "Women, People of Color Disproportionately Affected by Economic Impacts of Pandemic," GBH, November 10, 2020, https://www.wgbh.org/news/national-news/2020/11/10/women-people-of-color-disproportionately-affected-by-economic-impacts-of-pandemic.

[9] John Guiniven, "Inside Job: Internal Communications in Tough Times," *Public Relations Tactics*, November 2009, p. 6.

Microsoft is one such company that understands the importance of maintaining a two-way dialogue with employees in today's challenging environment. Recognizing the link between employee satisfaction, communication, and leadership, Microsoft CEO Satya Nadella held an intimate discussion with top leadership to discuss how to help the rest of the organization connect with the company's mission. Importantly, then, he opened up the discussion to the rest of the company and leadership, providing the 18,000 managers at Microsoft with tools and resources connected to communicating mission. Kathleen Hogan, the company's Chief People Officer, notes,

> The ability to connect our own purpose to the mission sustains us. When you can zoom out and see how we are making a difference, that's energizing in the face of the day-to-day challenges. While strategy will evolve, your culture and sense of purpose should be long-lasting. Culture paired with a purpose-driven mission allows your employees to use your company platform to realize their own aspirations and passions.[10]

Today's employees are increasingly demanding participation in the conversations at work that drive organizational change. Allowing this participation is vital to keeping employees at all levels of the organization engaged—regardless of job role or responsibility—fostering a more genuine sense of community in companies large or small. In light of this development, communication must be a two-way process. Employees today expect that when their opinions are solicited and they take the time to share feedback, senior management will listen—and act upon it. As the employee experience continues to evolve as an increasing strategic priority, the nature of how to best produce a positive experience has considerably changed under COVID-19, with a recent McKinsey survey finding that employees working remotely seeing positive effects on their work and feeling more engaged.[11] The ramifications for the employee experience in the future are not yet entirely clear, both in terms of the extent to which remote work will be a continuing norm and what this will mean for communicating with employees who aren't gathered in the same geographic location as frequently as they once were. However, many early insights from the pandemic are likely beneficial to carry forward into the next phase of work: continue to prioritize straightforward, honest, and frequent communication with employees, while remaining attuned to their underlying needs.

Organizing the Internal Communication Effort

The best way to assess the effectiveness of a company's internal communication efforts is by determining what employees' attitudes are about the firm. This assessment can be done through an internal *communication audit*. Based on the audit results, communications professionals can design the right program for the organization.

[10]Ron Carucci, "Balancing the Company's Needs and Employee Satisfaction," *Harvard Business Review*, November 1, 2019, https://hbr.org/2019/11/balancing-the-companys-needs-and-employee-satisfaction.

[11]Jonathan Emmett, Gunnar Schrah, Matt Schrimper, and Alexandra Wood, "Open Interactive Popup COVID-19 and the Employee Experience: How Leaders Can Seize the Moment," McKinsey & Company, June 29, 2020, https://www.mckinsey.com/business-functions/organization/our-insights/covid-19-and-the-employee-experience-how-leaders-can-seize-the-moment.

For example, Hyundai, winner of *PRWeek*'s 2020 Employee Engagement Campaign of the Year, recognized that they had a lot of work to do when it came to the gap between sales and employee sentiment. Though Hyundai had just been named North American Car of the Year, employees felt disconnected from the brand and turnover was high. To combat this, the company's in-house communications team looked to reignite employee brand passion to help them better serve as brand ambassadors (and to help make them just happier on the job). They launched the #HyundaiLife campaign, connecting with employees through less formal mechanisms like social media and encouraging employees to share their own experiences with the company. At the end of the day, paying attention to the results of their internal audit paid off: 76 percent of participants said the program lifted their engagement levels and 67 percent said it influenced their peers, colleagues, and teams.[12]

Once it knows how employees really feel about the internal communications they receive, management can create a detailed plan to implement or adjust the internal communication infrastructure to meet its needs. Depending on available resources, audit results, and its goals, management could also consider contracting with a third-party communications consultancy. Failure to implement visible changes in a timely manner following a communication audit, or regular employee surveys, can damage employee morale to a level below where it would be if management had never solicited feedback.

Where Should Internal Communications Report?

In the past, internal communications reported to the human resources area, as traditionally this function dealt with all matters related to employees' welfare. Increasingly, the function is falling under the communications umbrella, with a range of surveys finding that approximately 50 percent of internal communications reporting to the communications or marketing department, as opposed to its historical position within human resources.[13,14] As Michael Collins, Managing Director and Chief Marketing Officer at the CFA Institute, notes,

> I believe there is a difference in employee communications and internal communications. I see employee communications as transmitting extremely important information about benefits, employment policy, hiring, recruiting, career planning, etc. Clearly, those data points are human resources functions and communicating them should originate in the human resources (HR) department, with execution by the HR team or supported by internal communications as part of the marketing and communications team.
>
> In my experience, internal communications serve a broader role that extends external branding, including the organization's mission, to an internal audience that encompasses not only employees but management and board members. In that sense, I've grown to see internal communications as its own discipline. It demands a precise skill-set, ranging

---

[12] "PRWeek US Awards 2020: The Winners," *PRWeek*, July 30, 2020, https://www.prweek.com/article/1686443/prweek-us-awards-2020-winners.

[13] "Employee Engagement Survey 2011," International Association of Business Communicators Research Foundation and Buck Consultants, https://www.iabc.com/wp-content/uploads/2014/10/2011_IABC_Employee_Engagement_Report.pdf.

[14] "Is Internal Communications a Marketing or HR Responsibility?" XCD, https://www.peoplexcd.com/insights/is-internal-communications-a-marketing-or-hr-responsibility.

careful and empathetic listening, clear and concise writing, oral and visual communications expertise, intellectual and emotional agility, and an almost journalistic sense of objectivity that enables telling a story straightforwardly with none-to-limited personal opinion.[15]

Ideally, both the corporate communication and the human resources departments in large companies have someone in charge of internal communications. In this case, the human resources professional has responsibility for perfunctory communications such as those regarding explanation of benefits and the new-hire experience. The corporate communications professional takes the lead for major announcements that affect employees, such as significant changes to benefits. If the head of the corporate communication department reports to the vice president in charge of that area and the head of the human resources department to his or her respective vice president, each should have a dotted-line relationship with the vice president in the other area. Other companies actually situate the communicators focused on routine human resources issues in the corporate communication area to create continuity between both general and HR-related communication strategy and execution. These approaches also will help ensure that the goals of each department are fully met and that the lines of communication are kept open between these two critical functional areas.

Large, multidivisional companies often have internal communications representatives within each division who report jointly to the chief of staff for divisional management and to a firmwide corporate communication department. Ideally, each division shares best practices for delivering high-level messages to the employees in their respective areas—understanding the particular needs and nuances of their employee base, which, in turn, affects both the content and tone of communications. However, the channels may be different across divisions; for instance, some divisions may have a Slack culture, whereas others may pay more attention to e-mail. In larger corporations, there might be vast differences in the online connectivity of employees; those working in production plants or call centers might have no e-mail access whatsoever, whereas other office employees are wholly reliant on e-mail access—whether in-office or remote—to get the job done.

In some cases, companies look outside their own organizations for help with internal communications. For example, in the United Kingdom, Pizza Hut, which operates via a franchise model and which does not have a broad internal communications group, turned to communications consultancy Hanover to help them figure out how to best interact with staff during the COVID-19 pandemic. Hanover helped them launch a campaign to ensure workers felt safe and important, building trust and engagement not just with employees but with the broader community. Hanover suggested they use WhatsApp as the go-to channel for communications, given that it most easily allowed for the creation of both franchise-oriented groups and new groups needed for discussions during the pandemic. Pizza Hut UK's general manager shared posts letting teams know how genuinely valued they were, and staff and community members alike shared their own thank-you posts.

---

[15] Michael Collins, "Does Internal Communications Belong to HR or Corporate Communications?" *Forbes*, March 15, 2019, https://www.forbes.com/sites/forbescommunicationscouncil/2019/03/15/does-internal-communications-belong-to-hr-or-corporate-communications.

Individuals also received recognition through "Delivery Heroes" Awards, which they could be nominated for by colleagues. All told, the campaign reached 7,500 team members, 60 franchisees, and 400 restaurant managers, with employees reporting they felt far more confident and safe returning to work given how easy and transparent communications had become, despite the considerable stresses of the pandemic. Ultimately, Pizza Hut and Hanover won *PRWeek* UK's Internal Communications and Employee Engagement Campaign of the Year.[16] As the importance of internal communication gains recognition, it is not surprising that public relations and consulting firms are developing capabilities in the area of internal communications or that companies are increasingly turning to them for assistance.

Regardless of where the internal communications is positioned and whether or not an outside consultant is used, it must work closely in conjunction with external communicators to integrate the messages disseminated to both internal and external audiences. This approach can help ensure that when significant company news breaks, employees will not be the last to hear about it.

When news about a company becomes public, whether through a breaking news report or a Tweet-storm, employees should already be equipped with the company's own version of the story so they feel they are being kept in the loop by their own team. This strategy also enables companies to maintain better control of their messages, without being at the whim of how the media position them.

In addition to providing employees with timely and strategic updates on company news to help them feel connected and empowered, companies should understand that employees are often members of multiple constituency groups. As David Verbraska, Vice President of Worldwide Policy and Public Affairs at Pfizer, writes, "employees wear many hats—they're stockholders, recruiters, customers, and members of the community. . . . Management must understand that the internal audience could be even more important to a company than the external for all the right business reasons, and there are consequences to not aligning the areas."[17]

Some companies view the label "internal communications" as archaic and believe that the future of the industry is one in which internal and external communications are housed together. Explains Chris Hannegan, principal in PwC's Organization and Workforce Transformation group, "[A]lready today there is no more distinction between internal and external communications. Companies must assume that all communications going to employees could find its way to external social media and that all external coverage of the company is being followed closely by employees."[18] The likelihood of memos or other communications leaking to the outside world with a click of the mouse means that internal communicators should always consider the ramifications of their messages being shared with external audiences, including reporters and investors. This risk can be managed with positive outcomes. Companies will "increasingly understand how to strategically place media coverage done solely for the benefit of targeting employees and, conversely, leak

---

[16] "PRWeek UK Awards Winners 2020: Internal Communications and Employee Engagement," *PRWeek*, https://www.prweek.com/article/1696264/prweek-uk-awards-winners-2020-internal-communications-employee-engagement.

[17] Richard Mitchell, "Closing the Gap: From the Inside Out," *PRWeek* (U.S.), November 22, 2004, p. 17.

[18] "Chris Hannegan, "What Will the Future of Employee Engagement Look Like?", Edelman Global Practices Insights, June 26, 2014, http://www.edelman.com/post/will-future-employee-engagement-look-like/.

internal stories or information to the media to inject the employee voice into a company's external narrative," writes Hannegan.[19] Many companies already enable their employees to share internal communications content externally via social media, and this trend will only increase.

Implementing an Effective Internal Communication Program

Once goals for an internal communication program are established and decisions are made about where the function should report, the program is ready for implementation. In smaller organizations, internal communications may be a part of everyone's job, because the ideal method of communicating with employees is one-on-one or in meetings with small groups of employees.

Even in larger organizations, however, this intimacy in the internal communication effort is a good start for building a more formal program. In this section, we explore some of the key steps in implementing an effective internal communication program, from personal, one-on-one mechanisms to programs that use technology to distribute messages broadly and instantaneously.

It is the job of the internal communications professional to determine which combination of communication channels is the most appropriate for each message, based on factors such as timing requirements and potential employee reactions. Channel selection can mean the difference between success and failure for an initiative, and it can have a significant impact on employee morale.

Communicate Up and Down

Many large companies are perceived as being faceless, unfeeling organizations, an impression that is only reinforced when no upward communication exists from employees to management. When high-level managers isolate themselves physically and psychologically from other employees, effective communication cannot happen. Given the wide availability of technologies such as Zoom or Microsoft Teams, there is little excuse today to find a way to at least approximate an in-person or more intimate interaction.

Companies should remember to involve individual supervisors when announcing important news. A 2020 study from Gallup found that record levels of employee engagement, reaching 35 percent in February (though notably this was before the pandemic), could be attributed in large part to the inclusion of lower-level managers in key communications practices.[20]

It should be the responsibility of the internal communications professionals to provide supervisors with the information, tools, and ongoing support that they need to present news to their direct reports. Additionally, management should strive to create an environment where all employees feel comfortable sharing candid feedback. A recent MIT Sloan survey found that 17.5 percent of employees feel that they cannot speak up at all in the work setting, and another 47.1 percent felt comfortable speaking up only on a narrow range

---

[19] Ibid.

[20] Jim Harter, "4 Factors Driving Record-High Employee Engagement in U.S.," Gallup, February 4, 2020, https://www.gallup.com/workplace/284180/factors-driving-record-high-employee-engagement.aspx.

of topics.[21] Emeritus Professor of Leadership at Harvard Business School and former Vice Chairman of Goldman Sachs Robert S. Kaplan writes of the importance of an open culture, now more than ever. In the current business environment, he explains that "external shifts may be difficult for senior leadership to recognize, and otherwise vocal employees at the 'point of attack' may not feel sufficiently informed or empowered to voice their views." It is imperative, writes Kaplan, that CEOs and other executives recognize that they can take steps to getting valuable input on key strategic questions from their teams.[22] Effective internal communications can generate a dialogue throughout the company, fostering a sense of participation that can make even the largest companies feel more personal in the hearts and minds of employees.

The best approach to communicating with employees is through informal discussions between employees and supervisors. Employees need to feel secure enough in their positions to ask questions and offer advice without fear of reprisals from top management. At Accenture, one of the world's largest consulting firms, senior management involvement begins pre-hire, with executives taking part in the final rounds of interviews. Once on board, each new employee is assigned a career counselor, who can mentor employees throughout their stay at the company. Employees can also join community groups based on their discipline. Neil Hardiman, who transferred to the Chicago office from Dublin, said, "As I would walk around the floors of the office, I would knock on the door and just say hello. . . . That led to some great contacts and connections for me within Chicago."[23]

Emkay, one of the nation's largest fleet-leasing companies, keeps employees in the know through quarterly town halls and departmental committees. Employees gain a sense of ownership through exposure to the company's most sensitive information, such as potential acquisitions and earnings projections.[24]

Conversations with management promote feelings that employees themselves are serving as catalysts for organizational change. As Peter Senge highlights with a quote from the ancient Chinese visionary Lao Tsu:

> The wicked leader is he who the people despise, the good leader is he who the people revere, the great leader is he who the people say, "We did it ourselves."[25]

Respecting employees as well as listening to and interacting with them form the basis for an effective internal communications program. Emkay CEO Greg Tepas encourages feedback from employees and allows information to flow up to the top ranks. According

[21] Ethan Burris, Elizabeth McCune, and Dawn Klinghoffer, "When Employees Speak Up, Companies Win," *MIT Sloan Management Review*, November 17, 2020, https://sloanreview.mit.edu/article/when-employees-speak-up-companies-win..

[22] McKinsey Insights, September 2011, www.mckinsey.com/insights/leading_in_the_21st_century/top_executives_need_feedback_and__heres_how_they_can_get_it.

[23] Robert Channick, "Emphasis on Communication with Employees Brings Good Words about These Companies," *Chicago Tribune*, April 17, 2011, https://www.chicagotribune.com/business/ct-xpm-2011-04-17-ct-biz-0417-top-workplaces-20110417-story.html.

[24] Ibid.

[25] Peter Senge, "The Leader's New Work: Building Learning Organizations," *Sloan Management Review* 32 (Fall 1990), pp. 7–23.

to Tepas, "You can accomplish more together if everyone is driving towards those common objectives and understands why you're doing it and how you're going to do it."[26] In the current business environment, marked by declining trust in institutions and a focus on reputation, listening to employees is one of the key steps a company can take toward maintaining brand credibility and trust. Writes Micho Spring, Global Chair of the Corporate Practice at Weber Shandwick, "[E]ngaging them can provide companies the best way to humanize and unify their enterprise voice—a strategic imperative in today's environment."[27]

Make Time for Face-to-Face Meetings (Even If They Are Virtual)

One means of ensuring that employees have access to senior management is to hold regular, in-person meetings with fairly large groups of employees. Such town hall meetings should take place frequently (at least quarterly) and should be used as opportunities for management to share company results and progress on key initiatives and to demonstrate responsiveness to prior employee feedback. Most important, such meetings should provide employees with an opportunity to ask questions of management in an open forum. If size and geography prevent employees from participating in person, video or telephone conferencing should be used to facilitate their inclusion.

Topics for these types of gatherings should be limited; rather than trying to tackle everything that is going on at the company, managers should survey employees beforehand to find out what is most important to them. Then a presentation can be built around one or two critical issues from the employee perspective, plus one or more messages that management wants to share. Too often, management only sets up such meetings when the company has an important announcement, reducing the likelihood of relevant dialogue.

Gatherings can also be creative to mobilize and inspire employees. To encourage its environmental sustainability platform, GE hosts treasure hunts where staffers examine ways in which the company can be more energy efficient.[28] And in the COVID-19 world, companies became even more creative with their end-of-year parties, with companies like Intel hosting a virtual reality holiday featuring unique avatars designed by every employee.

Certainly, large-scale events are an effective means to reach out to the greatest number of employees at one time, but managers should not overlook the importance of meeting with employees in smaller groups. If they are seeking feedback or opinions about key initiatives, managers may find that employees are more forthcoming when not in a large-group setting. Increasingly, and particularly as a consequence of the pandemic, companies are turning to virtual settings to accomplish these smaller settings and to create new opportunities for more intimate face-time. However, companies ought to be wary of too easily slipping into over-scheduling of these smaller events, however well-intentioned they may seem. Researchers at the Harvard Business School and New York University found

[26] Channick, "Emphasis on Communication with Employees Brings Good Words about These Companies."

[27] "Employees Rising: Seizing the Opportunity in Employee Activism," Weber Shandwick, https://www.webershandwick.com/uploads/news/files/employees-rising-seizing-the-opportunity-in-employee-activism.pdf.

[28] Channick, "Emphasis on Communication with Employees Brings Good Words about These Companies."

that the number of meetings employees had to attend actually increased by 12.9 percent during the pandemic,[29] which of course leads to concerns regarding employee fatigue, burnout, and lost productivity. At the same time, the best organizations found their productivity increasing by 5 percent or more during this time period.[30] Thus, like so many other things in business and in life, moderation is key to make the most of meetings, both small and large, in-person and virtual.

Communicate and Monitor Online

Beyond use for meetings such as Zoom, companies must carefully consider the plethora of other digital options available to communicate internally with their teams. One classic, and still broadly adopted approach, is the company intranet. Introduced in the late 1990s, intranets provided a new channel through which companies could reach their employees quickly and broadly with important news on events and key management initiatives. While nearly 85 percent of organizations still maintain such platforms,[31] the utility of the company intranet has been increasingly called into question, in part because of the trend toward becoming the company "junk drawer,"[32] with poorly organized information and minimal search functionality. Employees seem to share the perspective that intranets possess limited utility, with a recent study from digital change consultancy Perficient finding that only 13 percent of employees use the intranet daily and 31 percent have never used it at all.[33] What, then, to do with the company intranet? Is it now a relic of the past, or does it still hold value for the future?

For some companies, maintaining some iteration of their current intranet may be the best decision, a consequence of the wealth of knowledge still held on these platforms and the extent to which they can be interwoven into employees' day-to-day operations. In these scenarios, a company intranet should be dynamic and engaging, with the home page regularly refreshed, so it becomes an employee's go-to resource for the latest company information. Ideally, it should be integrated into an employee's everyday workflow, serving as a resource employees can turn to in order to answer key questions on company operations.

Another key function of intranets, however, extends beyond knowledge management as discussed above, to providing space for easy collaboration. It is in this particular area that many companies have elected to turn to other, more modern communication tools. Two tools that have come to dominate the space are Slack and Microsoft Teams, which as of

[29] Richard Holden, "Vital Signs: Shorter Meetings but Longer Days—How COVID-19 Has Changed the Way We Work," *The Conversation*, August 6, 2020, https://theconversation.com/vital-signs-shorter-meetings-but-longer-days-how-covid-19-has-changed-the-way-we-work-143894.

[30] Eric Garton and Michael Mankins, "The Pandemic Is Widening a Corporate Productivity Gap," *Harvard Business Review*, December 1, 2020, https://hbr.org/2020/12/the-pandemic-is-widening-a-corporate-productivity-gap.

[31] "State of the Intranet 2020," Simpplr Research, https://www.simpplr.com/wp-content/uploads/2020/06/State-of-the-Intranet-2020-eBook-Simpplr-Research.pdf.

[32] Dhiraj Sharma, "Don't Let Your Company's Intranet Become a Junk Drawer," *Harvard Business Review*, May 8, 2020, https://hbr.org/2020/05/dont-let-your-companys-intranet-become-a-junk-drawer.

[33] Mark Polly, "Increasing Employee Engagement—Salesforce Community Cloud #DF16," Perficient, October 6, 2016, https://blogs.perficient.com/2016/10/06/increasing-employee-engagement-salesforce-community-cloud-df16.

the end of 2020 have combined daily active users of over 125 million.[34,35] Forces that have led to the widespread adoption of these tools include not only the need for easier collaboration, but also as a means for better managing company knowledge, a function historically within the domain of the intranet. Companies ought to be careful, then, not to duplicate currently offered functionalities in a way that leads to confusion or inefficiency. Notably, a recent survey of 200 IT decision-makers found that 91 percent of organizations had at least two messaging apps,[36] betraying that many companies already find themselves in this exact position.

Finally, social media is a key area for companies to consider within the context of internal communications. In many ways, social media represents a more external communication tool—one that is utilized as an extension of the marketing function through paid posts on Instagram and Facebook or in brand building through a company's Twitter presence. However, employees, driven in large part by Millennials and Gen Z-ers joining the workforce, also voice their own perspectives and interact with fellow employees on these externally facing tools, leading to the strange position where internal communications have suddenly become externally facing. Moreover, employees also interact with companies' more official social media posts, in ways that, when carefully managed, can actually amplify what initially was meant to be just an external communication. For example, LinkedIn content shared by employees sees an increased reach of 30 percent beyond content shared by the company alone.[37]

Given this intersection of the internal and external, companies need to introduce their own social media policies. IBM was one of the first organizations to introduce guidelines for employee blogging in 2005. Today, IBM's guidelines are not just limited to blogging; they have been revised and renamed "IBM Social Computing Guidelines" to accommodate new forms of social media.[38] Despite the near ubiquity of online presences for employees, today only 51 percent of companies have a social media policy.[39] The consequences of the absence of such a policy, or a less-than-transparent one, can be considerable. In highly regulated industries such as finance, social media can be a legal minefield and a danger to corporate reputation. Every tweet, post, and poke made by employees must be recorded and archived, or firms can be held liable. Ex-CFO of clothing retailer Francesca's Gene Morphis learned just how real these risks are. In 2012, after a positive board meeting,

[34] Jared Spataro, "Microsoft Teams Reaches 115 Million DAU—Plus, a New Daily Collaboration Minutes Metric for Microsoft 365," Microsoft, October 28, 2020, https://www.microsoft.com/en-us/microsoft-365/blog/2020/10/28/microsoft-teams-reaches-115-million-dau-plus-a-new-daily-collaboration-minutes-metric-for-microsoft-365.

[35] David Curry, "Slack Revenue and Usage Statistics (2021)," Business of Apps, March 22, 2021, https://www.businessofapps.com/data/slack-statistics.

[36] Matthew Finnegan, "Slack or Teams? Many Businesses Opt for Both," Computerworld, June 20, 2019, https://www.computerworld.com/article/3403675/slack-or-teams-many-businesses-opt-for-both.html.

[37] Jason Miller, "The Amazing Multiple Benefits When an Employee Shares Content," LinkedIn, January 31, 2017, https://business.linkedin.com/en-uk/marketing-solutions/blog/posts/content-marketing/2017/The-amazing-multiple-benefits-when-an-employee-shares-content.

[38] www.ibm.com/blogs/zz/en/guidelines.html.

[39] Meghan M. Biro, "Why Annual Social Media Policy Reviews Are Necessary," *The Entrepreneur*, March 27, 2017, https://www.entrepreneur.com/article/285920.

Morphis tweeted: "Board meeting. Good numbers=Happy Board." Unfortunately for Morphis, official earnings had not yet been released to all investors, and his Twitter followers were, therefore, privy to insider information, an SEC violation. He was fired shortly thereafter.[40] Hallowed investment bank Goldman Sachs was also thrown for a loop when a disgruntled employee of 11 years resigned in an open letter published online by *The New York Times*, which labeled the firm "as toxic and destructive as I have ever seen it." The letter quickly went viral, leaving Goldman Sachs with a PR disaster on its hands and an immediate stock price drop of 3.4 percent, a loss of $2.15 billion.[41]

Online communication channels are often expedient and engaging, but they must also be monitored to safeguard any potential leak of information or otherwise damaging information. They should also not be used as a substitute for personal, face-to-face communication between all levels of management and employees, as we will see later in the chapter.

Communicate Visually

We know that people are increasingly turning to online video, social media, and websites, in addition to television and traditional news outlets, to get their news. Similarly, employees are becoming more visually oriented in their consumption of information, particularly given increased use of company intranets. As a result, many companies have developed ways to communicate with employees through this powerful medium, now including everything from basic webcasts to multi-media presentations allowing for employee interaction.

Many large corporations have elaborate video production studios that create seamless mechanisms for communicating with employees through visual channels. Even if your company does not have its own studio, outside vendors can provide these services as needed.

These studios are often used to create "video shorts" that can be made available to employees in outlying areas, helping them feel like part of the core organization no matter where they are situated—a function that is increasing in importance as a consequence of the movement toward increasing remote work.

Johnson & Johnson offers an excellent example of a company that recognizes the importance of visuals for internal communications. The company launched their "J&J News Center" in September 2013, originally as a home for press releases. However, it quickly came to realize the value of increasing visuals not only to offer greater insight into the company's mission and operations to outsiders, but perhaps more importantly, to its day-to-day employees. Susan Rucci, manager of J&J's Social Media Content, noted, "As the digital landscape is changing, J&J is adapting and evolving as well, so we have redesigned the center to visually showcase our stories. We noticed a really strong visual—whether it is a photo, graphic, or quote—can be really impactful immediately." Ernie Knewitz, VP of Media Relations, echoed her sentiment when he noted,

---

[40] Ryan Holmes, "Social Media Compliance Isn't Fun, But It's Necessary," HBR Blogs Network, August 23, 2012, http://blogs.hbr.org/2012/08/social-media-compliance-isnt.

[41] Christine Harper, "Goldman Roiled by Op-Ed Loses $2.2 Billion," Bloomberg, March 15, 2012, https://www.bloomberg.com/news/2012-03-15/goldman-stunned-by-op-ed-loses-2-2-billion-for-shareholders.html?mrefid=twitter.

"The news center is a tool for engagement to drive trust and stimulate conversations about the company and what we are doing around the world." Visual communication, then, provides unique opportunity for engagement both with internal and external constituencies, making it a particularly powerful tool in the communications arsenal.

Moreover, managers should not see expenditures on such communication as frivolous or wasteful but rather as an investment in the firm, a way to make each employee feel more connected, while also "humanizing" senior management. In contrast to the sometimes impersonal nature of e-mail communication, these communications can offer employees a personal touch—literally bringing a company's leaders and vision to life without the time and expense of traveling. If such a production is well done, it can be a tremendous morale booster as well as a visual history of the company that can be used for years to come.

And visual communication does not always have to be high-tech. At Colgate-Palmolive's Mennen plant, for example, ubiquitous white boards revealed details about breakdowns, production goals, sick leaves, birthdays, vacation schedules, and numbers of units coming off each line. A special racecar billboard depicted the productivity of each line relative to the others—a visual measure of success and a source of motivation and pride. Verizon added a high-tech twist to the low-tech bulletin board. The company provides electronic downloads for supervisors to insert in the board. Each month the content is updated to ensure employees receive up-to-date messages.[42]

Focus on Internal Branding

In this chapter, we have discussed the importance of clear, two-way communication about strategy and direction. Internal branding is also important to building morale and creating a workplace where employees are "engaged" with their jobs. Although communicators do inform employees about new advertising campaigns, they seldom recognize the need to "sell" employees on the same ideas they are trying to sell to the public.

Internal branding is especially critical when an organization is undergoing changes such as a merger or a change in leadership. Over the course of two years, Citrix employees witnessed a restructuring of the workforce, executive turnover, product line adjustments, changes to the composition of the board, a new strategy, and a layoff. Despite efforts to maintain stability and help employees navigate all this change, the 2017 Global Employee Survey confirmed that trust in leadership had declined and employees lacked confidence in the company's new direction, as well as their own ability to contribute to it. Engagement overall had fallen significantly as well. All this led the communications team to select one overarching goal for 2018: Engage employees around the Citrix story. Two approaches drove the department's activities: a focus on strategy, storytelling, and enterprise engagement; and providing communications and messaging consulting support. These activities centered around "The 2020 Goals"—broad, unifying objectives the company also embedded in its performance, development, and rewards programs, ensuring alignment with business priorities.

[42] Kelly Kass, "Verizon Equips Employees with All the Right Tools," Simply Communicate, http://www.simply-communicate. com/case-studies/company-profile/verizon-equips-employees-all-right-tools.

Most significantly, the team created a Center of Excellence to ensure consistent messaging across the organization's various communication functions. Messages were cascaded through multiple channels, including employee meetings (which were increased to a bimonthly schedule), the intranet, a Five-Minute Manager Update (designed to provide managers with weekly action items) and other internal programs. As a result, Citrix saw an 80 percent improvement in its Net Promoter Score, along with significant other improvements in employee perceptions. Ultimately, Citrix won PR Daily's 2018 Employee Engagement Campaign of the year for their efforts.[43]

Internal branding campaigns can also be launched when results of internal audits reveal that employees are not connecting with a company's vision or when morale is low. When internal and external marketing messages are misaligned, the customer experience will suffer, with adverse effects on the company. For example, one health care company marketed itself as putting the welfare of its customers as its number-one priority, while telling employees that the number-one priority was cutting costs.

Internal branding campaigns are not just for times of leadership change, mergers, crisis, or low employee morale. For example, when the Alzheimer's Society sought to launch a rebranding effort in 2018, it started first with the internal communications, turning to employees and current ambassadors. The charity introduced its new brand and five-year strategy through the use of its internal TV channel, which it used to premier a film explaining the upcoming changes and the thoughts behind them. The company also included in-person activities centered around Forget Me Not Day, with leadership traveling to centers across the country and the use of the hashtag #unitedagainstdementia to streamline everyone's social media presence. The end result of the campaign was highly successful, with 91 percent of employees and volunteers now viewing themselves as charity ambassadors, both during the normal course of their work and in their day-to-day lives.[44]

Even when employees *understand* the company's brand promise or key customer deliverable, it is not until they *believe* it that they can really help the company carry it out. Just as external branding campaigns aim to create emotional ties among consumers to your company, internal branding's goal is to do the same with employees. Focusing attention on this important area will generate improved employee morale and, ultimately, better results for the company.

Management's Role in Internal Communications

A common thread in the company examples discussed in this chapter is the involvement in internal communications of CEOs and other senior leaders within organizations. This involvement is critical because these individuals are the "culture carriers" and visionaries within a company, and all communications relating to organizational strategy start with them. Increasingly, CEOs and senior managers—in the tradition of John Pierpont

---

[43] "Citrix Communicators Focus on a Single Goal when Engagement Flags after Momentous Changes," *PR Daily*, https://www.prdaily.com/awards/employee-communications-awards/2018/winners/employee-engagement.

[44] "The 10 Best Internal Communications Case Studies of 2018," McCann Synergy, February 13, 2019, https://www.mccannsynergy.com/the-10-best-internal-communications-case-studies-of-2018.

Morgan's desk on the trading floor—are even positioning themselves in the midst of their employees physically, working at standard desks or giving up their larger, more formal offices to demonstrate a flatter hierarchy. Senior leadership is also being more thoughtful about where they sit in meetings, too, electing to choose a spot on the side of conferences tables as opposed sitting at the imposing head.[45] The visibility of senior management helps create a culture of transparency, a critical issue in the current business environment. In Slack's most recent State of Work publication, they found that 80 percent of employees want their work environments to be even more transparent, a wake-up call for executives.[46]

Robert Dilenschneider, founder of corporate strategic counseling and public relations firm The Dilenschneider Group, describes the type of leader the twenty-first-century corporate landscape demands:

> What's needed now is a different kind of CEO: men and women who shed the trappings of imperial power, work with their boards of directors in new, dynamic relationships and find fresh ways to unleash the creative potential of their people, from middle managers to front-line workers. This will require a big shift in attitude from change-averse managers. They'll need to get off their private jets and fly with everyone else, shed the large personal staffs that coddle and isolate them and spend real time with the workers who are on the factory floors, behind the sales counters or in the office cubicles.[47]

Physical presence and interaction are an important start. Senior managers, however, also need to work closely with internal communications professionals to ensure their messages are received and, most important, understood by all employees. The "understanding" component is crucial but sometimes overlooked. Donald Sheppard, former CEO of Sheppard Associates, an independent consulting agency specializing in internal communication strategy, says, "You can have a vision of 'we want to be this'—that's nice, but the person out there in the plant in Michigan or in India needs to understand how that applies to him or her and what he or she needs to do differently. That can't be done at any macro level."[48]

Conclusion

Over the last several years, "management by walking around" and other management philosophies basically have come to the same conclusion: managers need to get out from behind their desks, put down their smartphones, and go out and get to know the people who are working for them. No other method works as well, and no "quick fix" will satisfy the basic need for interaction with other employees.

---

[45] Jeanne Sahadi, "Where the CEO Sits Matters," *CNN Business*, May 21, 2019, https://www.cnn.com/2019/05/20/success/ceos-office/index.html.

[46] "Trust, Tools and Teamwork: What Workers Want," Slack, October 3, 2018, https://slack.com/blog/transformation/trust-tools-and-teamwork-what-workers-want.

[47] Robert L. Dilenschneider, "When CEOs Roamed the Earth," *The Wall Street Journal*, March 15, 2005, p. B2.

[48] Lin Grensing Pophal, "Follow Me", *HR Magazine*, Vol. 45, Number 2, February 2000.

With all the sophisticated technology available to communicate with employees today, such as Slack, Teams, e-mail, social media, and Zoom meetings, the most important factor in internal communications begins with the manager who has a basic responsibility to his or her employees. That responsibility is to listen to what they have to say and to get to know who they really are as individuals. We have come a long way from Upton Sinclair's *The Jungle* to the modern American corporation. Today's employees do want high-tech and sophisticated communications, but they also want personal contact with their managers. Understanding this fact is the cornerstone of an effective internal communication program.

Go Travel

Dan Cassidy, a 2017 graduate of the Tuck School of Business at Dartmouth College, was sitting in his apartment, having spent a long day on Zoom meetings. He had just signed out of a meeting with his boss, Catherine Callahan, the Vice President of Human Resources at Go Travel. "Dan, I know we've all been stressed about much of what is going on with COVID, but unfortunately we are going to have to let a decent amount of our team go," she said. "I'm hoping that the CEO will buy my plan for voluntary severance and expedited vesting schedules for those who had taken a chance on working at a startup like ours."

Go Travel had never laid off anyone in the nearly 10 years of its existence. In fact, it had been considered a high-flying darling of Silicon Valley that had nowhere to go but up. The global pandemic, however, had changed that, and as the Director of Employee Relations, Dan would be responsible for telling employees about the new policy within the next couple of days.

As he stared out his apartment window to the beautiful southern California hills, many thoughts were going through his head. How should he identify the issues involved for all employees? Should he get the people in corporate communication involved? Who would be the best person to release the information? What about communication with other Go Travel constituencies? And what would be the long-term effects of what would be reported in the media as a "major downsizing"?

GO TRAVEL BACKGROUND

Go Travel was started by Linda Bosworth, a brilliant UCLA graduate, following her graduation in 2010. With a vision for changing the travel experience in her head, Bosworth had built the firm up to unicorn status, valued at well over a billion dollars with millions of venture-capital dollars funneled in over its short lifetime.

As the business grew, Bosworth gradually turned the day-to-day operation of Westwood over to professional managers, including MBAs from top business schools. But the bulk of employees were young college graduates, eager to work at a high-flying startup but also significantly burdened by student debt.

Even though at the start of the COVID-19 pandemic, many CEOs anticipated needing to make difficult decisions regarding their workforce, Bosworth was originally optimistic that no one would have to face being furloughed or fired: "You, the employees of Go Travel, are the most important assets that we have. Despite the difficult times this company now faces, you have my assurance that I will never ask any of you to leave for economic reasons."

CORPORATE COMMUNICATION AT GO TRAVEL

The company relied on a small staff of communication professionals to handle its communication efforts. All of the various activities that could be decentralized (e.g., internal communications, investor relations) were housed in the appropriate functional areas. This organization developed naturally as the company grew to become one of the most popular luggage brands in the United States.

The main outreaches to employees were annual meetings, where slide-heavy presentations from Bosworth and other top company executives would draw upwards of the entire employee workforce. Bosworth, as a young owner and CEO, enjoyed much attention from the press as a result of her meteoric rise in the business world. She relied on an outside consultant,

Craig Stevens, to handle her own public relations. Stevens also had a tremendous amount of influence over the communications department at the company itself.

The VP of Corporate Communication, Eric Ridgeway, was actually one of the several employees who would be affected by the current plan to trim the workforce. He had been hired early on as a favor to Bosworth's father. Ridgeway had spent 25 years at a large rival to Go Travel before signing on at the company, and although he had a media background, he was still newer to selling to the primarily millennial consumer that Go Travel targeted. The problems associated with Ridgway made the communications effort more difficult for both Dan Cassidy and the outside counsel advising him through the process.

THE VOLUNTARY SEVERANCE AND EXPEDITED VESTING PROGRAM

The Although the CEO was very much against the programs that were about to be implemented, she had been convinced by both Callahan, the Head of Human Resources, and her Board of Directors that something had to be done immediately, or the company itself would be at risk.

The way the programs would work, about half the employees were going to furloughed for an as-yet decided period of time, and another 25 percent of employees would be let go. The intention was to only let the lowest-performing employees go, and thus, a product manager who had received less than excellent performance appraisals for two consecutive years would be a prime candidate for voluntary severance with limited benefits, whereas a manager approaching four years with the company would be offered severance with full vesting. Although both of these programs were "voluntary," the supervisors responsible for identifying candidates were urged to get the weaker people to agree as soon as possible.

COMMUNICATING ABOUT THE PLANS

As Cassidy signed into work the following day, he saw that a meeting had been added to his calendar with his supervisor, Catherine Callahan, as well as Bosworth and Craig Stevens. "Well Dan, how are you going to pull this one off?" joked Bosworth. Cassidy responded, "Quite honestly, Linda, given your position on this issue, my feeling is that you need to get involved with the announcement tomorrow."

As the discussion progressed, however, it was obvious to Dan that he was the one that his boss and the head of the company wanted to take the heat. After two hours, Bosworth looked Dan squarely in the eye and said: "This was not my idea in the first place, but I know we have no choice but to adopt the voluntary severance packages for Go Travel. Unfortunately, I have conference calls with our investors all day tomorrow, so you and Catherine are going to have to take responsibility this time."

Before Dan could fully digest what Bosworth had told him, he was distracted by a *Wall Street Journal* notification about another tech company that had botched their COVID-19 workforce plan. He could not help but wonder if he, too, would become the focus of such an article if he mismanaged the difficult conversations ahead.

CASE QUESTIONS

1. Create a strategy for communicating change at Go Travel that you could give to Bosworth.
2. How do changes in the workforce affect how Cassidy ought to think about communicating the new policy?
3. What advice would you give Cassidy about how communications to employees are structured at Go Travel?

CHAPTER EIGHT

Investor Relations

As companies strive to maximize shareholder value, they must continually communicate their progress toward that goal to the investing public. Accordingly, investor relations is an essential subfunction of a company's corporate communication program. While explaining financial results and giving guidance on future earnings are critical investor relations activities, companies today need to go "beyond the numbers"—as Collins and Porras explain in their book *Built to Last*:

> Visionary companies pursue a cluster of objectives, of which making money is only one—and not necessarily the primary one. Yes, they seek profits, but they're equally guided by a core ideology—core values and sense of purpose beyond just making money. Yet, paradoxically, the visionary companies make more money than the more purely profit-driven comparison companies.[1]

Investor relations professionals therefore need to link communications to a company's strategy and "vision" as frequently as possible. Increasingly, the investor relations (IR) function is getting involved in activities traditionally handled by public relations and media relations professionals and communicating with many of the same constituencies. In addition to a solid understanding of finance, IR professionals, therefore, also need strong communication skills.

In this chapter, we begin our examination of this important subfunction with an overview of investor relations and a brief look at its evolution over the years. We then turn to the goals of investor relations and provide a framework for IR. After discussing important investor constituency groups and how IR reaches them, we look at how the function fits into an organization and conclude with a discussion of investor relations in the changing business environment.

Investor Relations Overview

The National Investor Relations Institute (NIRI) defines investor relations as "a strategic management responsibility that integrates finance, communication, marketing and securities law compliance to enable the most effective two-way communication between a company, the financial community, and other constituencies, which ultimately contributes to a company's securities achieving fair valuation."[2] Many practitioners and academics emphasize that "the modern day investor relations professional realize[s] that investors

[1] James C. Collins and Jerry I. Porras, *Built to Last* (New York: Harper Business, 2002), p. 8.

[2] NIRI corporate website, www.niri.org.

are not interested in seeing a company's 10K or 10Q, but instead are interested in understanding the company's business and its value. To create this better understanding, companies have to expand their communications with shareholders from obligatory financial disclosure to include . . . intangible and non-financial aspects of business."[3]

As these descriptions illustrate, investor relations is both a financial discipline and a corporate communication function. Changes in the business and regulatory environment over the past decade have affected the way corporations decide how, to whom, and to what extent they convey financial and operating results.

Investors want understandable explanations of financial performance as well as nonfinancial information about companies. A popular study from Ernst & Young's Center for Business Innovation reveals that analysts and investors rely on a broad range of nonfinancial indicators when making investment decisions, including quality of employees, innovation, the credibility of management, and the execution of corporate strategy.[4] Indeed, according to consulting firm McKinsey, best-in-class companies look beyond basic financial reporting, recognizing that maintaining good communications with analysts and investors involves "shift[ing] focus away from short-term performance and toward the drivers of long-term company health as well as their expectations of future business conditions and their long-range goals."[5]

Increasingly, the understanding of long-term company health has expanded to include the notion of corporate social responsibility (as discussed in Chapter 4), and thus the ability to speak to this portion of a company's mission has also landed upon the shoulders of investor relations professionals. Suzanne Fallender, Director of Corporate Responsibility at Intel noted, "I expect we will see investor focus on ESG continue to evolve . . . In response we also will likely see companies take a more integrated approach to their disclosure and investor outreach activities, with tighter alignment between CSR, investor relations, and corporate governance teams."[6]

To ensure that a company presents itself clearly and favorably on all these fronts, then, IR professionals must have both financial acumen and solid communication skills. Access to senior management is also necessary so that the IR function is connected to the company's strategy and vision. An IR department organized in this way is positioned to instill confidence in investors in both good times and bad.

The Evolution of Investor Relations

In the early part of the twentieth century, corporate secrecy was a great concern for companies. Disclosure of any kind was seen as potentially harmful to the interests of the corporation. This perception changed in the 1930s with the passage of two federal securities acts that required public companies to file periodic disclosures with the U.S. Securities and Exchange Commission (SEC). Despite the new reporting responsibilities brought about by the enactment of the Securities Act of 1933 and the Securities Exchange Act of 1934, corporations were interested only in mandatory disclosure, which required little in the way of an investor relations function.

[3] Institute for PR, "Investor Relations," www.instituteforpr.org/investor-relations, January 2011.

[4] "Measures that Matter," Ernst & Young Center for Business Innovation, May 2010.

[5] Peggy Hsieh, Timothy Koller, and S.R. Rajan, "The Misguided Practice of Earnings Guidance," *McKinsey Quarterly*, May 2006.

[6] Susan McPherson, "Corporate Responsibility: What to Expect in 2019," *Forbes*, January 14, 2019, https://www.forbes.com/sites/susanmcpherson/2019/01/14/corporate-responsibility-what-to-expect-in-2019.

Investor relations did not begin to resemble the discipline we know today until the 1950s. A decade later, the National Investor Relations Institute (NIRI) officially recognized the IR function. NIRI was established as a professional association of corporate officers and investor relations consultants who were responsible for communicating with corporate management, the investing public, and the financial community. Around the same time, the Chicago-based Financial Relations Board (FRB), now a unit of The Interpublic Group, became the first public relations firm dedicated to helping its clients develop relationships with investors.

By the 1970s, FRB had pioneered the distribution of investment profiles that laid out a company's long-term financial goals and strategies. Prior to this innovation, information reached potential investors through presentations by company representatives to local stockbroker clubs or analysts' societies.

Further regulatory changes altered the landscape for IR in the 1970s. With the enactment of the Employee Retirement Income Security Act (ERISA) in 1974, pension fund managers were legally held responsible for acting in the best interests of their beneficiaries. This new responsibility made pension fund managers more demanding of their portfolio companies. For instance, they sought more detailed explanations of company results, particularly when companies underperformed.

In the 1980s, state and local laws enabled pension funds to increase the equity allocation in their portfolios. That share rose to 36 percent in 1989 from 22 percent in 1982, making institutional investors an even more important constituency for the IR departments of corporations. At the same time, inflation caused many individual investors to flee the stock market, and by the end of the 1980s, institutional investors represented 85 percent of all public trading volume.

The first conference calls were held for hundreds of institutional investors at a time in the 1980s. Soon thereafter, quarterly conference calls were standard practice at many companies. A decade later, the Internet provided yet another channel for communicating company financials to large numbers of investors. Organizations began to create investor relations areas within their corporate websites to post information such as news releases, annual reports, 10-Ks (SEC required annual filing) and 10-Qs (SEC required quarterly filing), and stock charts.

Even with mass communications such as conference calls and webcasts, however, IR professionals still arranged for periodic private meetings between large institutional investors or sell-side analysts with the chief financial officer (CFO) or the chief executive officer (CEO). These meetings allowed the analysts to ask specific questions and get management's feedback on their own earnings models and projections.

These practices changed with the enactment of legislation designed to put individual investors on a level playing field with large institutions. The 1990s saw a resurgence of individual investor participation in the stock market and, at the same time, deepening concerns that these individual players were not afforded the same access to company information as their institutional counterparts. This theory was supported when two studies showed that volatility and trading increased immediately after quarterly conference calls (which were only open to institutional investors).[7]

---

[7] Steve Davidson, "Understanding the SEC's New Regulation FD," *Community Banker*, March 2001, pp. 40–42.

In response, in late 2000, the SEC passed Regulation Fair Disclosure, commonly referred to as "Reg. FD," prohibiting companies from disclosing "material nonpublic information" to the investment community (e.g., institutional investors, analysts) that has not already been disclosed to the general public. One of the immediate effects of this legislation was the opening up of conference calls to *all* investors, inviting individuals into a previously closed forum that allowed them to hear about company results and strategy directly from senior management. Generally, it set a more formal and coordinated tone for guidance—companies could no longer give "selective guidance"; that is, they could no longer provide some investors with information on earnings projections before others. Some of the other implications of Reg. FD for IR are discussed later in this chapter.

Over the last 50 years, IR has gained the respect and attention of senior management, who increasingly acknowledge it as a vital corporate communications function. The majority of the largest publicly held corporations in the United States and a growing number of small and mid-sized companies are now members of NIRI; as of 2021, NIRI had more than 2,800 members representing 1,600 publicly held companies and $9 trillion in stock market capitalization.[8]

Beginning in mid-2007, investor relations became an even more prominent force in business, both for the United States and, as globalization continued to break down borders, the global economy. A global recession, kick-started in part by the subprime mortgage crisis, prompted markets in North America, Europe, and Asia to sink at alarming rates. The turbulence that began in the United States quickly spread around the world, throwing investors and financial analysts into a frenzy. Equity markets both in the United States and abroad tumbled; in January 2008, world equity markets suffered a $5.2 trillion loss, according to Standard & Poor's.[9]

What became known as the Great Recession lasted 17 months, from October 2007 through March 2009, with the S&P 500's total loss reaching 56.4 percent. In February 2007, the market had fallen to its lowest level since 1997.[10] Less than a decade later, the memory of the recession continues to have implications for business executives. Investor relations is all the more important as local markets shift and merge into a global economy and as increased globalization enables one country's recession to initiate a domino effect around the world. Moreover, the range of ways for companies to reach their investors, and for investors and other important constituencies to find out about companies, has expanded exponentially in the decades since the field's original founding to include a wide range of social media channels and more sophisticated levels of webcasts and company websites than ever before. Given that investors today demand more communication, more transparency, and more access to companies than they have in the past, corporations competing for their investment dollars need to create IR

---

[8] National Investor Relations Institute website, www.niri.org/FunctionalMenu/About.aspx.

[9] "World Equity Markets Lost $5.2 Trillion in January," February 8, 2008, http://money.cnn.com/2008/02/08/news/economy/world_markets/.

[10] "11 Historic Bear Markets," MSNBC, www.msnbc.msn.com/id/37740147/ns/business-stocks_and_economy/t/historic-bear-markets/#.TxXfh6US2Hc.

programs that deliver on these requirements. In the next section, we explore how organizations can accomplish this.

A Framework for Managing Investor Relations

How do companies attract and retain investors? When you consider that annual turnover velocity (defined as share turnover in $/market capitalization) reached an all-time high of 179 percent in 2009 and then hit a historic low of 49 percent in August of 2018.[11] The following section addresses the key objectives of investor relations and also provides a framework for the implementation of a successful IR program.

The Objectives of Investor Relations

Although the structure of an investor relations program will vary from one organization to the next based on the size of the company, the complexity of its businesses, and the composition of its shareholder base, the main goal of any IR program is the same: to position the company to compete effectively for investors' capital. To achieve this goal, companies need to focus on the following objectives:

1. *Explain the company's vision, strategy, and potential to investors and intermediaries such as analysts and the media.* One of the most critical duties of an IR professional is to get messages about company results and potential future results across as understandably as possible to the investing public. We further examine the various investor constituencies later in this section, though it is important to note that the media now include a much wider range of individuals than had traditionally been classified in this group thanks to the rise of social media.

2. *Ensure that expectations of the company's stock price are appropriate for its earnings prospects, the industry outlook, and the economy.* IROs need to understand investor concerns and expectations for their organizations and relay this information to management to develop so that there is a high-level understanding of what the market anticipates from the company. If management does not see the company as being able to meet market expectations, it needs to work with IR to craft a communication plan to explain why and to manage expectations appropriately. Conversely, if management feels that the company's potential is not reflected in its stock price (that the stock is undervalued), an IR strategy should be developed to help investors see that potential and, accordingly, drive the stock to appropriate levels.

3. *Manage stock price expectations.* Industry research points to the direct impact of investor relations on company stock prices. Specifically, a recent survey by Rivel Research Group found that, after surveying buy-side analysts, nearly 75 percent felt that good IR impacts share price, with "super" IR increasing share price by a median of 10 percent and "poor" IR reducing share price by nearly 20 percent.[12] Such data, then, point to the

---

[11] "United States Annualized Turnover Rate: NYSE Group: Current Month," CEIC, https://www.ceicdata.com/en/united-states/nyse-turnover/annualized-turnover-rate-nyse-group-current-month.

[12] "Is Investor Relations Responsible for the Share Price?" *Bloomberg Professional Services*, July 1, 2015, https://www.bloomberg.com/professional/blog/is-investor-relations-responsible-for-the-share-price.

FIGURE 8.1
Investor
Relations
Framework

Source: Adapted from
Markus Will and
Anna-Lisa Wolters,
"Interdependencies of
Financial
Communications and
Corporate Reputation,"
*Proceedings of the 5th
International Conference
on Corporate
Reputation, Identity, and
Competitiveness,* Paris,
France, May 17–19,
2001. p. 14.

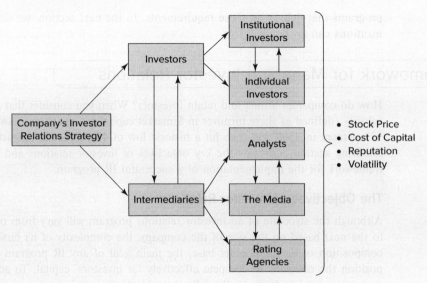

imperative to maintain strong relationships with the analyst community in order to accurately depict a company's financial performance. Obscuring or ineffectively communicating company strategy and vision is ultimately reflected in share price, and thus IR professionals have a foundational role to play in allowing a company's strategy to be most effectively reflected in its market pricing.

Now that we understand what investor relations is designed to accomplish, let's look at how it achieves these objectives. Figure 8.1 depicts how the IR function communicates both directly and indirectly with investors. The indirect communication occurs through intermediaries such as analysts, the media, rating agencies, and even the general public, given the broader access to company information that the rise of social media and other informal communications channels has enabled. Communication with these constituencies influences stock price, volatility, and, in turn, the firm's cost of capital and reputation.

Types of Investors

A company's IR strategy should address both retail investors (individual shareholders) and institutional investors (pension funds, mutual funds, insurance companies, endowment funds, and banks). These constituencies, however, place different demands on the IR department and require the use of different communication channels. For example, individuals do not as frequently look for incredibly detailed information but may require less-frequent but more complicated events such as stock split transactions. Conversely, institutions can place greater demands on IR departments in terms of information requests, but institutions also provide companies with access to larger, fairly concentrated pools of capital, affording them greater efficiencies in message delivery and market impact (defined as the combination of trading volume and price movement).

Institutional Investors

As of 2017, institutional investors owned 80 percent of the U.S. equity market.[13] The proportion of U.S. equities held by institutional investors has been growing, creating concern among market participants about the impact this may have on market volatility and information asymmetry between individual investors and more resource-heavy institutional investors. Moreover, the latest research suggests that it is not just overall ownership by institutional investors as an entire class, but rather the top 10 institutional investors, including BlackRock, Vanguard, and Fidelity, that have a significant impact on stock market volatility. The 2020 study highlighted that these institutions trade in larger volumes, which has a greater impact on stock prices and swings in price, even greater than the impact produced by smaller institutions' investments that combine to equal the same total volume of these larger institutions.[14] Overall, there is continuing debate about the influence and systemic risk produced by the asset management industry, but the importance of this subset of investors is clear.

IR departments can identify and target multiple categories of institutional investors. For instance, institutions can be broken down into groups based on portfolio turnover (high, moderate, and low) as well as investment styles (e.g., growth, value, income, index). By grouping investors into smaller constituencies with similar characteristics, IROs can efficiently communicate their message to appropriate target audiences. For example, explaining a company's vision and outlook to index investors will yield little benefit because index fund managers do not have the discretion to change portfolio holdings away from index weightings.

IR professionals (or their agencies) can use databases to gather information on institutional stock holdings, turnover rates, and basic portfolio characteristics to identify institutions whose portfolio characteristics closely coincide with their company's price/earnings (P/E) ratio, yield, market capitalization, and industry classification. A company with a low price/book ratio, for instance, might focus on marketing itself to mutual fund managers who specialize in "value" investments. A small company will similarly target small-cap managers and possibly start raising awareness among mid-cap managers if it is approaching a larger capitalization. This kind of research will prevent the company from spending too much time communicating with uninterested investors.

Having identified those institutions whose investing criteria match its characteristics, the company should develop a plan to interest them in investing for the long term. IROs can then reach those institutions in a variety of ways, including day-to-day phone contact and one-on-one meetings with analysts. For meetings with representatives of large, influential institutions the company would like to have a relationship with, the CEO and/or CFO are often involved.

More formal gatherings are another way to access large groups of institutional investors. For example, CEOs often address analyst or brokerage societies, industry conferences, and conferences geared toward particular kinds of organizations (such as small-cap, high-tech firms). Companies also host their own meetings in major financial centers such as New York and Boston and invite institutional investors who either own or might want to buy the company's stock.

[13] "80% of Equity Market Cap Held by Institutions," Pensions & Investments, April 25, 2017, https://www.pionline.com/article/20170425/INTERACTIVE/170429926/80-of-equity-market-cap-held-by-institutions.

[14] Chris Flood, "Top 10 Institutional Investors Fuel Market Volatility, Study Finds," *Financial Times*, August 8, 2020, https://www.ft.com/content/00bb26e7-16ac-45b1-b56e-74f8f0aa7e42.

Individual Investors

Just over half of all Americans (55 percent) own equities, either individually or through funds.[15] Like institutions, individual investors are not a monolithic constituency group. They may own stock directly or through mutual funds, company stock plans, or 401(k) plans. They may actively trade securities to generate trading profits on an intraday basis, apply "buy-and-hold" strategies to save for retirement, or anything in between.

Compared with institutions, individual investors have smaller account sizes and generate lower trading volume. In addition, as mentioned previously, they tend to require different types of information than institutional investors.

We talked in Chapter 2 about the blurring lines between a company's constituency groups. As an example, individual investors also can be employees of the company whose stock they are investing in, through a 401(k) program, bonus compensation in the form of company stock, or options. Employees read about the financial performance of their own companies in the media and expect to see information that is consistent with what they are hearing internally. Companies thus should be prepared to respond to employees' concerns about depictions of their organization appearing in the press that are inconsistent with management's own messages to them.

Reaching individuals is more difficult than connecting with institutions, as they are more numerous and harder to identify. The channels companies use to communicate with individual investors include direct e-mails to affinity groups (e.g., current shareholders, employees, customers, suppliers), the brokerage community to promote their stocks with individuals, and visibility generated through the media and advertising (see Chapter 4 for more on financial advertising).

In recent years, digital platforms have emerged that have increased individual investor access to both the stock market and as to information more broadly about equity investments that previously had been controlled by more narrow IR channels. A prime example of the ways that democratized trading platforms and online information can collide comes from the Robinhood-GameStop saga of early 2021, when individual investors on the Robinhood trading platform drove GameStop stock exorbitantly high largely as a consequence of information exchanged across the Reddit forum Wall Street Bets. Initially, investors, driven by conversations on Reddit, sought to drive up the stock artificially in order to create a "short squeeze" that punished several large hedge funds who had taken short positions. Later, broader media coverage of the squeeze inspired even greater individual investor participation from those who hoped to quickly realize large gains from the skyrocketing stock.[16] Ultimately, however, the outcomes individual investors faced ranged widely, from one man who turned $500 into $203,411 in less than four weeks[17] to another individual who took out a $20,000 loan to purchase shares only to witness the stock dive

[15] Teresa Ghilarducci, "Most Americans Don't Have a Real Stake in the Stock Market," *Forbes*, August 31, 2020, https://www.forbes.com/sites/teresaghilarducci/2020/08/31/most-americans-dont-have-a-real-stake-in-the-stock-market.

[16] Andy Serwer with Max Zahn, "How the Tale of Reddit, GameStop, Robinhood Is Really About 5 Big Trends," Yahoo!finance, January 30, 2021, https://www.yahoo.com/lifestyle/how-the-reddit-gamestop-robinhood-story-is-part-of-5-bigger-trends-130701087.html.

[17] Gregory Zuckerman, "For One GameStop Trader, the Wild Ride Was Almost as Good as the Enormous Payoff," *The Wall Street Journal*, February 3, 2021, https://www.wsj.com/articles/for-one-gamestop-trader-the-wild-ride-was-almost-as-good-as-the-enormous-payoff-11612348200.

80 percent shortly thereafter.[18] While the GameStop example is certainly one of the more extreme ones highlighting the challenges inherent in investing in individual stocks as an individual investor, it also highlighted the broader avenues available for individuals to both participate in the stock market and obtain information pertaining to those investments—trades the IR professionals must continue to contend with in the future.

Intermediaries

Investors often learn about corporations through sources other than the company itself. In particular, traditional news media and the analyst community are conduits, though as the GameStop example highlighted above, social media platforms have also emerged as key channels of influence. Companies often provide information to more traditional media channels and analysts through conference calls highlighting quarterly achievements, press conferences announcing annual financial results, and face-to-face meetings to discuss company developments and strategy. Reporters and analysts often present management with probing and difficult questions and report the company's responses to the investing public. Accordingly, management should present honest answers and messages that are consistent with what the organization communicates to investors directly.

Media

We learned in Chapter 6 that the business world is a frequent area of focus for media coverage. Business network news hosts regularly discuss earnings announcements on their programs and often invite equity research analysts to appear and comment on developments within companies they follow.

Media coverage—including social media coverage—of business can have a dramatic effect on a company's stock price. For example, Elon Musk sent shares of his own company, Tesla, down 12 percent in May 2020 when he tweeted that the stock price was "too high."[19] Conversely, shares of the health tech company Signal Advance rose 1,500 percent when he tweeted "Use Signal" in January 2021.[20] Musk's immediate impact on stock prices underscores the effect powerful individuals can have on the stock market by using channels such as Twitter to directly interact with investors and raises questions regarding how best to balance the right of individuals to directly invest in the markets with the need to protect less sophisticated participants from misleading or even spurious information.

Traditional media channels also significantly impact stock prices, and these channels are more likely to cover negative news than positive news. Additionally, recent research has found that the tone adopted by the first reports on a company's performance considerably impacts the tone adopted by later reports, indicating the need for IROs to pay attention to who first reports on their company's latest news.[21]

[18] Rachel Louise Ensign, "Here's Who Bet Big and Lost Big on GameStop," *Financial News*, February 15, 2021, https://www.fnlondon.com/articles/heres-who-bet-big-and-lost-big-on-gamestop-20210215.

[19] Jessica Bursztynsky, "Tesla Shares Tank after Elon Musk Tweets the Stock Price Is 'Too High'," *CNBC*, May 1, 2020, https://www.cnbc.com/2020/05/01/tesla-ceo-elon-musk-says-stock-price-is-too-high-shares-fall.html.

[20] Brian Sozzi, "Elon Musk Tweet Sends This Stock Up 1,500% in 24 Hours—May Be a Sign of Market Bubble," Yahoo!finance, January 11, 2011, https://finance.yahoo.com/news/elon-musk-tweet-sends-this-stock-up-1500-in-24-hours-may-be-a-sign-of-market-bubble-175845075.html.

[21] Agatha Bordonaro, "How Does News Coverage Affect the World of Finance?" Columbia Business School, April 7, 2017, https://www8.gsb.columbia.edu/newsroom/newsn/5061/how-does-news-coverage-affect-the-world-of-finance.

Certainly, having a strong media relations function coordinated with the IR department will be beneficial to a firm's investor relations effort by maximizing access to media outlets and ensuring consistency in the messages each group sends to the media.

Additionally, for low-visibility companies looking to attract investors, obtaining the right kind of media coverage can be a critical component of an IR strategy. In response to the influence of the financial media, some IR and PR consulting firms offer "financial media relations" programs to help companies target media strategically.

As we discuss in the next section, the media also play an important role in bringing the views of prominent analysts to the investing public, giving a voice to this other very influential intermediary.

Sell-Side Analysts

IR functions target the financial community through "buy-side" and "sell-side" analysts. Buy-side analysts typically work for money management firms (e.g., mutual funds or pension funds) and research companies for their own institutions' investment portfolios. They sometimes use sell-side research in their analysis, but many perform proprietary analysis, including company visits and their own review of company financials. As such, for the purposes of our investor relations framework, buy-side analysts belong in the institutional investor constituency group and are not intermediaries.

Sell-side analysts, however, cover stocks within certain industries and generate detailed research reports that offer "buy," "sell," or "hold" recommendations. This research is then provided to clients of investment banks such as JP Morgan Chase or retail brokerages such as Charles Schwab. Thus, sell-side analysts are intermediaries between a company and existing and potential investors. According to research from UCLA Accounting Professor Michael Brennan, strong IR can increase interest in the company from both investors and sell-side analysts. Brennan's research shows that sell-side analysts are able to positively affect the trading of stocks by improving market liquidity, increasing trading volume, and tempering reaction to news affecting the company.[22]

In the late 1990s and with the crash of the Internet bubble in 2000, sell-side analysts came under fire for continuing to issue "buy" recommendations on severely underperforming stocks. The media raised awareness of the inherent conflicts of interest in the job of a sell-side analyst working for an investment bank. Traditionally, companies covered by a firm's research team were also important banking clients who could take their business elsewhere or cut off the analysts' access to information if offended by an unfavorable rating.

Even when the Internet bubble burst in early 2000, many analysts maintained sky-high valuations on companies whose stocks were simultaneously plummeting to maintain their firm's investment banking relationships with the companies they covered. Investors, who had come to view these analysts as trusted advisors, felt betrayed and misled. Media coverage of these "star analysts" was just as prevalent as it had been in the dot-com heyday, but its angle on the analysts was decidedly changed. A *Vanity Fair* article characterized the group as "superstar analysts who were no longer objective observers of the market: they were insiders with inherent conflicts of interest."[23] Mary Meeker, once dubbed

[22] Michael Brennan and Claudia Tamarowski, "Investor Relations, Liquidity and Stock Price," *Journal of Applied Corporate Finance* 12, no. 4 (2000).

[23] Robin Londner, "Street Cleaning," *PRWeek*, July 23, 2001, p. 17.

"Queen of the Net," appeared on the cover of *Fortune* magazine in a feature article entitled "Can We Ever Trust Wall St. Again?".[24]

The burst of the bubble ushered in an era of analyst regulation that changed the landscape for communicating with the sell-side analyst community. One of the responses to this, as discussed earlier in the chapter, was the passage of Reg. FD, which not only was passed to attempt to correct the information asymmetry between institutional and individual investors, but also to correct the extent to which analysts were able to access key company performance metrics that broader parts of the investment community could not.

Additionally, in April 2003, the Securities and Exchange Commission, the New York Stock Exchange (NYSE), the National Association of Securities Dealers (NASD), and the New York attorney general announced the $1.4 billion Global Analyst Research Settlement with 10 of the largest U.S. investment banks. The Global Settlement was the result of a long investigation by the New York district attorney that found evidence of investment banks inappropriately influencing the work of research analysts. The settlement sought to eliminate the inherent conflicts of interest in the job of a sell-side analyst working for an investment bank. The settlement imposed $1.4 billion in fines and penalties on 10 of the largest U.S. investment banks, mandated structural changes to ensure research and coverage decisions were independent, and prohibited improper interactions between a firm's investment banking and research functions. In particular, analyst compensation could no longer be based directly or indirectly on investment banking revenues, and research analysts were prohibited from participating in investment banking sales efforts, such as pitches and roadshows.[25]

The Great Recession brought even further changes to the relationship between the IR community and the analyst community. In the wake of the crisis, IR professionals had to juggle increasingly complex responsibilities pertaining both to regulations and their use of technology, and as a consequence considerably shifted their approach to interacting with the analyst community. Greater emphasis has been placed on working more cooperatively with analysts, providing them with answers to key data requests within the same day as opposed to delaying servicing requests from analysts deemed more antagonistic. Additionally, earnings calls trended toward reduced durations, from one-hour calls to 45 minutes, to emphasize data as opposed to salesmanship, allowing analysts to make their own interpretations of company performance as opposed to intentionally misguiding them. Similarly, many firms eschewed large investor days for smaller earnings events, once again to emphasize data and direct reporting as opposed to seeking to influence analysts via over-the-top gatherings.[26]

Today, much of these changes have persisted, be it a consequence of regulatory enforced ones (like Reg. FD) or shifting attitudes toward the IR–analysts relationship that ensued following the Great Recession. Overall, however, analysts remain an important intermediary for a company's IR strategy. IROs should also be prepared to communicate strategically with and handle downgrades from analysts with a communication plan.

---

[24] Peter Elkind, "Can We Ever Trust Wall St. Again?" *Fortune*, May 14, 2001, p. 69.

[25] SEC Fact Sheet on Global Analyst Research Settlement, www.sec.gov/news/speech/factsheet.htm.

[26] "Buy Side, Sell Side and Investor Relations: Strengthening the Triangle," *Bloomberg Professional Services*, April 19, 2016, https://www.bloomberg.com/professional/blog/buy-side-sell-side-and-investor-relations-strengthening-the-triangle.

Rating Agencies

In the United States, examples of rating agencies include Standard & Poor's (S&P), Moody's Investors Service, and Fitch Ratings. These agencies analyze companies in much the same way that buy-side and sell-side analysts do, but with a specific focus on their creditworthiness. The ratings that these agencies assign to a company reflect their assessment of the company's ability to meet its debt obligations. This rating, in turn, determines the company's cost of debt capital (the interest rates at which it borrows).

These agencies make their ratings available to the public through their ratings information desks and published reports. The highest ratings are AAA (S&P, Fitch) and Aaa (Moody's), and the lowest are D (S&P) and C (Moody's), representing companies that are in default of existing loan agreements. Companies rated BBB/Baa or above are considered "investment grade," and those below are considered not investment grade, or "high yield." The more pejorative term *junk bonds* also refers to below-investment-grade bonds. The lower the rating, the higher the agency's assessment of the company's potential to default on its loans, thus making it more expensive for the company to raise capital by issuing debt.

Debt ratings affect more than a firm's cost of capital. Senator Joseph Lieberman, chair of the Senate Committee on Governmental Affairs, put it this way:

> The credit raters hold the key to capital and liquidity, the lifeblood of corporate America and of our capitalist economy. The rating affects a company's ability to borrow money; it affects whether a pension fund or money market fund can invest in a company's bonds; and it affects stock price. The difference between a good rating and a poor rating can mean the difference between success and failure, prosperity and bad fortune.[27]

Credit rating analysts are similar to equity research analysts when it comes to their relationship with a company, with the obvious exception that they will focus a great deal more on the company's debt structure. Additionally, many buy-side and sell-side analysts rely on the research and ratings of credit analysts as a component of their own assessment of the company overall, especially for firms within capital-intensive industries characterized by heavy debt loads.

Credit rating analysts at the major rating agencies came under fire after the 2008 debt crisis for many of the same reasons equity analysts were under fire in 2001. The rating agencies had lost credibility with the investing public due to perceived conflicts of interest and a lack of willingness to downgrade both corporate and sovereign debt until significantly after the crisis hit.[28] The rating agencies were also blamed and held directly responsible for some of what happened in the credit crisis. As a result, they faced numerous lawsuits, investigations, and much public and media criticism. Following a broad swath of investigations, Moody's ultimately agreed to pay nearly $864 million in 2017 to settle with U.S. federal and state authorities over its ratings of risky securities, with S&P settling in 2015 for $1.375 billion.[29] Despite their considerable role in the financial crisis, these

---

[27] Statement by Chair Joseph Lieberman, "Rating the Raters: Enron and the Credit Rating Agencies," U.S. Senate Committee on Governmental Affairs website, March 20, 2002, www.senate.gov/~gov_affairs/03202002lieberman.htm.

[28] "Rating Agencies under Fire, But Big Reform Unlikely," CNBC, May 13, 2010.

[29] Karen Freifeld, "Moody's Pays $864 Million to U.S., States over Pre-crisis Ratings," *Reuters*, January 13, 2017, https://www.reuters.com/article/us-moody-s-credit/moodys-pays-864-million-to-u-s-states-over-pre-crisis-ratings-idUSKBN14X2LP.

credit ratings agencies continue to exert influence in financial markets and thus remain an important area of focus for the IR community.

Developing an Investor Relations Program

Now that we understand who the key investor constituencies are, let's look at how IR functions are structured to communicate with them: in-house, delegated to an agency, or some combination of the two. This section also takes a closer look at some of the activities that make IR such an important function within a company.

How (and Where) Does IR Fit into the Organization?

A company's IR function can be structured in a number of ways, from fully in-house to fully outsourced. In-house IR teams are typically small: according to a recent survey by *IR Magazine*, the average size of a corporate IR department is two people. At smaller organizations, the CFO might handle IR responsibilities directly and use an agency to perform some of the more routine report-writing tasks.[30]

When companies do turn to agencies for assistance, they can choose from agencies that specialize in IR work, such as Kekst CNC, Abernathy MacGregor, and the Financial Relations Board, or full-service PR firms that have strong IR specialty groups, such as Fleishman-Hillard or Burson Cohn & Wolfe. Agencies can help with projects and activities across the spectrum of IR, from report-writing and arranging analyst conferences to higher-end services such as bankruptcy and litigation communications, mergers and acquisitions, and initial public offerings. In the last decade agencies also have focused on fully understanding Reg. FD so that they can help companies with their disclosure policies. Reg. FD has a goal of creating an even playing field between institutional and individual investors; however, it also adds a burden to the company to identify and disclose all material information to all constituents at the same time.

The division of responsibilities between what is done in-house versus what is handled by the agency depends on several factors, including the size of the firm and its IR objectives. However it is arranged, the individuals responsible for a company's IR efforts should have access to senior management, including the CEO and CFO. This situation appears to be the case for in-house IR professionals—an overwhelming majority of IROs report directly to the CEO or the CFO.[31]

Given the increasing overlap between IR and areas such as media relations, in some organizations, IR and corporate communications are linked or part of the same group. According to a recent E&Y survey, 84 percent of IR teams are in regular contact with the corporate communications department, with 44 percent meeting on a monthly basis and 6 percent meeting quarterly.[32] Whether they are part of the same official group or in separate ones, however, the takeaway is the same: IR professionals and communications professionals need to be in regular contact.

[30] Global Survey of Budget and Team Structure," *IR Magazine*, https://media.irmagazine.com/library/xbinsight/research_resourcesv4-4final.pdf.

[31] Evan Traver, "Investor Relations (IR)," Investopedia, https://www.investopedia.com/terms/i/investorrelations.asp.

[32] "Taking It to Heart," EY, https://assets.ey.com/content/dam/ey-sites/ey-com/en_gl/topics/growth/ey-investor-relations-20180920.pdf.

Annual Reports: More Than Just the Numbers

The SEC's reporting requirements create the need for a number of documents to be produced periodically, such as the annual report, form 10-K, and form 10-Q. Companies can file these reports electronically with the SEC, and investors can download them from the SEC's online database, EDGAR, or the company's own website in addition to, or instead of, receiving hard copies.

Among all these documents, the annual report is the most time-consuming, expensive, and high-profile endeavor. An annual report is a company's equivalent to a "coffee table piece" and is used by companies as an image vehicle and a reporting tool. Annual reports have played a role in shaping corporate reputation and public perception for decades. An annual report gives a company the opportunity not only to share and explain results for the prior year, but also to communicate the company's vision. Investors can obtain the financial information contained in a printed annual report faster online, yet there is still great demand for the printed piece. The 2012 NIRI annual report reveals that the majority of NIRI members produce both print and electronic versions of their annual report, while 5 percent issue an electronic version exclusively, and 7 percent put out just a printed report.[1]

Annual reports typically have themes that are carried through the piece in graphics and text. Thompson Reuter's highly regarded 2013 annual report had the theme "The World Cannot Wait." The theme emphasized Thompson Reuter's role in helping clients stay ahead of the curve with its global information platforms. The annual report was a dynamic website with downloads, photographs, data, and client stories embedded throughout. The annual report won awards for its report narrative, reporting of financials, information accessibility, and creativity.[2]

Thompson Reuters reflects another prominent theme in annual reports today: the rise of sustainability reporting. Its report was addressed to "Our Shareholders and Stakeholders," emphasizing the importance of multiple stakeholder groups, and included not only the typical sections on strategy, vision, and financials, but also a special report on corporate responsibility. In their 2013 annual reports and 10-Ks, 51 percent of the world's largest companies included CR information.[3] According to KPMG: "[T]he direction of travel is clear and with more than half of companies researched now including CR data in their financial reports, this can arguably be considered as standard global practice."[4]

Today, annual reports are used as reporting vehicles, brand builders, recruiting pieces, marketing brochures, corporate image books, and strategic positioning tools. Even as more companies post their annual reports online in new, innovative ways, it doesn't appear that the hard-copy version will go away.

[1] NIRI Annual Report 2012, www.niri.org/Main-Menu-Category/resource/publications/Executive-Alert/2013-Executive-Alert-Archive/NIRI-Annual-Report-2012-Survey-1413.aspx.

[2] League of American Communications Professionals 2013 Vision Awards, www.lacp.com/2013vision/awards-annual-report-competition-thomson-reuters.htm.

[3] The KPMG Survey of Corporate Responsibility Reporting, 2013.

[4] Ibid.

Using IR to Add Value

As mentioned previously, the investor relations function assumes a marketing role with respect to a company's equity and debt, which involves much more than producing and distributing annual and quarterly reports, responding to shareholder inquiries, and sending information to securities analysts. IR plays both proactive and reactive roles within an organization.

Proactively, IR targets investors to whom they can market the company's shares and provides regular informational updates and explanations of performance to the marketplace. Proactive communications can go beyond traditional analyst calls and include activities such as "field trips" for analysts and portfolio managers. Plant tours and meetings or lunches with key company executives can provide investors and potential investors with a true feel for the company and its management.

IROs also craft communication strategies in response to certain internal or external events. Internal events such as mergers, acquisitions, or the sale of a part of the business allow time to confer with the CEO and CFO, develop a communication strategy around the event, and script answers to anticipated questions and concerns. External events, however, such as an unanticipated crisis (see Chapter 10) require much more rapid damage control.

Companies with extensive IR resources can conduct research to identify their most influential shareholders and seek to understand what motivates them, allowing management to predict more accurately the effect on share price of various events or announcements. The Investor Relations Charter states that identifying key influencers within the shareholder community ought to include the identification of potential shareholders who are most likely to place a fair valuation on the company's securities.[33] Given, however, developments in the IR community as a consequence of the Great Recession, as well as the ability of a smaller group of large institutional investors to more materially impact stock prices and market volatility, less emphasis has been placed on looking to guide a small subset of shareholder attitudes as opposed to more broadly sharing insights with the larger investment community.

When a crisis hits, or a company undergoes some structural change that the market reacts to negatively, investors have already lost money as the stock price usually adjusts downward nearly instantaneously. Either shareholders can join in the selling, or they can continue to hold the company's stock, hoping that it will recover. To ensure that shareholders do not sell, companies must be prepared with swift, honest communications to investors when the stock price starts spiraling downward.

Management must identify the problem (or perceived problem), what caused it, and, importantly, develop a strategy to address it. In these types of "damage control" situations, channel choice matters: a webcast or conference call with the CEO or CFO will carry much more weight than a press release posted to the company website.

Similarly, when a company is not performing as well as it should, IR professionals should proactively communicate to analysts and investors what management is doing about the situation. Such candor is definitely in the company's best interests. As Thomas Garbett says:

> Information reduces risk. The stock market, as a process, arrives at a stock price based upon all known elements relating to the company. Some of the unknown factors add to the price, others subtract. Areas about the company that are unknown usually contribute to the minus side of the price equation.[34]

Investor Relations and the Changing Environment

The chapters thus far have referenced the instigators for the dramatically changing business climate, including the rise of digital communications and stakeholder empowerment. The rise in social media and overall digitization of communication has meant that investor relations and corporate communications must be in greater contact with one another than

[33] "Investor Relations Charter Competency Framework," NIRI, 2015, https://www.niri.org/NIRI/media/NIRI/Certification/IR_Competency_Framework.pdf.

[34] Thomas F. Garbett, *How to Build a Corporation's Identity and Project Its Image* (Lexington, MA Lexington Books, 1988), p. 99. CCBN company website, www.ccbn.com/about/faqs.html (accessed April 11, 2002).

ever before. Moreover, IR departments increasingly must leverage a broader range of channels to influence investor perception, given the extent to which shareholders now turn to more than just quarterly and annual reports to gain a sense of a company's prospects. A recent survey from Greenwich Associates found that 80 percent of institutional investors turn to social media as part of their regular workflow and 30 percent of these investors state that information obtained through social media has directly influenced investment decisions.[35] Clearly, then, IR professionals cannot ignore the role of social media or assume that it only impacts "less sophisticated" individual investors. Additionally, almost all of the *Fortune* 500 companies have dedicated investor relations pages that make stock quotes and charts, news releases, webcasts, and company financial statements available to anyone with Internet access. Investors find this kind of instantaneous access to information reassuring, particularly during periods of market volatility and uncertainty. Earnings webcasts are also quite popular. These events enable participants to witness firsthand how companies' top executives handle themselves and can bring an otherwise two-dimensional upper management to life for current and potential investors.

Activist investors also continue to remain increasingly influential in the realm of investor relations and are not just a trend that appears likely to go away anytime soon. According to *IR Magazine's* 2020 report on IR issues crossing the minds of CFOs, 45 percent of CFO respondents stated that their company had experienced some level of shareholder activism over the last three years, most frequently directly communicated to management. Additionally, 80 percent of survey respondents stated their company provided an activist-oriented presentation to leaders at least annually. However, given that the digital platforms have effectively shifted power more toward shareholders, particularly activist shareholders, as a consequence of the ease by which individuals can access information on social media and broader online reports, larger swaths of IR departments are considering increasing the pace at which they communicate with activist groups (and key stakeholders more generally) to match the uptick in information that is more broadly being made available to the public.[36]

Overall, investor relations is even more important to companies against this backdrop of increasing transparency and higher rates of information exchange. Clear, full disclosure of business results will put companies in a strong position in the competition for investor capital.

Conclusion

Many activities fall under the IR function, from planning and running annual meetings and putting together reports for SEC filings to targeting and marketing the company's shares to investors. These activities should be approached no differently from any other communication activity: companies need to follow a communication strategy that includes a clear understanding of the company's objectives and a thorough analysis of all of its constituencies so that appropriate messages can be crafted and delivered.

[35] "Social Media Influencing Investment Decisions at Global Institutions," Coalition Greenwich, https://www.greenwich.com/press-release/social-media-influencing-investment-decisions-global-institutions.

[36] Chris Ruggeri, "Activism, Guidance and Purpose: The IR Issues on the Minds of CFOs," *IR Magazine*, February 19, 2020, https://www.irmagazine.com/reporting/activism-guidance-and-purpose-ir-issues-minds-cfos.

Unfortunately, quantifying IR's direct effect on stock price and/or a company's cost of capital is challenging. Today's equity markets are influenced by many factors beyond companies' control, and thus, although it is still used as a broad indicator, stock price does not single-handedly signal an IR success or failure. Anecdotal evidence, however, does provide a basis for the simple conclusion that IR is a required communication function in today's marketplace.

No company can afford to deal with the current investment community without developing an effective investor relations function, whether it is fully in-house, fully contracted to an outside agency, or a combination of the two. The price paid for overlooking this advice is far greater than the investment made in the personnel that staff this important function.

Steelcase, Inc.

Perry Grueber sat at his desk at Steelcase, Inc., on a bright day in July 2000, thinking about the work that lay ahead for him. Grueber had just joined Steelcase, a maker of office furnishings and workspace solutions, as Director of Investor Relations. Steelcase was dedicated to improving IR at the company and had promised Grueber the resources he required to make the department an effective tool for communicating to key constituencies.

When Grueber accepted his job in May, Steelcase was trading at $11.56 per share, just above its all-time low of $10.38 per share and down 70 percent from a high of $37.94. Steelcase's operating performance was mostly to blame for the declining share price; however, the company's communications with its investors also had played a role. The company had high turnover in its institutional shareholder base and, since the time of its IPO, had not actively marketed itself to sell-side analysts. These analysts, in return, expressed little interest in the company. At the same time, insider sales were increasing, sending more shares into the market amid soft demand. Grueber needed a new IR strategy to help Steelcase turn its situation around. As he settled into his new office at the company's headquarters in Grand Rapids, Michigan, he began to assess the challenge that lay before him objectively.

HISTORY OF STEELCASE, INC.

Steelcase was founded in 1912 by Peter Wege, Henry Idema, and 12 other investors under the name Metal Office Furniture. Wege hoped to capitalize on the

Source: This case was prepared by Thomas Darling under the supervision of Professor Paul A. Argenti at the Tuck School of Business at Dartmouth. Information was gathered from public and corporate sources, including interviews with Perry Grueber at Steelcase in May 2002. © 2008 Trustees of Dartmouth College. All rights reserved. For permission to reprint, contact the Tuck School of Business at 603-646-3176.

benefits of metal furniture over its more flammable wooden counterparts. This original vision found success early on, as government architects began to specify metal in their designs and turned quickly to Metal Office Furniture to fill their demand. Early company successes included the development of the metal wastebasket and the later invention of the suspension cabinet, which became the foundation for all modern filing cabinets.

Company sales in 1913, the first full year of operations, were $76,000. As revenues began to increase, Metal Office Furniture hired a media consultant, who created the trademark Steelcase name in 1921. World War II and the resulting war material contracts benefited the company, and the boom years of the 1950s and 1960s catapulted Steelcase further forward in terms of revenues and profits. By the late 1960s, Steelcase had become the largest manufacturer in the office furniture industry. It retained that status through the year 2001, when the company reported revenues of $4.1 billion.

Steelcase's founder, Peter Wege Sr., died in 1947. Wege's partner Henry Idema died four years later in 1951, and control of the company fell to Henry Idema's son Walter. The Idemas began a tradition of family stewardship over the company that continued when Walter Idema's son-in-law Robert Pew II assumed leadership in 1966. Pew became Executive Chairman in 1974 and retained that title until his retirement in 1999, although James P. Hackett became President and CEO in 1994. By 2000, Steelcase as a company retained the imprint of the vision and the direction it had received through the founding families' descendants.

IDENTITY, VISION, AND REPUTATION

Steelcase built its image from the set of values held by founders Peter Wege and Henry Idema, clearly articulated in its organizational goals: "Steelcase aspires to transform the ways people work . . . to help them work more effectively than they ever thought they could."[1] Every employee read the company's core values statement:

"At Steelcase, We:

Act with integrity
Tell the Truth
Keep commitments
Treat people with dignity and respect
Promote positive relationships
Protect the environment
Excel"[2]

Steelcase had a history of "putting people before profits"[3] and dealing fairly with its employees. As Grueber explained, "There is very much a family atmosphere . . . I've never seen a better benefits package and it is not just executive benefits; it's all the way down the line." Tenure with the firm averaged nearly 18 years. The values embodied in Steelcase's treatment of its employees applied to other constituencies as well, including dealers, vendors, and the communities in which Steelcase operated.

As Grueber described it, Steelcase prided itself in "communicat[ing] values through actions. It's not just the corporate line." For example, shortly after becoming CEO, James Hackett voiced his concern that Steelcase's offices did not communicate the company's goal of transforming the way people work to be more effective. Outdated headquarters designs from the 1960s and 1970s isolated executives in their offices. When company management wanted to conduct brainstorming or other creative sessions, they often "fled headquarters."[4]

James Hackett challenged senior management to trade their traditional offices for a new office environment one floor below. This office overcame the existing separation and used a quarter less space. The offer contained an escape clause, allowing management to move back to the traditional offices after

a trial period. But the redesigned offices proved to be an unmitigated success, increasing workplace effectiveness and becoming the prototype for a new line of systems furniture called Pathways.[5]

Internally, all members of Steelcase acted in a way that reinforced the company's message of open communication at every level. As Grueber explained, "Executives all have an open-door policy. If you came to visit our offices, you would see that our senior executives reside in an open-plan environment. They don't have enclosed offices and so, we go to great lengths to live our vision."

Externally Steelcase's strong values helped create a dealership network that was the envy of the industry and demonstrated the extent to which Steelcase's values shaped its business. Steelcase relied heavily on its dealers to support its "made to order" business model and made a point of treating them with respect, as primary purchasers of their products and as fellow businesspeople whose own businesses would prosper as Steelcase's had prospered.

THE INITIAL PUBLIC OFFERING

During its time as a private company, Steelcase had developed a much-admired reputation stemming from its well-articulated identity, vision, strategy, and culture. Although Steelcase intended to continue its focus as defined by the original families into the future, the company also believed that it had reached a point where it would benefit from a changeover to public ownership. This change would provide increased liquidity to the company's founding families and give them the ability to diversify their holdings. As the list of Steelcase heirs grew, liquidity became more important to these private owners. Many of the family members wanted to diversify their long-term holdings and allow for distributions to charities and other philanthropic activities. During its 90 years as a private company, Steelcase had grown to become a member of the *Fortune* 500 and the largest manufacturer of office solutions in the United States. By 1998, the private ownership structure for this organization was simply too inflexible.

---

[1] Steelcase, Inc., website, "Our Company: Overview," http://www .steelcase.com/servlet/OurCompany.

[2] Ibid.

[3] Conversation with Perry Grueber.

[4] Marc Spiegler, "Changing the Game," *Metropolis Feature*, July 1998, http://www.metropolismag.com/html/content/0798/jl98game.htm.

[5] Ibid.

The economic environment at the end of the 1990s was prime for Steelcase's initial public offering. Data from the Business and Industrial Furniture Manufacturer's Association (BIFMA) forecast double-digit increases in office furniture shipments throughout the first three quarters of 1997.[6] Steelcase was the leader in this growing furniture shipment industry, which was already worth $10 billion in 1996. Furthermore, the U.S. economy overall was still growing at an impressive pace (though the Asian crisis had sparked some doubt in late 1997), white-collar job growth remained strong, and companies were flush with cash from the booming stock market.

Steelcase came to market on February 18, 1998, with a 9.4-million-share offering priced at $28 per share; the proceeds went entirely to family stakeholders. The offering proved very popular with money managers and was oversubscribed to such a degree that the number of shares was increased from 9.4 million to 12.5 million and the IPO price quickly exceeded the originally projected range of $23–$26 per share. On the first day of trading, Steelcase shares rose from the opening offer to close at $33.63, up approximately 20 percent.

After the IPO, 156 million total shares were outstanding, with 12.5 million in public hands, and the balance owned by the founding family. Employees received a gift of 10 shares each and options allowing them to purchase shares at below-market rates. One-third of the IPO shares went to employees. Institutions were the largest purchasers of the 12.5 million shares sold to the public.

STEELCASE AS A PUBLIC COMPANY (IPO TO JUNE 2000)

Steelcase hit an all-time closing high of $37.94 per share on March 13, 1998, less than one month after the IPO. Almost everything that followed with respect to the company's stock price, however, was disappointing. Uncertainty caused by the 1997 Asian crisis and the 1998 Russian default significantly

disturbed many companies' capital expenditures. In addition, as the year 2000 approached and "Y2K" fears loomed, corporate spending was focused almost solely on technology and information systems. Although traditional indicators of furniture system demand remained strong, those indicators did not translate into end demand for Steelcase's products.

In 1999, just as the company's profitability started to weaken, Steelcase purchased the remaining 50 percent of Strafor, a previous joint venture interest in Europe and Africa with annual sales of $500 million. Because the two companies concentrated on different aspects of the furniture business, the addition of Strafor's business to the balance sheet had a material effect on several of Steelcase's financial ratios. All of Steelcase's products were "made to order." This business model had allowed it to carry only a small amount of inventory, and Steelcase's dealers typically paid for purchases in less than 30 days. Strafor did not have the same inventory constraints. Also, many of Strafor's customers were accustomed to paying closer to 90 days after receiving an order. With the Strafor acquisition, inventory at Steelcase rose and inventory turnover fell. At the same time, however, a new customer base increased Steelcase's collection risk. The softness in the balance sheet reinforced investor concerns over deteriorating earnings performance.

Steelcase performance in 1999–2000 was mediocre. Sales slumped or, at best, remained flat. Cost control initiatives and a cut in bonuses brought earnings up in 1999, but gains were erased by a significant fall in earnings reported in 2000.[7] Steelcase had expected a certain amount of business in 1999 that never materialized, throwing off the company's cost structure and causing the gross margins to drop.

Sagging sales turned into a flood of orders in early 2000, coming in from companies that had delayed renovation projects until after Y2K. Investors expected Steelcase to bounce back quickly. Unfortunately, the company had underestimated the costs associated with serving a rush of new orders. According to Grueber, "As the surge in business came in 2000, when our

---

[7] Note that Steelcase operates on a fiscal year ending in February, and all references to financial statements are for the year ending in February.

[6] Mahua Dutta, "Steelcase Builds IPO," *IPO Reporter*, February 16, 1998.

system should have been there to meet the needs without any difficulty, the customer service requirements were so rigorous in terms of delivering product, getting it there on time, and the pricing environment so tough that we had further erosion of our gross margins and operating margins." Profitability and operating margins continued to slump.

At the time of the IPO, Steelcase had no debt on its balance sheet. It had positive earnings of $1.40 per share (including shares issued through the IPO) and an overall strong demand for its product. Two years later, Steelcase faced increasing volatility in end demand and a weaker balance sheet. The company was unsure of what strategy to communicate to investors. "The market just didn't understand what was happening," said Grueber, "and we were not in a position to articulate a great strategy."

THE INVESTOR RELATIONS EFFORT (1998–2000)

STRUCTURE

Because of its large size and market-leading position, Steelcase had the potential to be a credible, attractive investment for multiple types of institutional investors. But institutions didn't flock to Steelcase shares. The company was large enough to be included on several indices; however, its percentage weighting was often adjusted to reflect its small float (the number of shares owned by the public, not including insiders). Many institutional investors chose to steer clear because of its relative illiquidity. SEC filings showed only 28 institutional holders of Steelcase in 2000, representing between 5 and 8 percent of the shares available to the public. With the exception of several small index players, turnover among institutions was well over 50 percent, meaning that the institutional shareholder base changed every two years.

When Perry Grueber arrived at the company to take over as Director of Investor Relations, he replaced Gary Malburg, who was both the Vice President of Finance and Treasurer and Head of IR. Malburg had been responsible for communicating with investors, answering questions, and assisting with the financial statements. However, because of significant and growing

responsibilities in the Treasury department, only about a quarter of his time was available for investor relations activities. The company's Corporate Communications Director, Allan Smith—who reported to the Vice President of Global Marketing and Communications, Georgia Everse—also assisted the IR effort, crafting and disseminating press releases and creating the company's annual report. The staff in these two divisions had few formal channels for interaction. Steelcase's internal structure lacked a clear conduit for IR staff to respond to the concerns of its shareholders.

Although IR had not been a priority at Steelcase, the company had not remained inactive in its attempts to communicate with existing shareholders following its IPO. It engaged the services of Genesis, Inc., a highly respected investor relations consulting company. According to Deborah Kelly, a partner at Genesis, "The good news was that Steelcase was widely respected by its core constituencies as the dominant force in the office furniture industry and as being guided by people with strategic vision and a solid grasp of trends."[8] Nonetheless, she continued, "there was frustration among investment analysts regarding performance."

Genesis's main responsibility was advising Steelcase in the creation of the company's annual report. Genesis also helped plan Steelcase's first "analyst day" in November 1999, an event hosted by the company for buy- and sell-side analysts and portfolio managers. Leading up to this "analyst day," Steelcase hired another outside consultant to perform a perception study of investors' opinions about company communications. The report produced from the study, according to Kelly, revealed that "investors were looking for a more proactive IR program that could help them better understand strategic objectives and they wanted to have greater access to management, so they could get more than just the phone answered." Analyst day helped open up the decision-making process to many analysts and portfolio managers, but this important first step lacked the vital follow-up that additional proactive communications might have provided. As he entered the company, Grueber had the opportunity to launch a renewed and sustained effort to implement strong IR strategies at Steelcase.

[8] This and all quotes are from interviews with Deborah Kelly in May 2002.

GUIDANCE AND REPORTING

In some ways, Steelcase resembled a public company even before its IPO in 1998; it had a board of directors, audited financial statements, and a large shareholder base. Once Steelcase became a public company, however, the previous shareholder makeup led to an "inner circle" mentality that proved difficult to change. Management was not used to the additional requests for information and sometimes assumed a defensive posture toward inquisitive analysts or investors. "Once we had come public," said Grueber, "we were providing the required elements but not a great deal of insight into decision making at the company or the strategic direction of the company."

Steelcase's reluctance to share publicly its inner decision-making processes extended a company approach to communications that had developed during its decades of heavy reliance on the controlling families' leadership. The families chose board members as their representatives, who then hired and supervised the management team. The company under this system earned a strong level of trust both in its direction and in the quality of the reported information. Very little information was ever questioned or requested by non-board members. Along with this trust, though, came a highly conservative outlook from company leadership with regard to the amount of information shared and prospective statements regarding business performance.

In each earnings release, Steelcase typically disclosed very specific guidance for the upcoming year or quarter. Grueber noted, "The company, due to its conservative nature, has been very cautious about selective disclosure throughout its public life. The way they communicated to the Street was through a press release." Due to advice from internal counsel and a desire to prevent selective disclosure, management never "walked the Street up or down" with its estimates.[9] Another major factor in Steelcase's conservative approach to its disclosures after it became public was

the lack of incentives to develop a strong quarterly forecasting discipline during its years as a private company. In addition, the company did not strive to build and maintain relationships with its analysts, so when it came time to disseminate information, it didn't have a receptive ear through the sell-side analysts.

Steelcase's inexperience with releasing company information to the analyst community cost it credibility in the years immediately following its IPO. Press releases assumed relatively high importance at Steelcase in a company environment that both lacked a strong channel for adjusting guidance and reflected the company's inherently conservative attitude toward providing information to outside parties. Unfortunately, if the information published in a current press release was inconsistent with earlier guidance, Steelcase could do very little to minimize the surprise the information caused investors. Several pre-announcements in 1998 and 1999 damaged Steelcase's reputation with investors and increased the perceived risks associated with owning the stock. As Genesis's Deborah Kelly explained, "They kept missing quarters and it was an unusually large number. For a company that has just gone public, usually you want to have 4–5 quarters in the bag. . . . Not here."

NEXT STEPS FOR STEELCASE

Overall, Steelcase put a tremendous amount of effort into its IPO and into readying itself for the rigor of being a public company. Unfortunately, assumptions about public company communications that Steelcase made based upon past experiences as a private company often led to disappointment for investors. In addition, the equity markets entered into an extremely turbulent period after the IPO, which caused significant shocks to equity values and corporate capital spending and also created a harsh environment for a newly public company to develop its investor relations acumen. Deborah Kelly summed up Steelcase's situation as follows:

> I think they put a lot of effort into getting a grasp for what being a public company meant from a communications perspective. They are such good people. They are a terrific management team in terms of doing the right thing, integrity, and caring about what happens. The shock was that they had spent so many years communicating with owners that I don't think they realized there

---

[9] "Walking the street" is a practice that includes providing material information to analysts during conversations, making excessive statements concerning future earnings prospects, or blatantly encouraging analysts to raise a lower earnings estimate. Some of these tactics have since been prohibited through the Regulations for Fair Disclosure, enacted in 2000.

might be a difference when you go public. It was kind of a shock that you had to do things a little differently and have a different sensitivity with this group.

As part of Steelcase's effort to readdress its corporate communication to investors, the company had hired Grueber, and now it was up to him to outline his goals and strategy for the IR department.

CASE QUESTIONS

1. As part of creating the full-time IR position, Steelcase had to decide where to place Grueber in the company hierarchy. Given the issues facing Steelcase when Grueber arrived, what are the strengths and weaknesses of placing Grueber under the CFO versus the corporate communications department?

2. What resources should Grueber ask for? How should he organize the function (reporting lines, internal staff versus agencies, etc.)?

3. What investor constituencies should Steelcase try to interest in the company's stock? What channels should Grueber use to attract them? What message would Steelcase deliver to them?

4. What mistakes did Steelcase make in its past IR efforts?

5. What are the biggest challenges facing Steelcase in mid-2000 and beyond? How would you position the IR function to handle those challenges?

6. What can you learn about Steelcase today through an online search of its website?

CHAPTER NINE

Government Relations

Government and business in the United States tend to have an adversarial relationship, as business attempts to minimize government involvement in the private sector and Washington attempts to manage the needs of all citizens by exerting its power over the corporate realm.

Government influences business activities primarily through regulation. Originally, government regulation managed market competition. The first government regulations applied to industries such as railroads and telecommunications, in which high barriers to entry facilitated the emergence of monopolies that could hurt the consumer. In these cases, regulation replaced Adam Smith's "invisible hand" to protect citizens from high prices, bad service, and discrimination.

Governmental regulation of monopolies has not prevented large corporations, however, from wielding impressive political and social power. The predominance of global corporate giants such as Amazon, Apple, and Alphabet transcends voting districts and political borders. Historically, some of the most politically active organizations in the United States are, in fact, domestic or multinational corporations and trade associations.[1] That political involvement changed considerably in 2010, when the Supreme Court ruled in *Citizens United* that the First Amendment prohibits the restriction of independent expenditures for political communications by corporations, among others, effectively uncapping political donations.[2] Perspectives on the ruling also diverge considerably (a quick Google search will reveal a *Wall Street Journal* headline stating, "Celebrate the Citizens United Decade"[3] while the *New York Times* has simultaneously declared, "After Citizens United, a Vicious Cycle of Corruption"[4]), but this is in many ways a reflection of the larger tensions that arise in the arena of government and business and the challenges inherent in finding the appropriate balance between the two.

In this chapter, we first examine the nature of the relationship between government and business. Then, we discuss the importance of government relations departments within companies and how the function itself has developed over the past few decades. After seeing how businesses today manage government affairs, we highlight some of the political activities that companies use to advance their agendas in Washington.

[1] Wendy L. Hansen and Neil J. Mitchell, "Disaggregating and Explaining Corporate Political Activity: Domestic and Foreign Corporations in National Politics," *American Political Science Review*, December 1, 2000, p. 891.

[2] "Citizens United v. Federal Election Commission," Cornell Law School, https://www.law.cornell.edu/supct/cert/08-205.

[3] Bradley A. Smith, "Celebrate the Citizens United Decade," *The Wall Street Journal*, January 20, 2020, https://www.wsj.com/articles/celebrate-the-citizens-united-decade-11579553962.

[4] Thomas Edsall, "After Citizens United, a Vicious Cycle of Corruption," *The New York Times*, December 6, 2018, https://www.nytimes.com/2018/12/06/opinion/citizens-united-corruption-pacs.html.

Government Begins to Manage Business: The Rise of Regulation

Government regulation began more than 100 years ago with state regulation of the railroad companies. By the mid-nineteenth century, trains had triumphed over rival forms of land transportation. Railroad systems opened travel opportunities to people all over the United States and drove the growth of industry, shipping goods quickly across long distances. However, the railroads also presented the country with enormous problems. Although proponents of a laissez-faire approach to the markets maintained that competition would regulate business, it failed to regulate the railroads and corruption ensued.

The federal government's regulation of business began in 1887, with the Act to Regulate Commerce and the establishment of the Interstate Commerce Commission (ICC). Then, in 1890, another critical piece of legislation was passed: the Sherman Antitrust Act. This act established a legal framework to prevent trusts from restricting trade and reducing competition and remains the main source of antitrust law in the United States. From the ICC and the Sherman Antitrust laws to the hundreds of regulations currently in place, covering topics that range from the environment to pornography to food quality, the government is actively engaged in business affairs. Each year the federal government passes laws, and even creates new agencies, to correct what it (and its constituencies) perceives as negative market externalities produced by private business.

Some examples of past bills that affected business include the Cigarette Labeling and Advertising Act (1965), which requires all cigarette packages to carry warnings about the hazards of smoking; the Clear Air Act Amendments (1970), which outlined procedures for monitoring air quality; the Employee Retirement Income Security Act of 1974 (ERISA), which set new federal standards for employee pension programs; and the Dodd-Frank Wall Street Reform and Consumer Protection Act (2010), which created the Consumer Financial Protection Bureau.

One of the most significant acts to affect business was the Sarbanes-Oxley Act of 2002, officially titled the Public Company Accounting Reform and Investor Protection Act. It came in the wake of a series of devastating corporate financial scandals, including those affecting Enron, Arthur Andersen, and WorldCom.

The act was designed to review dated legislative audit requirements and, by doing so, protect investors by improving the accuracy and reliability of corporate disclosures. The act covers issues such as establishing a public company accounting oversight board, auditor independence, corporate responsibility, and enhanced financial disclosure. It also eliminated some of the most egregious practices in the accounting world, such as using auditing as a loss leader to encourage companies to buy their higher-profit consulting services. It also mandated that companies test their internal financial controls to help ensure that fraud doesn't happen.[5]

In the United States, the government philosophy has alternated between laissez-faire (less regulation) and interventionist (more regulation) policies, reflecting differing views on what sort of market involvement best advances the public interest. Historically, business has resisted new regulations, especially laws that mandate costly additions to existing procedures. One example of these regulations is the "best available technology" clauses

---

[5] American Institute of Certified Public Accountants website, https://www.aicpa.org.

of many environmental laws, which demand that polluting companies maximize investment in "clean" equipment when they update their facilities. Historically, American industry has complained that regulations hurt American businesses and their efforts to compete with foreign rivals. However, the American business position toward environmental regulation has evolved of late, particularly over the past decade. PwC's Annual CEO Survey reports that 24 percent of CEOs cite climate change as an "extreme concern," citing a need for increased attention to threats to supply chain stability and greater investment in the creation of a "green economy."[6] Business leaders are increasingly shifting toward a collaborative as opposed to an antagonistic approach to environmental regulation, recognizing that the long-term vitality of operations is much more closely intertwined with environmental health than previously recognized.

The Reach of the Regulatory Agencies

Through the years, regulatory agencies have evolved into sophisticated organizations. Franklin D. Roosevelt's New Deal gave government incredible power to regulate business. The Securities and Exchange Commission (SEC) was created to stabilize financial markets and the National Labor Relations Board to remedy labor problems. The Federal Communications Commission (FCC) regulated radio, television, and telephones, and the Civil Aeronautics Board (CAB) regulated the airlines. The safety rulemaking powers would later be transferred to a new agency, the Federal Aviation Administration (FAA), and then undergo yet another restructuring as part of Homeland Security after the terrorist attacks of September 11, 2001. More recently, Sarbanes-Oxley (SOX) increased the power of the Public Company Accounting Oversight Board (PCAOB), a congressionally created private-sector, nonprofit corporation. The PCAOB has sweeping powers over the nation's external auditors with respect to their auditing of publicly held companies. This description is only a small selection of the regulatory agencies that have emerged over the last century. Regulation covers most industries and can be complex to navigate given the overlapping jurisdictions of some regulatory agencies and the ability of firms to operate across regulatory boundaries.

Government is involved in virtually all stages of business development. Many enterprises cannot begin operations until they receive a license from a regulatory agency such as the ICC, the FCC, or the Food and Drug Administration (FDA). Once an enterprise has its license to operate, the same government agencies must then inspect and approve its products. The Consumer Product Safety Commission (CPSC) helps set safety standards for consumer products, and most products must pass its "tests" before they ever reach the market.

Beyond approving which products become available to the public, the government also can influence the prices of goods and services. Agricultural goods, forest products, and metals are examples. Using congressionally approved formulas, federal agencies set floor prices, volume-based subsidies, and quota systems that shape the prices in these markets. The government also heavily influences the prices set by transportation, communications, and utility companies—industries that provide the basic infrastructure for society.

[6] "Navigating the Rising Tide of Uncertainty," PwC, 2019, https://www.pwc.com/ee/et/publications/pub/pwc-23rd-global-ceo-survey.pdf.

Since the days of the Sherman Antitrust Act, the U.S. government has continued its efforts to prevent monopolies and other anticompetitive business practices. One example is the Federal Trade Commission's (FTC) rejection of a merger between Staples and Office Depot. The FTC argued that, if they merged, each superstore would lose its largest competitor. Without the check that direct competition between Staples and Office Depot had placed on prices, the merged office supply store would gain considerable control over what it charged its customers. The FTC viewed the joining of Staples and Office Depot as more of a threat to consumers than a benefit and so prevented the merger.[7] A more recent example of the involvement of the FTC in market dynamics is the move in early 2020 to examine all prior acquisitions made by Alphabet, Amazon, Apple, Facebook, and Microsoft.[8] The move is amidst increasingly vocal calls to break up big tech (or at least considerably mitigate its influence) on the part of individual citizens and politicians of all political persuasions alike[9] and is on the heels of a 2019 record-breaking $5 billion fine issued by the FTC against Facebook, which actually resulted in a 1.8 percent increase in the company's stock.[10] The notion that big tech is unassailable is of increasing concern, and the FTC's investigation into acquisition practices could have considerable implications for the continued dominance of this handful of companies.

In the next section, we look at how business has responded to government regulation and ways in which companies work with lawmakers to ensure their own voice is heard when drafting business-specific legislation.

How Business "Manages" Government: The Rise of Government Relations

In light of the government's heavy involvement in commercial affairs, business eventually realized that instead of fighting regulation, a more effective approach would be advocating its own positions to key political decision makers. Companies began to protect their interests with well-crafted lobbying and negotiating tactics, particularly when they were facing substantial opposition from consumer and community groups that politicians were eager to appease.

One of Wall Street's largest investment banks, Goldman Sachs, is a good example of a politically active organization in a sometimes controversial industry. The bank has been the 28th largest organizational donor (including all unions and private organizations) from 1990 to 2021, distributing $69,998,697 in political donations. During the 2008 election cycle, a period of great economic and regulatory uncertainty

---

[7] John M. Broder, "FTC Rejects Deal to Join Two Giants of Office Supplies," *The New York Times*, April 5, 1997, p. 7.

[8] "FTC to Examine Past Acquisitions by Large Technology Companies," Federal Trade Commission, February 11, 2020, https://www.ftc.gov/news-events/press-releases/2020/02/ftc-examine-past-acquisitions-large-technology-companies.

[9] Lauren Feiner, "FTC Will Examine Prior Acquisitions by Alphabet, Amazon, Apple, Facebook and Microsoft," *CNBC*, February 11, 2020, https://www.cnbc.com/2020/02/11/ftc-will-examine-prior-acquisitions-by-big-tech-companies.html.

[10] Wal van Lierop, "Step Up Or Break Up: The Challenge For Big Tech," *Forbes*, October 9, 2020, https://www.forbes.com/sites/walvanlierop/2020/10/09/step-up-or-break-up-the-challenge-for-big-tech.

for securities firms facing the fallout of the economic crisis, Goldman Sachs made $6,025,681 in political donations, a 36 percent increase from 2000; in 2020, its political donations were $5,454,671—a decrease from the donation level of the past but nonetheless placing Goldman as one of the top organizational donors nationally.[11]

In 2020, the top five lobbying groups were the National Association of Realtors, the U.S. Chamber of Commerce, Pharmaceutical Research & Manufacturers of America, the American Hospital Association, and Blue Cross/Blue Shield, which collectively contributed over $238 million to their lobbying efforts. Facebook and Amazon also joined the top 10, contributing $19.6 million and $18.7 million, respectively.[12]

In the interaction between business and Capitol Hill, powerful lobbies and trade unions are prevalent—subjecting the government to a multitude of pressures. As Alfred D. Chandler Jr., an economic historian, wrote, "the visible hand of management [has] replaced what Adam Smith referred to as the invisible hand of market forces. . . . [As business has] acquired functions hitherto carried out by the market, it [has become] the most influential group of economic decision makers."[13]

Businesses use a number of tactics to further their own agendas in Washington. In this section, we look at the rise of the government relations function within companies.

The Government Relations Function Takes Shape

In the late 1960s and early 1970s, government regulations placed on certain industries significantly raised the cost of doing business. Thus, "It became apparent to American business leaders that in order to win in Washington, they would have to adapt the rules to their advantage, and that meant playing Washington's game."[14] "Playing the game" became the job of a company's government relations, or government affairs, department. This function concentrated specifically on the positive and negative effects of policy and policy changes, as well as monitoring shifts in ideology and agendas on Capitol Hill and accurately identifying emerging trends. By being knowledgeable about government and getting involved in the development of regulatory policy, business could better protect itself from damaging regulations while taking advantage of any positive opportunities that governmental regulation created (especially vis-à-vis a competitor).

Since the 1980s, government relations departments have improved their effectiveness by studying the methods of other companies, hiring consultants, organizing popular support, learning to use the media properly, making alliances, creating political action committees, and establishing connections with influential Washington insiders. By applying business and marketing techniques to politics and combining traditional organizational tools with advanced technology (e.g., computerized association memberships, the Internet,

---

[11] "Top Spenders," OpenSecrets.org, 2021, https://www.opensecrets.org/federal-lobbying/top-spenders.

[12] Ibid.

[13] Walter Adams and James W. Brock, *The Bigness Complex: Industry, Labor, and Government in the American Economy* (New York: Pantheon Books, 1986).

[14] Sar A. Levitan and Martha R. Cooper, *Business Lobbies: The Public Good and the Bottom Line* (Baltimore, MD: Johns Hopkins University Press, 1984), pp. 4–5.

electronic and paper newsletters), business has increased its influence over Washington's policymakers. More than 50 percent of *Fortune* 500 corporations had representatives in Washington or retained counsel there.[15]

Many companies, such as Bridgestone/Firestone and today's big tech companies, including Facebook, Google, and Amazon, have learned the costs associated with *not* having a Washington presence. When the National Highway Traffic Safety Administration forced Bridgestone/Firestone to recall millions of tires—after more than 40 deaths were linked to problems with tire treads—the company had no Washington office in place and had lost most of its outside consultants. The company needed to seek out new representation in the midst of a highly publicized crisis. Bridgestone/Firestone learned from this mistake and now has a dedicated Washington office and several consultants.[16]

Similarly, while big tech companies like Facebook, Google, and Amazon now appear to be regular players in Senate investigations into their influence, they were not nearly as politically active just a short while ago. In fact, one decade ago, Amazon employed just two registered lobbyists, and Facebook's lobbyists had only just been granted actual office space, having previously led their D.C. operations out of an employee's living room.[17] Since then, however, these companies have collectively spent over half a billion in lobbying efforts, particularly increasing their spending practices following heightened scrutiny during the Russian Facebook hacking scandal during the 2016 election cycle.[18] While it remains to be seen whether this increased investment in lobbying will allow big tech to maintain its influence in Washington or if such spending will only be added to the ever-growing list of transgressions attributed to the industry, it is clear that the approach taken in the early 2010s will remain a thing of the past.

The FiscalNote conducted a survey in 2020 to define the responsibilities and focus areas of public affairs executives. Over 80 percent of respondents noted that they follow at least 3 governmental issues closely, with 25 percent noting they follow 6 to 10 and 18 percent following over 20 issues. At the same time, however, the majority of respondents felt that their team sizes were too small for the amount of information they must contend with, underscoring just how fraught the position has become, with its tension between increased complexities of serving in a public affairs role and limited resources devoted in terms of actual team sizes.[19]

It is no surprise, then, that Fortune 100 companies spend a considerable amount of time and money employing outside lobbyists to work on their behalf. The extent to which public affairs outsource their government relations strategy has remained relatively steady over the past decade, with 41 percent of public affairs executives reporting that they

[15] Hansen and Mitchell, "Disaggregating and Explaining Corporate Political Activity," p. 891.

[16] Shawn Zeller, "Lobbying: Saying So Long to D.C. Outposts," *National Journal*, December 1, 2001, http://www.nationaljournal.com.

[17] "Tech Giants Led by Amazon, Facebook, and Google Spent Nearly Half a Billion on Lobbying over the Past Decade, New Data Shows," *The Washington Post*, January 22, 2020, https://www.washingtonpost.com/technology/2020/01/22/amazon-facebook-google-lobbying-2019.

[18] Ibid.

[19] "The State of Public Affairs," FiscalNote, 2020, https://fiscalnote-marketing.s3.amazonaws.com/FN-State-of-PA-2020_FNL1_191212_171654.pdf.

outsource their government relations strategy, compared to 39 percent a decade prior.[20] Additionally, the number of registered lobbyists has remained steady as well, with 12,000 lobbyists actively working in Washington, helping clients to spend $3.5 billion on their efforts in 2019.[21]

What is most notable, however, is the amount of money invested on behalf of lobbying efforts. The external lobbying consultants in Washington to whom companies often turn for advice and guidance on political activities command rates on average of $15,000 as a baseline amount per month, reaching up to $50,000 for the full range of services.[22] Though big tech often comes the most under fire for their political influence and money spent on lobbying efforts, the pharmaceutical and health products industry takes the lead, having spent over $300 million on lobbying efforts in 2020. Moreover, between 2014 and 2017, Fortune 100 companies spent $2 billion lobbying Congress, receiving $3.2 billion federal grants during that time period.[23] Additionally, they received $393 billion in federal contracts during that same time period.[24] Adam Andrzejewski of *The Washington Post* puts this into perspective by noting that, "This amount is equivalent to all federal student loans each year; all aid to the state government of California; or eighty percent of the entire payroll of the executive federal agencies, i.e. Homeland Security, Veterans Affairs, Health & Human Services, Internal Revenue Service, etc."[25]

Considering the extensive amounts spent by corporations on lobbying efforts, they must be diligent in measuring the returns they are receiving for such efforts. As with other corporate communications functions, companies measure their impact by turning to KPIs. The FiscalNote 2020 survey cited earlier found that 82 percent of participants measured success according to the percent of legislation objectives met and achieved, with costs reduced or avoided listed as the second most important objective by 74 percent of participants. A results-focused approach will help ensure that a government affairs program stays strategically on track.[26]

The Ways and Means of Managing Washington

An internal staff of government relations professionals and senior leaders who are engaged in the issues that affect their companies are two important components of any business's strategy to stay tapped into Washington. In this section, we look at some of the specific activities that companies use to advance their positions with lawmakers.

[20] "Americans Concerned About Election Integrity and Government Response to COVID-19," Public Affairs Council, https://pac.org/public-affairs-pulse-survey-2020.

[21] Tala Hadavi, "Lobbying in Q1 Topped a Record $938 Million, but Lobbyists Say Their Profession Is Misunderstood," *CNBC*, October 5, 2020, https://www.cnbc.com/2020/10/05/q1-lobbying-spend-was-record-938-million-but-lobbyists-decry-stereotype.html.

[22] "Top Tier Lobbying Five Tier Pricing," Lobbyit.com, https://lobbyit.com/pricing.

[23] Adam Andrzejewski, "How the Fortune 100 Turned $2 Billion in Lobbying Spend into $400 Billion of Taxpayer Cash," *Forbes*, May 14, 2019, https://www.forbes.com/sites/adamandrzejewski/2019/05/14/how-the-fortune-100-turned-2-billion-in-lobbying-spend-into-400-billion-of-taxpayer-cash.

[24] Ibid.

[25] Ibid.

[26] Ibid.

Coalition Building

The 1970s saw a great "political resurgence of business." Many of the methods used by government relations departments today became established or perfected during this period. In particular, coalition building emerged as a popular form of political influence. Many businesses previously acted to defend only their individual interests when faced with legislative problems, without considering the ways in which their own concerns might coincide with those of other groups or organizations. When a particular company was in trouble, it often battled Washington alone, even when the same issues applied to many other corporations within its industry.

The times of each business standing alone in Washington ended when legislation that affected most, if not all, businesses became more common than the earlier regulations that had affected one or a small collection of industries. Laws concerning consumer safety and labor and wage reform led the wave of these broader regulations. Companies soon learned the benefits of working together. When one company was affected by new regulations, it would find other firms in a similar position to form ad hoc committees. In these committees, the companies forged alliances of support on the business level, which then translated into channels for expressing their views in a greater number of congressional districts and states.

Although loosely formed ad hoc coalitions are still common, companies also often join established industry associations that pool financial and organizational resources for representing their positions in Washington. The Consumer Electronics Association (CEA), for example, advocates that industry's collective viewpoint on issues that include government regulation of broadband, consumer home recording rights, and copyright protection. The Pharmaceutical Research and Manufacturers of America Group advocates on behalf of the pharma industry, looking to present a unified vision on pharmaceutical regulation and cost control, while also spending more than any other industry lobbying group in 2020.

By joining forces through either ad hoc coalitions or more formalized industry associations, companies can assert greater power and have a better chance of affecting legislative outcomes than they would have acting alone.

CEO Involvement in Government Relations

Large and small companies alike strengthen their government relations programs through actively involving senior management in political activities. As they have recognized the importance of gaining a seat at the policy discussion table for their companies, increasing numbers of CEOs are stepping into the policy debate. This trend does not surprise most executives. As John de Butts, former Chairman of AT&T, remarked, "So vital . . . is the relationship of government and business that to my mind the chief executive officer who is content to delegate responsibility for that relationship to his public affairs expert may be neglecting one of the most crucial aspects of his own responsibility."[27]

The vast majority of CEOs surveyed in 2020 (over 95 percent) indicated that they were in some way politically active on behalf of their organization.[28] Other activities drawing

[27] James W. Singer, "Business and Government: A New 'Quasi-Public' Role," *National Journal*, April 15, 1978, p. 596.

[28] Edward Segal, "How And Why Corporate Lobbying Will Continue to Matter During the Biden Administration," *Forbes*, January 26, 2021, https://www.forbes.com/sites/edwardsegal/2021/01/26/how-and-why-corporate-lobbying-will-continue-to-matter-during-the-biden-administration.

CEO participation were correspondence to federal legislators or regulators, endorsement of the company's political action committee, direct lobbying of federal legislators, and attendance at candidate fundraisers.[29]

Perhaps no example better underscores the prime importance of CEO involvement in the government relations function than during the House Judiciary Committee's 2020 antitrust panel that represents the culmination of a years-long investigation into the anticompetitive behavior of tech's largest companies. CEOs of all four big companies—Facebook's Mark Zuckerberg, Google's Sundar Pichai, Apple's Tim Cook, and Amazon's Jeff Bezos—sat before the committee, testifying on behalf of their companies and seeking to better position their roles in such contentious issues as Internet privacy, free speech, and outside political influence.[30] That the CEOs of these oftentimes harsh competitors would testify collectively, attempting to present a unified vision for the industry while also trying to limit culpability for the individual companies they lead, was something previously thought incredibly unlikely to ever happen. Their faces plastered across the front pages of *The New York Times, The Wall Street Journal,* and *The Washington Post,* among many other newspapers and sites, underscored just how intimately intertwined CEOs must be not only with their individual company's governmental relations efforts but also with those of the entire industries in which they operate. Long gone are the days, then, in which CEOs and entire industries could attempt to avoid Washington's focus and purely devote efforts to their business's operations; in many ways these have become one and the same now.

Lobbying on an Individual Basis

When business leaders realized the importance of having a say in the activities on Capitol Hill, they turned to lobbying groups to help them successfully advance their viewpoints with congressional decision makers. (Lobbying is any activity aimed at promoting or securing the passage of specific legislation through coordinated communications with key lawmakers.) In recent decades, as government intervention has grown, so has the number of organizations in Washington that present the views of business to Congress, the White House, and the regulatory agencies.

Individuals lobby the government in several ways at several different levels, with office visits and other meetings (formal or informal) with lawmakers and regulatory agencies becoming increasingly important as the Internet makes it easier for congressional and other governmental offices to become deluged with electronic communications. Political fundraisers have long been an informal opportunity for individuals to (albeit briefly) lobby those running for election. In addition, developing a working relationship with staff members (in addition to the politician) is an effective way of influencing decisions. Other individuals work through intermediaries; for example, a local businessperson may lobby local government to request help from their representatives in Congress (these requests can carry more weight, as they go from one level of government to another). Additional methods of individual lobbying efforts include letter writing; inserting op-ed pieces or editorials in print

[29] "CEOs More Politically Involved."

[30] "Facebook, Google, Twitter CEOs Clash with Congress in Pre-Election Showdown," *The Washington Post,* March 25, 2021, https://www.washingtonpost.com/technology/2020/10/28/twitter-facebook-google-senate-hearing-live-updates.

news media; and, for executive branch agencies, providing comments during the rulemaking process.

Companies employ a variety of data to convince government officials to meet with them. For example, many companies track their employment/economic footprint by county, state, and congressional district. Some companies, including those involved in government contracting, open offices in many different congressional districts in order to increase the number of politicians willing to advocate on their behalf (and on behalf of the employment they provide).

These techniques and others can have a significant impact in Congress. The U.S. Chamber of Commerce, for one, has conducted very effective and sophisticated grassroots campaigns to increase its influence. With state and local chapters that contain thousands of members, the Chamber of Commerce has a wide base from which to work. By 1980, it had established 2,700 "Congressional Action Committees" that consisted of executives who were personally acquainted with their senators and representatives. These executives received information about events in Washington through bulletins from the Chamber's Washington office and remained in touch with their representatives so that they might contact them when called upon to do so. In 2013, they were the largest single lobbying group in the United States, with annual spending of more than $74 million.[31]

This method of lobbying through far-reaching constituencies has produced good results: "within a week [the Chamber of Commerce] . . . can carry out research on the impact of a bill on each legislator's district and through its local branches mobilize a 'grassroots campaign' on the issue in time to affect the outcome of the vote."[32] Today, the Chamber of Commerce—once poorly regarded in Washington—has a grassroots network of 50,000 business activists, an expansive membership of 3 million businesses, 830 business associations, and 116 American Chambers of Commerce abroad.[33]

Political involvement activities by companies include direct lobbying by public affairs executives, visits to company locations by candidates/public officials, attending candidate fundraisers, soliciting PAC contributions, participation in coalitions, employee newsletters on political/legislative affairs, and grassroots/grasstops activism.[34]

Returning to our Microsoft example, this company's lobbying efforts, which included its "grassroots" website campaign, clearly have paid off. In 2001, Microsoft's lobby against copyright violators resulted in a government crackdown on software piracy. Later that year, in the wake of the September 11 terrorist attacks, Microsoft led the charge in persuading the Bush administration to allot more than $70 million to improve "cybersecurity" in America.[35]

Success stories like Microsoft and the U.S. Chamber of Commerce have prompted many major corporations to establish campaigns that target individuals. In addition to achieving desired legislative outcomes, "a prudently managed grassroots program can be a team-building exercise. Providing information about legislation that will affect current

[31] "Top Spenders," 2013, OpenSecrets.org, https://www.opensecrets.org/federal-lobbying/top-spenders?cycle=2013.

[32] Graham Wilson, *Interest Groups in the United States* (New York: Oxford University Press, 1981).

[33] American Chamber of Commerce website, www.uschamber.com.

[34] Foundation for Public Affairs, "State of Public Affairs 2011–2012," 2011.

[35] Jeffrey H. Birnbaum, "How Microsoft Conquered Washington," *Fortune*, April 29, 2002, pp. 95–96.

and future company activities will be of interest to many employees at all ranks. . . . [B]uilding a grassroots program with employees makes them part of the team."[36] Using individuals in lobbying is one of the most popular methods for companies and their employees to get involved in politics. Blogs have become an important part of grassroots campaigns, as they can be targeted to niche groups of constituents very easily.

Political Action Committees

Another popular method of getting involved in government is the formation of political action committees (PACs). The idea for this movement came from organized labor, which created official committees responsible for raising and dispersing money to support political campaigns. In 1980, 1,200 companies had their own PACs; today there are 4,874.[37] Approximately 58 percent of *Fortune* 500 companies currently have a PAC.[38] Industry leaders such as Honeywell, Blue Cross/Blue Shield, and AT&T have some of the largest and most active PACs, giving between $2.4 and $3.2 million to candidates in 2012.[39] Nineteen percent of Walmart's 60,000 domestic managers contribute to its PAC, mostly through payroll deductions that average $8.60 a month.[40]

To target their funding efficiently, PAC administrators need to have access to information about each political candidate and the races they support. The Business-Industry Political Action Committee (BIPAC) was formed to meet these information needs. Although this group does contribute directly to candidates, its most important role is to research candidates and identify close races. BIPAC provides weekly newsletters to PAC managers, along with providing daily updates on congressional races through the BIPAC website. By using their national organization, individual PACs remain well informed and are able to direct their funds intelligently.

PACs have arisen out of an increased political awareness in corporate managers. They provide a simple framework for getting employees involved in political issues that could determine their employers' well-being into the future. Employee involvement is key, as federal election law prevents direct corporate contributions to party committees and candidates. Data from OpenSecrets, a non-profit aimed at increasing political transparency and accountability, found that PACs donated over $500 million during the 2020 election cycle.[41]

Data from the Center for Responsive Politics indicates that PAC contributions account for 27 percent of political donations, with business PACs responsible for 20 percent of political donations.[42] The amount of money that businesses contribute to politicians in any given election cycle is staggering. According to the Center for Responsive Politics, business interests contribute far more money to candidates and political parties than do labor unions or ideological groups.

[36] Gerry Keim, "Corporate Grassroots Program in the 1980's," *California Management Review* 28, no. 1 (Fall 1985), p. 117.

[37] Federal Election Commission website, www.fec.gov.

[38] Tim Reason, "Campaign Contributions at the Office," *CFO Magazine*, July 12, 2004.

[39] Data from OpenSecrets.org, www.opensecrets.org/pacs/toppacs.php?Type=C&cycle=2012.

[40] Cummings, "Joining the PAC," p. A1.

[41] "Political Action Committees (PACs)," OpenSecrets.org, 2020, https://www.opensecrets.org/political-action-committees-pacs/2020.

[42] Data from OpenSecrets.org, www.opensecrets.org/overview/blio.php.

Conclusion

Corporate America's relationship with various levels of government extends far beyond licenses, safety standards, and product prices. Today, the influence of private business on public affairs, and vice versa, has become so established that we often assume changes in one arena will lead to changes in the other.

In America, defining the roles of government and business with regard to each other is an ongoing and ever-evolving process. When the last edition of this text was published, much of the focus on lobbying and potentially undue political influence on the part of corporations was focused predominantly on the banking industry, coming out in the wake of the Great Recession and revelations regarding banking's influence in Washington. Today, that conversation has shifted considerably, now focusing on big tech and the many ways in which those industries exert influence not just over Washington but also over many aspects of everyday life. The themes, however, remain the same. Individual companies and entire industries would be foolish to ignore or even take an antagonistic approach toward governmental interactions and regulations given the inevitability of some sort of focus on the part of Washington turning toward corporations. At the same time, companies must balance the need not to ignore this challenge with the obligation to ensure that influence is not unduly wielded; whether they like it or not, overstepping influence, as illustrated by the more recent investigations into big tech, can also result in considerable damage to a company and arguably more broadly to society.

Case 9-1

Disney's America Theme Park: *The Third Battle of Bull Run*

On September 22, 1994, Michael Eisner, CEO of the Walt Disney Company, one of the most powerful and well-known media conglomerates in the world, stared out the window of his Burbank office, contemplating the current situation surrounding the Disney's America theme park. Ever since November 8, 1993, when *The Wall Street Journal* first broke the news that Disney was planning to build a theme park near Washington, D.C., ongoing national debate over the location and concept of the $650 million park had caused tremendous frustration. Eisner thought back over the events of the past year. How could his great idea have run into such formidable resistance?

THE CONTROVERSY COMES TO A HEAD

Eisner's secretary had clipped several newspaper articles covering two parades that took place on September 17. In Washington, D.C., several hundred Disney opponents from over 50 anti-Disney organizations had marched past the White House and rallied on the National Mall in protest of the park. On the same day in the streets of Haymarket, Virginia, near the proposed park site, Mickey Mouse and 101 local children dressed as Dalmatians had appeared in a parade that was filled with pro-Disney sentiment. Eisner was particularly struck by the contrast between the two pictures: one showing an

Source: This case was written by Elizabeth A. Powell, Assistant Professor of Business Administration, and Sarah Stover, MBA 1997. It was written as a basis for class discussion rather than to illustrate effective or ineffective handling of an administrative situation. Copyright © 2001 by the University of Virginia Darden School Foundation, Charlottesville, VA. All rights reserved. To order copies, send an e-mail to dardencases@virginia.edu.

anti-Disney display from the National Mall protest and another of Mickey and Minnie Mouse being driven through the streets of Haymarket during the exuberant community parade.

Despite the controversy depicted in the press, on September 21, Prince William County, Virginia, planning commissioners had recommended local zoning approval for Disney's America, and regional transportation officials had authorized $130 million in local roads to serve it. It appeared very likely that the project would win final zoning approval in October. At the state level, Virginia's Governor George Allen continued his strong support of the park's development.

Over the past three weeks, however, Eisner had been ruminating over a phone call he received in late August from John Cooke, President of the Disney Channel since 1985. Although Cooke had no responsibility for Disney's America, he had more experience in the Washington, D.C. political scene than any of Disney's other highest-ranking managers and was one of Eisner's most trusted executives. Cooke was not encouraging about the park's prospects. Quite familiar with many of the park's opponents, he believed they would not give up the fight under any circumstances. Given the anti-Disney coalition's considerable financial resources, the nationally publicized anti-Disney campaign could go on indefinitely, inflicting immeasurable damage on Disney's fun, family image. Cooke advised Eisner to think very seriously about ending the project.

Since the mid-1980s, Eisner's business strategy was to revitalize Disney by broadening its brand into new ventures. Although promising at first, now the wisdom of some of the ventures seemed less certain. The worst example, EuroDisney, the new Disney park located outside Paris, continued to flounder. The numbers for fiscal year 1994, due in just a couple of days on September 30, didn't look promising. Estimates said net income would be down to $300 million from $800 million the year before, mostly because EuroDisney lost $515 million from operations and $372 million from a related accounting charge.[1]

The good news was that due to cost cutting, EuroDisney's losses were actually less than in the previous year, while the bad news was that attendance was also down. Prince al-Waleed bin Talal bin Adulaziz of Saudi Arabia had agreed to buy 24 percent of the park and build a convention center there, thus relieving some of the financial pressure, but it seemed that the negative press coverage of that park's troubles would never end.

The Disney's America problem was particularly bothersome, however. Eisner realized that the controversy surrounding the park, coupled with the many other highly publicized problems of 1994, was damaging Disney's image. Due to publicity about its highly visible corporate problems, Disney's image as a business threatened to tarnish its reputation for family-friendly fun and fantasy.

Personally, Eisner was particularly fond of the Disney's America concept. He had helped develop the original idea and had personally championed it within the Disney organization. He recalled the early meetings during which several Disney executives, including himself, had brainstormed an American history concept. He and the other executives had strongly believed that Disney had the unique capability of designing an American history theme park that would draw on the company's technical expertise and offer guests an entertaining, educational, and emotional journey through time. They envisioned guests, adults and children alike, embracing a park dedicated to telling the story of U.S. history. Eisner had hoped the park would be part of the personal legacy he would leave behind at Disney. As he told a *Washington Post* reporter, "This is the one idea I've heard that is, in corporate locker room talk, what's known as a no-brainer."[2]

[1] The Walt Disney Company Annual Report, 1995. See also Kim Masters, *The Keys to the Kingdom* (New York: William Morrow, 2000), p. 299.

[2] William M. Powers, "Michael in Eisnerland: Disney's Chairman's Sense of Wonder, Will to Win Drive for Virginia Theme Park Plan," *Washington Post*, January 23, 1994, p. H1.

THE DISNEY'S AMERICA CONCEPT AND LOCATION

The idea of building an American history theme park originated in 1991 when Eisner and other Disney executives attended a meeting at Colonial Williamsburg in southeastern Virginia. The executives were impressed by the restored pre-Revolutionary capital. Disney had already been thinking about locations for theme parks that were on a somewhat smaller scale than the company's massive ones. Visiting Williamsburg helped Disney make the connection to a new park based on historical themes.

Disney's attention soon shifted focus to Washington, D.C. As the third-largest tourist market in the United States and the center of American government, the nation's capital seemed a natural location for an American history park. The abundance of historical sites in the area broadened its appeal as a center of American history. Disney's other parks were located on the fringes of developed urban centers (Anaheim, Orlando, Tokyo, and Paris). The parks gained advantages from their proximity to urban centers, but due to their peripheral locations, Disney was able to acquire lower-priced land and ensure a safe environment for visitors, far from inner-city congestion and crime.

Disney needed a location with easy access to an airport and an exit off an interstate highway. Executives hoped to find land that had already been zoned for development as well as local and state politicians who would be open to economic growth. In Prince William County, located in the heart of Virginia's Piedmont region, Disney found all these things. Dulles International Airport was located just east of Prince William County. U.S. Interstate 66 (I-66), the main traffic artery connecting Washington, D.C., with its western suburbs, could transport tourists straight from Washington's monuments and museums into Prince William County, a distance of about 35 miles.

The political and economic context also made Prince William County attractive to Disney. Virginia had long been a pro-growth state, and its governors were constantly under pressure to bring in new business. Democratic Governor Doug Wilder would leave office in November 1993, having lost some notable campaigns to bring growth to Virginia's economy. Polls showed that he would likely be replaced by Republican George Allen, the son of a former Washington Redskins American football coach and a graduate of the University of Virginia. If elected, Allen would be under instant pressure to create state economic growth. Most Prince William County officials were also "pro-growth," though not well prepared for it. The county's growing population of middle-class residents (up 62 percent since 1980) paid the highest taxes in the state of Virginia due to a dearth of economic development within the county. The Virginia legislature set an ambitious goal in 1990 to attract 14,000 jobs and $1 billion in nonresidential growth to the county to fund more and better schools and county administrative services, in addition to reducing residential taxes paid by each family.

In the spring of 1993, Peter Rummell, President of Disney Design and Development, which included the famous Imagineering group, as well as the real estate division, identified 3,000 acres in Prince William County near the small town of Haymarket (population 483). The largest property was a 2,300-acre plot of land, the Waverly Tract, owned by a real estate subsidiary of the Exxon Corporation. Waverly was already zoned for mixed-use development of homes and office buildings, yet due to a weak real estate market, Exxon had never broken ground on the undeveloped farmland. For a modest holding price, Exxon was willing to option the property. Using a scheme that had worked years before in Orlando, the Disney real estate group bought or put options on Waverly and the remaining 3,000 acres without revealing the company's corporate identity in any of the transactions.

THE VIRGINIA PIEDMONT

The northeast corner of Virginia comprises the Piedmont region. The region contains countless significant sites related to U.S. history, including, for example, the preserved homes of four of the first five U.S. presidents: Washington, Jefferson, Madison, and Monroe. According to Pulitzer Prize–winning historian David McCullough, "This is the ground of our Founding Fathers. These are the landscapes—small towns, churches, fields, mountains, creeks, and rivers—that speak volumes."[3] Thomas Jefferson loved the agrarian life he found on the farms east of the Blue Ridge Mountains. In his letters, he exulted over the region's "delicious spring," "soft genial temperatures," and good soil.[4]

The region is also home to more than two-dozen Civil War battlefields. The U.S. Civil War was fought largely over the issue of slavery, pitting northern states against the southern states that had seceded from the union. Just a few miles from the Waverly tract is Manassas National Battlefield Park, land that is protected and preserved by the U.S. National Park Service, commemorating two major Civil War battles. The first battle in 1861 was the Civil War's first major land engagement. The second, in 1862, marked the beginning of Confederate General Robert E. Lee's first invasion of the North. On what would become some of the bloodiest soil in U.S. history, Lee reflected at Bull Run in 1861, "The views are so magnificent, the valleys so beautiful, the scenery so peaceful. What a glorious world the Almighty has given us. How thankless and ungrateful we are, and how we labor to mar His gifts."[5]

Although largely rural and predominantly middle class, the region was also notable as home to some of America's most wealthy and influential citizens. The largest estates suggested the presence of privilege at every turn: perfect fences built from stone or wood, carefully manicured pastures, large barns requiring lots of hired help, a few private landing strips, and long private lanes lined with boxwood or dogwood that led to magnificent private homes.

The Piedmont also had a history of successfully fighting local development projects. In the late 1970s, the Marriott Corporation had proposed building a large amusement park, and, in the late 1980s, a

[3] Richard L. Worsnop, "Historic Preservation," *The CQ Researcher*, October 7, 1994, p. 867.

[4] Rudy Abramson, "Land Where Our Fathers Died," *Washingtonian Magazine*, October 1996, p. 62.

[5] "Making a Stand," *Conde Nast Traveler*, September 1994, p. 148.

development group had planned to develop a major shopping mall in the area. Both projects were defeated by local opposition.

DISNEY'S PLANS REVEALED

To keep its land acquisition secret, Disney had done little to work with local government and communities, but by late October of 1993, Eisner learned that Disney's plans had begun to leak.[6] It would only be a matter of days before the news would hit the media, so in the meantime Disney had to act quickly. Behind the scenes, Eisner contacted outgoing Governor Wilder and Governor-elect Allen. Both gave their immediate support and agreed to attend a public announcement scheduled for November 11. The company hired a local real estate law firm, and also retained the services of Jody Powell, former Press Secretary to President Jimmy Carter, who ran the Powell Tate public relations firm.

On November 8, 1993, a brief item appeared in *The Wall Street Journal* stating that Disney was planning to build a theme park somewhere in Virginia. That same day, Disney officials confirmed the story but provided no additional details. The next day, a *Washington Post* reporter identified Prince William County as the targeted area. Disney spokespeople confirmed the location and added some details. Disney officials briefed reporters and legislators, stating that they had investigated possible obstacles to the project, including environmental and historic preservation concerns, and believed there would be no serious problems.[7] They also stated that they had studied traffic patterns on I-66 and believed additional theme park traffic would not exacerbate rush-hour congestion.[8] Because 65 percent of Prince William County residents commuted to jobs in other northern Virginia counties, traffic congestion was a primary concern. On November 10, the *Post* ran the first full news story, headlined "Disney Plans Theme Park Here; Haymarket, VA: Project to Include Mall, Feature American History."

As local discussion increased, Disney held an upbeat news conference on November 11 and also issued a press release. Rummell, flanked by the governors and local officials, revealed an architectural model of the theme park and the surrounding development plans. The park logo featured a bold close-up of a stylized bald eagle rendered in navy blue, draped in red and white striped bunting, and with the words, "Disney Is America" emblazoned in gold across the eagle's chest.

Disney's America was presented as a "totally new concept . . . to celebrate those unique American qualities that have been our country's strengths and that have made this nation the beacon of hope to people everywhere." Disney would draw upon its entertainment experience in multimedia and theme park attractions. Disney officials emphasized the park's focus on the Civil War. Guests would enter the park through a detailed Civil War–era village and then ride a steam train to explore nine areas, each devoted to an episode from American history. One of these included a Civil War fort, complete with battle reenactments. Other exhibits included "We the People," depicting the immigrant experience at Ellis Island, and "Enterprise," a factory town featuring a high-speed thrill attraction called "The Industrial Revolution."

Disney officials predominantly sold the park on its economic benefits to the local area, stating that the park would directly generate about 3,000 permanent jobs[9] along with 16,000 jobs indirectly.[10] Around the park, the company would develop resort hotels, an RV park, a 27-hole public golf course, a commercial complex with retail and office space, and 2,300 homes.[11] Disney projected $169 million in tax revenues for the first 10 years after the park opened in 1998 and nearly $2 billion over its first 30

[6] Michael D. Eisner, *Work in Progress* (New York: Random House, 1998), p. 323.

[7] Kirsten Downey and Kent Jenkins Jr., "Disney Plans Theme Park Here; Haymarket, VA: Project to Include Mall, Feature American History," *Washington Post*, November 10, 1993, p. 59.

[8] Ibid.

[9] Spencer S. Hsu, "Disney Project Runs into Concern about Traffic Pollution," *Washington Post*, November 12, 1993, p. A18.

[10] Lisa Gubernick, "The Third Battle of Bull Run," *Forbes* 400, October 17, 1994, p. 68.

[11] Ibid.

years.[12] In addition, Disney would donate land for schools and a library and reserve up to 40 percent green space as a buffer around the core recreational area.[13]

In part, the announcement came off better in print than at the conference. In the press release, Bob Weis, Senior Vice President of Walt Disney Imagineering, was quoted as saying, "Beyond the rides and attractions for which Disney is famous, the park will be a venue for people of all ages, especially the young, to debate and discuss the future of our nation and to learn more about its past by living it." In the conference, however, Weis said of the attractions, "We want to make you a Civil War soldier. We want to make you feel what it was like to be a slave, or what it was like to escape through the Underground Railroad." Weis's intended meaning was to refer to the new technology of virtual reality that would be used, but critics quickly jumped on the statement. *Washington Post* columnist Courtland Milloy contrasted the description to "authentic history" that would have to portray atrocities like slave whippings and rape.[14] Author William Styron wrote that he believed the comment suggested that slavery was somehow a subject for fun or that the escape route used for slaves was similar to a subway system.[15]

PIEDMONT OPPOSITION

Almost immediately after Disney confirmed its plans to build a park in Prince William County, anti-Disney forces began organizing their opposition. To many who were alarmed, the plans seemed already so well-developed that they gave the impression of a *fait accompli*. Just days after Disney's formal announcement, a meeting was held at the home of Charles S. Whitehouse, a retired foreign service officer who had owned property in the Virginia hunt

[12] Ibid.

[13] Park Net, National Park Service, "More Battles: The Horse and the Mouse, Battling for Manassas," http://www.cr.nps.gov/history/ _online books/mana/adhi11b.htm (last modified August 8, 2001).

[14] Ibid.

[15] Chris Fordney, "Embattled Ground," *National Parks*, November/ December 1994, p. 28.

country since the early 1960s. The dozen guests included William D. Rogers, former Undersecretary of State under Henry Kissinger and now a senior partner in a powerful Washington law firm; Joel McCleary, a former aide in the Carter White House and former Treasurer of the Democratic National Committee; and Lavinia Currier, great-granddaughter of Pittsburgh financier Andrew Mellon. William Backer, a former New York advertising executive who had created slogans for Coca Cola ("Coke– It's the Real Thing") and Miller Beer ("If you've got the time, we've got the beer"), also attended. The group worried that the proposed development would undermine the upper Piedmont's "traditional character and visual order."

The phrase came from the charter of the Piedmont Environmental Council (PEC), a rural-preservation group co-chaired by Whitehouse. Many of Whitehouse's guests had donated considerable amounts of time and money to the organization, which fought development and bought land and easements to preserve the area. The PEC was originally founded in 1927 by a group of prominent landowners. Over the years, it fought successfully against uranium mining and plans for a "western bypass" highway.

The group discussed the options for stopping Disney's encroachment upon the hunt country. There was the possibility of derailing the project during the Virginia legislature's next session. Rogers discussed some of the legal options. Backer suggested a negative publicity campaign, possibly at a national level, to force an image-conscious company like Disney to retreat. He argued for a subtle approach rather than a straight-on NIMBY (Not In My Backyard) campaign. He didn't want the opposition campaign to be viewed simply as a group of wealthy landowners who wanted to prevent a theme park from disturbing their fox hunting. As the meeting ended, Backer agreed to come up with a slogan.

A few days later, Backer presented his "Disney, Take a Second Look" slogan to the group. Backer's angle was to convince Disney that it should reassess the idea of building a theme park amid the beauty of the Piedmont. Although the campaign addressed Disney directly, it would remind anyone who saw it of the Piedmont's unspoiled and now-threatened natural beauty. Within a few days, the slogan was running in radio ads and incorporated on a letterhead. The logo accompanying the slogan showed a balloon, with a barn and farmhouse inside, drifting away in the breeze.

This initial meeting was followed by dozens of others in the coming weeks and months. One week after the gathering at the Whitehouse home, over 500 people attended a meeting at the Grace Episcopal Church in The Plains, Virginia, about seven miles west of the Disney site. The meeting's attendants represented a wide range of economic backgrounds, but they were united in their preference for the rural life they enjoyed.

Megan Gallagher, Whitehouse's Co-Chairman of the Piedmont Environmental Council, led the meeting, reminding the group of other local protest movements that had stopped big projects. Other speeches rounded out the audience's concerns: the park's estimated 9 million annual visitors would spark low-density ancillary development like that around Anaheim and Orlando. The pristine countryside would be overcome by cheap hotels, restaurants, and strip malls. Already problematic traffic congestion would be exacerbated. The park would create low-wage jobs and not provide the tax base that the Disney plan promised. During the meeting, the Piedmont Environmental Council, which had already committed $100,000 of its $700,000 annual budget to the project, emerged as the leading opposition group.

A few days after the meeting at Grace Episcopal Church, another meeting organized by the Prince Charitable Trusts of Chicago, another land preservation group, was held at a local restaurant. This meeting brought together several regional and national environmental groups concerned about the Disney's America project. Eventually, the Prince Charitable Trusts would give over $400,000 to 14 different anti-Disney groups that conducted studies, gave press conferences, and attacked Disney from every possible environmental angle. The largest grant went to the National Growth Management League, which mounted a local advertising campaign under the name "Citizens Against Gridlock." The campaign depicted I-66, already one of northern Virginia's busiest and congested highways, as "Disney's parking lot."

In early December, the PEC held a news conference in a Washington hotel to increase the reach of its "Second Look" campaign. It retained a prominent Washington law firm as well as a public relations firm. The group began recruiting and organizing dozens of volunteers. It sent out a fundraising letter seeking $500,000 in contributions. It also commissioned experts to assess the park's impact on the environment, urban sprawl, traffic, employment, and property taxes.

DISNEY'S CAMPAIGN

Soon after the public announcement, Disney undertook concerted efforts to win over state and local government, as well as constituencies within proximity of the proposed site. Virginia's new Governor, George Allen, immediately promoted the Disney project. He believed Disney's worldwide reputation would make Virginia an international tourist destination, bringing millions of travelers to the state. In numerous press releases, Allen endorsed Disney's belief that the project would create 19,000 jobs and bring millions of new tax dollars to state and municipal coffers.

By early January, Disney asked the state to bear some of the costs of the new park. Disney requested $137 million in state highway improvements and $21 million to train workers, move equipment from Orlando, pay for advertising, and put up highway signs directing tourists to the park. These funds would have to be guaranteed by the end of the current state legislative session to allow Disney to move ahead with development in early 1995. Now focusing on Virginia's state capital, Disney retained a well-connected Richmond law firm to handle its lobbying efforts. It also hired a Richmond event-planning firm to organize two large receptions. Lobbying expenses alone reached almost $450,000, including $32,000 for receptions and $230 for the Mickey Mouse ties given to state legislators.

Allen supported Disney's request and argued the highway improvements Disney planned would ease traffic problems that already existed in northern Virginia, in addition to accommodating the extra traffic generated by the park. The state's support of the project, he said, would send a message that Virginia was "open for business."

Disney officials met with African-American legislators and promised to ensure that minorities got a good shot at contracts and jobs. They invited a dozen officials from area museums and historic sites, including Monticello and Colonial Williamsburg, to a meeting in Orlando to discuss their plans for portraying history in the northern Virginia park. In Richmond, Disney lobbyists portrayed opponents as wealthy landowners who simply did not want Disney in their backyards.

Disney sought and received strong support from the Prince William business community, especially realtors, contractors, hotels, restaurants, and utility companies. The Disney staff also poured tremendous effort into harnessing the support of local citizens, spending hours preaching the message of neighborliness to local groups. Groups formed to support the park, including the Welcome Disney Committee, Friends of the Mouse, Youth for Disney, and Patriots for Disney. Members of these groups attended state legislative hearings, gave testimony, and handed out bumper stickers and buttons. Disney sent newsletters to 100,000 local households and retained a second Washington public relations firm to handle grassroots support.

Disney also entered negotiations with the National Park Service at the Manassas park, which was three miles away. The company agreed to limit the height of its structures to 140 feet so they would not be visible from the park and to develop a special transit bus system that would transport 20 percent of Disney guests and 10 percent of employees. The company promised to promote historic preservation and the Manassas National Battlefield Park within Disney's America and immediately donated money to an allied nonprofit group.

THE PEC'S CAMPAIGN

The PEC mounted a strong effort in Richmond as well, including hiring two full-time lobbyists.[16] Its

campaign was based on the premise that the park was a bad business deal for Virginia. The PEC claimed that the park would generate fewer jobs than Disney and Governor Allen had promised—6,300 rather than 19,000—and that the jobs would not pay well. They accused Allen of exaggerating the tax benefits. They emphasized the traffic and air pollution that would be caused by the park. They also suggested 32 other sites in the Washington area that would be more suited to the project than the current site. Finally, they suggested that the state should not have to fund any of the park's development. The PEC spent over $2 million in its campaign against Disney, including lobbying and public relations.[17]

THE VOTE

On March 12, 1994, when the Virginia state legislature voted on a $163 million tax package for Disney, the results clearly favored Disney. This wasn't even a close call for the state government officials. Disney won 35 to 5 in the Virginia Senate and 73 to 25 in the House of Delegates. Things were looking up for the Disney's America project, although a new bumper sticker appeared in the Piedmont that said, "Gov. Allen Slipped Virginia a Mickey."

THE HISTORIANS AND JOURNALISTS TAKE OVER

Disney officials were elated after their victory in Richmond. It seemed likely that construction could begin in early 1995 after all. Meanwhile, Disney's opponents were not ready to give up the fight. Public debate on local issues such as traffic congestion and pollution had failed to keep Disney out of the Piedmont, and the anti-Disney crowd realized they needed to change the theme of their campaign. They needed a grander, more significant argument—something that would gain national attention.

The kernel of that argument had appeared in December 1993, in an editorial written to the

---

[16] Ibid.

[17] Ibid.

Washington Post by Richard Moe, President of the National Trust for Historic Preservation and former Chief of Staff for Vice President Walter Mondale.[18] In his article, Moe suggested that Disney's development would engulf "some of the most beautiful and historic countryside in America."[19] He predicted that the park would reduce attendance at authentic northern Virginia historic landmarks, including the Manassas battlefield. Moe also questioned Disney's ability to seriously portray American history when the success of its other theme parks was based on simply showing visitors a good time.

Moe's article was followed by a similar piece published in mid-February 1994 by the *Los Angeles Times*, the newspaper serving Disney's southern California headquarters. This editorial was written by Pulitzer Prize-winning journalist Nick Kotz, whose Virginia farm happened to be located three miles from the Disney site. Like Moe, Kotz based his article on the premise that Disney's park would desecrate land that should be considered a national treasure. He suggested that Disney would cheapen and trivialize its historic value. After the article was published, Kotz met with Moe over breakfast at the Mayflower Hotel in Washington to discuss anti-Disney strategy. This meeting was one of many that would follow among a growing network of the nation's most elite journalists and historians who were becoming increasingly concerned over Disney's plans.

As the network grew, several prominent historians joined the fight against Disney and formed a group that became known as Protect Historic America. An early recruit was David McCullough, the author of several best-selling books, including a Pulitzer Prize-winning biography of Harry Truman. McCullough was very well known, particularly of late for his narration of the highly acclaimed Ken Burns "Civil War" series on PBS. Another prominent member was James McPherson, a Princeton University professor and author of the Pulitzer

Prize-winning *Battle Cry of Freedom*. Exhibit 9.1 provides a list of many prominent authors and historians who joined Protect Historic America in its early stages.

By May, Protect Historic America was prepared to launch a national campaign in partnership with Moe's National Trust for Historic Preservation. Using funds donated by Piedmont residents, the group placed a full-page ad in the May 2 edition of the *Washington Post*, asking Eisner to reconsider the Haymarket site. The ad included a tear-away response form at the bottom and generated over 5,000 responses. Nine days later, on May 11, the group held a news conference at the National Press Club that featured McCullough and Moe, among others. The prominent journalists in the group virtually assured that the conference would receive national news coverage.

During the well-publicized news conference, the speakers argued that Disney threatened the Piedmont countryside, including historic towns and battlefields. The region's rich heritage made it valuable to all Americans. David McCullough stated, "We have so little left that's authentic and real. To replace what we have with plastic, contrived history is almost sacrilege."[20] James McPherson, in a written statement presented to reporters, said, "A historical theme park in Northern Virginia, three miles from the Manassas National Battlefield, threatens to destroy the very historical landscape it purports to interpret."[21]

The press conference, along with personal correspondence from McCullough and McPherson, convinced over 200 historians and writers to endorse the fight against Disney. Several historians wrote articles in national publications, attacking the Disney project. C. Vann Woodward, the noted Southern historian, wrote an article for the *New Republic* in which he stated:

> What troubles us most is the desecration of a particular region . . . historians don't own history, but it isn't

---

[18] Ibid.

[19] Richard Moe, "Downside to Disney's America," *Washington Post*, December 21, 1993, p. A23.

[20] Larry Van Dyne, "Hit the Road, Mick," *Washingtonian Magazine*, January 1995, p. 59.

[21] Paul Bradley, "Prominent Historians Join Disney Foes," *Richmond Times-Dispatch*, May 12, 1994, p. B1.

EXHIBIT 9.1   **The Third Battle of Bull Run: The Disney's America Theme Park. Partial List of Historians and Authors in the Anti-Disney Campaign**

James David Barber	Professor of political science, Duke University
Frances Berry	Professor of American social thought, history, and law, University of Pennsylvania
William R. Ferris	Director, Center for the Study of Southern Culture, and professor of anthropology, University of Mississippi
Barbara J. Fields	Professor of history, Columbia University
Shelby Foote	Author of four-volume *Civil War*, which was made into a popular PBS miniseries
George Forgie	Associate professor of history, University of Texas at Austin
John Hope Franklin	Former president, American Historical Association
Ernest B. Furgurson	Journalist and historian
Gary Gallagher	Chairman, History Department, Pennsylvania State University
John Rolfe Gardiner	Piedmont Virginian and author of novels set in the Piedmont region
Doris Kearns Goodwin	Professor of government, Harvard University
Ludwell H. Johnson III	Professor emeritus of history, College of William and Mary
Richard M. Ketchum	Editorial director, American Heritage Books
Nick Kotz	Journalist, author of four books on American history and politics
Glenn LaFantasie	Deputy historian and general editor of the *Foreign Relations of the United States* series, U.S. State Department
David Levering Lewis	Professor of history, Rutgers University
David McCullough	Author, Pulitzer Prize winner, *Truman*
James McPherson	Professor of history, Princeton University, and Pulitzer Prize winner, **Battle Cry of Freedom**
Holt Merchant	Professor of history, Washington and Lee University
Richard Moe	President, National Trust for Historic Preservation
W. Brown Morton III	Chairman, Department of Historic Preservation, Mary Washington College
Neil Irvin Painter	Professor of American history, Princeton University
Merrill D. Peterson	Professor emeritus and former chairman, History Department, University of Virginia
James L. Robertson Jr.	Professor of history, Virginia Polytechnic and State University
George F. Scheer	Author specializing in colonial and Revolutionary War history
Arthur Schlesinger Jr.	Author of 16 books on American history
William Styron	Author, Pulitzer Prize winner, *The Confessions of Nat Turner*
Dorothy Twohig	Associate professor of history, University of Virginia
Tom Wicker	Former Washington bureau chief of *The New York Times*
Roger Wilkins	Former advisor to President Johnson and professor of history, George Mason University
C. Vann Woodward	Professor emeritus of American history, Yale University

Source: Paul Bradley, "Prominent Historians Join Disney Foes," *Richmond Times-Dispatch*, May 12, 1994, p. B1.

Disney's America either. Nor is it Virginia's. Every state . . . in the country sent sons to fight here for what they believed, right or wrong. They helped make it a national heritage, not a theme park.[22]

The historians and journalists attempted to limit their arguments to the importance of preserving the Piedmont land and its historic heritage. Concerned that they would be regarded as cultural elitists, they tried to avoid the argument that Disney should not attempt to portray history in a theme park. There were several notable deviations from this strategy, however. McCullough once referred to Disney's plans as "McHistory."[23] Shelby Foote, a Civil War

[22] C. Vann Woodward, "A Mickey Mouse Idea," *New Republic*, June 20, 1994, p. 16.

[23] Sarah Skolnik, "The Mouse Trapped: Horton Gives a Hoot; Professor James Oliver Horton Retained by Walt Disney Company as a Consultant," *Regardie's Magazine*, September 1994, p. 44.

historian, made it clear that he believed Disney would sentimentalize history as it had done to the animal kingdom.[24] Commentator George Will asked facetiously, "Is the idea to see your sister sold down the river, then get cotton candy?"[25] Around this same time period, a lively online discussion took place on the H-Civwar listserve, whose members included academics and historians who were Civil War buffs.[26]

DISNEY'S RESPONSE

Following the May 11 press conference, a Disney spokesperson reiterated the park's intended effect: "Disney's America will bring America's history to life, celebrate America's diversity, provide a road map to other attractions throughout the region, and encourage Americans to go further into their history."[27] Governor Allen also defended Disney after the press conference, saying, "I majored in history. I love history, and I think it's one of the best selling points for tourism. As much as I respect Shelby Foote and enjoyed the *Civil War* series, we shouldn't set ourselves up as censors." He added, "Hopefully, it will get people interested and want to go see the real thing."[28]

At Disney the situation seemed reminiscent of a 1991 controversy over an exhibit on Abraham Lincoln, which was criticized for its cursory treatment of slavery. Disney responded by redesigning the exhibit with the help of Eric Foner, a history professor from Columbia University who had made the complaint. To avoid costs associated with designing and redesigning an entire park based on varying interpretations of history, Disney had already begun to seek advice as early as mid-December 1993.[29] The company turned again to Foner, as well as other historians. As Weis put it, "We all share a common

interest to make sure that our treatment of history is sensitive, honest, and balanced."[30] Disney invited a group of historians to Orlando to help them envision what Disney had in mind for Disney's America. Though at first skeptical, some came away thinking that Disney's America might work.[31] James Oliver Horton, a professor of African-American history and American studies at George Washington University, who also designed exhibits for the Smithsonian, took the view that Disney's technological expertise might indeed help audiences learn more about history.[32]

Even with this much foresight, the strength of Protect Historic America's objections caught Eisner off guard. In April, the U.S. Transportation Department had decided to assess the environmental impact of Disney's proposed development. In light of impending federal involvement and PHA's national campaign, Eisner decided to personally visit Washington in mid-June to meet with reporters and editors from the *Washington Post*, Interior Secretary Bruce Babbitt, U.S. House Speaker Thomas Foley, and 30 other legislators. Eisner defended the company's intentions and expressed his frustration openly to the press, saying:

> I'm shocked because I thought we were doing good. I expected to be taken around on people's shoulders. . . . If this was any other city in the country, the (Federal government) wouldn't even be interested. . . . (I was unaware) so many wealthy people (lived west of Washington). . . . Disney's America will offer an alternative approach to history that may have more effect on people than conventional history. . . . It's private land that is in the middle of a historic area, but it's not in the middle of a battlefield. . . . We have a right to do it. . . . If people think we will back off, they are mistaken.[33]

Then Eisner threw in at least one other comment that came back to haunt him, "I sat through many history classes where I read some of their stuff, and I didn't learn anything."[34] A few days later, PHA

[24] Bradley, "Prominent Historians Join Disney Foes," p. B1.

[25] Van Dyne, "Hit the Road, Mick," p. 122.

[26] Archived by Avon Edward Foote, "Disney Documents Plus," last modified March 26, 2002, http://www. chotank.com/disvasav2.html.

[27] Bradley, "Prominent Historians Join Disney Foes," p. 1.

[28] Ibid.

[29] Eisner, *Work in Progress*, p. 326.

[30] Skolnik, "The Mouse Trapped," p. 44.

[31] Eisner, *Work in Progress*, pp. 329–31.

[32] Park Net, National Park Service, "More Battles."

[33] William F. Powers, "Eisner Says He Won't Back Down," *Washington Post*, June 14, 1994, p. A1.

[34] Ibid.

responded with a full-page advertisement in *The New York Times*. The ad headlined "The Man Who Would Destroy American History" reiterated the quote and commented, "Unfortunately, he means it."[35] In an attempt to generate some positive publicity for Disney, Eisner's visit coincided with the Washington movie premier of *The Lion King*. The plan backfired when the event attracted over 100 protesters from the PEC and other organizations, including a couple dressed as lions carrying a sign reading "Michael Eisner, the Lyin' King."

CONGRESSIONAL HEARING

Protect Historic America's leaders next met with several U.S. senators and congressional representatives. As a result, Arkansas Senator Dale Bumpers, Chairman of the subcommittee with jurisdiction over national parks, agreed to hold a hearing on the issue, which was held on June 21. McCullough, McPherson, and Moe represented the historians' point of view, while Governor Allen and several Disney executives presented their side of the issue. The historians presented a legal brief prepared *pro bono* for the hearing by a Washington law firm, stating that the Interior Department had a responsibility to investigate the project, given its proximity to the Manassas battlefield and Shenandoah National Park. They added that Virginia's historic landmarks were threatened, and because the landmarks were national treasures, the federal government had a responsibility to protect them. Allen and the Disney officials countered, arguing that the park was a local land use issue that should be handled within the state of Virginia.

Most of the congresspeople sympathized with Disney, believing that Congress and the federal government should stay out of the situation, and Bumpers said he would take no further action. Although it had no legislative impact, the hearing spurred thousands of newspaper stories, cartoons, and editorials nationwide, greatly increasing national awareness of the issue. Protect Historic America's clipping service pulled over 10,000 items covering the hearing. At this point, national television and radio shows began

covering the issue in depth, and political cartoonists were having a field day.

THE DEBATE CONTINUES

Despite outraged or lampooning overtones in the press, a few columnists supported Disney in the debate. For example, columnist Charles Krauthammer wrote,

> Those who fear that a children's entertainment will destroy real history have little faith in history. Disney's America is an amusement for kids who bring their parents along for the ride. The issue of urban sprawl is serious. The suggestion of cultural desecration is not. As the kids would say, "Lighten up, guys."[36]

In another instance, William Safire of *The New York Times* called the opposition group "a little band of well-credentialed historians, litigating greens, liberal columnists, and self-protected landowners."[37]

Overwhelmingly, however, press opinion sided with the historians, and the criticism became increasingly vicious over time. Pat Buchanan suggested that Eisner should "take his billions and go back to Hollywood . . . where they are impressed by . . . swagger."

Eisner remained steadfast as he continued in his attempt to build public support for the project. On July 12, *USA Today* printed Eisner's retort to the historians' arguments to build national support for the project. Eisner wrote, "When we began developing plans for a northern Virginia park to celebrate America's heritage, we expected to encounter hurdles. . . . But we did not expect that our creative reputation and talent for educating while entertaining would be attacked with such invectiveness." He continued, "We see Disney's America as a place where people can celebrate America, her people, struggles, victories, courage, setbacks, diversity, heroism, dynamism, pluralism, inventiveness, playfulness, compassion, righteousness, tolerance. . . . [O]ur goal is to instill visitors with a desire to see and learn more."[38]

---

[35] Van Dyne, "Hit the Road, Mick," p. 123.

[36] Charles Krauthammer, "Who's Afraid of Virginia's Mouse," *Time*, June 6, 1994, p. 76.

[37] Quoted in Van Dyne, "Hit the Road, Mick," p. 123.

[38] Michael D. Eisner, *USA Today*, July 12, 1994, p. 10A.

On September 12, Protect Historic America and the National Trust for Historic Preservation invited journalists and politicians to a program at Ford's Theater in Washington celebrating Virginia as the "Cradle of Democracy." Foote, Styron, and several other authors gave readings from their work, and each guest received a binder of anti-Disney news clippings.[39] Don Henley, co-founder of the rock group the Eagles, also read a brief passage and donated $100,000. Several years earlier, Henley had been involved in the fight to save nineteenth-century American essayist Henry David Thoreau's Walden Pond in Massachusetts. Then, just five days after the Ford's Theater event, the anti-Disney national mall demonstration and the pro-Disney parade in Haymarket took place concurrently.

THE DECISION

Eisner watched the beautiful California sunset and pondered the situation. Could he come up with an argument that would sway public opinion in Disney's favor? Would the public tire of the issue, or would the debate continually resurface? How many lawsuits would Disney have to become involved in, and what would be the cost of litigation? What would the historians do once the park opened? Would Disney continually be engaged in a costly process of redesigning exhibits that were objectionable to various factions of historians? Could the park's theme be changed or repackaged?

If Eisner ended the Disney's America project now, the company would upset countless Virginia

politicians, including Governor Allen, who had fought on its behalf. The various groups of Piedmont residents who had supported Disney and were counting on the park to provide jobs and tax revenues would be upset as well. Giving up now would mean that Disney had lost a very public, hard-fought campaign. Eisner had said publicly that Disney would not give in, so ending now would risk going back on his word. But were these previous commitments worth the costs of keeping them in light of the vocal opposition and the risk to Disney's reputation?

Eisner considered the options. He had reached the point where he needed to make a decision regarding Disney's America so he could focus more closely on other business concerns.

CASE QUESTIONS

1. What are the key issues that Eisner must consider in this situation from a government relations perspective?
2. Where is Disney most vulnerable, from a communications standpoint?
3. How could Disney have better anticipated the opposition to its new theme park proposal?
4. What advice would you give Eisner?

[39] See Protect Historic America, "Reaching the People: News Media Coverage of the Controversy over the Siting of 'Disney's America,'" Washington, D.C., May 11, 1995.

CHAPTER TEN

Crisis Communication

Unlike many of the other topics covered in this book, a crisis is something *everyone* can relate to. The death of a close relative, the theft of one's car, or even a broken heart—all can become crises in one's personal life. Organizations face crises as well. PwC's 2019 Global Crisis Survey found that "near 7 in 10 (69 percent) leaders have experienced at least one corporate crisis in the last 5 years—with the average number of crises being 3."[1] Tokyo Electric Power Co. (Tepco), for example, experienced a crisis when the earthquake and tsunami that hit Japan in March 2011 disabled its Fukushima Daiichi nuclear power plant. This led to nuclear leaks and mandatory evacuation of the surrounding area. Several universities, charitable organizations, and private investment groups also experienced a crisis in December 2008 when they suddenly learned that they had lost all of the money that they had invested with Bernie Madoff, who had been operating a Ponzi scheme.[2]

Today, because of the increasingly digital makeup of the media and the ever present social networking community, a breaking corporate crisis is likely to be reported within minutes by interested individuals via social media platforms such as Twitter and Facebook. The news will then be reported throughout the online world and, of course, by traditional media organizations on their websites as well. Thus, a more sophisticated media environment, as well as a new emphasis on technology in business, has created the need for a more sophisticated *response* to crises.

This chapter first defines what constitutes a crisis. It turns next to a discussion of several prominent crises of the last quarter century. Once we define what crises are all about, the focus shifts to how organizations can prepare for such events. Finally, the chapter offers approaches for organizations to follow when crises do occur.

What Is a Crisis?

Imagine for a moment that you are sleeping in bed on a warm evening in southern California. Suddenly, you feel the bed shaking, the light fixtures swaying, and the house trembling. If you are from California, you know that you are in the middle of an earthquake; if you are from New England, you might think that the world is coming to an end. Now picture yourself on a friend's boat, out for a leisurely sail on a sunny afternoon. Two hours later you discover that you have been having such a good time that you didn't notice

---

[1] "PwC's Global Crisis Survey 2019," PwC, https://www.pwc.com/gx/en/forensics/global-crisis-survey/pdf/pwc-global-crisis-survey-2019.pdf.

[2] "2011 Crisis Preparedness Study," Burson-Marsteller and Penn Schoen Berland, https://www.ropella.com/talon/pdfs/B-M_and_P_S_B_Crisis_Preparedness_Study_2011.pdf.

yourself moving farther and farther away from shore into open ocean. Storm clouds are gathering on the horizon, and the sun seems to be mysteriously setting a bit early.

All of us would agree that, in these situations, we as individuals would be facing crises. If the earthquake turns out to be "the big one," or if your friend is a novice sailor and you are in fact drifting into a severe storm, these scenarios could become life-threatening situations.

Organizations also face crises that occur naturally: a hurricane rips through a town, leveling the local waste management company's primary facility; the earthquake we imagined earlier turns the three biggest supermarkets in the area into piles of rubble; a tsunami devastates a coastal area, crippling the local tourism industry for months if not years in its aftermath; a ship is battered at sea by a storm and sinks with a load of cargo destined for a foreign port. Although all of these incidents create havoc and most can't be predicted, they all can be planned for to some degree.

Natural disasters cannot be avoided, but there are many crises—those caused by human error, negligence, or, in some cases, malicious intent—that planning could have prevented in the first place. In fact, most of the crises described later in this chapter—such as the infamous crises that beset Tylenol, Perrier, Volkswagen, and several online retailers and banks—were *human-induced crises* rather than natural disasters. Such crises can be more devastating than natural disasters in terms of the costs they entail for companies, in both dollars and reputation.

All human-induced crises cannot be lumped together, however. One type includes cases in which the company is clearly at fault, such as cases of negligence. A perfect example of this is the devastating 2010 oil spill in the Gulf of Mexico that occurred when BP pumped 4.9 million barrels of oil into the water during three long months, putting more than 400 species of animals at risk and causing lasting damage to the local fishing and tourism industries. This is a crisis that could have been avoided. Financial or accounting frauds constitute another example of human-induced crises—a type increasingly exposed under the scrutiny required by the Sarbanes-Oxley Act. A devalued stock price and significant legal expenses are not the only aftereffects that a company must address following a human-induced crisis; often the most serious challenge is the damage to the company's reputation and the subsequent loss of trust with key constituencies. In 2015, Volkswagen's reputation took a major hit when it was revealed that the company had knowingly misled the world's governments and customers by using software to manipulate exhaust emissions during government testing. Although the company has committed itself to rebuilding its reputation following "Dieselgate," Volkswagen continues to deal with the ramifications, including ongoing SEC charges and negative press coverage into 2020 and beyond.[3]

A second type of human-induced crisis includes cases in which a company becomes a victim. Examples include Target, Uber, MyFitnessPal, and other major corporations, which were targeted by online information theft attempts, discussed later in this chapter. The company falls prey to circumstances in these situations, just as when natural disasters unexpectedly hit. A company's role as either the perpetrator or the victim in a crisis is the distinction upon which public perception often hinges. The general public's attitude

---

[3] "Exhausted by Scandal: 'Dieselgate' Continues to Haunt Volkswagen," Knowledge @ Wharton, May 21, 2019, https://knowledge.wharton.upenn.edu/article/volkswagen-diesel-scandal.

toward a company in crisis is more likely to be negative for crises that could have been avoided, such as the 2008 financial disaster caused by failures in regulation and oversight and fueled by dishonesty and greed, as opposed to crises that organizations had no control over, such as the devastating 2010 earthquake in Haiti that destroyed more than 30,000 commercial properties. Whatever the cause, in all crisis situations, constituencies will look to the organization's *response* to the crisis before making a final judgment. If a company responds well, some crises, such as the Tylenol tragedy, end up actually increasing the overall credibility of the organization involved.

Thus, to define *crisis* for organizations today is a bit more complicated than to simply say that it is an unpredictable, horrible event. For the purposes of this chapter, a crisis will be defined as follows:

A crisis is a major catastrophe that may occur either naturally or as a result of human error, intervention, or even malicious intent. It can include tangible devastation, such as the destruction of lives or assets, or intangible devastation, such as the loss of an organization's credibility or other reputational damage. The latter outcomes may be the result of management's response to tangible devastation or the result of human error. A crisis usually has significant actual or potential financial impact on a company, and it usually affects multiple constituencies in more than one market.

Crisis Characteristics

Although all crises are unique, they do share some common characteristics, according to Ray O'Rourke,[4] the former Managing Director for Global Corporate Affairs at the investment bank Morgan Stanley. These include (1) *the element of surprise*—such as Philip Morris finding carcinogens in its filters or Pepsi learning of reports of a syringe found in a Diet Pepsi can; (2) *insufficient information*—the company doesn't have all the facts right away, but very quickly finds itself in a position of having to do a lot of explaining (the Perrier example later in this chapter is instructive here, in that it took the company more than a week to figure out what was going on after reports of benzene contamination surfaced); (3) *the quick pace of events*—things escalate very rapidly (even before Exxon's crisis center was up and running after the *Valdez* incident, the state of Alaska and several environmental groups were mobilized); (4) *intense scrutiny*—executives are often unprepared for the media spotlight, which is instantaneous, as answers and results normally take time. Think of how much air time Tony Hayward, then CEO of BP, received in 2010 during the oil spill in the Gulf of Mexico.

What makes crises difficult for executives is that the element of surprise can lead to a loss of control. It's hard to think strategically when overwhelmed by unexpected outside events. In addition, the media frenzy that typically surrounds a crisis can prompt a siege mentality to ensue, causing management to adopt a short-term focus. Attention shifts from the business as a whole to the crisis alone, forcing all decision making into the shortest time frame. This has been true in crisis situations even before the Internet dramatically changed the pace of reporting. For example, in the early 1990s, the public relations firm Burson-Marsteller was hired six days after the Perrier benzene scare began, and already

[4] Ray O'Rourke, presentation to Corporate Reputation Conference, New York University, January 1997. At the time of this presentation, O'Rourke was with public relations firm Burson-Marsteller.

it had to undo three different explanations from the company—none of which were true. Perrier's uncoordinated and off-the-cuff statements only increased the likelihood that the crisis would escalate. When panic sets in, organizations typically fail to coordinate.

Part of the problem in dealing with crises is that organizations tend to not understand or acknowledge how vulnerable they are until *after* a major crisis occurs. Lack of preparation can make crises even more severe and prolonged when they do happen. Let's take a closer look at some major crises from the past 40 years to bring our definition to life.

Crises from the Past 40 Years

For baby boomers, the defining crisis of their time was the assassination of President John F. Kennedy. Virtually everyone who was alive at that time can remember what he or she was doing when the news was announced that President Kennedy had been shot. Generation Xers in the United States today probably feel the same way about the explosion of the space shuttle *Challenger* in January 1986. People near the United States and even internationally will remember the terror attacks of September 11, 2001 in New York City as a defining moment for the new millennium. These events have become etched in the public consciousness for a variety of reasons.

First, people tend to remember and be moved by negative news more than positive news. Americans in particular seem to have a preoccupation with such negative news. The front headlines of many media outlets underscore this point. Viewers rarely see "good" news stories because they just don't sell to an audience that has become accustomed to the more dramatic events that come out of the prime-time fare on television or that are more easily captured in short YouTube clips.

Second, the human tragedy associated with a crisis strikes a psychological chord with most everyone. Two high-speed trains collide and fall off of a bridge, killing 35 and injuring hundreds in eastern China; Hurricane Katrina devastates New Orleans and the U.S. government bungles its response; a deranged shooter opens fire on a crowd in Las Vegas, killing 60 and wounding over 400: such events make us realize how vulnerable we all are and how quickly events can make innocent victims out of ordinary people.

Third, crises associated with major corporations stick in the public's mind because many large organizations lack credibility in the first place. A public predisposed to distrust big oil companies could not be completely surprised by what happened during BP's Deep Horizon oil spill or by the nationwide sex discrimination class action lawsuit against Walmart, which was the largest civil rights class action ever certified against a private employer and which, though the Supreme Court ruled in favor of Walmart in 2011, has continued to see regional and individual gender discrimination suits filed against it into the 2020s.[5] Indeed, these events validated the public's suspicions, and the public appears to have taken as much pleasure in the turmoil that these corporations faced in the aftermath. In other cases, crises have such a significant impact on the public because they take it by surprise. Consider the investment bank Lehman Brothers.

---

[5] Bryce Covert, "Nearly Two Decades Ago, Women Across the Country Sued Walmart for Discrimination. They're Not Done Fighting," *Time*, May 9, 2019, https://time.com/5586423/walmart-gender-discrimination.

Before filing for Chapter 11 bankruptcy, it was one of the four largest investment banks in the world. After the U.S. Government denied aid to Lehman and to other banks during the early days of the subprime mortgage crisis, Lehman filed for bankruptcy on September 15, 2008. At the time, it held assets of $691 billion. It was the largest bankruptcy in U.S. history and affected thousands of jobs and the lifesavings of many. As we look at other major crises, we start to see more clearly why these events linger in the public psyche.

1982: Johnson & Johnson's Tylenol Recall

Johnson & Johnson's (J&J's) Tylenol recall in the early 1980s is held by many as "the gold standard" of product-recall crisis management. Although nearly 40 years have passed since the crisis, the lessons to be learned from it are still relevant. Johnson & Johnson's handling of the crisis was characterized by a swift and coordinated response and a demonstration of concern for the public that only strengthened its reputation as "the caring company."

In late September and early October of 1982, seven people died after taking Tylenol capsules that had been laced with cyanide. At the time, Tylenol had close to 40 percent of the over-the-counter market for pain relievers. Within days of the first report of these poisonings, sales had dropped by close to 90 percent.

Certainly the irony of something that is supposed to relieve pain turning into a killer made this episode one of the most memorable in the history of corporate crises. However, many experts on crisis communication, marketing, and psychology have praised Johnson & Johnson for its swift and caring response that was primarily responsible for turning this disaster into a triumph for the company. Despite losses exceeding $100 million, Tylenol came back from the crisis stronger than ever within a matter of years.

What did Johnson & Johnson do? First, it did not simply *react* to what was happening. Instead, it took the offensive and removed the potentially deadly product from shelves. (In the end, 31 million bottles of Tylenol were recalled.) Second, it leveraged the goodwill it had built up over the years with constituencies ranging from doctors to the media and decided to try to save the brand rather than come out with a new identity for the product. Third, the company reacted in a caring and humane way rather than simply looking at the incident from a purely legal or financial perspective. Thousands of J&J employees made more than 1 million personal visits to hospitals, physicians, and pharmacists around the nation to restore faith in the Tylenol name.[6] Fourth, when J&J reintroduced Tylenol to the market, the product was packaged in triple-seal tamper resistant packaging.

Why did the company go to these lengths? Despite its decentralized structure, Johnson & Johnson's management is bound together by a document known as the "Credo." The Credo is a 341-word companywide code of ethics that was created by Robert Wood Johnson in 1943, and it is carved in stone at company headquarters in New Brunswick, New Jersey, today. It acknowledges: "We believe patients, doctors, and nurses, to mothers and fathers." Then-CEO James Burke made sure that the principles of the Credo guided the company's actions during the Tylenol crisis, helping J&J react to tragedy without losing focus on what was most important.

[6] Harold J. Leavitt, "Hot Groups," *Harvard Business Review*, July 1, 1995, p. 109.

What is most amazing is not that J&J handled this crisis so formidably but that the perception of the company was actually *strengthened* by what happened. As Burke—who was brought in early as the lead person handling the crisis—explained, "We had to put our money where our mouth was. We'd committed to putting the public first, and everybody in the company was looking to see if we'd live up to our pretensions."[7] J&J management did, and the public rewarded them for it. Within three months of the crisis, the company regained 95 percent of its previous market share.[8] Nearly four decades later, Johnson & Johnson ranks consistently on Interbrand's annual list of the 100 Top Global Brands,[9] with a market cap worth of $400 billion as of December 2020.[10]

1990: The Perrier Benzene Scare

Another classic crisis in business history is the 1990 Perrier benzene scare. Perrier Sparkling Water faced a contamination crisis of its own nearly 10 years after the Tylenol episode. Although Perrier's contamination crisis did not lead to any deaths, or even reported illnesses, it still demanded resolution and an explanation from the public and the media. Perrier's actions during the 1990 benzene scare provide as many lessons in how *not* to handle a crisis as J&J's did of how to handle one effectively.

In February 1990, Perrier issued the following press release:

> The Perrier Group of America, Inc. is voluntarily recalling all Perrier Sparkling Water (regular and flavored) in the United States. Testing by the Food and Drug Administration and the State of North Carolina showed the presence of the chemical benzene at levels above proposed federal standards in isolated samples of product produced between June 1989 and January 1990.[11]

This press release marked the beginning of the end of Perrier's reign over the sparkling water industry. In 1989 Perrier, one of the most distinguished names in bottled water, sold 1 billion bottles of sparkling water, riding high on the wave of 1980s health consciousness. Then in January 1990, a technician in the Mecklenberg County Environmental Protection Department in Charlotte, North Carolina, discovered a minute amount of benzene, 12.3 to 19.9 parts per billion (less than what is contained in a non–freeze-dried cup of coffee), in the water.[12] After receiving confirmation from both the state and federal officials, Mecklenberg briefed Perrier Group of America about the contamination.

Two full days after the crisis broke, after recalling more than 70 million bottles from North America (but before identifying the source of the contamination), Perrier America president Ronald Davis confidently announced that the problem was limited to North America. Officials had reported a cleaning fluid containing benzene had been mistakenly used on a production line machine.[13] The real cause of the contamination—defective filters

---

[7] Brian O'Reilly, "Managing: J&J Is on a Roll," *Fortune*, December 26, 1994, p. 109.

[8] Ibid.

[9] "Best Global Brands 2019," Interbrand, https://www.interbrand.com/best-brands/best-global-brands/2019/ranking.

[10] "Johnson & Johnson," Google Finance, https://www.google.com/finance/quote/JNJ:NYSE?sa=X&ved=2ahUKEwja1buV2sLt AhWGHzQIHcyKAskQ3ecFMAB6BAgBEBk.

[11] Perrier press release, The Perrier Group, February 10, 1990.

[12] "When the Bubble Burst," *Economist*, August 3, 1991, p. 67.

[13] Ibid.

at its spring[14]—was discovered less than three days later, and contrary to what Ronald Davis had previously announced, six months' worth of production would be affected, covering Perrier's entire global market.[15] The firm was forced to change its story.

Without an official crisis plan of its own, Perrier relied on the media to communicate its story during the crisis, which proved to be a fatal decision. The press only served to expose the lack of internal communication and the lack of global coordination within the company. At a news conference in Paris, when Perrier-France announced that it was also issuing a recall due to the presence of benzene, the President of Perrier's international division, Frederik Zimmer, offered the explanation that "Perrier water naturally contains several gases, including benzene."[16] From the contradictory messages released to the press, it was clear that the U.S. operations were not communicating well—if at all—with their European counterparts. Moreover, yet another story emerged to explain the presence of benzene, and it contradicted the previous explanations: according to Perrier officials, "the benzene entered the water because of a dirty pipe filter at an underground spring at Vergeze in southern France."[17] All of this hurt the company's credibility.

The cost of the recall and eventual relaunch of the product—ushered in by a pricey advertising campaign—meant that customers found the new 750-mL bottles selling at the same price as the old one-liter bottles. Perrier's pre-crisis 1989 market share of 44.8 percent plummeted to 20.7 percent by 1991.

The Perrier benzene crisis illustrates not only the consequences of having a *reactive* strategy to deal with crises but also the problems of not having a coordinated and fact-based approach to crisis communication.

2015: Volkswagen Emissions Scandal

A third more modern case in crisis management, but one that is already a classic, is the 2015 Volkswagen Emissions Scandal. In September 2015, the U.S. Environmental Protection Agency (EPA) discovered that Volkswagen (VW) cars being sold in the United States had a "defeat device" installed, in which the software that managed the cars' diesel engines could detect when they were being tested for compliance with emissions rules and accordingly change the performance metrics of the engine in order to pass testing. Wildly, the degree to which these devices were cheating testing was not by a few percentage points, but by many multiples: engines were emitting nitrogen oxide pollutants up to 40 times above what was allowed in the United States.[18]

Given the degree to which VW blatantly broke the law, it should come as no surprise that the company's initial response to the crisis was equally as flippant. Martin Winterkorn, the CEO at the time, attempted to chalk up the scandal to the result of "the mistakes

---

[14] "Handling Corporate Crises; Total Recall," *Economist* 335 (June 3, 1995), p. 61.

[15] Ibid.

[16] "Poor Perrier, It's Gone to Water," *Sydney Morning Herald*, February 15, 1990, p. 34.

[17] Ibid.

[18] Russell Hotten, "Volkswagen: The Scandal Explained," *BBC News*, December 10, 2015, https://www.bbc.com/news/business-34324772.

of a few people," despite regulators quickly uncovering that the defeat device was placed on millions of cars and had been in place for many years.[19] Though he abruptly resigned a few weeks into the scandal, his replacement, Matthias Muller, similarly failed to embrace any appropriate level of accountability, declaring in an NPR interview, "We didn't lie."[20] The company's new Chief Communications Officer perhaps captured it best when he bluntly noted, "A crisis like this, the company was not prepared for. We don't know the right way out."[21]

The hit to Volkswagen's financial performance—and overall reputation—was swift and severe. Days after the scandal broke, VW recorded a $7.3 billion write-off in earnings in anticipation of fines and litigation costs, and the company lost 46 percent of its value during the first two months of the scandal.[22] Similarly, it fell to dead last in a Harris Poll ranking Americans' attitudes toward the 100 most visible companies.[23]

Years later, however, VW still grapples with the ramifications of its actions. Its initial write-off of $7.3 billion turned out to be a massive underestimate; to date, the company has booked $35 billion of charges to earnings, although there is considerable reason to believe this number will end up being much higher. Though the company's stock has clawed back from its October 2015 nadir, as of late 2020, it still sits 35 percent below its pre-scandal price; taking into account the overall growth and health of the stock market in the five years following 2015 makes this number only look worse. Over 30,000 employees were let go as a result of the crisis, and over $1.2 billion was paid in damages to U.S. dealers to compensate them for their losses. Finally, over 20 executives have faced criminal charges in connection with the scandal, ranging from fraud and embezzlement to aiding and abetting those crimes.[24] With the trial of disgraced-CEO Winterkorn still not even scheduled, one of the few certainties remaining in VW's future is that it will continue to be haunted by shades of unethical actions that began well more than a decade ago.

The Online World—Data Theft and Beyond

With smartphones, personal computers, the Internet, and the cloud now integral parts of the fabric of business, organizations face new challenges and the potential for crises that they have not dealt with before. Globally, more than $11 billion is lost to software piracy (the illegal copying of software programs) every year.[25] In 2017, the WannaCry virus downed more than 200,000 computers in over 150 countries, which Europol called

---

[19] Danny Hakim, "VW's Crisis Strategy: Forward, Reverse, U-Turn," *The New York Times*, February 26, 2016, https://www.nytimes.com/2016/02/28/business/international/vws-crisis-strategy-forward-reverse-u-turn.html.

[20] Ibid.

[21] Ibid.

[22] Geoff Colvin, "5 Years In, Damages from the VW Emissions Cheating Scandal Are Still Rolling In," *Fortune*, October 6, 2020, https://fortune.com/2020/10/06/volkswagen-vw-emissions-scandal-damages.

[23] Hakim, "VW's Crisis Strategy: Forward, Reverse, U-Turn," *The New York Times*.

[24] "Eight More Volkswagen Employees Charged in Diesel Scandal," *Reuters*, September 23, 2020, https://uk.reuters.com/article/us-volkswagen-emissions/eight-more-volkswagen-employees-charged-in-dieselscandal-idUKKCN26E2VA.

[25] "Piracy Prevention," Apple, https://www.apple.com/legal/intellectual-property/piracy.html.

"unprecedented in range."[26] Industries from healthcare to oil and gas were affected, and it ultimately resulted in $4 billion in losses.[27]

Cybersecurity attacks aren't confined to major attacks on well-known businesses, however; as of late 2019, 43 percent of cyberattacks targeted small businesses, costing these companies $200,000 on average and resulting in bankruptcy for many.[28] Similarly, the movement toward predominantly (or exclusively) online or mobile business platforms further exposes a considerable amount of the world to the threats of cyberattacks.

For example, in 2016, Uber suffered a breach in which the names, home addresses, drivers licenses, and other personal information of over 57 million users and drivers were stolen. Perhaps worse, however, was Uber's response to the breach: the company elected to pay the hackers $100,000 to cover up the breach and did not reveal the issue until over a year later. Ultimately, Uber's actions angered consumers and resulted in the introduction of a bill by three Senators that required jail time for executives who fail to disclose such data breaches.[29]

Hacking into Reputations

Today, the majority of online thieves are opting for more surreptitious tactics to steal confidential information. Malware, phishing, SQL injection attacks, and many other hacking techniques have unfortunately both proliferated over the years and increased in sophistication, resulting in confidential information being stolen both from individual users as well as broader databases that store the personal information of millions.[30]

The proliferation of such online security threats has resulted in crisis situations for countless companies worldwide that now must redouble their efforts to defend themselves against attacks. They must successfully protect themselves if they wish to maintain the confidence and trust of their customers. The battle is not an easy one, especially as technological advances enable cyber-criminals to become more creative. Malicious cyber activity is estimated to cost the U.S. economy alone between $57 billion and $107 billion annually.[31] In fact, by 2025, cybercrime is projected to cost the world $10.5 trillion annually, through damaged and destroyed data, lost productivity, intellectual property theft, and more.[32]

---

[26] "Cyber-Attack: Europol Says It Was Unprecedented in Scale," *BBC News*, May 13, 2017, https://www.bbc.com/news/world-europe-39907965.

[27] Daniel Kurt, "The 10 Most Expensive Cyberattacks of All Time," Investopedia, November 11, 2020, https://www.investopedia.com/financial-edge/0512/10-of-the-most-costly-computer-viruses-of-all-time.aspx.

[28] Scott Steinberg, "Cyberattacks Now Cost Companies $200,000 on Average, Putting Many Out of Business," *CNBC*, October 13, 2019, https://www.cnbc.com/2019/10/13/cyberattacks-cost-small-companies-200k-puttingmany-out-of-business.html.

[29] Juliana De Groot, "The Biggest Moments in Cybersecurity History (in the Past 10 Years)," Data Insider, December 26, 2019, https://digitalguardian.com/blog/biggest-moments-cybersecurity-history-past-10-years.

[30] "Common Types of Cybersecurity Attacks," Rapid7, https://www.rapid7.com/fundamentals/types-of-attacks.

[31] "The Cost of Malicious Cyber Activity to the U.S. Economy," The Council of Economic Advisers, February 2018, https://www.whitehouse.gov/wp-content/uploads/2018/03/The-Cost-of-Malicious-Cyber-Activity-to-the-U.S.-Economy.pdf.

[32] Steve Morgan, "Cybercrime to Cost the World $10.5 Trillion Annually by 2025," *Cybercrime Magazine*, November 13, 2020, https://cybersecurityventures.com/hackerpocalypse-cybercrime-report-2016.

Given the inevitability of data breaches, why has this problem reached crisis level for so many companies? In part, some of the challenge lies in finding qualified individuals to lead an organization's cybersecurity efforts. Chief Information Security Officers (CISOs) have a tenure considerably shorter than other positions in the C-suite, although over the past decade, this number has been inching up from an average of approximately two years to over four.[33] This reflects both the increasing respect for the position and the challenges that persist in successfully holding such a role.

Doubts about online security have cast a shadow on many online retailers and banks' corporate reputations. And in the online arena, reputation may indeed be everything. A recent survey by PwC found that 69 percent of consumers believe companies are vulnerable to cybersecurity attacks, but only 25 percent believe that companies handle their personal data responsibly.[34] This gap between perceived level of threat versus perceived level of protection and responsibility represents not only considerable shortcoming on the part of companies but also the immense challenges in tackling such a rapidly evolving challenge.

What are companies doing to battle back? The most effective reactions have focused on clear, consistent communications disseminated to customers prior to and in the immediate wake of an online attack. Most important, communications should concentrate on consumer education. MyFitnessPal, for example, suffered a data breach in which the accounts of over 150 million app users were compromised. Unlike other companies, such as the Uber example cited earlier in which the company took over a year to disclose their breach, MyFitnessPal discovered and publicly disclosed the breach within one week. Moreover, the company had segmented sensitive user information, such as birthdays and credit cards, such that this information was not directly linked to user accounts. The combination of their actions—both prior to and in the aftermath of the attack—helped not only to reduce the impact of such a breach but also to maintain company's credibility afterward.[35]

Online Opinions: Louder Than Ever

Data theft is only one type of threat companies need to guard against online. Another dimension companies must contend with is how easily the online world can propagate just about anything about a company—whether true or false, positive or negative, an isolated incident or a widespread issue.

In one of the earliest iterations of this, a dissatisfied Dunkin' customer used the Internet to share his bad experience at a store in the summer of 1999. When the customer could not get his choice of skim milk with his coffee and could not find a corporate website to lodge a complaint, he created his own, writing: "Dunkin' Donuts sucks. Here's

---

[33] "Age and Tenure in the C-Suite: Korn Ferry Study Reveals Trends by Title and Industry," *Business Wire*, January 21, 2020, https://www.businesswire.com/news/home/20200121005146/en/Age-and-Tenure-in-the-C-Suite-Korn-Ferry-Study-Reveals-Trends-by-Title-and-Industry.

[34] "Consumer Intelligence Series: Protect.me," PwC, https://www.pwc.com/us/en/services/consulting/library/consumer-intelligence-series/cybersecurity-protect-me.html.

[35] Daniela Perlmutter, "Responses To 2018 Data Breaches—The Good, The Bad and The Ugly," Cyberint blog, July 29, 2019, https://blog.cyberint.com/responses-to-2018-data-breaches-the-good-the-bad-and-the-ugly.

Why."[36] Although the site started out as a small section of this individual's personal web page, it was not long before Yahoo! picked up the page in its consumer opinion section. Because Dunkin' had no official forum for customer suggestions or complaints, this fledgling site—out of the company's control—effectively became that forum. The complainant eventually purchased new web space and the domain name www.dunkindonuts.org, moving the discussion to a place with a seemingly official name[37] and ultimately wasting two years of Dunkin's time and lawyers' billable hours in the back-and-forth attempt to regain control of the domain name.

While an incident identical to the 1999 Dunkin' debacle would not likely occur today (nearly every company has an online presence and offers multiple channels for consumers to get in touch with them), companies still must contend with negative online content potentially going viral and a far greater number of channels in which this can take place. As of 2019, over 1.7 billion websites were online enabling information (and disinformation) to spread like wildfire.[38] These electronic diaries often push a very specific agenda, and this can be an agenda that can tarnish a company's reputation if read and shared by any of the estimated 3 billion people who go online.[39] In fact, a 2019 Pew Research Center survey revealed that 80 percent of U.S. adults go online daily, with one in three adults saying they are online "almost constantly."[40] Moreover, the means by which consumers interact with companies is, of course, not just limited to websites, but extends to a broad range of channels. For example, more than 150 million people message businesses directly through Instagram every month,[41] and 76 percent of the 330 million Twitter users follow brands through the social media platform.[42,43] Because postings tend to remain online for long periods of time—and are often not removed at all—anything shared online can have a much longer-lasting impact than those transmitted through traditional vehicles such as print media, which is often recycled to the curb the next day.[44] With data preservation services proliferating due to cloud and blockchain technologies, online information may never disappear entirely.[45]

[36] Joanna Weiss, "Dunkin' Donuts Complaint-Site Saga Shows Business Power of Internet," *Boston Globe*, August 25, 1999, Online Lexis-Nexis Academic, April 2002.

[37] Ibid.

[38] Martin Armstrong, "How Many Websites Are There?" Statista, October 28, 2019, https://www.statista.com/chart/19058/how-many-websites-are-there.

[39] Khalid Saleh, "How Much of the World Population Is Online – Statistics and Trends," Invesp, April 11, 2020, https://www.invespcro.com/blog/world-population-online.

[40] Andrew Perrin and Madhu Kumar, "About Three-in-Ten U.S. Adults Say They Are 'Almost Constantly' Online," Pew Research Center, July 25, 2019, https://www.pewresearch.org/fact-tank/2019/07/25/americans-going-onlinealmost-constantly.

[41] Christina Newberry, "Social Media Customer Service: Everything You Need to Do It Well," *Hootsuite*, September 8, 2020, https://blog.hootsuite.com/social-media-customer-service.

[42] Ying Lin, "10 Twitter Statistics Every Marketer Should Know in 2020," Oberlo, May 30, 2020, https://www.oberlo.com/blog/twitter-statistics.

[43] James Quilter, "How Retailers Can Reach Twitter Users," Twitter, April 9, 2018, https://blog.twitter.com/en_gb/topics/marketing/2018/twitter-retail-research.html.

[44] Caspar van Vark, "Your Reputation Is Online," *Revolution*, March 4, 2004, p. 42.

[45] Liehuang Zhu, Keke Gai, and Meng Li, "Blockchain-Enabled Cloud Data Preservation Services," in *Blockchain Technology in Internet of Things*, July 2019, pp. 43–52, https://www.researchgate.net/publication/334720615_Blockchain-Enabled_Cloud_Data_Preservation_Services.

FIGURE 10.1
**KFC'S UK &
Ireland Twitter
Post Detailing
Their Initial
Apology for the
Chicken
Shortage**

Source: KFC
Corporation

THE **CHICKEN** CROSSED THE
ROAD, **JUST** NOT TO OUR
RESTAURANTS...

WE'VE BROUGHT A NEW DELIVERY PARTNER ONBOARD, BUT
THEY'VE HAD A COUPLE OF TEETHING PROBLEMS - GETTING
FRESH CHICKEN OUT TO 900 RESTAURANTS ACROSS THE
COUNTRY IS PRETTY COMPLEX!

WE WON'T COMPROMISE ON QUALITY, SO NO DELIVERIES
HAS MEANT SOME OF OUR RESTAURANTS ARE CLOSED, AND
OTHERS ARE OPERATING A LIMITED MENU, OR SHORTENED
HOURS.

SHOUT OUT TO OUR RESTAURANT TEAMS WHO ARE WORKING
FLAT OUT TO GET US BACK UP AND RUNNING AGAIN.

The near-permanence of online postings, however, may offer opportunities for companies to build even better customer rapport and provide a record of their ability to ward off customer concerns that otherwise could have devolved into a crisis. Today, 64 percent of consumers prefer to message a brand rather than call,[46] and, as a result, many product or service complaints that typically would occur in the more private confines of a phone call are made public via postings on Twitter and Facebook. For example, in February 2018 in the United Kingdom, KFC infamously ran out of—of all things—chicken after switching delivery partners. The company was forced to close nearly 800 out of 900 U.K. locations,[47] and customers were quick to express their displeasure on social media, racking up over 53,000 mentions of the shortage on Twitter alone in less than 48 hours.[48]

As opposed to hiding behind formal corporate jargon or remaining silent on the issue altogether, however, KFC immediately took to Twitter to apologize for the major blunder, posting to their UK handle a witty apology, declaring, "The chicken crossed the road, just not to our restaurants..."[49] followed by a more detailed explanation of the error (see Figure 10.1). The company took their apology one step further when they ran a full-page ad in the British papers, featuring a photo of their classic red-and-white-striped chicken basket with their KFC logo replaced by three letters: "FCK" (see Figure 10.2). It was then this tongue-in-cheek ad that suddenly went viral, with articles, TV discussions, and social media sites posting, discussing and overall, it seems, laughing at the company's hilarious *mea culpa*. By May 2018, their campaign had reached over 1.02 billion individuals—far

[46] "5 Reasons Travel Brands Should Focus on Messaging," Facebook for Business, April 6, 2020, https://www.facebook.com/business/news/insights/5-reasons-messaging-is-taking-flight-with-travelers.

[47] apology

[48] Alex Brownsell, "KFC: A Very Fcking Clever Campaign," Campaign, November 21, 2018, https://www.campaignlive.co.uk/article/kfc-fcking-clever-campaign/1498912.

[49] "The Colonel is working on it." KFC Twitter, February 17, 2018, https://twitter.com/KFC_UKI/status/964838797841190912/photo/1.

FIGURE 10.2
KFC's Full-Page
Newspaper Ad in
The Sun

Source: KFC ad in *The Sun* on February 23, 2018.

WE'RE SORRY

A chicken restaurant without any chicken. It's not ideal. Huge apologies to our customers, especially those who travelled out of their way to find we were closed. And endless thanks to our KFC team members and our franchise partners for working tirelessly to improve the situation. It's been a hell of a week, but we're making progress, and every day more and more fresh chicken is being delivered to our restaurants. Thank you for bearing with us.

Visit kfc.co.uk/crossed-the-road for details about your local restaurant.

exceeding the 53,000 negative Twitter mentions.[50] In the end, KFC's response allowed them not just to return to business as usual, but it also even appeared to bolster the brand's reputation and recognition, with its impression score actually *increasing* post-crisis for those consumers who already ate at the chain and, with its campaign reaching 29 percent of the UK public, up from 7 percent pre-crisis.[51] What could have been a textbook example of a logistical failure, then, ultimately became a textbook example of deft use of social media for crisis management.

The importance of a strong online presence extends beyond companies themselves but to the individuals who work for them, particularly those in the C-suite. In 2015, only 39 percent of Fortune 500 CEOs had an online presence, but that number has steadily risen to 62 percent as of August 2020.[52] For those who do have a social media presence, LinkedIn is a top choice, with 94 percent of such social media active CEOs turning to this platform.[53] CEOs do also turn to other channels, such as Twitter or even their

[50] Brownsell, "KFC," Campaign.

[51] Ibid.

[52] Elissa Liu, "Most Fortune 500 CEOs Are on Social Media in 2020," Influential Executive, August 8, 2020, https://influentialexecutive.com/how-many-fortune-500-ceos-social-media-2020.

[53] Ibid.

company's own websites, to directly interact with end-users and consumers, but such approaches can be met with mixed results. For example, on Earth Day in 2018, Amazon CEO Jeff Bezos created a firestorm when tweeting about his luxury dog-sledding vacation he was enjoying right in the middle of particularly acrimonious employee strikes over low wages and poor warehouse conditions. Such a tweet led to a flood of responses, from employees, politicians, and even celebrities alike who decried Bezos' tone-deaf social media presence.[54] Though Bezos ultimately issued an apology and Amazon later raised its minimum wage to $15 an hour that year, Bezos' blunder underscored just how thin a line exists between being perceived as open and casual (and therefore more approachable) on social media platforms and falling into less professional and even offensive language in a way that ultimately impacts the entire organization. Not every individual (or organization for that matter) has the team behind KFC's accounts that allows them to pursue the witty, tongue-in-cheek tone that they do.

Crises of the Past Decade

In the "new economy," companies must recognize the increasing influence of the Internet on a growing number of their constituencies (see Chapters 6 and 7 for more on media and investor constituencies, respectively) and the greater consumer concern about online privacy and security. Companies must take their operating environment into account when planning for and handling crises.

These are just some of the other major crises that organizations have faced in the past 10 years:

- In March 2019, the second Boeing 737 Max in just a few months crashed, claiming the lives of all those on board. Executives blamed recent faulty software for the crashes, but further details emerged to suggest that the company had knowledge of the risks to flights for years in advance. Boeing was ultimately forced to ground the Max into 2020, had to compensate families for their losses, and faced considerable legal fees, amounting to a nearly $19 billion loss to the company.

- In April 2018, two Black men sitting inside a Philadelphia Starbucks were arrested for not making a purchase in the store. Much of the incident was filmed and uploaded to YouTube, promoting immediate public outcry. Though Starbucks' CEO Howard Schultz promptly issued an apology and closed more than 8,000 stores a month later for racial sensitivity training, the company faced continued criticism for what some viewed as an attempt to put a band-aid on a far more widespread and pernicious issue.

- In March 2018, a Cambridge Analytica employee named Christopher Wylie came forward to *The New York Times* and *The Guardian* to reveal how Facebook had made the private data of over 50 million users available without their consent to Cambridge Analytica for political advertising, resulting in fines from the UK Information Commissioner's Office, an immediate drop in Facebook's stock, and ongoing public outrage regarding the company's handling of user data.

---

[54] Michelle Cheng, "The 5 Biggest Corporate Social Media Fails of 2018," *Inc.*, November 30, 2018, https://www.inc.com/michelle-cheng/biggest-corporate-social-media-fails-2018.html.

- In December 2017, members of the Sackler family, owners of Purdue Pharma, testified before the House Oversight Committee for their and their company's role in opioid crisis that has claimed over 400,000 lives in the United States. The company had come under increasing scrutiny after the link between their drug, oxycontin, and the crisis had been increasingly clear, all while the Sackler family made over $12 billion. Horrifyingly, as of December 2020, the family has still refused to take any level of accountability for their actions, with Dr. Kathe Sackler, a member of the Purdue board for over 20 years, declaring, "There's nothing I can find that I would have done differently."

- In April 2017, a doctor heading home to Louisville, Kentucky, was violently removed from an overbooked United Airlines flight. The scene was recorded and posted online by fellow passengers, capturing his face being bloodied and his limp body ultimately being dragged off the flight. Just as shockingly, United took more than 24 hours to issue what amounted to a very tepid apology, initially siding with employees until CEO Oscar Munoz stated he "apologize[d] for having to reaccommodate these customers."

- In February 2017, Uber opened an internal investigation in sexual harassment within the company after Susan Fowler, a former engineer, made public her experience with sexual harassment and discrimination during her time at the company. The investigation uncovered more than 200 reports of inappropriate conduct and resulted in the firing of more than 20 employees, including Travis Kalanick, its then-CEO.

- In the summer of 2016, Mylan came under attack for its repeated price hikes on EpiPen, which had taken the life-saving injector's list price up several hundred percent over several years. The price hikes and public outrage prompted a Department of Justice investigation that resulted in a $465 million fine levied against the company.

- In September 2015, the EPA discovered that Volkswagen had installed "defeat devices" in several its diesel-powered cars in order to cheat emissions tests. The defeat devices were ultimately discovered to have been placed in over 11 million cars throughout the globe, and it led to considerable fallout for the company, ranging from SEC investigations to the resignation of its CEO.

- In March 2014, Malaysian Airlines flight 370 disappeared while flying from Kuala Lumpur to Beijing. The company's slow response and poor coordination with its government antagonized victims' relatives, strained relations with China, and wasted manpower and time through searching for the plane in wrong locations. Four months later, Malaysian Airlines flight 17 was destroyed by a surface-to-air missile while flying over Ukrainian insurgents.

- In late November 2013, criminals hacked into Target Brand's point-of-sale devices and stole more than 40 million credit card numbers and 70 million records of personal information. Target's Chairman, President, and CEO, Gregg Steinhafel, lost his job as a result of his failure to swiftly react.

- In September 2013, Barilla (a pasta company) faced a boycott from many consumers after company Chairman (and family heir) Guido Barilla told an Italian broadcaster that the company supports the traditional family and invited gays and others to "eat pasta from another brand" if they disagreed. In response, Barilla apologized, the company established a diversity advisory board, and it planned a more inclusive advertising campaign.

- In March 2013, Celebrity chef Paula Deen was sued for a hostile workplace subject to sexist and racist slurs. By the time the lawsuit was dismissed in August, companies such as Walmart, QVC, Home Depot, Caesars, Sears, and Novo Nordisk canceled endorsement deals, and The Food Network canceled her cooking program. Deen and her advisors avoided "litigating in the court of public opinion" and, as a result, left her open to social media attacks (on Twitter, #PaulasBestDishes featured mock-racist recipe names, such as "Lettuce from a Birmingham Jail") that ultimately led to the ending of so many of her business relationships.

- In January 2012, the *Costa Concordia* cruise ship hit a reef off the coast of Italy and partially sunk, killing 32 people and setting in motion a bizarre chain of events that damaged the reputation of its owner, Carnival Corporation, and Carnival's CEO, Micky Arison while also bringing heightened scrutiny to the safety of cruise lines. Further scrutiny arrived the next month after a fire on the *Carnival Triumph* caused the ship to lose power and propulsion. The on-board experience was harrowing; with more than 4,000 people on board and only a few functional bathrooms, the journey quickly became known as the "poop cruise."

How to Prepare for Crises

The first step in preparing for a crisis is to understand that any organization, no matter what industry or location it is in, can find itself involved in the kinds of crises discussed in the previous section. The 2019 PwC Global Crisis Survey not only found that nearly 70 percent of leaders had experienced some sort of crisis in the past five years, but that almost every single leader (95 percent) anticipated experiencing some sort of business crisis in the near future.[55] This is to say nothing of the near-universal impact that the 2020 COVID-19 pandemic had on businesses and the entire world. Although those crises listed in this chapter may be some of the most noteworthy ones from recent history, those left out were likely just as devastating to the companies involved. Obviously, some industries— the chemical industry, Big Pharma, consumer packaged goods, mining, forest products, energy-related industries such as oil and gas and electric utilities, and online retailers—are more crisis-prone than others, but today, every organization is at risk.

The terror attacks of September 11, 2001, proved to be an important test of many companies' crisis plans. For other companies, the attacks underlined the importance of having a plan in place. A survey of nearly 200 CEOs conducted by Burson-Marsteller and *PRWeek* magazine in late 2001 revealed that a full 21 percent of CEOs surveyed "had no crisis plan and were caught unprepared" by the events of September 11. Fifty-three percent acknowledged that their plan was good but "not totally adequate for such events." In response to the question of whether they had readdressed their crisis communication plan since the September 11 disaster, 63 percent indicated that they intended to do so.[56] According to a recent survey, crisis management is one of the top priorities among most

[55] "PwC's Global Crisis Survey 2019," PwC.

[56] Jonah Bloom, "CEOs: Leadership through Communication—The *PRWeek* and Burson-Marsteller CEO Survey 2001 Finds U.S. Corporate Leaders Emulating the Strong, Open, Communicative Style of Rudy," *PRWeek*, November 26, 2001, pp. 20–29.

Fortune 1000 companies' senior managers. According to respondents, this is mostly due to a recent crisis in their own company or those witnessed in the media, and an increased sense of vulnerability to natural disasters.[57]

Many companies located in the World Trade Center also had been tenants of the Twin Towers at the time of a previous terrorist attack. In 1993, an explosion blew out three of the underground floors of the World Trade Center, forcing the evacuation of more than 30,000 employees and thousands of visitors from the entire complex and a rescue operation lasting 12 hours.[58] After the 1993 bombing, many organizations developed or refined their evacuation plans from the Trade Center. When the second attack occurred in 2001, this preparation helped save many lives.

For example, the World Trade Center's largest tenant, Morgan Stanley Dean Witter, cited its own evacuation plan as critical to saving the lives of all but six of its 3,700 employees on September 11. A Morgan spokesman attributed the smooth evacuation to companywide familiarity with the plan: "Everybody knew about the contingency plan. We met constantly to talk about it."[59]

Although crisis management is perceived as a top priority by senior managers, companies routinely fail to practice what they preach. According to a March 2020 survey by *PRNews*, 62 percent of corporations have crisis plans, but very few routinely update them.[60] While the COVID-19 pandemic has in many ways further elevated "crisis consciousness," it is yet unclear whether this will translate into concrete action or if the gap between those corporations that have a dated plan and one that is more fitting to the times will further close.

Assess the Risk for Your Organization

As mentioned earlier, some industries are more prone to crises than others. But how can organizations determine whether they are more or less likely to experience a crisis? Publicly traded companies are at risk because of the nature of their relationship with a key constituency—shareholders. If a major catastrophe hits a company that trades on one of the stock exchanges, the likelihood of a selloff in the stock is enormous. Such immediate financial consequences can threaten the organization's image as a stable ongoing operation in addition to the damage the crisis itself inflicts.

Although privately held companies do not have to worry about shareholders, they do have to worry about the loss of goodwill—which can affect sales—when a crisis hits. Often the owners of privately held companies become involved in communication during a crisis to lend their own credibility to the organization. So all organizations—public, private, and not-for-profit—are at some risk if a crisis actually occurs. The next section examines how a company can plan for the worst no matter what.

[57] www.disaster-resource.com/articles/98nuggs.shtml.

[58] Carol Carey, "World Trade Center," *Access Control & Security Systems Integration*, July 1, 1997.

[59] Daren Fonda, "Girding against New Risks: Global Executives Are Working to Better Protect Their Employees and Businesses from Calamity," *Time*, October 8, 2001, p. B8.

[60] Seth Arenstein, "62% Have Crisis Plans, But Few Update Them or Practice Scenarios," *PRNews*, February 5, 2020, https://www.prnewsonline.com/crisis-survey-CSA-practice.

Identify Potential Crises

The person in charge of corporate communication should first call a *brainstorming session* that includes the most senior managers in the organization as well as representatives from the areas that are most likely to be affected by a crisis—for example, the head of manufacturing in some cases because of the potential for industrial accidents in the manufacturing process. It also might include the Chief Information Officer because of the danger to computer systems when accidents happen. In the case of the explosion during the first World Trade Center attack in 1993, most of the organizations were service organizations. After the loss of lives, the loss of critical information was one of the worst outcomes of the explosion.

During the brainstorming session, participants should work together to develop ideas about potential crises. They should be encouraged to be as creative as possible during this stage. The facilitator should allow participants to share their ideas, no matter how outrageous, with the group and should encourage all participants to be open-minded as they think about possible crisis scenarios.

Once an inventory of possible crises exists, the facilitator should help the group to determine which of the ideas developed have the most potential to actually occur. It might be useful, for example, to ask the group to assign probabilities to the potential crises so that they can focus on the more likely scenarios rather than wasting time working through solutions to problems that have a very low probability of occurring. But even at this stage, participants must not rule out the worst-case scenario. The risk for an oil spill the size of the BP spill occurring was very low according to outside projections. Thus, neither the oil company nor governmental agencies prepared for the worst possible accident.

Determine Effect on Constituencies

Once the probability of risk has been assigned to potential crises, organizations need to determine *which constituencies would be most affected by the crisis*. Crisis communication experts spend too little time thinking about this question. Why is it so important? Because some constituencies are more important than others, organizations need to look at risk in terms of its effect on the most important constituencies.

When the World Trade Center came under attack on September 11, 2001, then-American Express CEO Ken Chenault phoned the company's headquarters across the street from the World Trade Center and instructed building security to evacuate employees immediately. As the day wore on, he contacted all his senior executives to check on their well-being.[61] Until Chenault was able to relocate the company's 3,000 employees to a new building across the river, AmEx's in-house communications staff worked from their homes to reach out to customers and let them know the company was open for business.[62] Two concerns guided Chenault in his actions following this crisis: employee safety and customer service.[63] Employees and customers, in this example, were the constituencies determined to be most affected by these events, and Chenault's actions reflected this determination.

Determining how to rank constituencies when a crisis actually happens is more difficult because so many other things are going on. But thinking about risk in terms of effect on

---

[61] Bloom, "CEOs: Leadership through Communication."

[62] "Corporate America's Reaction," *PRWeek*, September 24, 2001, p. 10.

[63] Bloom, "CEOs: Leadership through Communication."

constituencies in advance helps the organization further refine which potential crises it should spend the most time and money preparing for. During the Tylenol crisis, for example, Johnson & Johnson could rely on its Credo to help the company set clear priorities and deal with its constituencies.

Set Communication Objectives for Potential Crises

Setting communication objectives for potential crises is different than figuring out how to deal with the crisis itself. Clearly, organizations must do both, but typically managers are more likely to focus on what kinds of things they will do during a crisis rather than what they will say and to whom. Communication takes on more importance than action when the crisis involves more intangible things such as the loss of reputation rather than the loss of lives. For each constituency, identify what that constituency's initial response to the crisis is likely to be and what you want them to hear during a crisis.

Analyze Channel Choice

Once the ranking of constituencies is complete, the participants in a planning session should begin to think about what their communication objective will be for each constituency. Whether this objective will be achieved often depends on the effectiveness of the communication *channel* the company selects to convey the message.

Perhaps the mass distribution of a memo would be too impersonal for a message to employees in a time of crisis. The company might consider personal or group meetings or a "town hall" gathering instead. The choice of communication channel often can reflect how sensitive a company is to its constituencies' needs and emotions. What would be the most efficient and most sensitive way to communicate with consumers or their families during a crisis? Johnson & Johnson's caring and highly personalized reaction to the Tylenol crisis—involving a host of personal visits to hospitals and pharmacies nationwide—won the company significant goodwill. In a time of crisis, constituencies crave information and are often more sensitive than usual to how information is conveyed to them. In the column of impersonal and inappropriate responses, however, lies the marketing firm Exactis and its CEO Steve Hardigree. In June 2018, security researcher Vinny Troia discovered that the company had exposed the data of over 340 million individuals, with information ranging from demographics to financial information to even personal interests.[64] Such a breach far exceeded Equifax's famous breach in scope and size. Initially, the company declined to make a public comment, and when CEO Hardigree finally addressed the public, he simply stated, "According to log reports there was no breach."[65] Failure on the part of Exactis to take ownership for the breach and to even acknowledge the concern that many individuals had over the exposure of their private, sensitive data resulted not only in widespread outrage but also ultimately—and unfortunately—the perfect example of how not to respond to a crisis.

Assign a Different Team to Each Crisis

Another important part of planning for communicating in a crisis is determining in advance who will be on what team for each crisis. Different problems require different

[64] Andy Greenberg, "Marketing Firm Exactis Leaked a Personal Info Database with 340 Million Records," *Wired*, June 27, 2018, https://www.wired.com/story/exactis-database-leak-340-million-records.

[65] Perlmutter, "Responses to 2018 Data Breaches."

kinds of expertise, and planners should consider who is best suited to deal with one type of crisis versus another. For example, if the crisis is likely to have a financial focus, the Chief Financial Officer may be the best person to lead a team dealing with such a problem. He or she also may be the best spokesperson when the problem develops. On the other hand, if the problem is more catastrophic, such as an airline crash, the CEO is probably the best person to put in charge of the team and to serve, at least initially, as head spokesperson for the crisis. In crises that result in loss of life, anyone other than the CEO will have less credibility with the general public and the media.

But managers should avoid putting senior-level executives in charge of communications for *all* crises. Sometimes the person closest to the crisis is the one people want to hear from. For example, the best spokesperson for a global company may be someone located in the country where the problem develops rather than a more senior manager from the head office due to considerations such as cultural issues, language differences, and local community concerns.

Assigning different teams to handle different crises helps the organization put the best people in charge of handling the crisis and communications. It also allows the organization to get a cross-section of employees involved. The more involved managers are in planning and participating on a team in a crisis, the better equipped the organization will be as a whole.

Plan for Centralization

Although organizations can employ either a centralized or decentralized approach to corporate communication for general purposes (as we discussed in Chapter 3), when it comes to crises, the approach must be completely centralized.

Conflicting stories from Perrier's U.S. and European divisions created problems in the company's handling of the benzene contamination scare, further compounding that crisis. Decentralized organizations often find it more difficult to communicate efficiently between divisions, especially if they have not given interdivisional communication full consideration in a crisis-planning phase. Planning for centralization can help strip away layers of bureaucracy, keep lines of communication open throughout the organization, and dissipate conflict, all of which are especially critical in a crisis.

What to Include in a Formal Plan

Every communications consultant will suggest that you develop a detailed plan for use in a crisis. These are formal in the sense that they are typically printed up and passed around to the appropriate managers, who may have to sign a statement swearing that they have read and agree to the plan. This step allows the organization to ensure that the plan has been acknowledged by the recipients and permits questions and clarifications to be discussed *in a noncrisis environment*. The last thing you want to happen is for a plant manager's first read of the plan to be when a real crisis occurs.

When developing a formal crisis communications plan, there are several key actions that should be executed to ensure the plan's competence. Pearson and Mitroff condense these specific actions in their Crisis Management Strategic Checklist below. As their checklist accurately indicates, corporate leaders must spend significant time and energy preparing what actions they and their company will take in times of crisis to help

Pearson and Mitroff's Crisis Management Strategic Checklist

STRATEGIC ACTIONS

1. Integrate crisis management into strategic planning processes.
2. Integrate crisis management into statements of corporate excellence.
3. Include outsiders on the board and on crisis management teams.
4. Provide training and workshops in crisis management.
5. Expose organizational members to crisis simulations.
6. Create a diversity or portfolio of crisis management strategies.

TECHNICAL AND STRUCTURAL ACTIONS

1. Create a crisis management team.
2. Dedicate budget expenditures for crisis management.
3. Establish accountabilities for updating emergency policies/manuals.
4. Computerize inventories of crisis management resources (e.g., employee skills).
5. Designate an emergency command control room.
6. Assure technological redundancy in vital areas (e.g., computer systems).
7. Establish working relationship with outside experts in crisis management.

EVALUATION AND DIAGNOSTIC ACTIONS

1. Conduct legal and financial audits of threats and liabilities.
2. Modify insurance coverage to match crisis management contingencies.
3. Conduct environmental impact audits.
4. Prioritize activities necessary for daily operations.
5. Establish tracking system for early warning signals.
6. Establish tracking system to follow up past crises or near crises.

COMMUNICATION ACTIONS

1. Provide training for dealing with the media regarding crisis management.
2. Improve communication lines with local communities.
3. Improve communication with intervening stakeholders (e.g., police).

PSYCHOLOGICAL AND CULTURAL ACTIONS

1. Increase visibility of strong top management commitment to crisis management.
2. Improve relationships with activist groups.
3. Improve upward communication (including "whistleblowers").
4. Improve downward communication regarding crisis management programs/accountabilities.
5. Provide training regarding human and emotional impacts of crises.
6. Provide psychological support services (e.g., stress/anxiety management).
7. Reinforce symbolic recall/corporate memory of past crises/dangers.

Source: Christine Pearson and Ian Mitroff, "From Crisis Prone to Crisis Prepared: A Framework for Crisis Management," *Academy of Management Executive* 7, no. 1 (1993), pp. 48–59.

safeguard corporate reputation and to communicate clearly and effectively with their stakeholders.

Research on crisis planning shows that the following information is almost always included in a crisis plan.

A List of Whom to Notify in an Emergency

This list should contain the names and numbers of everyone on the crisis team as well as numbers to call externally, such as the fire and police departments. The list should be kept updated as people leave the company or change responsibilities.

An Approach to Media Relations

Frank Corrado, the President of a firm that deals with crisis communications, suggests that the cardinal rule for communicating with all constituencies in a crisis should be "Tell It All, Tell It Fast!"[66] To a certain extent, this recommendation is true, but one should be extremely careful about applying such a rule too quickly to the media. Perhaps a friendly amendment to Corrado's rule might be, "Tell as much as you can, as soon as you can," so that you do not jeopardize the credibility of the organization. For example, Perrier's hasty communication with the media, in the absence of accurate information, was a crippling mistake.

If the organization has done a good job of building relations with the media when times are good, reporters will be more understanding when a crisis occurs. Having a reserve of goodwill with the media is what helped Johnson & Johnson during the Tylenol crisis. Generally, the person who has the best relationships with individual reporters is probably the right person to get involved with them during a crisis. By agreeing ahead of time that all crisis-related inquiries will go to a central location, organizations can avoid looking disorganized.

A Strategy for Notifying Employees

Employees should be seen as analogous to families in a personal crisis. Employees finding out from the media about something that affects the organization can be likened to a family member hearing about a personal problem from an outsider. An organization should take pains to ensure that a plan for employee notification is created with employee communication professionals in advance and is included in the overall crisis plan.

A Location to Serve as Crisis Headquarters

Although consultants and experts who have written about crises suggest that companies need to invest money in a special crisis center, all companies really need to do is identify ahead of time an area that can easily be converted to such an operation. A contingency location should be determined in the event of a natural disaster or terrorist attack affecting the safety or security of the chosen location. Gathering the appropriate technology (e.g., laptops, cell phones, mobile hot spots, etc.) as quickly as possible when a crisis hits is also important. This headquarters location should be shared ahead of time with all key internal and external constituencies. All information ideally should be centralized through this office. Other lines of communication should then flow through the headquarters for the duration of the crisis.

In addition to a physical crisis headquarters, companies that plan to communicate via social media and the company website should have details in place such that activating a new webpage, banner announcement, etc., can be done with a minimum amount of technical involvement.

A Description of the Plan

Companies should have their crisis plans documented in writing. In addition to communication strategy, a crisis plan should address logistical details, for example, how and where the families of victims should be accommodated in the case of an airline crash.

Following the development of an overall plan, all managers should receive training about what to do if and when a crisis strikes. Several public relations firms and academic consultants now offer simulations that allow managers to test their crisis management

[66] Frank Corrado, *Media for Managers* (New York: Prentice Hall, 1984), p. 101.

skills in experiential exercises. Companies including MasterCard, Southwest Airlines, and General Motors use simulations to help their organizations work out the kinks before a real crisis hits.[67] Managers searching for the right training should be sure that the simulation or training session includes a heavy emphasis on communication in addition to management of the crisis itself.

Beyond managers, all employees should be versed in and trained regularly on the company's emergency procedures and plans. Involve all employees in continuity of business tests; although a genuine crisis cannot be simulated, test runs will help ensure familiarity with emergency plans throughout all levels of the organization. Unfortunately, simulation testing is another area where considerable gaps exist between companies' perceptions of what is important and the actions they actually take. According to a recent Deloitte Crisis Management Survey, 90 percent of respondents were confident in their organization's ability to deal with a corporate scandal, but only 17 percent had actually tested this assumption via a simulation.[68]

Communicating During the Crisis

All the planning that an organization can muster will only partially prepare it for an actual crisis. The true measure of success is how it deals with a problem when it occurs. If the plan is comprehensive enough, managers will at least start from a strong position. What follow are the most important steps to take when communicating during a crisis. Every crisis is different, which means that managers must adapt these suggestions to meet their needs, but crises have enough common elements for this prescription to be a starting point for all crisis management.

Step 1: Get Control of the Situation

The first step is for the appropriate manager to get control of the situation as soon as possible. Such control involves defining the real problem with the use of reliable information and then setting measurable objectives, including communications objectives, for handling it. Failing to take this seemingly obvious, but crucial, first step can be devastating to crisis management efforts, as seen in the Perrier case. Perrier lacked sufficient information to *define* its benzene problem in the first place—though its spokespeople tried to convince the public otherwise—which only compromised its attempts to mitigate the crisis.

When a crisis erupts, everyone in the organization should know who needs to be contacted, but in large global organizations, this knowledge is often unrealistic. Therefore, the corporate communications department can initially serve as a clearinghouse. The Vice President for Corporate Communication at the head office should know the composition of crisis teams and can then turn the situation over to the appropriate manager.

Step 2: Gather as Much Information as Possible

Understanding the problem at hand is the right place for communicators to begin dealing with a crisis. This understanding often involves managing information coming from many sources.

---

[67] "Crises: In-House, in Hand," *PRWeek*, January 21, 2002, p. 13.

[68] "Stronger, Fitter, Better: Crisis Management for the Resilient Enterprise," Deloitte, 2018, https://www2.deloitte.com/content/dam/Deloitte/at/Documents/risk/at-global-crisis-management-survey-2018.pdf.

As information becomes available, someone should be assigned to mine that information: if it is an industrial accident, how serious is it? Were lives lost? Have families already been notified? If the incident involves an unfriendly takeover, what are the details of the offer? Was it absurdly low? Have any plans been made for the company to defend itself?

Many corporations have been criticized for reacting too slowly during a crisis because they were trying desperately to gather information about the incident. If it is going to take longer than a couple of hours to get the right information, a company spokesperson should communicate this delay to the media and other key constituencies right away to make it clear that the company is not stonewalling. No one will criticize an organization for trying to find out what is going on, but a company can face harsh treatment if its constituencies think that management is deliberately obstructing the flow of information.

Step 3: Set Up a Centralized Crisis Management Center

At the same time managers are getting in touch with the right people and gathering information, they also should be making arrangements for creating a crisis center as described earlier in this chapter. This location will serve as the platform for all communications during the crisis. Organizations also should provide a comfortable location for media to use during the crisis, including whatever technical infrastructure is necessary for them to communicate with their editors. All communications about the crisis should come from this one, centralized location.

Step 4: Communicate Early and Often

The organization's spokesperson needs to say whatever he or she can as soon as possible. Particularly if the crisis involves threat to lives and property, communicators should try to shield constituencies from panic by allaying some of the probable fears that people will have about the situation. Employees, the media, and other important constituencies should know that the crisis center will issue updates at regular intervals until further notice. Even if they retain public relations firms to assist them in handling a crisis, companies need to put good *inside* people on the front lines of crisis communication and should encourage managers to adopt a team approach with others involved.

Above all else, companies must avoid silence and delayed responses or their constituencies will fill any information voids with criticism and rumors, using powerful tools such as Twitter, Facebook, and LinkedIn. As mentioned earlier in the chapter, Uber discovered the lesson the hard way during its 2016 data breach that they only brought to light in 2017. The space between the time of the breach, the discovery of the breach, and its ultimate disclosure was filled with an immense level of criticism via a range of online platforms as a consequence of the company's reticence. Furthermore, Uber's standing as a startup, as opposed to a company with a multi-decade reputation, meant that they had considerably less goodwill and long-term brand trust to draw on from during such a time.

Communicating early and often is much easier said than done. Larry Kamer, CEO of Kramer Consulting Group, notes that "nine and a half times out of 10 you have to communicate before the facts are in."[69] So companies need to communicate values, such as concern for public safety, and to show a commitment to coming to the aid of people affected by the crisis, even if they do not have all the details yet.

[69] John Frank, "What Can We Learn from the Ford/Firestone Tire Recall? As John Frank Explains, Unlike the Tylenol Crisis, the Problem Is That They Just Can't Seem to Put a Lid on It," *PRWeek*, October 9, 2000, p. 31.

Step 5: Understand the Media's Mission in a Crisis

Members of the media work in an extremely competitive environment, which explains why they all want to get the story first. They are also more accustomed to a crisis environment in their work. What they are looking for is a good story with victims, villains, and visuals.

The Pepsi syringe hoax had all of these sensational elements. As we have seen, CEO Craig Weatherup recognized the impact that visuals would have in reassuring the public that the tampering claims it was facing were simply impossible. The video footage of Pepsi canning procedures and the grocery-store surveillance tape, shown on television, and the full-page newspaper ad are all examples of Pepsi's using the media to help it beat a crisis.

Step 6: Communicate Directly with Affected Constituents

Using the media to get information out is critical for companies, but it's even more important that they communicate with their employees, sales staff, organized leadership, site security, operators, and receptionists, as these will be the media's best sources of information in the crisis. External constituencies need to be contacted as well. These include the other three key constituencies besides employees—customers, shareholders, and communities—as well as suppliers, emergency services, experts, and officials.

Several companies received praise from their customers for their direct communications surrounding the March 2011 hacking of mass e-mail service Epsilon's address files. Epsilon provided mass e-mail service for many respected companies, including Brookstone, Kroger, Marriott Rewards, and The College Board. Upon learning of the security breach, Best Buy, for example, quickly posted press releases and sent e-mails to customers informing them of the security breach. These e-mails contained clear details about what had happened; what data had and had not been compromised; the steps that Best Buy was taking to investigate the breach; and resources for further information.[70]

When designing the communication plan, companies also should consider which constituencies are the top priority, and what information is the most important for each constituency to receive first. Companies must keep in mind the increasingly blurred lines between constituencies and should consider that any communication meant for one constituency may not be read exclusively by that constituency.

Step 7: Remember That Business Must Continue

To the managers involved, the crisis will most certainly be uppermost in their minds for the duration, but to others, the business must go on despite the crisis. In addition to finding suitable replacements ahead of time for those who are on the crisis team, managers must try to anticipate the effects of the crisis on other parts of the business. For example, if an advertising campaign is under way, should it be stopped during the crisis? Have officers stopped trading on the company's stock? Will it be necessary for the organization to move to a temporary location during the crisis? These and other questions related to the ongoing business need to be thought through by managers both on and off the crisis team as soon as possible.

---

[70] "Epsilon Hacking Exposes Customers of Best Buy, Capital One, Citi, JPMorgan Chase and Others," *Los Angeles Times*, April 4, 2011, http://latimesblogs.latimes.com/technology/2011/04/epsilon-cutsomer-files-email-addresses-breached-including-best-buy-jpmorgan-chase-us-bank-capital-on.html.

FIGURE 10.3
Four Essential Crisis Communication Steps

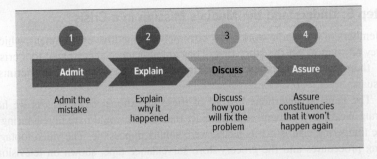

1 Admit	2 Explain	3 Discuss	4 Assure
Admit the mistake	Explain why it happened	Discuss how you will fix the problem	Assure constituencies that it won't happen again

Step 8: Make Plans to Avoid Another Crisis Immediately

After the crisis, corporate communications executives should work with other managers to ensure the organization will be even better prepared the next time it faces a crisis. Companies that have experienced crises are more likely to believe that such occurrences will happen again and also will recognize that preparation is key to handling crises successfully.

Johnson & Johnson's experience in 1982 helped the company to deal with another episode of Tylenol contamination four years later when a New Yorker died after taking cyanide-laced Tylenol capsules. There is no better time than the period immediately following a crisis to prepare for the next one, because motivation is high to learn from mistakes made the first time.

Ultimately, the above crisis communications steps can be distilled down to four key ones (see Figure 10.3): (1) admit a mistake was made; (2) explain why it happened; (3) discuss how you will fix the problem; and (4) assure constituencies it will not happen again. Armed with this paradigm, as well as the more detailed steps outlined above, your organization will be well-prepared to weather the storms of any future crises you may face.

Conclusion

Webster's Dictionary traces the word *crisis* back to the Greek word *krisis*—meaning a decision, from the verb *krinein*, to decide.[71] Today we know crises as pivotal times of instability during which leadership and decision making can determine the ultimate outcome of the situation—for better or for worse. As we've seen, sometimes companies can emerge even more respected in the wake of a well-handled crisis.

In this chapter, we explored some real-life examples of how companies across a number of industries dealt with crises of their own and saw that planning and preparation are key to effective crisis management and communication. As British author Aldous Huxley put it, "The amelioration of the world cannot be achieved by sacrifices in moments of crisis; it depends on the efforts made and constantly repeated during the humdrum, uninspiring periods, which separate one crisis from another, and of which normal lives mainly consist."[72]

[71] *Merriam-Webster Online Dictionary*, https://www.merriam-webster.com.
[72] Aldous Huxley, *Grey Eminence: A Study in Religion and Politics* (London: Chatto & Windus, 1941), chapter 10.

Case 10-1

Carnival Corporation: The *Costa Concordia* Crisis

It was called "the most significant event in modern maritime history."[1] On January 13, 2012, the *Costa Concordia* ran aground off the coast of the island of Giglio in Italy, partially sinking and resulting in the evacuation of over 4,000 passengers and crew. *The New York Times* deemed the wreck "a drama that seemed to blend tragedy with elements of farce,"[2] and *Vanity Fair* dubbed it "a tale of monumental human folly."[3] Indeed, the wreck of the *Costa Concordia* combined tragedy, farce, and folly across its multiple actors and many strange twists of fate: a courageous search and rescue operation by international divers; a potential environmental catastrophe in an Italian marine reserve; bizarre stories of the captain's actions and behavior; and passenger accounts of a disorganized and terrifying evacuation process. The wreck even drew comparisons to the *Titanic* tragedy of 1912,[4] helped in no small part by the fact that it had supplanted the *Titanic* as the largest passenger ship ever wrecked.[5] Ultimately, three years passed before rescue crews finally salvaged the *Costa Concordia* off the shores of Giglio, a solemn reminder of a tragedy that resulted in 32 deaths.

In the weeks following the tragedy, the absence of one man in the crisis management of the incident was universally noted and publicized by the global media. Micky Arison, the chairman and CEO of Carnival Corporation & plc, had not made a public appearance or in-person statement about the tragedy, choosing only to acknowledge the incident through company-released statements and his Twitter account.

His apparent lack of involvement prompted *The New York Times* to ask in the first line of an article, "Where is Micky Arison?"[6] Crisis management experts criticized Mr. Arison's handling of the situation and *The Independent*, an Italian newspaper, ran an article with the headline, "Concordia's Invisible U.S. Owner Branded a 'Disgrace.'"[7] Supporters of Mr. Arison, however, stated that his handling of the crisis was in line with his historical management style and that he was handling the situation in a "textbook fashion."[8]

Further confusion was sewn when on January 19th both Carnival Corporation and Mr. Arison announced that both parties would be "taking a break" from communicating via social media to focus on the tragedy.[9] Until this date, Carnival Corporation had been engaging in active communication with concerned customers through its social media accounts, providing answers to questions on topics ranging from safety to navigation. In addition, it seemed Mr. Arison was choosing to shut down the one channel he had been using to communicate with the public and media. Was this decision a calculated part of a larger crisis-communications plan? Or was it a sign that the company and its leader of over 30 years were struggling to gain control of an international disaster? Would Mr. Arison's and Carnival's reputations be permanently damaged by their crisis-communications decisions?

CARNIVAL CORPORATION & PLC

Carnival Cruise Line was founded in 1972 by Ted Arison, an Israeli-American businessman who was one of the pioneers of the modern cruise industry.

[1] Phillip Knightley, "The Unbelievable Crash," *The Khaleej Times*, January 23, 2012, https://www.khaleejtimes.com/article/20120123/ARTICLE/301239881/1098.

[2] "Rescue Efforts Resume on Stricken Cruise Liner," *The New York Times*, January 19, 2012.

[3] Bryan Burrough, "Another Night to Remember," *Vanity Fair*, April 10, 2012.

[4] "Many Make Concordia, Titanic Comparisons," *The Columbus Dispatch*, January 16, 2012.

[5] Burrough, "Another Night to Remember."

[6] Mike Esterl and Joann S. Lublin, "Carnival CEO Lies Low After Wreck," *The Wall Street Journal*, January 23, 2012.

[7] Michael Day, "Concordia's Invisible US Owner Branded 'a Disgrace'," *The Independent*, January 25, 2012.

[8] Esterl and Lublin, "Carnival CEO Lies Low After Wreck."

[9] Facebook and/or Twitter accounts of Carnival Corporation and Micky Arison, accessed on May 29, 2012.

Carnival Cruise Line had since become Carnival Corporation & plc ("Carnival"), the world's largest cruise ship operator. As a British-American company, Carnival was headquartered in both Southampton, Hampshire, England and Miami, Florida, United States. The company similarly employed a dual approach to its organizational structure, operating two unique companies with separate shareholder bodies, a consequence of the merger between Carnival Corporation and P&O Cruises in April 2003. As part of the merger agreement, P&O Princess, relisted as Carnival plc, remained a separate entity that generally maintained its executive team and predominant British shareholder base. The company was also dual listed, with Carnival Corporation stock trading on the New York Stock Exchange (NYSE) and Carnival plc stock trading on the London Stock Exchange (LSE).

As of January 2012, Carnival included 10 cruise lines, each operating under individual brand names (see Exhibit 1). As shown, the 10 brands operated a combined fleet of over 101 ships, totaling 190,000 lower berths (cruise industry term found by multiplying the number of passenger beds by two). Additionally, the company had 10 ships on order for delivery by 2016.

Carnival Corporation structured executive control of its organization and assets by geographic location with four operating groups spread across the globe. Carnival Corporation controlled operations in North America; Costa Crociere S.p.A controlled operations in Europe (except the United Kingdom); Carnival UK controlled operations in the United Kingdom; and Carnival Australia controlled operations in Australia and the South Pacific. These entities reported to the executive management of Carnival Corporation & plc, led by Chief Executive Officer Mickey Arison, and were united by a shared mission statement, emphasizing the company's commitment to excellence and accessibility:

"Our mission is to deliver exceptional vacation experiences through the world's best-known cruise brands that cater to a variety of different lifestyles and budgets, all at an outstanding value unrivaled on land or at sea."[10]

The company deemed itself "The World's Most Popular Cruise Line." Indeed, based on passenger volume, Carnival was the "most popular," accounting for an estimated 51.6 percent of worldwide cruising revenue in 2011.[11] Carnival attributed its success to its "ability to manage brand autonomy, with each major cruise line maintaining separate sales, marketing, and reservation offices, as well as through the industry's most aggressive shipbuilding program."[12]

MICKY ARISON[13]

Born in Israel in 1949, Micky Arison was the son of the late cofounder of Carnival Cruise Lines, Ted Arison. After dropping out of the University of Miami, Mr. Arison started working in the sales department of his father's growing cruise line. In 1979, Mr. Arison became President of Carnival and focused on aggressively growing the business to capitalize on the rapid growth of passenger travel in the cruise industry during the 1980s. In 1987, Mr. Arison took Carnival public and became the Chairman in 1990. He had led the company in an aggressive growth strategy, acquiring several other cruise lines, including Seabourn, Holland America, Cunard, and Costa Cruises. With the acquisition of British-based P&O Cruises in 2002, Mr. Arison created the largest global cruise company, effectively controlling nearly 50 percent of global passenger volume. Mr. Arison remained the Chairman of the Board and CEO of Carnival Corporation and plc as of January 2012.

In 2011, *Forbes* magazine named Mr. Arison the 169th wealthiest person in the world with an estimated wealth of U.S. $5.9 billion.[14] In 2009, as the

[10] "Nearly 500 on 2 Princess Cruise Ships Stricken by Norovirus," *CNN*, February 5, 2012, http://www.cnn.com/2012/02/05/health/ships-outbreak/index.html.

[11] "Market Share Statistics," *Cruise Market Watch*, accessed on May 29, 2012, http://www.cruisemarketwatch.com/market-share.

[12] "Mission and History," Carnival Corporation & plc, accessed on May 29, 2012, http://phx.corporate-ir.net/phoenix.zhtml?c=200767&p=irol-history.

[13] Biographical information for Micky Arison compiled from the Carnival Corporation & plc website and Wikipedia: http://phx.corporate-ir.net/phoenix.zhtml?c=140690&p=irol-govBio2&ID=155632 and http://en.wikipedia.org/wiki/Micky_Arison.

[14] "The World's Billionaires," *Forbes*, accessed on May 29, 2012, http://www.forbes.com/lists/2011/10/billionaires_2011.html.

EXHIBIT 10.1 Carnival Corporation & plc's Cruise Lines

CARNIVAL
CORPORATION & PLC

Carnival

Established: 1972
Tagline: The World's Most Popular Cruise Line
Ships: 23
Berths: 58,279

Costa
CRUISING ITALIAN STYLE

Acquired: 2000
Tagline: Europe's Number One Cruise Line
Ships: 14
Berths: 31,714

P&O CRUISES

Merged: 2003
Tagline: A World of Choice
Ships: 7
Berths: 14,610

AIDA

Acquired: 2002
Tagline: The Ultimate Club Ships for German Guests
Ships: 9
Berths: 16,442

PRINCESS CRUISES
escape completely

Merged: 2003
Tagline: Let Princess Take You on a Complete Escape from the Ordinary
Ships: 16
Berths: 36,800

Holland America Line
A Signature of Excellence

Acquired: 1989
Tagline: A Signature of Excellence
Ships: 15
Berths: 23,492

ibero
cruceros

Founded: 2007
Tagline: Nada Como Lo Nuestro
Ships: 3
Berths: 4,176

P&O CRUISES
This is how to holiday

Merged: 2003
Tagline: The Company that Invented Cruising
Ships: 4
Berths: 6,242

CUNARD

Acquired: 1998
Tagline: Impeccable White Star Service
Ships: 3
Berths: 6,670

SEABOURN

Acquired: 2001
Tagline: Intimate. Luxury.
Ships: 6
Berths: 1,974

Source: Carnival Corporation & plc website, http://phx.corporate-ir.net/phoenix.zhtml?c=200767&p=irol-products.

Chief Executive Officer of Carnival, Mr. Arison earned a salary of U.S. $7.2 million, composed of a base salary, cash bonus, stock grants, and other compensation.[15] Since 1995, Mr. Arison had also been the owner of the Miami Heat, an NBA Miami-based professional basketball team.

TRAGEDY ON THE WATER[16]

On Friday, January 13, 2012, the *Costa Concordia* set sail from Civitacchia, a port outside of Rome, with 3,206 passengers and 1,023 crew on board. The *Costa Concordia* was to conduct a seven-day cruise visiting the ports of Savona, Marseille, Barcelona, Palma, Cagliara, and Palermo before returning to Civitacchia. The *Costa Concordia* was under the command of Captain Schettino. To conduct a close sail past the island of Giglio, the alarm system for the ship's computer navigation system was manually shut off, and the ship was steered on a five-mile diversion toward the island. According to Captain Schettino, he had previously conducted similar sail-pasts of the island. In interviews after the accident, Captain Schettino stated, "I was navigating by sight because I knew those sea beds well. I had done the move three, four times."[17] Captain Schettino recounted to investigators that when he saw waves breaking on the reef, he ordered the ship to be turned abruptly, inadvertently swinging the side of the hull into the reef. He acknowledged, "I have to take responsibility for the fact that I made a judgment error. This time I ordered the turn too late."[18] At approximately 9:45 p.m. local time, the ship collided with Le Scole, a chartered area of the reef off the

shore of Giglio. The collision resulted in a 160-foot gash in the *Concordia*'s port side below the water line, effectively cutting steel from the ship's hull and lodging a huge rock in the aft end of the gash. Within minutes, according to testimony by the head of the engine room, the generators and engines of the ship were underwater.

The ship lost propulsion power and relied solely on backup emergency electric power. The remaining inertia of the ship enabled it to continue to sail past Giglio Porto. At 10:10 p.m., the *Costa Concordia* turned south and began to list starboard 20 degrees. At 10:44 p.m., the ship came to a final rest at a 70-degree angle on Punta del Gabbianera, partially submerged in 20 meters of water. (See Exhibit 2 for a map detailing the ship's final course.) The captain testified that the ship did not sink in deeper waters due to his actions and orders in the aftermath of the collision. Contradicting this statement, the chief of the Italian Coast Guard stated that it was only due to fortunate winds and tides that the ship did not sink in deeper water.

At the time of the collision, most passengers were dining in one of the ship's multiple restaurants. Passengers reported hearing a loud bang and then feeling the ship shake. Following the loud bang, a voice-over the ship's intercom system attributed the bang to an electrical failure. According to one steward, "We told the guests everything was [okay] and under control, and we tried to stop them panicking."[19] In describing the experience, one passenger noted, "The boat started shaking. The noise—there was panic, like in a film, dishes crashing to the floor, people running, people falling down the stairs."[20] Passengers reported feeling the ship list to starboard in the aftermath of the collision. A passenger took video of a crew member relating the following statement shortly before the official evacuation order was given: "We have solved the problems we had and invite everyone to return to their cabins."[21]

[15] "2010 Top 200 U.S. CEOs," *Equilar*, accessed on May 29, 2012, http://www.equilar.com/CEO_Compensation/Carnival_Micky_Arison.php.

[16] Details concerning the wreck of the *Costa Concordia* obtained through a variety of media sources. Direct quotes have been appropriately referenced to the source material. All other facts and details surrounding the incident are part of the public domain.

[17] Stacy Meichtry, "Italy Probes Captain's Call with Boss," *The Wall Street Journal*, January 19, 2012, https://www.wsj.com/article/SB10001424052970204468004577168762570407898.html.

[18] "Costa Concordia: Captain Schettino 'Turned Too Late'," *BBC News*, January 18, 2012, https://www.bbc.com/news/world-europe-16620807.

[19] "Italy Cruise Ship Costa Concordia: Search for Missing," *BBC News*, January 15, 2012, https://www.bbc.com/news/world-europe-16561904.

[20] "Cruise Captain 'Committed Errors', Says Ships Owners," *BBC News*, accessed on May 29, 2012, https://www.bbc.com/news/world-europe-16570281.

[21] "Everything Is Under Control, Go Back to Your Cabins," *Corrierre Della Sera*, January 16, 2012, http://www.webcitation.org/65NzqXCoF.

EXHIBIT 10.2 *Costa Concordia's* **Final Course**

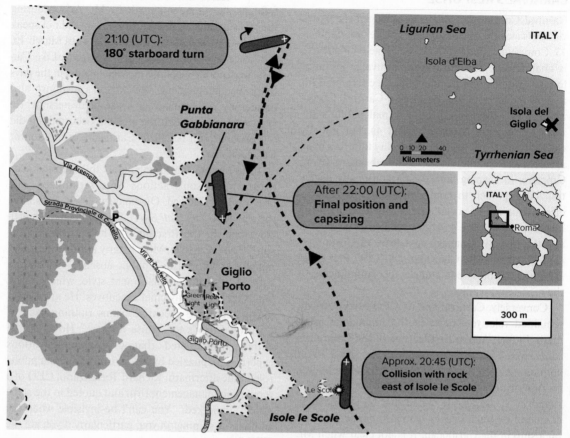

21:10 (UTC):
180° starboard turn

Punta Gabbianara

After 22:00 (UTC):
Final position and capsizing

Giglio Porto

Green Light Red Light

Giglio Porto

Approx. 20:45 (UTC):
Collision with rock east of Isole le Scole

Le Scole

Isole le Scole

Via Arenella

Strada Provinciale di Castello

Via di Castello

Ligurian Sea

ITALY

Isola d'Elba

Isola del Giglio

0 10 20 40
Kilometers

Tyrrhenian Sea

ITALY

Roma

300 m

Note: The timing detailed in this diagram varies slightly from the timing detailed in the case, a consequence of multiple contradictory accounts of the event.

Source: Wikipedia, http://en.wikipedia.org/wiki/File:Location_of_Costa_Concordia_cruise-ship_disaster_(13-1-2012).png.

Multiple conflicting accounts exist regarding what exactly occurred during the ensuing evacuation of the ship. Of importance to note is that 600 passengers who boarded in Rome had not participated in an evacuation drill prior to the accident. Passengers reported a chaotic and disorganized evacuation process, with contradictory orders given by various crew members. By the time the ship came to a final stop, the listing caused serious problems for the launching of the lifeboats. It was widely reported that some passengers jumped into the water to escape the sinking ship. In response to accusations that the crew was unprepared for the evacuation, Costa CEO Pier Luigi Foschi attributed the crew's apparent lack of training to poor leadership from the ship's officers and a language barrier.[22] In the end, passengers evacuated from the ship by lifeboat, helicopter, or by jumping and swimming to safety. All told, 32 people lost their lives in the aftermath.

[22] "Most of the Costa Concordia's Crew Were Entertainers and Bartenders, Not Qualified Seamen," *National Post*, accessed on May 29, 2012, http://news.nationalpost.com/2012/01/17/most-of-the-costa-concordias-crew-were-entertainers-or-bartenders-not-qualified-seamen.

CARNIVAL'S RESPONSE

Carnival Corporation first acknowledged the wreck via messages on Facebook and Twitter on January 13. Communication via these social media platforms is unapologetic and illustrates Carnival's hesitancy to take ownership of the incident. (See Exhibit 3 for a social media response timeline for Carnival Corporation.) The company made a formal public statement on January 14 (see Exhibit 4), but initially elected to place primary responsibility for crisis management and communication to its subsidiary, Costa Crociere, in keeping with their traditionally decentralized approach to communications. Costa Crociere set up a web portal specifically to address the incident and provide real-time updates to the public, and the executive management team of Costa Crociere (including the Chairman and CEO Pier Luigi Foschi) held press conferences to communicate to the media and public.

Conversely, Carnival and its CEO Micky Arison remained relatively quiet in the immediate aftermath. In fact, Arison first learned of the *Costa Concordia* wreck via social media, when he saw a Tweet containing a reference to the accident while he was on one of his company's ships near the Caribbean island of St. Bart's. He stated that he immediately emailed Pier Luigi Foschi, who also happened to be on a ship in the Caribbean. It is not clear when Mr. Arison and Mr. Foschi found out the true extent of the disaster that would result in the death of 32 passengers and the complete loss of a $515 million vessel.

In the immediate aftermath of the tragedy, Mr. Arison chose not to travel to the site of the accident, make any in-person public statements, nor grant any interviews. According to reports, Mr. Arison managed the crisis from Carnival's offices in Miami, Florida, relying on Mr. Foschi to be the company's public face and primary communicator. A longtime acquaintance of Mr. Arison stated that, "He wants to distance Carnival from this disaster. If he talks, Carnival is speaking."[23] Despite his apparent desire to distance himself, Mr. Arison communicated with stakeholders

via social media and Carnival's website. (See Exhibit 5 for public statements made by Mr. Arison during the crisis period.) However, Mr. Arison did not speak publicly in-person about the accident until March 10, 2012, nearly two months after the tragedy. Like Carnival's corporate response on social media in the days following the incident, Mr. Arison's response also lacked any real apology or sense of ownership. He expressed remorse that the incident occurred but did not apologize on behalf of Carnival Corporation or Costa Crocier.

In the weeks that immediately followed the accident, Mr. Arison's actions were scrutinized and, oftentimes, criticized. On January 23, 10 days after the accident, *The Wall Street Journal* printed an article asking in the first line: "Where is Micky Arison?"[24] In the article, Mike Esterly and Joann Lublin noted that Mr. Arison's public absence was "in line with Mr. Arison's management style, which is less hands-on than many chief executives. He gives great independence to executive teams running each of Carnival Corp.'s ten cruise lines... ." However, the authors also noted that crisis-communications experts were puzzled by Mr. Arison's lack of a public role in the aftermath. Richard Torrenzano, CEO of a reputation management firm and quoted in the same article, remarked, "You can't be invisible when the spotlight is shining on you, particularly if you are the CEO."[25]

Other organizations and news outlets were even less understanding. The Italian newspaper *La Republica* asked in an article, "Who is this mysterious boss and how has he managed to remain like a ghost since the tragedy?"[26] The president of the U.S.-based International Cruise Victims group was quoted in *The Independent*, "The response, or lack of it, by Carnival is disgraceful."[27] Adding to the criticism, Jim Walker, a leading U.S. lawyer specializing in maritime law, wrote, "Arison admittedly expressed condolences from the comfort of his 200-foot luxury yacht in the

[23] Esterl and Lublin, "Carnival CEO Lies Low After Wreck."

[24] Ibid.

[25] Ibid.

[26] Day, "Concordia's Invisible US Owner Branded 'a Disgrace'."

[27] Ibid.

EXHIBIT 10.3   Social Media Response Timeline of Carnival Corporation

JANUARY 13:

Our thoughts are with guests and crew of the Costa Concordia. We are keeping them in our hearts in the wake of this very sad event.

JANUARY 14:

Our hearts go out to everyone affected by the grounding of the Costa Concordia and especially the loved ones of those who lost their lives. They will remain in our thoughts and prayers in the wake of this tragic event. We wish to recognize and thank the Italian Coast Guard and everyone in Italy who has provided such extraordinary assistance

JANUARY 14:

Carnival Corp. statement on Costa Concordia just posted here: tinyurl.com/7un6pho

JANUARY 17:

Some of you are asking if it's safe to go on a cruise. The safety of Carnival Cruise Lines' passengers and crew is our number one priority and we have an excellent record of safe operation throughout our company's history. Cruising continues to be one of the safest means of travel and marine accidents are an extremely rare occurrence. All of our ships meet or exceed international safety and training requirements, and are equipped with the most advanced navigation technology, which our officers are expertly trained to use. Here's a link to additional information on cruise ship safety on the website of Cruise Lines International Association: http://cruiseindustryfacts.com/safety-and-security/ship-safety/

JANUARY 17:

Many of you have asked about our ships navigation systems and if we have equipment to detect rocks and depth. All of our ships are equipped with the most advanced navigation technology and our officers are expertly trained in its use. Our ships are equipped with two independent depth sensors that can detect variations in ocean floor depth. Further, we have several radars, GPS, electronic charts, gyros etc for safe navigation in all conditions. All bridge systems have a redundant back-up system in case of system malfunction. As part of our comprehensive bridge team management system, we always have multiple people on the bridge watch.

JANUARY 18:

Many of you will recognize this (hello, past guests), but for the benefit of those who haven't seen it before, what follows is the safety video shown onboard all Carnival Cruise Lines ships. We use this to help inform our guests of procedures to follow in an emergency situation.

JANUARY 19:

Hi, everyone. Out of respect for all those affected by the recent events surrounding our sister line, Costa cruises, we are going to take a bit of a break from posting on our social channels. We will still be actively listening and answering any questions you have about your past or upcoming cruises, but for now, the majority of our time will be spent focusing on all those affected by this event. We thank you again for all your support.

JANUARY 24:

During the last two weeks, the amount of support all of you have shown has been truly amazing – and we thank you from the bottom of our hearts. Our sister line, Costa Cruises, and parent company Carnival Corporation & plc, remain focused on taking care of all guests, crew and the families affected by this tragic event.

In addition to saying thank you to everyone, we've decided to resume some posting on our social channels – and will start back up by answering your questions about cruising and Carnival, as well as providing you with content and resources to help you better prepare and plan for your upcoming vacations. We thank you again for your continued support. We have the best fans in the world.

Note: Carnival posted the same messages via both Facebook and Twitter, breaking up messages as necessary to accommodate the Twitter character limit.

Source: Carnival Cruise Line's Facebook and Twitter pages, accessed April 2012.

EXHIBIT 10.4 Press Release from Carnival Corporation

JANUARY 14—OFFICIAL CARNIVAL NEWS RELEASE:
On January 13, 2012, Costa Cruises' vessel, the Costa Concordia, departed from Civitavecchia, Italy with approximately 3,200 passengers and 1,000 crew members on a seven-day voyage. At approximately 10:00 pm CET, the vessel struck rock off the coast of Isola del Giglio, Italy and sustained significant damage causing the ship to list severely. The order was given to abandon ship and deploy the lifeboats.

Tragically, there are reports of some deaths and injuries. This is a terrible tragedy and we are deeply saddened. Carnival Corporation & plc offers our sympathies and heartfelt condolences to all of the Costa Concordia guests, crew members and their families. Carnival Corporation & plc and Costa Cruises are committing our full resources to provide assistance and ensure that all guests and crew are looked after.

We want to express our deep gratitude to the Italian Coast Guard and local authorities and community members who have gone to extraordinary lengths to assist in the evacuation of the ship and provide support for our guests and crew.

We are working to fully understand the cause of what occurred. The safety of our guests and crew members remains the number one priority of Carnival Corporation & plc and all of our cruise lines.

Costa Concordia was sailing on a Mediterranean cruise from Civitavecchia (Rome) with scheduled calls at Savona, Italy; Marseille, France; Barcelona, Spain; Palma de Mallorca; Cagliari and Palermo, Italy.

Source: Carnival Corporation & plc website, http://phx.corporate-ir.net/phoenix.zhtml?c=200767&p=irol-overview.

EXHIBIT 10.5 Micky Arison Public Response Timeline

JANUARY 13—TWEET:
Tonight our thoughts and prayers are with the passengers and crew of the Costa Concordia.

JANUARY 17—TWEETS:
"Since Friday night, I've been focused on the response to this tragedy. I want to thank you all for your support this week."
"I am deeply saddened by reports of more deaths following the grounding of #Concordia."
"My condolence statement is attached phx.corporate-ir.net/phoenix.zhtml"
Link to following Public Statement on company website:

We are deeply saddened by the reports of additional deaths following the grounding of the Costa Concordia. On behalf of the entire Carnival Corporation & plc team, I offer our heartfelt condolences to all of those families affected by this tragedy.

Our immediate priority continues to be supporting rescue and recovery efforts and looking after our guests and crew members, along with securing the vessel to ensure there is no environmental impact. My senior management team and I have been in continuous contact with the Costa executive team in Italy and we have our senior level technical experts on the ground to provide additional support for this tragic and highly unusual incident.

While this is a terribly sad time for everyone involved, we want to recognize the tremendous efforts of Concordia's crew, who along with the Italian Coast Guard and authorities, helped to evacuate more than 4,000 passengers and crew members from the ship in very difficult conditions. And we continue to offer our deep gratitude to the Italian authorities for their support and ongoing efforts.

JANUARY 18 –TWEET
"I gave my personal assurance that we will take care of each &every one of our guests, crew and their families click bit.ly/zPLVY7"
Link to following on company website:

"I give my personal assurance that we will take care of each and every one of our guests, crew and their families affected by this tragic event. Our company was founded on this principle and it will remain our focus," said Micky Arison, chairman and CEO of Carnival Corporation & plc.

In this spirit, Costa has been arranging lodging and transportation for affected passengers and crew members to return home. Every passenger and crew member or their family is being contacted and the company has offered its assistance and counseling as needed, and will be addressing personal possessions lost on board. Costa has also begun the process of refunding all voyage costs including both passenger cruise fares and all costs incurred while on board. Our senior management teams are working together to determine additional support.

JANUARY 19—TWEET
"We just announced a comprehensive Audit &Review of Safety & Emergency Response Across All our Cruise Lines-link bit.ly/w10Lbk"
Link to following on company website (excerpt only):

Following the tragic Costa Concordia accident, Carnival Corporation & plc, parent company of Costa Cruises and nine leading cruise lines around the world, today announced a comprehensive audit and review of all safety and emergency response procedures across all of the company's cruise lines.

Carnival Corporation & plc and the cruise industry as a whole have maintained an excellent safety record over the years. "However, this tragedy has called into question our company's safety and emergency response procedures and practices," said Micky Arison, chairman and CEO of Carnival Corporation & plc. "While I have every confidence in the safety of our vessels and the professionalism of our crews, this review will evaluate all practices and procedures to make sure that this kind of accident doesn't happen again."

JANUARY 19—TWEET
"I won't be as active on Twitter for the next while. Helping our @costacruises team manage this crisis is my priority right now. Thnx"

JANUARY 24—TWEET
"In response2 numerous tweets recvd on inaccurate media reports please C link costacruises.com/B2C/USA/Info/c"

Link to Costa Concordia status update page on Costa Cruises website.

JANUARY 27—MICKY ARISON ATTENDS FIRST MIAMI HEAT GAME SINCE THE DISASTER. UP TO THIS DATE, MICKY ARISON HAD NOT SPOKEN IN-PERSON NOR HAD ANY INTERVIEWS RELATED TO THE TRAGEDY.

JANUARY 30—TWEET
"Thnx for ur gr8 support this weekend @MiamiHEAT fans. No let down 2nite #LetsGoHeat"

MARCH 10—FIRST PUBLIC INTERVIEW ON DISASTER WITH *THE MIAMI HERALD* (EXCERPTS)
"Obviously, I am very sorry it happened. When you have 100 ships out there, sometimes unfortunate things happen, but as I said, it was an accident. We as a company do everything we can to encourage the highest of safety standards."

"I have a lot of faith in Pier and his team. I believe they'll work their way through this. It was a terrible, terrible, terrible accident, but that's what it was."

In response to attending Miami Heat basketball game two weeks after tragedy:

"No matter what I would've done, I think I would've been criticized. I did what I thought was right and in the best interest of the company. During the weeks after the event, I stayed focused on this issue and did not attend games, but once I felt that it was appropriate to go back to my other job, I went back."

Sources: Micky Arison's Twitter account accessed April 2012; and "Micky Arison on Costa Concordia Accident: 'I am Very Sorry It Happened,'" *The Miami Herald*, accessed on May 29, 2012, http://www.miamiherald.com/2012/03/09/2684790/carnivals-micky-arison-speaks.html.

Miami area. But carefully crafted corporate PR statements go only so far."[28]

Mr. Arison further angered critics when he attended a Miami Heat basketball game two weeks after the accident prior to making any in-person public statements or interviews about the tragedy. In response, Arison answered critics during an interview with *The Miami Herald*, "No matter what I would've done, I think I would've been criticized. I did what I thought was right and in the best interest of the company. During the weeks after the event, I stayed focused on this issue and did not attend games, but once I felt that it was appropriate to go back to my other job, I went back."[29]

A CRISIS-COMMUNICATIONS DISASTER OR SUCCESS?

Mr. Arison opened the first quarter earnings call on March 9, 2012, with an acknowledgment of the *Costa Concordia* disaster, offering condolences to the passengers, crew, and families of the victims. Mr. Arison related on the call, "First, the cruise industry remains incredibly safe and maintains one of the best safety records of any form of recreational travel in the world. The safety and security of our guests are job one, and we learn from everything we can from this incident and apply all lessons learned."[30] At Carnival's first annual meeting since the wreck in April 2012, Chief Operating Officer Howard S. Frank noted that booking volume increased 3 percent in the five weeks leading up to April 1 (excluding bookings for the Costa Line), after plunging 9 percent in the month-and-a-half after the incident. He stated

that the company had reduced pricing in an effort to increase passenger bookings.[31] Then in May 2012, Costa Chief Executive Officer Pier Luigi Foschi told *The Independent*, "Starting from the middle of March we resumed our marketing activity [of Costa Cruises]. Bookings now are higher than we forecasted and higher than they were a year ago. The [customers] who knew us in the past have been loyal."[32]

However, with a slate of upcoming lawsuits, both civil and criminal, on the company's docket, and criticism persisting throughout the online world, the question still lingered: had Carnival safely sailed past this crisis or would the company be permanently run aground by what had transpired?

CASE QUESTIONS

1. In what ways did Carnival Corporation and Costa Crociere's responses to the *Costa Concordia* crisis align with and deviate from the "What to Say in a Crisis" paradigm?

2. What role did Carnival's decentralized approach to communications play in the company's initial response to the crisis? What other options did Carnival have beyond delegating the initial response to Costa Crociere?

3. What key constituencies should Carnival have first engaged with in the immediate aftermath of the crisis? For example, how should the company

[28] Ibid.

[29] "Micky Arison on Costa Concordia Accident: 'I Am Very Sorry It Happened,'" *The Miami Herald*, accessed on May 29, 2012, http://www.miamiherald.com/2012/03/09/2684790/carnivals-micky-arison-speaks.html.

[30] "Carnival Corporation CCL Q1 2012 Earnings Call Transcript," *Morningstar*, accessed on May 29, 2012, http://www.morningstar.com/earnings/36291308-carnival-corporation-ccl-q1-2012.aspx.

[31] "At Carnival's Annual Meeting, Talk of Shipwreck and Taxes," *The Miami Herald*, accessed on May 29, 2012, http://www.miamiherald.com/2012/04/11/2742198/concordia-disaster-likely-to-dominate.html.

[32] Simon Calder, "Business? It's Never Been Better, Says Costa Cruise Line Boss Pier Luigi Foschi," *The Independent*, May 8, 2012, http://www.independent.co.uk/travel/news-and-advice/business-its-never-been-better-says-costa-cruise-line-boss-pier-luigi-foschi-7720679.html.

have balanced the need to apologize to passengers, crew members, and families who lost loved ones with potential legal liability this could open them up to?

4. Was Mr. Arison right in not taking a public role in the management of the crisis? How should his response be viewed in light of his otherwise active social media presence? What are the implications for leaders more generally in maintaining a presence online?

5. Was the increase in bookings an indication that Carnival Corporation and Costa Crociere

executives had successfully navigated the parent company and subsidiary through the crisis? Had Carnival Corporation managed the crisis effectively?

Source: This case is derived from two earlier cases ("Carnival Corporation–Case A" and "Carnival Corporation–Case B") written in 2012 by Professor Paul A. Argenti and Research Assistant of the Tuck School of Business at Dartmouth. They were combined and modified by Research Assistant Anne Bozik under Professor Argenti's supervision in 2020.

Aaker, David A. *Building Strong Brands*. New York: Free Press, 1996.

Aguilar, Francis Joseph. *General Managers in Action: Policies and Strategies*, 2nd ed. Oxford: Oxford University Press, 1992.

Ailes, Roger, and Jon Kraushar. *You Are the Message*. Garden City: Currency Doubleday, 1995.

Angell, Marcia, M. D. *Science on Trial: The Clash of Medical Evidence and the Law in the Breast Implant Case*. New York: W.W. Norton, 1996.

Argenti, Paul A. "BuildingTrust through Reputation Management," *Public Trust in Business*, Cambridge University Press, 2012.

———. "Collaborating with Activists: How Starbucks Works with NGOs to Enhance Its Emphasis on Social Responsibility." *California Management Review*, Fall 2004.

———. "Communications and Business Value: Measuring the Link." *Journal of Business Strategy*, November 2006.

———. "Lessons from 9/11" in the Japanese version of *Harvard Business Review*, May 2011 (Reissued).

———. "The Good, the Bad and the Trustworthy," *Strategy + Business*, Winter 2011.

———, and Courtney Barnes. *Digital Strategies for Powerful Corporate Communications*. New York: McGraw Hill, 2009.

——— and ———. "The Employee Care Revolution." *Leader to Leader*, Summer 2004.

———, and Georgia Aarons. "Digital Strategies for Enhancing Reputation," *Reputation Management*, Bloombury, Fall 2012.

———, and Janis Forman. *The Power of Corporate Communication: Crafting the Voice and Image of Your Business*. New York: McGraw Hill, 2002.

———, Robert Howell, and Karen Beck. "The Strategic Communication Imperative." *Sloan Management Review*, Spring 2005.

Aristotle. *The Art of Rhetoric*. Cambridge: Harvard University Press, 1975.

Barton, Laurence. *Crisis Leadership Now: A Real-World Guide to Preparing for Threats, Disaster, Sabotage, and Scandal*. New York: McGraw Hill, 2008.

Blythe, Bruce. *Blindsided: A Manager's Guide to Crisis Leadership*. Brookfield: Rothstein Publishing, 2015.

Byrne, John A. *Informed Consent*. New York: McGraw Hill, 1996.

Chajet, Clive, and Tom Shachtman. *Image by Design: From Corporate Vision to Business Reality*, 2nd ed. New York: McGraw Hill, 1997.

Collins, James C., and Morten T. Hansen. *Great by Choice: Uncertainty, Chaos, and Luck, Why Some Thrive Despite Them All*. New York: Harper Business, 2011.

D'Aveni, Richard A. *Strategic Capitalism: The New Economy Strategy for Winning the Capitalist Cold War*. New York: McGraw Hill, 2012.

DeBower, Herbert F. *Modern Business*, vol. 7, *Advertising Principles*. New York: Alexander Hamilton Institute, 1917.

Dozier, David M., Larissa A. Grunig, and James E. Grunig. *Manager's Guide to Excellence in Public Relations and Communication Management*. Mahwah: Lawrence Erlbaum, 1995.

Eccles, Robert G., and Michael Krzus. *One Report: Integrated Reporting for a Sustainable Strategy*. New York: John Wiley & Sons, 2010.

Edsell, Thomas. *The Age of Austerity: How Scarcity Will Remake American Politics*. New York: Doubleday, 2011.

Eichenwald, Kurt. *Conspiracy of Fools*. New York: Broadway Books, 2005.

Fombrun, Charles J. *Reputation: Realizing Value from the Corporate Image*. Boston: Harvard Business School Press, 1996.

Forty, Adrian. *Objects of Desire: Design and Society from Wedgewood to IBM*. New York: Pantheon, 1986.

Friedman, Milton. "The Social Responsibility of Business Is to Increase Its Profits." *The New York Times Magazine*, September 13, 1970.

Gaines-Ross, Leslie. *Corporate Reputation: 12 Steps to Safeguarding and Recovering Reputation*. Hoboken: John Wiley & Sons, 2008.

Garbett, Thomas F. *Corporate Advertising*. New York: McGraw Hill, 1981.

———. *How to Build a Corporation's Identity and Project Its Image*. Lexington: Lexington Books, 1988.

Garten, Jeffrey. *The Mind of the CEO*. New York: Basic Books, 2001.

Goodman, Michael B., and Peter B. Hirsch. *Corporate Communication: Strategic Adaption for Global Practice*. New York: Peter Lang Publishing, 2010.

Goss, Mimi. *What Is Your One Sentence?: How to Be Heard in the Age of Short Attention Spans*. Upper Saddle River: Prentice Hall, 2013.

Gottschalk, Jack, ed. *Crisis Response: Inside Stories on Managing Image under Siege*. Detroit: Gale Research, 1993.

Gupta, Sunil, and Donald R. Lehmann. *Managing Customers as Investments: The Strategic Value of Customers in the Long Run*. Upper Saddle River: Wharton School Publishing, 2005.

Handler, Edward, and John R. Mulkern. *Business in Politics*. Lexington: Lexington Books, 1982.

Hattersley, Michael E., and Linda McJannet. *Management Communication: Principles and Practice*. New York: McGraw Hill, 1997.

Heath, Jim F. *John F. Kennedy and the Business Community*. Chicago: University of Chicago Press, 1969.

Hoffman, Paul. *The Dealmakers*. Garden City: Doubleday, 1984.

Hsieh, Tony. *Delivering Happiness: A Path to Profits, Passion, and Purpose*. New York: Grand Central Publishing, 2010.

Hutton, James G., and Francis J. Mulhem. *Marketing Communications: Integrated Theory, Strategy & Tactics*. West Patterson: Pentagram, January 2002.

Huxley, Aldous. *Grey Eminence: A Study in Religion and Politics*. London: Chatto & Windus, 1941.

Isaacson, Walter. *Steve Jobs*. New York: Simon & Schuster, 2011.

Keller, Keven. *Strategic Brand Management: Building, Measuring, and Managing Brand Equity*. Upper Saddle River: Pearson/Prentice Hall, 2008.

Klein, Naomi. *No Logo: Taking Aim at the Brand Bullies*. New York: Picador USA, 1999.

Lasswell, Harold D. "The Structure and Function of Communication in Society." In Lyman Bryson, ed. *The Communication of Ideas: A Series of Addresses*. New York: Institute for Religious and Social Studies, 1948, pp. 203–243.

Lorenz, Christopher. *The Design Dimension: Product Strategy and the Challenge of Global Marketing.* New York: Blackwell, 1986.

Low, Jonathan, and Pam Cohen Kalafut. *Invisible Advantage: How Intangibles Are Driving Business Performance.* Cambridge: Perseus Books, 2002.

McLean, Bethany, and Peter Elkind. *The Smartest Guys in the Room.* New York: The Penguin Group, 2004.

McLuhan, Marshall, and Bruce R. Powers. *The Global Village: Transformations in World Life and Media in the 21st Century.* New York: Oxford University Press, 1989.

Munter, Mary. *Guide to Managerial Communication*, 7th ed. Upper Saddle River: Prentice Hall, 2006.

Olins, Wally. *Brand New: The Shape of Brands to Come.* New York: Thames and Hudson, 2014.

Peters, Thomas J., and Robert H. Waterman Jr. *In Search of Excellence: Lessons from America's Best-Run Companies.* New York: Harper & Row, 1982.

Poe, Marshall T. *A History of Communications: Media and Society from the Evolution of Speech to the Internet.* New York: Cambridge University Press, 2011.

Postman, Neil. *Amusing Ourselves to Death: Public Discourse in the Age of Show Business.* New York: Penguin, 1985.

Riley, Charles A., II. *Small Business, Big Politics: What Entrepreneurs Need to Know to Use Their Political Power.* Princeton: Peterson's/Pacesetter, 1995.

Schenkler, Irv, and Tony Herrling. *Guide to Media Relations.* Upper Saddle River: Pearson/Prentice Hall, 2004.

Schultz, Howard, and Joanne Gordon. *Onward: How Starbucks Fought for Its Life Without Losing Its Soul.* Emmaus: Rodale, 2012.

Schultz, Majken, Mary Jo Hatch, and Mogens Holten Larsen, eds. *The Expressive Organization.* Oxford: Oxford University Press, 2000.

Shannon, Claude Elwood, and Warren Weaver. *The Mathematical Theory of Communication.* Champaign: University of Illinois Press, 1964.

Shelby, Annette Nevin. "Organizational Business, Management and Corporate Communication: An Analysis of Boundaries and Relationships." *Journal of Business Communication*, 30, no. 3 (June 1993).

Slywotzky, Adrian. *Value Migration: How to Think Several Moves Ahead of the Competition.* Boston: Harvard Business School Press, 1996.

van Riel, Cees B. M. *Principles of Corporate Communication.* London: Prentice Hall, 1995.

Vogel, David. *Fluctuating Fortunes: The Political Power of Business in America.* New York: Basic Books, 1989.

Waite, Thomas J. "Keeping to the Fairway." Case commentary, *Harvard Business Review*, April 2003.

Wallis, Allen W. *An Over Governed Society.* New York: The Free Press, 1976.

Weidenbaum, Murray L. *Business, Government, and the Public.* Englewood Cliffs: Prentice Hall, 1990.

Welch, Jack, and John A. Byrne. *Jack: Straight from the Gut.* New York: Warner Business, 2001.

Wilson, Graham. *Interest Groups in the United States.* New York: Oxford University Press, 1981.

Yankelovich, Daniel. *Profit with Honor: The News Stage of Market Capitalism.* New Haven: Yale University Press, 2006.

Index